Contemporary Cases in Women's Rights

Contemporary Cases in Women's Rights

Leslie Friedman Goldstein

The University

of Wisconsin Press

The University of Wisconsin Press
114 North Murray Street
Madison, Wisconsin 53715

3 Henrietta Street
London WC2E 8LU, England

5 4 3 2 1

Printed in the United States of America

Library of Congress Cataloging-in-Publication Data
Goldstein, Leslie Friedman, 1945–
    Contemporary cases in women's rights / Leslie Friedman Goldstein.
    352 p.   cm.
    Includes bibliographical references and index.
    ISBN 0-299-14030-X.   ISBN 0-299-14034-2 (pbk.)
    1. Women—Legal status, laws, etc.—United States—Cases.
2. Women's rights—United States—Cases.   3. Abortion—Law and
legislation—United States—Cases.   4. Sex discrimination against
women—Law and legislation—United States—Cases.   I. Title.
    KF478.A4G65   1994
    342.73'0878—dc20
    [347.302878]   93-20926

To the memory of
Ethel Friedman Greenberg

Contents

Introduction

This book is meant to serve as an introduction to current issues facing the American judiciary that bear with particular force on women's rights. A number of those issues concern the right to obtain an abortion: To what degree may that right be burdened by a requirement of parental consent for minors, or of a husband's consent for a married woman? Does forbidding medical personnel at federally funded health clinics to mention abortion to patients violate the First Amendment's protection for freedom of speech?

Some of the issues being debated by judges in cases of recent years still revolve around equal job opportunity or equal educational opportunity for women. But when they reach the U.S. Supreme Court, such cases typically present a complicated context of rights in conflict: employers' right to protect themselves from future lawsuits for negligence may compete with the right of fertile women to work in environments dangerous to a fetus (and competing with both may be a fetus's right to protection from harms that will egregiously damage its later life). A woman's right to sue an employer or an educational institution for sex discrimination competes with a societal perception that massive award damages in our ever-more–litigious society may be starting to cause more harm than good. The right of women to protect themselves from what many see as a kind of group-libeling perpetuated by pornography against women in general competes with the First Amendment freedom of the press claims of the pornographer. The rights of women feeling harassed by sexually oriented remarks in the workplace or school compete with the free speech rights of persons making the remarks.

Finally, some of the cases involve sexual violence. Current statutes do not seem to successfully secure women's right to be safe from rapists or from violent boyfriends or husbands. In attempts to improve the situation, some judges are producing innovative interpretations of old statutes, or of common law principles. Those efforts naturally arouse debate, and the cases included here will present some of their arguments.

Because of the complexity of these issues, this book will prove useful in coursework not only in "Law and Social Change" or "Women and Law" but also in "Contemporary Moral Problems" or "Philosophy and Public Affairs." The emphasis here is on cutting-edge, contemporary issues; Supreme Court cases of the last several years are included, as are some lower-court cases of national significance. Readers will not need any background knowledge of earlier judicial decisions; chapters or sections of chapters are provided to introduce and explain the evolution of legal doctrine that provides the backdrop to each of the cases. Readers who are familiar with earlier Supreme Court decisions, or students using this book as an up-to-date supplement for older casebooks on women's rights, such as *The Constitutional Rights of Women* (1988),* can skip or skim the historical segments of the book.

The cases in this book are organized into three basic categories: reproductive rights (Chapters 1, 2, and 3), the right to be free of sex discrimination (Chapter 4), and the right to be free of sexual violence (Chapter 5). To some degree, the placement of a case in a given category is arbitrary, because these abstract categories overlap considerably in real life. For instance, workplace fetal protection policies can be analyzed as sex discrimination as the Supreme Court chose to do, or as infringements on reproductive freedom.† Sexual harassment often has elements of sexual violence (offensive touching or even rape), but the Supreme Court analyzed it (as did the Equal Employment Opportunity Commission) as sex discrimination. The way that a judge frames a question structures the answer that will be produced, and the reader should be alert to the phenomenon.‡

Because these issues are unfolding even as this book goes to press, I hope to engage readers in the very dialogues that go on between dissenting and majority justices in these cases. For that reason, questions for discussion are presented at the end of each case. They aim to present food for thought. *Bon appétit*!

---

* Leslie F. Goldstein, *The Constitutional Rights of Women* (2d ed., Madison: University of Wisconsin Press, 1988).

† The general right to reproductive freedom is a right against the government, not against private employers, but Congress has codified into law a right to be free of discrimination based on pregnancy at the hands of private (as well as governmental) employers. For examples of the Court's viewing policies restrictive of pregnant employees as an infringement of reproductive freedom, see *Cleveland Board of Education v. LaFleur*, 414 U.S. 632 (1974) (school policy requiring teachers to take unpaid leave from the time they are five months [or more] pregnant until the semester after their babies are three months old held unconstitutional), and *Turner v. Department of Employment Security*, 423 U.S. 44 (1975) (law denying unemployment benefits to women more than six months pregnant held unconstitutional). Compare *Geduldig v. Aiello*, 417 U.S. 484 (1974) (state's denial of medical disability benefits for maternity costs in a comprehensive employee health insurance package held not sex discrimination, and therefore not unconstitutional; this practice became illegal in 1978 when Congress passed the Pregnancy Discrimination Act).

‡The reader unfamiliar with the court system and legal citation and terminology may find it helpful to read Appendix A before starting the main body of the text. Regarding the sections of the case decisions which appear, certain editorial alterations have been made:

All omitted text has been marked with ellipses.

In a few instances some repetitious citations and note numbers have been silently omitted.

The style of the cases has been altered to generally conform with the suggestions of *A Uniform System of Citation*, fourteenth edition.

No change has been made in the content of the cases themselves. Within judicial opinions brackets indicate material added by the author of this book unless the brackets appear within quotations or parentheses internal to the opinion.

Contemporary Cases in Women's Rights

CHAPTER 1

Historical Evolution
of the Right of Privacy

By far the most controversial judicial initiative concerning women's rights in the United States was the nation-wide legalization of abortion in the *Roe v. Wade* decision of 1973.[1] The decision spurred an enormous and intense anti-abortion, or "pro-life," political movement, which in turn stimulated a number of abortion restrictions at the state level, several prohibitions on abortion funding at the national level, and even some nonnegligible efforts to amend the U.S. Constitution to ban abortion. The movement had a pronounced effect on the presidential races of the 1980s and 1992. Ronald Reagan pledged in 1980 and again in 1984 to appoint to the Supreme Court justices who would be "pro-life." George Bush repeated the pledge in 1988 and 1992. The Democratic Party platform of those years endorsed the constitutional right to privacy, from which federal judges had derived the constitutional right to obtain an abortion, free from undue government interference.

The intensity of the political conflict over abortion heated up in the late 1980s, when personnel turnover on the Supreme Court reached the point that Reagan and Bush appointees constituted a majority on the Supreme Court. Two cases in particular, *Webster v. Reproductive Health Services* (1989)[2] and *Rust v. Sullivan* (1991),[3] left many legal scholars with the distinct impression that *Roe v. Wade* was about to be overturned by a substantial majority on the Court. The Justice Department under Presidents Reagan and Bush had argued for this overruling in a number of cases, and President Bush instructed his solicitor general to continue that effort in *Planned Parenthood v. Casey*.[4]

This time, however, three of these appointees balked. Together, Sandra Day O'Connor, Anthony Kennedy, and David Souter co-authored an opinion in which they joined the two remaining abortion (or "pro-choice") liberals, Justices Harry Blackmun and John Paul Stevens, to strike down one of the Pennsylvania abortion restrictions and to reaffirm their commitment to what they called the "essential holding" of *Roe*, insisting that to do otherwise would foster the politicization of the Supreme Court. This trio of abortion moderates argued that the abandonment of *Roe* under the political circumstances of 1992[5] would create the public impression that constitutional law was a mere political football, changing sides whenever electoral fortunes did. Their detailed arguments on when precedents should be abandoned versus when they should be followed will be presented in the next chapter. For now, it is simply worth noting that the co-authoring of a judicial opinion itself is a very rare procedure. Normally, one justice writes an opinion and indicates the names of those who concur. This move to co-authorship was evidently meant to depict a highly united front, and thus to discourage further efforts to whittle away at the pro-*Roe* majority. Those efforts, no doubt, will nonetheless continue, despite the election in November 1992 of a moderately pro-choice[6] president, Bill Clinton, in an election where abortion was said to be a more salient issue than ever before.[7]

The remaining sections of this chapter will trace the steps by which the Supreme Court took itself into the midst of this intensely controversial policy domain. The Court's first giant step in that direction was the acknowledgment of an unwritten, fundamental, constitutional right of privacy. The next major step was to extend that right to cover the choice to seek an abortion. But courts typically take many more small steps than large ones, so there is much more to the story. This story has its roots in events that reach far back, before the judiciary began discussing a constitutional "right of privacy."

Early Judicial Invocation of Unwritten Rights

The Constitution itself, in the Fourth Amendment, declares, "The right of the people to be secure in their persons, houses, papers, and effects, against unreasonable searches and seizures, shall not be violated." That declaration, however, describes not a general right of privacy, but a conditional one; if the government meets the conditions of demonstrating to a magistrate "probable cause" (i.e., grounds for a reasonable person to believe the probability) that, say, evidence of a crime will be found in a particularly described place or on a particular person, then the magistrate may issue a search warrant to enter said place or to search said person, and the resulting search will not be "unreasonable" under the terms of the Fourth Amendment. A general right of privacy, then, evolves not directly from the Fourth Amendment but rather from developments in Court history concerning the Fourteenth Amendment.

The Fourteenth Amendment states, in relevant part:

> No State shall make or enforce any law which shall abridge the *privileges or immunities* of citizens of the United States; nor shall any State deprive any person of life, liberty, or property, without *due process* of law; nor deny to any person within its jurisdiction the *equal protection* of the laws. [Emphasis added to indicate names of clauses.—Au.]

The Supreme Court early on took the clause from this passage that seemed to say "no state may abridge the fundamental rights of American citizens"—the "privileges or immunities" clause—and rendered it a nullity; they literally interpreted it as adding nothing to the Constitution that had not already been there before the Fourteenth Amendment.[8] The spirit of that clause, however, lived on; lawyers continued to argue for decades that the Fourteenth Amendment created a rule that the states were no longer free to abridge basic citizen rights (such as the right to freedom of religion or the right to be free of coerced self-incrimination); this (highly plausible) reading of the Fourteenth Amendment would mean that it profoundly restructured the American system of rights and their judicial enforcement. Finally, around the turn of the century the Court began to accept the idea that the Fourteenth Amendment really had put the shield of the national Constitution between citizens' basic rights and the power of the citizens' own state government. Steering away from overruling their own precedent that had emptied the privileges or immunities clause of any meaning,[9] however, the Supreme Court instead inserted this meaning into the due process clause of the same section of the amendment (see italics in quotation at the bottom of p. 4).

Thus, the Court in 1897, in *Chicago, B. & Q. Railroad Co. v. Chicago*,[10] ruled that the Fifth Amendment command "nor shall private property be taken for public use, without just compensation" was applicable to the state governments because taking property without just compensation was taking it "without due process of law," as forbidden to the states by the Fourteenth Amendment. In 1905, in *Lochner v. New York*,[11] the Court ruled that "freedom of contract"—in this case freedom to hire someone, or to be hired, for more than sixty hours a week—was such a fundamental freedom that it is constitutionally protected; in order for a law abridging this right to meet the requirements of "due process of law," said law must be really necessary (must have a "direct relation, as a means to an end") for furthering a substantial government interest. (Eliminating "some small amount of unhealthiness" in workers did not qualify as a substantial enough interest, according to the Court.)

While the Court soon was persuaded—first, concerning women,[12] and later, workers in general[13]—that limiting the length of the workday might in fact improve public health to a substantial, not just a trivial, degree, it was not until 1937 that the majority of the Court abandoned the idea that "freedom of contract" was a fundamental right and therefore protected by the due process clause. They had used that idea as the core of their argument in striking down minimum wage laws twice, first in 1923[14] and again in 1936.[15] These decisions angered President Franklin Roosevelt, as did other decisions striking down major portions of New Deal programs he had created to raise the country out of the Great Depression. Reelected by a massive margin in 1936, he proceeded in 1937 to submit to Congress his notorious Court-packing bill, which proposed to increase the number of justices on the Supreme Court from nine to fifteen. (Three justices had been consistently voting to uphold the kind of economic regulations that Roosevelt favored; six additional sympathetic judicial appointees would give him a solid, nine-to-six majority.) Rather than endure this blatant political takeover of the Supreme Court, two justices who had often voted against Roosevelt programs lined up with the three pro–New Deal, pro–minimum wage justices to produce the "switch in time that saved nine." Upholding a minimum wage law in 1937, this new majority declared that freedom of contract had no special constitutional protection and overruled their earlier precedents to the contrary.[16] (Similarly, they reversed direction on other aspects of the New Deal, upholding a variety of programs that would have been unconstitutional under the logic of their cases from the early 1930s.[17])

During the four decades from 1897 to 1937, when the Supreme Court had been using the due process clause to accord constitutional protection to economic rights, they had also used the clause to protect a number of noneconomic rights, such as freedom of speech[18] and freedom of press.[19] Having abandoned freedom of contract in 1937, but wishing to retain protection for these other, noneconomic rights, the Supreme Court in 1938 produced a set of guidelines for the sorts of rights that would be viewed as protected by the phrase "due process of law." They articulated these guidelines in what has become the most famous footnote in Supreme Court history, footnote 4, of the case *U.S. v. Carolene Products*.[20] Essentially, that footnote said that "due process of law" required that the government meet stringent standards of justification (the kind formerly demanded when government regulated freedom of contract) for only three kinds of frowned-upon laws: (1) "legislation [that] appears on its face to be within one of the specific prohibitions of the Bill of Rights"; (2) legislation that restricts those political processes essential to the functioning of a democratic lawmaking process (e.g., the right to vote); and (3) legislation that seems to attack "discrete and insular minorities," such as racial or religious groups.

Thus, according to this explanatory footnote, freedom of speech and press, since they *are* mentioned in the Bill of Rights, would remain protected. Freedom of contract, not mentioned in the Bill of Rights (or elsewhere in the Constitution), would not be protected.

Marital and Procreative Freedom: Skinner v. Oklahoma (1942) *and Its Predecessors*

The footnote in *U.S. v. Carolene Products* implied but did not spell out an abandonment of other non–Bill of Rights freedoms that had been protected in the pre-1938 period. For instance, in *Meyer v. Nebraska*, a 1923 case striking down a law that forbade the study of German prior to ninth grade, the Supreme Court said that the due process clause protects the freedom "to acquire useful knowledge, to marry, establish a home and bring up children, to worship God according to the dictates of [one's] own conscience...."[21] In *Pierce v. Society of Sisters*, a 1925 case striking down a law that prohibited private schools, the Court added to the list of fundamental rights protected by the due process clause "the liberty of parents ... to direct the upbringing and education of children under their control."[22] Some of these rights do have echoes in the Bill of Rights, e.g., the freedom to worship God according to personal conscience. But the freedom to marry, for instance, is no more explicitly protected in the Constitution than was the now rejected freedom of contract.

Did the *Carolene Products* footnote mean to imply that the freedom to marry and to raise children was no longer a constitutionally protected right of Americans? That question was to remain in a kind of legal limbo for twenty-seven years, until 1965, although the Court somewhat indirectly addressed it in a compulsory sterilization case in 1942, only four years after the footnote had been set forth. The 1942 case, *Skinner v. Oklahoma*,[23] unanimously struck down a criminal statute that provided that persons convicted three times of crimes of "moral turpitude" would be considered "habitual criminals" and were to be sterilized. The statute categorized theft as a crime of moral turpitude and but did not so categorize embezzlement. The Supreme Court noted, "In terms of fines and imprisonment, the crimes of larceny and embezzlement rate the same under the Oklahoma code," and on that basis asserted that the sterilization law violated the equal protection clause[24] because it punished two such similar crimes differently. (In light of both existing and subsequent precedent, this was an extraordinary application of the equal protection clause; typically, the federal courts assume that states have leeway to decide which crimes deserve harsher punishment than others.) In passing, the Court did make an effort to fit this decision into the rubric of *Carolene Products* by implying that this law, because it dealt with procreation, had racial overtones, and thus was at least potentially an attack on a "discrete and insular minority." What the opinion said in this context in *Skinner* was the following:

> We are dealing here with legislation which involves one of the basic civil rights of man. Marriage and procreation are fundamental to the very existence and survival of the race. The power to sterilize, if exercised, may have subtle, far-reaching and devastating effects. In evil or reckless hands it can cause races or types which are inimical to the dominant group to wither and disappear.... [T]he individual whom the law touches ... is forever deprived of a basic liberty.[25] (316 U.S. 535, 541.)

With the *Skinner* decision declaring fundamental another unwritten freedom—the freedom to marry and procreate—the Supreme Court arguably was turning its back on its own *Carolene Products* restrictions of only a few years earlier. But the picture was murky, since, as noted, *Skinner* did contain this strained effort to squeeze its equal protection argument into the "discrete and insular minorities" piece of the *Carolene* framework.

Contraceptive Freedom and Marital Privacy: Poe v. Ullman (1961) and Its Predecessor

The *Skinner* precedent no doubt encouraged certain activists interested in what might be called the other side of the freedom to procreate, the freedom to contracept, or to avoid procreation. One such activist, Wilder Tileston, a physician affiliated with the Connecticut Birth Control League, took a case to the Supreme Court the very next year to challenge Connecticut's still extant 1879 law that made it a crime to use "any drug . . . or instrument for the purpose of preventing conception."[26] He claimed that this statute posed a threat to the lives of some of his patients. The Supreme Court refused to decide his case on the grounds that his own constitutional rights were not involved. If his patients felt that they were being threatened with the deprivation of life without due process of law, then they, not he, said the Court, would have to bring a case presenting that claim.[27]

In general, federal courts insist that only litigants with proper "standing" may present a case to them: to have standing, a litigant must have an actual, concrete, personal stake in the controversy; she or he must stand to gain or lose something by the outcome of the case. The Court's standing requirements are applied with varying degrees of stringency, depending whether it is eager or reluctant to decide certain cases. The Court's refusal to allow Dr. Tileston to present the constitutional claims of third parties (his patients) indicated that the justices were not eager to declare a national, unwritten constitutional right to use contraception. On the other hand, the fact that the case progressed as far as it did—in that the Supreme Court actually issued an opinion explaining why it would not issue an opinion "on the merits"—means that at least initially four justices out of nine felt that the case was worth deciding. The Supreme Court has a "rule of four" for deciding which cases to hear. After hearing the case and discussing it, the justices then (puzzlingly) lined up unanimously against actually deciding it. Americans were to live without an official constitutional right to marital or contraceptive privacy for another two decades.

Tileston's attorney, Morris Ernst did not abandon the contraceptive freedom cause. In 1961 he returned to the Supreme Court, along with two other attorneys for Planned Parenthood, Harriet Pilpel and Nancy Wechsler, to argue (in an *amicus curiae,* or "friend of the court," brief) against the Connecticut statute, this time in the case *Poe v. Ullman.*[28] For the seventeen years since Tileston's case, Planned Parenthood, successor to the Birth Control League, had been unsuccessfully lobbying the Connecticut legislature to repeal the 1879 statute. In this their second try, their litigation effort achieved at least a number of dissents against the Supreme Court's refusal to hear the case. The Supreme Court majority refused to decide *Poe v. Ullman* on the grounds that the law was a dead letter; the state had never completed a prosecution of anyone under it, and contraceptives were openly dispensed in Connecticut drugstores without any police response. The state's attorney, Ullman, had indicated that the state might prosecute only if someone opened a publicly advertised birth control clinic, and the Court majority preferred to postpone a decision in the hope that this hypothetical prosecution possibility would never become actual.

Two of the four dissents to the Court's refusal to decide, however, did argue squarely for an unwritten constitutional right to contraceptive freedom for married couples. Justice Douglas argued that "due process of law" could not be confined to protect only the liberties listed in the Bill of Rights; he pointed to precedents protecting the nonitemized rights "to travel," and "to marry, establish a home, and bring up children." He indicated his own view that an additional unwritten right was the right to privacy. He derived this right from "the totality of the constitutional scheme under which we live" and pointed to the Third Amendment prohibition on stationing soldiers in private homes. He then reasoned that this law was unconstitutional because an effort to enforce it would require "an inquiry into the relations between man and wife," thereby invading "the privacy that is implicit in a free society."[29]

Justice Harlan, too, dissented. At a number of points he cited the precedent of *Skinner* (which had been authored by Justice Douglas). He also cited the *Meyer* and *Pierce* precedents. His basic argument was that the due process clause calls upon the judiciary to identify those rights that are fundamental—as he put it, those "interests [that] require particularly careful scrutiny of the state need asserted to justify their abridgment." One of those interests in a free society had to be the right of married couples to "privacy in the conduct of the most intimate concerns of an individual's personal life." Justice Harlan argued that even though a right to the privacy of family life was nowhere explicit in the Constitution, both the Third and Fourth amendments contained indirect allusions to it. Moreover, judges are bound to consider the "rational purposes and historic roots" of constitutional provisions, not just their bare words. Such a consideration yields the conclusion that the right of privacy in marital life is fundamental in our constitutional order. Because this law intrudes "the whole machinery of the criminal law into the very heart of marital privacy, requiring a husband and wife to render account before a criminal tribunal of their uses of that intimacy," it should be judged unconstitutional, he argued.[30] His conclusion was to be shared by a Court majority only four years later.

Victory for Marital Privacy and Contraception: Griswold v. Connecticut (1965)

In 1965, the U.S. Supreme Court took up for the third time this 1879 statute from Connecticut. Finally the state had enforced the ordinance, and—contrary to concerns that had been voiced in the *Poe* dissents of Douglas and Harlan— seemed to have managed to do so without physical intrusion into anyone's home and without forcing marital partners to discuss intimate details. Following the *Poe v. Ullman* dismissal, Planned Parenthood did open up a public birth control clinic in that state. Police proceeded to arrest both Estelle Griswold, executive director of Planned Parenthood, and Dr. C. Lee Buxton (the same man who had brought the suit *Poe v. Ullman*) for the crime of being an accessory to a crime. The latter was the crime of using contraception; the act that made them accessories was Buxton's prescribing contraceptives to a married woman. Each of them was fined $100. They appealed their case to the U.S. Supreme Court, and, facing this issue for the third time in twenty-three years, the justices finally decided to decide the case.

Writing for the Court, Justice Douglas this time steered clear of the reasoning in his *Poe v. Ullman* dissent. There he had argued frankly that, while the Court should continue to reject the discredited "freedom of contract," it should nonetheless be willing to use the due process clause to protect other fundamental rights not specified in the Bill of Rights (or other parts of the constitutional text). Here he hedged on that position, arguing instead that the explicit rights of the Constitution not only contain implicit ones (e.g., speech and peaceable assembly imply a right of political association), but also contain "penumbras, formed by emanations from those [explicit] guarantees that help give them life and substance." (A penumbra is a kind of hazy shadow around the edges of a thing.) He then asserted that zones of privacy were created by penumbras of the First Amendment (implied right of associational privacy), as well as the Third (prohibition on soldiers in private homes), Fourth (freedom from unreasonable searches), Fifth (protection against coerced self-incrimination), and Ninth amendments. (The Ninth states that the enumeration of rights in the Constitution "shall not be construed to deny or disparage others retained by the people.") He concluded that the marital relationship fell within a constitutionally protected zone of privacy and that this restriction on the use of contraceptives, even by married couples, swept "unnecessarily broadly" into this area of protected freedom. That reference to the "unnecessary" breadth of the restriction was an allusion to a standard test for laws that are challenged as abridgments of constitutionally protected rights (e.g., freedom of speech); in order to have a restriction on a protected freedom upheld, a state must be able to demonstrate to the judges that the restriction goes no further than is "necessary for attaining a compelling governmental interest." Although he alluded to this test in the *Griswold* opinion, Douglas did not elaborate upon his application of it to this law, other than to say that the law failed the test.

Justice Goldberg authored a concurring opinion on behalf of three (including himself) of the five justices who made up the group for whom Douglas's majority opinion spoke. This opinion particularly emphasized that the Ninth Amendment should be viewed as a guide to the construction of the Constitution. Goldberg argued that the Ninth Amendment indicated an interpretation of the due process clause that would read it as protecting *all* rights (not just the explicit ones) that are fundamental to the "traditions and [collective] conscience of our people" or that are part of the "fundamental principles of liberty and justice which lie at the base of all our civil and political institutions."[31] Like Justice Douglas, although somewhat more explicitly, Justice Goldberg also invoked the compelling interest (or "necessity") test. "Absent a showing of a compelling subordinating state interest," he argued, the state must permit both procreative and contraceptive freedom to married couples.

Justices Harlan and White each wrote separate concurring opinions. Harlan specifically disagreed with the tone of the Court opinion, for he felt it too much hewed to the idea that if a right was not specifically listed in the Constitution or covered by a penumbra of a clause of the Constitution, then it was not a protected right. Harlan reiterated his idea, detailed in his *Poe v. Ullman* dissent, that the due process clause protects all "basic values implicit in the concept of ordered liberty," whether or not those values are alluded to elsewhere in the Constitution. For the explanation of his views, he referred readers back to his *Poe* dissent. There he had indicated that the state does have legitimate authority to promote morality[32] but that the prohibition of extramarital sexuality (whether fornication, adultery, or homosexuality) had a constitutional status different from a regulation of the details of marital intimacy. If the people of Connecticut chose to view contraception as immoral, they could discourage it in a variety of ways (e.g., forbid the manufacture of certain products within their own borders, offer financial rewards for large families), but using the criminal law to trample upon the intimacy of the married couple was transgressing constitutional bounds.

Justice White, too, authored a separate concurrence, refusing to join Douglas's suggestion that the First, Third, Fourth, Fifth, and Ninth amendments somehow implied a right to marital, procreative privacy. Instead, like Harlan, White based his views squarely on the due process clause. But unlike Harlan,[33] he particularly stressed the long line of Supreme Court precedents that had noted the protected constitutional status (under the due process clause) of the "right to marry, establish a home, and bring up children" (*Meyer*) and the idea that procreation is among "the basic civil rights of man" (*Skinner*). Having established the point that contraceptive freedom within marriage was a constitutionally protected liberty, White then invoked the standard test for statutes regulating such liberty: to be valid they must be proven "reasonably necessary for the effectuation of a legitimate and substantial state interest, and not arbitrary or capricious in application." Next he applied this test. Connecticut had argued that its interest in the ban was to discourage premarital and extramarital sex by intensifying the fear of pregnancy. Justice White pointed out the obvious; by applying the ban to sex within marriage, the statute swept more broadly than its stated goal necessitated, and therefore it was unconstitutional.

Justices Stewart and Black each wrote vehement dissents. Stewart noted specifically that just because a law is "asinine" does not make it unconstitutional. Both of them argued that the *Meyer* and *Pierce* line of cases, upholding unwritten constitutional rights, had later been discredited (except to the extent that the specific rights embraced in those cases could be legitimately inferred from written clauses of the Constitution, such as freedom of speech). They argued that it was utterly implausible to claim that statements referring to "freedom of speech," or a right to assemble peaceably for redress of grievance, or a right "against unreasonable searches and seizures," somehow create a right to use a contraceptive device. (Griswold and Buxton had been arrested by means of impeccable arrest warrants.) Black and Stewart both insisted that "fundamental values" were something for the American people to discern and implement through the electoral/legislative process, and that decisions where justices imposed unwritten values, to override those implemented by elected legislatures, amounted to unconstitutional power grabs by those justices.

It is perhaps worth noting that Justices Black and Stewart (the dissenters) were considered, respectively, a liberal and a moderate. Their view that it was illegitimate for the judiciary to be declaring an unwritten right of marital, procreative privacy has been abandoned by all the justices since 1965, even those considered most conservative in the use of judicial power (Rehnquist and Scalia). Justice Black died before any other contraception case would be decided, and Justice Stewart switched sides in the next contraception case, *Eisenstadt v. Baird*,[34] on the grounds that *Griswold* was now a valid precedent, which had to be followed. Justice Rehnquist implied (without stating) in *Roe v. Wade* (1973) that he disagreed with the logic of *Griswold;* this implication was carried in his insistence that a century-old criminal statute could not plausibly be viewed as contrary to our national traditions (and on that grounds a violation of due process).[35] By 1977, however, he seemed to accept the view that at least "decisions on the part of married couples as to procreation" are protected by the due process clause as a traditional liberty.[36] Even Justice Scalia, by all accounts the most conservative of the justices, has accepted the doctrine that marital privacy is a national tradition and for that reason is protected by the due process clause.[37] Thus, the U.S. Supreme Court now acknowledges that the due process clause accords to justices the power to decide which liberties are "fundamental" under our national traditions, and to override the considered views of any elected legislature to the contrary. This reading of the due process clause, of course, accords considerable power to nonelected judges. Evidently, judges, like other humans, find it difficult to give up power.

From Marital to Extramarital Privacy and an Abortion Forecast: Eisenstadt v. Baird (1972)

Every justice in the *Griswold* majority had emphasized the close link between the nature of marriage—a central institution in our national traditions—and the right of privacy that *Griswold* was singling out for protection. Several of them had made a point of acknowledging that they did not question the state's power to punish sexual behavior outside of marriage. Still, it did not take birth control activists long to detect a certain illogic in a national policy that would allow married couples but not unmarried people to avoid unwanted pregnancies.

By 1972 such activists had reached the U.S. Supreme Court with a case challenging a Massachusetts law that prohibited the distribution of contraceptives by anyone other than licensed physicians who were prescribing for married persons or pharmacists filling such prescriptions. Bill Baird, a prominent advocate of birth control, initiated that case, *Eisenstadt v. Baird*,[38] by getting himself arrested during a lecture at Boston University when he handed a package of Emko Vaginal Foam (a generally nonprescription, spermicidal contraceptive) to an unmarried coed. Since he was not a physician, Baird was arrested (as he had intended) for the felony of distributing a nonprescription contraceptive. The Massachusetts Supreme Court upheld his conviction; the federal district court dismissed his appeal that claimed the law he violated was an unconstitutional infringement on the right of privacy; the federal circuit court of appeals overturned his conviction; and the U.S. Supreme Court handed down the opinion for his case on March 22, 1972.

The reasoning for *Eisenstadt v. Baird* was announced under the pronounced shadow of the question of abortion. Only three months earlier the justices had heard oral argument for what were to become the two landmark abortion cases, *Roe v. Wade* and *Doe v. Bolton*.[39]

By the time of the *Eisenstadt* decision, a number of federal courts had already issued opinions extending the constitutional right to privacy to cover the freedom of a woman, married or single, to choose an abortion. Abortion policy had become a topic of heated controversy in the United States in large part because of a feminist movement that mushroomed in the 1967–1972 period. As of 1967 abortion was a crime in every state of the union. As early as 1968 lawyers had begun to argue, in both law review articles and litigation, that laws prohibiting abortion violated a woman's right to privacy.[40] By 1969 one state court (California Supreme Court) and one federal court (for the District of Columbia) had declared abortion prohibitions unconstitutional. These pioneering courts had done so not on right-to-privacy grounds but rather on grounds that the laws in question were so vague as to deny fair warning to would-be violators (and thus to deny "due process of law").[41] By 1970, however, three states—Wisconsin, Texas, and Georgia—lost their anti-abortion statutes at the hands of federal judges using right-to-privacy reasoning. Four other states (New York, Washington, Alaska, and Hawaii) legalized abortion by statute in 1970. Several others came close to doing so.[42] In 1971 another federal court declared the criminal abortion statute of Illinois an unconstitutional invasion of the right to privacy. Also in 1971 the U.S. Supreme Court settled the appeal concerning the District of Columbia statute by ruling that the statute was not void on vagueness grounds but that the word "health" in the statute certainly included mental health. In other words, the Court interpreted the D.C. law to permit abortion for reasons of psychological stress.[43]

Then, with abortion policy across the nation in an apparent state of flux, and with only seven justices on the Supreme Court (due to the recent retirements of Justices Black and Harlan), on December 13, 1971, the Supreme Court heard arguments for the appeals of the Texas (*Roe v. Wade*) and Georgia (*Doe v. Bolton*) abortion decisions.[44] (The justices were eventually to announce, in June 1972, that they wanted the Texas and Georgia cases reargued in the fall of 1972, when the Court would be back at a full complement of nine justices.) Having heard arguments for the *Roe* and *Doe* abortion cases and before announcing that they were to be set for reargument, the Supreme Court handed down its decision in *Eisenstadt v. Baird* in March of 1972.

Because the Massachusetts law that Baird violated prohibited him from giving a contraceptive to married as well as unmarried persons (since he was neither a doctor nor a pharmacist) the Supreme Court could have simply thrown out the Massachusetts law as they had thrown out the Connecticut law—because it swept overly broadly into the area of marital privacy, keeping married people from access to nondangerous contraceptives such as condoms. Two of the justices (White and Blackmun) indeed relied on this reasoning, still maintaining that the right of privacy was peculiarly a right of the marital couple. Justice Burger dissented on the grounds that, even though some contraceptives are not dangerous, since birth itself can be dangerous, a state can reasonably require that people obtain professional medical advice about the choice of a contraceptive best for their circumstances.

Four justices out of the *Eisenstadt* seven insisted on pushing beyond the *Griswold* plateau; with the stroke of a pen the right of marital privacy was transformed to a right of individual privacy. Justice Brennan's formulation of that new right structured it in terms that seemed with full self-awareness to lay the groundwork for a constitutional right to seek an abortion. He wrote: "If the right of privacy means anything, it is the right of the *individual*, married or single, to be free from unwarranted governmental intrusion into matters so fundamentally affecting a person as the decision whether to bear or beget a child."[45]

The choice not to "beget" a child is about contraception; the decision "whether to bear a child" would seem to describe a decision about abortion. In light of the timing of this announcement, one must at least suspect that Brennan intended to establish the groundwork for the conclusion that the right to privacy encompasses the abortion decision. It was to be less than a year before the Supreme Court in a 7–2 decision announced that very conclusion, in *Roe v. Wade* and *Doe v. Bolton*.

(Lest the reader be wondering what else besides abortion and contraception the Supreme Court regarded as "matters so fundamentally affecting a person as the decision whether to bear or beget a child," it can be noted that in 1977 the Court included in that category the right of grandparents and their grandchildren to inhabit the same household, zoning laws to the contrary notwithstanding.[46] In 1986 the Court by a 5–4 vote excluded from constitutional protection an asserted right of adults to engage in private, consensual sodomy—i.e., oral or anal sex.)[47]

The Right to Abortion: Roe v. Wade *and* Doe v. Bolton (1973)

The Supreme Court consolidated the *Roe* and *Doe* cases even though they dealt with rather different abortion statutes. The Texas statute at issue in *Roe* was the traditional anti-abortion law, and was typical of American state laws at the time. It prohibited as a serious crime any abortion except one necessary "for the purpose of saving the life of the mother." Suit against it was brought by the pseudonymous Jane Roe (years later, publicly identified as Norma McCorvey, an unwed, impoverished, sometime carnival worker/sometime waitress) who found herself pregnant.[48] By the time of completing even her first round in court, she would no longer be pregnant, so her lawyers, aware that the wheels of justice grind slowly and also interested in general abortion reform, framed the suit as a class action on behalf of all women who find themselves with unwanted pregnancies (as well as doctors wishing to help them). Faced with a claim for abortion by a no-longer-pregnant woman, the U.S. Supreme Court decided to be lenient (both in *Roe* and *Doe*) with its standing requirement,[49] explaining its grant of jurisdiction as follows:

> The usual rule in federal cases is that an actual controversy must exist at stages of appellate . . . review. . . .
> But when, as here, pregnancy is a significant fact in the litigation, the . . . gestation period is so short that the pregnancy will come to term before the usual

appellate process is complete. If that termination makes a case moot . . . appellate review will be effectively denied. Our law should not be that rigid. . . . Pregnancy provides a classic justification for a conclusion of nonmootness. It could truly be "capable of repetition, yet evading review." (*Roe*, 410 U.S., at 125.)

The *Doe v. Bolton* lawsuit challenged Georgia's much more liberal abortion statute. That law basically tracked the model abortion reform law proposed in 1962 by the prestigious American Law Institute (ALI).[50] Georgia allowed abortion for bona fide Georgia residents in an accredited hospital upon verification by three licensed physicians and a three-member hospital staff abortion committee that either (1) continued pregnancy would endanger the pregnant woman's life or "seriously and permanently" injure her health; (2) the fetus would "very likely be born with a grave, permanent and irremediable mental or physical defect"; or (3) the pregnancy resulted from rape or incest. While considered lenient for its time, the statute nonetheless resulted in hardship for many women, and the pseudonymous Mary Doe was a case in point. Twenty-two years old, impoverished, and with a history of psychiatric hospitalization, she had already borne three children, two of whom—because of her inability to care for them—had been placed in foster homes and the third of whom was given up for adoption. On the grounds of a serious threat to her mental health, her physician recommended an abortion. Doe was unable to win approval, however, from the Grady Memorial Hospital abortion committee. She then did get approval at the Georgia Baptist Hospital, but the latter refused to accept her as a charity patient. She then went to court to challenge the statute, and like Roe gave birth long before the appeals process ended.

Both Roe and Doe won a declaration of unconstitutionality in their first round in federal court but both failed to obtain what their lawyers requested: a court order forbidding enforcement of the abortion law against anyone in the future. In order to obtain that injunction, both Roe and Doe appealed to the U.S. Supreme Court.

The opinions that finally came down for those two cases[51] had enormous legal impact. All but four states still had laws on the books declaring abortion to be a serious crime. Nine states had had their abortion law declared unconstitutional in either state or federal court,[52] but none of those decisions could have the definitive effect of a U.S. Supreme Court decision (since it is the court of final appeal for interpreting the Constitution, and its decisions apply to the entire country). *Roe* legalized abortion nationwide for approximately the first six months of pregnancy—technically until the point of fetal viability.[53]

The reasoning in both *Roe* and *Doe* followed the compelling interest test approach discussed above. First, the Court reiterated that Americans do have a fundamental, constitutionally protected "right to privacy," which right has application in matters of marriage, procreation, contraception, family relationships, and child rearing and education (and it identified relevant precedents for each of these). With the apparent purpose of showing the relation of abortion to our society's traditions, Justice Blackmun prefaced his right of privacy discussion with a lengthy excursus on the history of abortion in Western civilization, going back to the ancient Greeks and up through British and then American common law, right up to the contemporary views of the American Medical Association, the American Bar Association, and the American Public Health Association. He took care to point out that before the late nineteenth century, North American laws tended to treat leniently abortion prior to quickening (the time, generally early in the fifth month, when the pregnant woman senses fetal movement), either ignoring it or treating it as a minor offense. He concluded his discussion of the right of privacy precedents with this remark:

> This right of privacy, whether it be founded in the Fourteenth Amendment's concept of personal liberty and restrictions upon state action, as we feel it is, or, as the District Court determined, in the Ninth Amendment's reservation of rights to the people, is broad enough to encompass a woman's decision whether or not to terminate her pregnancy.[54]

Having established that freedom in the decision to terminate one's own pregnancy was part of constitutionally protected privacy, Blackmun then had to weigh the state's various interests in checking this freedom, in order to decide whether any of them were "compelling" enough to justify the Texas ban on abortion or the various limits on abortion in the Georgia statute. He took up specifically the state interest or duty in preserving fetal life (the basic justification put forth by Texas for its law) and the question of protecting the pregnant woman's health. The Court majority evidently found at least plausible the arguments of the pro-choice attorneys that late nineteenth century abortion laws had been adopted primarily for the latter purpose. Blackmun took pains to explain that before 1900, "[a]bortion mortality was high" and remained so "perhaps until as late as the development of antibiotics in the 1940's."[55] Blackmun framed his discussion of the health concern around his conclusion that times had changed dramatically, to the point that "[m]ortality rates for women undergoing early abortions, where the procedure is legal, appear to be as low as or lower than the rates for normal childbirth."[56] Abortion late in pregnancy, however, still posed substantial health risks to women, and these legitimate health and safety concerns could not be ignored.[57]

Concerning the state's interest in preserving fetal life, Blackmun first took up the claim of Texas that the fetus was a person "from the moment of conception," and was therefore protected by the mandate of the Fourteenth Amendment due process clause: "nor shall any state deprive any person of life, liberty, or property without due process of law." Blackmun noted that all three branches of the federal government had a consistent record (for instance, when counting persons for the census, as mandated in Article I, section 2, clause 3 of the Constitution) of treating personhood for legal purposes as beginning at birth. Concerning the claim that Texas ought to be free nonetheless to protect prenatal life from its ostensible beginning at conception, Blackmun wrote, "We need not resolve the difficult question of when life begins."[58] He then catalogued various views on the subject: the arguments for dating life from conception, from quickening, from viability, or from live birth itself. While maintaining that the Court did not have to resolve the question of when life begins, Blackmun nevertheless, went on to conclude:

> [W]e do not agree that, by adopting one theory of life, Texas may override the rights of the pregnant woman that are at stake. We repeat, however, that the State does have an . . . important and legitimate interest in protecting the potentiality of human life. . . .
>
> With respect to the State's important and legitimate interest in potential life, the "compelling" point is at viability. This is so because the fetus then presumably has the capability of meaningful life outside the mother's womb. State regulation protective of fetal life after viability thus has both logical and biological justifications. If the State is interested in protecting fetal life after viability, it may go so far as to proscribe abortion during that period, except when it is necessary to preserve the life or health of the mother.[59]

In other words, while Blackmun claimed *not* to need to resolve the question of when life begins, still he *did* select that point before which the state may not act to protect prenatal life. And that point was viability.

As to the state's interest in protecting maternal health, Blackmun acknowledged that this interest, too, is "important and legitimate." Of this interest, he wrote:

> [T]he "compelling" point, in light of present medical knowledge, is at approximately the end of the first trimester [of pregnancy]. This is so because of the now-established medical fact . . . that until the end of the first trimester mortality in abortion may be less than mortality in normal childbirth. It follows that, from and after this point, a State may regulate the abortion procedure to the extent that the regulation reasonably relates to the preservation and protection of maternal health. Examples of permissible state regulation in this area are requirements as to the qualifications of the person who is to perform the abortion; as to the licensure of that person; as to the facility in which the procedure is to be performed, that is, whether it must be a hospital or may be a clinic or some other place of less-than-hospital status; as to the licensing of the facility; and the like.[60]

This discussion of the two points of compelling justification for state intervention established the contours of the Court's framework for analyzing the constitutionality of abortion statutes. In the first trimester of pregnancy, the state had to leave the abortion decision to the woman in consultation with her attending physician, except that the state did have legitimate authority to decide who counts as a licensed physician and to forbid abortions by anyone else.[61] (Blackmun did not explain how, if maternal health was not a compelling enough interest to justify other sorts of licensings for abortion prior to the fourth month of pregnancy, it nonetheless justified this particular one in the first three months.) After the first trimester, the state could "regulate the abortion procedure in ways that are. reasonably related to maternal health." And after the point of fetal viability, the state could proscribe abortion "except where it is necessary, in appropriate medical judgment, for the preservation of the life or health of the mother."[62]

· Blackmun applied this *Roe* framework to the Georgia law in *Doe v. Bolton*. The Court ruled that the requirement that abortions be performed only in hospitals accredited by the Joint Commission on the Accreditation of Hospitals lacked a reasonable basis because Georgia imposed this rule on no other type of surgery (unlike the requirement that both the surgeon and hospital be licensed by the state). Using the same reasoning, the Court invalidated the requirements for committee approval and for approval from two doctors in addition to the attending physician. As to the rule that only Georgia residents could obtain abortions in Georgia, the Court declared that this violated the constitutional right to travel freely among the states, implied by clause 1 of Article IV, section 2.[63]

Post-**Roe** *Abortion Restrictions*

The successful efforts of the pro-choice movement in four state legislatures, in a number of federal and state courts, and most impressively in *Roe v. Wade* proved an enormous stimulus to a counter-lobbying effort, which dubbed itself the pro-life movement. Pro-life lobbyists attained their earliest successes in state legislatures, where they secured passage of a number of restrictions on the newly legalized practice of abortion. These restrictions in turn were soon tested in litigation at the U.S. Supreme Court, where they met with only limited success.

The first such challenge was presented in 1976 in the case *Planned Parenthood v. Danforth*.[64] The Court divided into a variety of factions over the several provisions of the Missouri statute at issue there, with the following results:

1. The Court ruled unanimously that *Roe* did not conflict with a provision that defined *viability* as "that stage of fetal development when the life of the unborn child may be continued indefinitely outside the womb by natural or artificial life-supportive systems."[65] Contrary to the claims of the litigants, *Roe* did not demand an inflexible line at the end of the second trimester of pregnancy.

2. The Court struck down by a 6–3 vote a statutory requirement that persons who perform abortions must "exercise that degree of professional skill, care and

diligence to preserve ... the fetus which such person would be required to exercise ... to preserve ... any fetus intended to be born,"[66] on the grounds that the provision did not contain an explicit exception for nonviable fetuses.

3. Against the litigants' insistence that *Roe* had forbidden regulations of any kind to interfere with abortion freedom during the first trimester, the Court unanimously upheld the following two regulations:

(a) The requirement that any woman obtaining an abortion, unless the abortion is needed to save her life, give the physician her prior consent, certifying in writing that the consent "is freely given and is not the product of coercion." (The Court explained as follows: "The decision to abort, indeed, is an important, and often a stressful one, and it is desirable and imperative that it be made with full knowledge of its nature and consequences. The woman is the one primarily concerned, and her awareness of the decision and its significance may be assured, constitutionally, by the State to the extent of requiring her prior written consent.")[67]

(b) The requirement that records of "maternal health and life data" be gathered, recorded, and maintained in confidentiality for seven years, with access thereto allowed for local, state, or national public health officers. (Against the argument that this imposed an extra burden of regulation and cost upon first-trimester abortions, which under *Roe* were supposed to be free of regulation, the Court replied that "we see no legally significant impact or consequence on the abortion decision or on the physician-patient relationship. . . .")[68]

4. By a 6–3 vote the Court struck down a law forbidding the saline amniocentesis abortion technique after the first twelve weeks of pregnancy. The majority reasoned that since amniocentesis was the most widely available, relatively safe abortion technique for that stage of pregnancy, and since its alternative, the prostaglandin method, was barely, if at all, available in Missouri at the time this statute passed, the measure appeared to be a thinly disguised attempt to render second-trimester abortions unavailable in Missouri.

5. By a 6–3 vote the Court declared unconstitutional a requirement of written consent of a married woman's husband to permit her to obtain an abortion, unless the abortion were necessary in order to save her life. The Court reasoned that, while it did not dispute the legitimacy of laws requiring two-parent consent to give up a child born in wedlock for adoption, or for artificial insemination of the wife or for voluntary sterilization of either spouse, abortion was different because "it is the woman who physically bears the child and who is the more directly and immediately affected by the pregnancy." Since, if the two spouses disagree, one will have to make the decision, "as between the two, the balance weighs in her favor."[69]

6. Finally the Supreme Court divided 5–4 to strike down the requirement that unmarried minors (i.e., under eighteen) obtain the written consent of a parent or guardian unless an abortion is necessary for preserving the young

woman's life. Here, however, the 5–4 vote was deceiving because two justices of the five (Stewart and Powell) wrote a separate opinion to indicate that they would uphold a parental consent requirement if an option were made available for a minor to go to a judge and "bypass" her parents by convincing the judge either that she were mature enough to make her own decision or that an abortion would be in her best interest. Thus, carefully read this decision turns out to be 6–3 *in favor of* upholding a parental consent requirement that is tempered by a judicial bypass option.[70] That implication of the ruling was later to be ratified in a number of cases.[71]

Between the 1976 *Planned Parenthood* case and 1983, abortion decisions essentially refined the reasoning of *Planned Parenthood* under various fact situations. Most of these concerned parental consent or notice provisions,[72] and one involved statutory definitions of viability and of the standard of care required for a viable fetus who might be accidentally (i.e., by physician misjudgment as to viability) delivered. In the latter, the Court ruled that viability was that point "when, in the judgment of the attending physician on the particular facts of the case before him, there is a reasonable likelihood of the fetus' sustained survival outside the womb, with or without artificial support."[73]

Roe v. Wade *Under Siege:* Akron I (1983) *and* Thornburgh v. ACOG (1986)

In the election campaign of 1980, Ronald Reagan promised to appoint pro-life judges, and his first appointment to the Court was a woman, Sandra Day O'Connor. Her first opinion on the abortion question turned out to be a dissent in the 1983 case *Akron v. Akron Center for Reproductive Health* (later referred to as *Akron I*)[74] in which she argued, in an opinion joined by Justices White and Rehnquist (the *Roe* dissenters), that the *Roe* three-stage, or trimester, framework should be abandoned because it was "on a collision course with itself," since medical technology would steadily move the date of viability to earlier in the pregnancy and steadily extend to a later point in the pregnancy that stage during which abortion was safer for a woman than childbirth. Strangely, Justice Burger, who had concurred in *Roe* but had been dissenting in favor of upholding abortion restrictions ever since *Planned Parenthood*, did not align with O'Connor's dissent; thus, the vote in *Akron I* was not the somewhat expected 5–4 but rather 6–3 on behalf of following *Roe v. Wade*. In addition to her "collision course with itself" reasoning, O'Connor criticized *Roe* for failing to acknowledge that the state's interest in protecting "the potentiality of human life" in the fetus amounted to a compelling interest not just in the third trimester but "*throughout* pregnancy" (her italics). She argued, "At any stage in pregnancy, there is the *potential* for human life" (her italics).[75] By this logic, it appeared that Justice O'Connor would vote to uphold virtually all abortion restrictions, for every abortion prohibition furthers the state's interest in the potentiality of life and is arguably necessary for that potential life to become actual.[76]

But at this point, Justice O'Connor complicated her argument by adding a second consideration; she explained that "not every regulation that the state imposes must be measured against the state's compelling interests and examined with strict scrutiny." She quoted an earlier precedent to the effect that "'the right in *Roe v. Wade* . . . protects the woman from *unduly burdensome interference* with her freedom to decide whether to terminate her pregnancy.'"[77] She characterized the concept of "undue burden" with phrases such as "state action 'drastically limiting the availability and safety of the desired service,'" or "the imposition of an 'absolute obstacle' on the abortion decision," or "'official interference' and 'coercive restraint' imposed on the abortion decision." She then added that, if there were no undue burden, the statute need satisfy only the very minimal "reasonableness" test; the state needed to show at least a rational connection between the law and some legitimate governmental goal. (Protecting potential life would always count as a legitimate purpose.)

Justice O'Connor did not make clear the relation between her two lines of reasoning. If potential life were not just a legitimate interest but even a "compelling interest" warranting state protection throughout pregnancy, it was not clear where the "unduly burdensome" test would come into play, because it would seem, for the sake of potential life, that states could totally prohibit abortion throughout pregnancy, and an outright prohibition is as burdensome as a regulation ever becomes. She closed this section of her reasoning with the rather cryptic remark, "[S]tate action 'encouraging childbirth except in the most urgent circumstances' is 'rationally related to the legitimate governmental objective of protecting potential life.'"[78] This left the impression that in "the most urgent" circumstances—say, threat to a mother's life, or perhaps grave threat to physical or mental health—the mother's right to choose against childbirth could be protected (i.e., an abortion prohibition would be ruled "unduly burdensome"), but absent such circumstances O'Connor would be willing to uphold absolute prohibitions on abortion as in furtherance of the compelling interest in potential life. At this point it appeared that if one or two (depending on the unreliable vote of Justice Burger) justices were to join the O'Connor group, the abortion freedom secured by *Roe v. Wade* would become a thing of the past, and the United States would return to the 1972 status quo.

The six-judge majority in *Akron I* all concurred in an opinion drafted by Justice Powell. This opinion devoted its lengthy first footnote to rebutting the proposition of Justice O'Connor that *Roe* should be abandoned. The footnote documented the number of justices and the number of precedents that had concurred with *Roe*'s "basic principle that a woman has a fundamental right to make the highly personal choice whether or not to terminate her pregnancy," and pointedly insisted, "We respect [the doctrine of following precedent, *stare decisis*] today, and reaffirm *Roe v. Wade*."

The majority (in Section II of Powell's opinion) reiterated the precedents that underlay the logic of *Roe* and recapitulated the law of abortion as it had evolved up until 1983: (1) During "approximately the first trimester" the state is forbidden to restrict a woman's freedom, in consultation with her (licensed) physician, to decide to have an abortion, with the qualification that "regulations that have no significant impact on the woman's exercise of her right [e.g., mandating confidential record-keeping] may be permissible where justified by important state health objectives"; (2) from approximately the end of the first trimester until the point of viability the state may adopt regulations reasonably tailored to the goal of promoting maternal health; (3) after viability, abortion may be forbidden except for purposes of preserving the life or health of the mother.

After this summary, Powell proceeded to acknowledge that abortion technology had changed since *Roe*. In 1973 it had been medically reasonable to require (because of techniques then prevalent) that second-trimester abortions be limited to full-service hospitals. Now, however, throughout the fourth month of pregnancy, abortions could safely be, and were routinely, performed in clinics, which were much less expensive and more widely available. Because of this change in medical reality, Akron's statute, which restricted *all* second-trimester abortions to full-service hospitals, was not truly "reasonably related" to promoting maternal health. Such a statute could be constitutional only if it kicked in after the fourth month (not third) of pregnancy, when such a restriction was now medically reasonable. So, as written, the statute was declared unconstitutional.[79]

Moreover, the majority declared unconstitutional Akron's parental consent provision for a minor under fifteen because of its vagueness in describing the judicial bypass option; they also declared unconstitutional on vagueness grounds its mandate that every aborted fetus be "disposed of in a humane and sanitary manner."

Finally, Akron's elaborate requirements ostensibly aimed at informed consent of the abortion-seeking patient were ruled unconstitutional by the Supreme Court. These included a twenty-four-hour waiting period between her signing a consent form and the performance of an abortion and a mandate that, before she signed, her physician must inform her of the following: the date when her fetus would become viable and what its approximate stage of development was; that "the unborn child is a human life from the moment of conception"; that a specific list (compiled in the statute) of abortion risks and complications are possible (whether they were likely in her case or not); that state agencies were available to help her with birth control, adoption, and childbirth; and, finally, in accordance with his/her own medical judgment, what risks might be likely with respect to her particular pregnancy and the particular abortion techniques the physician planned to use. With respect to the last item on the list, the Court ruled that while a state might reasonably require that this information be provided to a patient, it was not reasonable to insist that the only person qualified to give this information was the attending physician. Therefore the Court struck down the requirement as reaching more broadly than necessary into the area of protected freedom. As to the other provisions—a twenty-four-hour wait, a litany of state-defined supposed risks, and a mandated assertion by the doctor that life begins at conception—the Supreme Court struck them down as not reasonably related to promoting maternal health.[80]

On the same day that *Akron I* was decided, the Supreme Court decided *Simopoulos v. Virginia*[81] and *Planned Parenthood v. Ashcroft.*[82] In *Simopoulos*, the Court ruled (8–1) that it was constitutional to require all second-trimester abortions to be performed either in a licensed clinic or, where appropriate, a hospital.

In *Ashcroft* five justices (Burger, Powell, O'Connor, Rehnquist, and White) formed a majority to rule constitutional Missouri's parental consent requirement with a judicial bypass provision for unmarried minors and also two new sorts of abortion regulations. The first required a pathology report for all abortions. The majority reasoned that this was a minimally burdensome regulation, similar to record-keeping requirements. The dissenters argued that this could add as much as forty dollars to the price of every abortion, and that pathology reports were not routine medical practice for comparable surgery (in other words, that the requirement amounted to an unreasonable burden on abortion). The second requirement mandated that for all post-viability abortions (i.e., those done to preserve a mother's life or health), a second physician be on hand to care for the fetus. The majority, interpreting the statute to imply an exception if delay of the second physician endangered the mother's life, reasoned that this rule was acceptable because it was closely related to the compelling interest in the life of the viable fetus. The dissent objected on the grounds that sometimes a mother's health necessitated employment of an abortion technique that inevitably destroys the fetus, and for these procedures the second physician requirement is simply irrational.

The *Ashcroft* decision made clear that the lines on permissible regulations of abortion seemed to have shifted slightly since *Roe*, but the *Akron I* decision, handed down on the same day, indicated that *Roe* still had the support of a six-justice majority.

Within three years, with no personnel change on the Court, that six was to dwindle to five in the case of *Thornburgh v. American College of Obstetricians and Gynecologists (ACOG)*;[83] Justice Burger joined the dissenters' camp arguing that the Court "should re-examine *Roe.*" He explained that what provoked him to change sides was the now-prevailing Court understanding of *Roe v. Wade* which he claimed was a more extreme version than *Roe* really warranted. If this extreme version of *Roe* was going to continue, then Burger would now be willing to abandon the *Roe v. Wade* precedent.

The particular actions that drove Burger into the anti-*Roe* camp were the majority's declarations of unconstitutionality of several Pennsylvania statutes. These had mandated the following:

1. Twenty-four hours before obtaining a woman's written consent to abortion, her physician was required to tell her (a) his/her own name; (b) the "fact that there may be detrimental physical and psychological effects [of the abortion] which are not accurately foreseeable"; (c) the "particular medical risks associated with the particular abortion procedure to be employed"; (d) the probable gestational age of the fetus; and (e) the "medical risks associated with carrying her child to term."

2. By the same deadline, the law also required that the woman be informed "that medical assistance benefits may be available for prenatal care, childbirth and neonatal care," that the father "is liable to assist" in the child's support even if the father has offered to pay for the abortion, and that the state has available printed materials that describe the fetus (detailing "probable anatomical and physiological characteristics for the unborn child at two-week increments") and list agencies offering alternatives to abortion. If she could not read the material, she could choose to have it read to her and if she had any questions, they were to be answered in her own language. Her written consent was supposed to indicate that all this had been done before the twenty-four-hour waiting period began.

3. Records were to be kept specifying the performing and referring physicians, the facility, the probable age of gestation, the basis for determination of nonviability, the method of payment for the abortion, the woman's political subdivision and state of residence, also her age, race, marital status, number of previous pregnancies, and date of last menstrual period. This material was to be available to the public except for the woman's name and the physicians' names.

4. For post-viability abortions, three rules applied: (a) a second physician had to be on hand to preserve the life and health of the fetus; (b) the abortion performer had to exercise the same degree of care for the fetus as she or he would for a fetus intended to be born; (c) the abortion technique selected had to be one that maximized the chances of fetal survival unless, in the physician's good faith judgment, this technique "would present a significantly greater medical risk to the life or health of the pregnant woman."

The five-justice majority declared all of these provisions unconstitutional. Blackmun reasoned, for the majority, that the information-mandating provisions were not aimed at truly informed consent because the physician was required to present the information whether or not his or her medical judgment viewed it as relevant to the particular patient. To the degree that the mandated information was irrelevant, these provisions did not truly promote health and therefore were unconstitutional. Moreover, by superimposing government views where professional medical judgment should prevail, the state was unconstitutionally interfering with the privacy of the doctor-patient relationship. As to the recordkeeping provisions, the Court reasoned that the detailed level of specificity of the information gathered and its availability to the public presented a specter of intimidation and harassment of abortion-procurers and abortion-providers that threatened the right of privacy. Finally, the post-viability abortion rules were struck down because, despite the statutory language protecting women from a pro-fetus abortion technique that "would present a significantly greater risk" to her health, the majority nonetheless reasoned that the statute mandated some degree of "trade-off" of maternal health for fetal survival, and that this government choice violated the Constitution. The rule for a second physician was struck down because the statute contained no exception, implied or express, for an emergency situation where physician delay might pose a threat to the woman's life.

In addition to Burger, Justices O'Connor and White contributed dissents to the *Thornburgh* decision, and Rehnquist joined both their dissents. Justice O'Connor made it a point to reiterate her views of *Akron I*, particularly her explication of the analysis that ought to replace the *Roe* framework. White wrote a lengthy dissent, forthrightly urging, "[T]he time has come to recognize that *Roe v. Wade*, no less than the cases overruled by the Court in the past . . . 'departs from a proper understanding' of the Constitution and to overrule it." He granted that the Court properly protected as fundamental a right to privacy "in connection with the conduct of family life, the rearing of children, marital privacy, the use of contraceptives, and the preservation of the individual's capacity to procreate," but insisted that the issues involved with abortion are different because it involves the destruction of a fetus which is "an entity that bears in its cells all the genetic information that characterizes a member of the species *homo sapiens* and distinguishes an individual member of that species from all others, and . . . there is no nonarbitrary line separating a fetus from a child or, indeed, an adult human being."[84] These facts rendered abortion unique, and thus not properly classed with matters like contraception or childrearing. Nor should freedom to choose abortion be viewed as part of the liberty protected by "due process" because it was not a liberty traditional to our society. Our laws against it ranged in age from 100 to 150 years.[85] Thus, White concluded, *Roe* was wrongly decided. Moreover, even if the right were somehow fundamental, it would be outweighed by the compelling governmental interest of "protecting those who will be citizens if their lives are not ended in the womb."[86]

And, finally, White argued that even without abandoning *Roe* all of these statutes should be found constitutional: the recordkeeping requirements did mandate confidentiality as to names and thus would not produce harassment and intimidation; the post-viability rules served the compelling interest in the life of a viable fetus, did forbid any significant risk to the mother's health, and (contrary to the majority reading) were worded in a way that encouraged the inference that any maternal health emergency would justify an abortion before waiting for a second physician to arrive; and the twenty-four-hour waiting period and informational requirements did further health, mental and physical, by assuring that consent was truly informed. He called the Court's reasoning on the last topic "nonsensical" because even if abortion freedom is a constitutional right, the practice of medicine is not, and government has always heavily regulated it in the United States.

Justice White's dissent provoked a special concurrence from majority-justice Stevens, which focused specifically on why *Roe v. Wade* should not be overruled. In effect, Justice Stevens presented a new rationale for *Roe*, evidently concerned that Justice Blackmun's original opinion had not been adequately cogent or powerful. Justice Stevens's starting point was the right of privacy; he reminded readers that White and other justices in the minority by now pretty routinely conceded that it did cover contraception. Stevens then wrote:

> For reasons that are not entirely clear . . . Justice White abruptly announces that the interest in "liberty" that is implicated by a decision not to bear a child that is made a few days after conception is *less* fundamental than a comparable decision made before conception. There may, of course, be a difference in the strength of the countervailing state interest, but I fail to see how a decision on childbearing becomes *less* important the day after conception than the day before. Indeed, if one decision is more "fundamental" to the individual's freedom than the other, surely it is the postconception decision that is the more serious. Thus, it is difficult for me to understand how Justice White reaches the conclusion that restraints upon this aspect of a woman's liberty do not "call into play anything more than the most minimal judicial scrutiny."

> . . .

> Justice White is also surely wrong in suggesting that the government interest in protecting fetal life is equally compelling during the entire period from the moment of conception until the moment of birth. . . . I should think it obvious that the State's interest in the protection of an embryo—even if that interest is defined as "protecting those who will be citizens,"—increases progressively and dramatically as the organism's capacity to feel pain, to experience pleasure, to survive, and to react to its surroundings increases day by day. The development of a fetus—and pregnancy itself—are not static conditions, and the assertion that the government's interest is static simply ignores this reality.
> . . .[I]t seems to me quite odd to argue that distinctions may not also be drawn between the state interest in protecting the freshly fertilized egg and the state interest in protecting the 9-month-gestated, fully sentient fetus on the eve of birth. Recognition of this distinction is supported not only by logic, but also by history and by our shared experiences.[87]

After the *Thornburgh* decision, the judicial battle lines around *Roe v. Wade* appeared to be very close indeed; only five justices out of nine still maintained support for *Roe*. At this point, two justices left the Court, one from each contingent: Chief Justice Burger and Justice Powell. President Reagan moved Rehnquist up into the role of Chief Justice; filled the former Rehnquist slot with Antonin Scalia, an Italian Catholic and a very conservative jurist; and filled the Powell vacancy with Anthony Kennedy, who was generally viewed as a moderate.[88] If Kennedy were to vote as Powell had, and Scalia as the recently anti-*Roe* Burger, then the close balance on the Court would not change. However, the next major abortion decision, *Webster v. Reproductive Health Services*[89] was to reveal an inclination on the part of both Scalia and Kennedy to scrap *Roe v. Wade*.

The *Webster* case presented a challenge to a group of statutes that contained a mixture of restrictions concerning abortion funding and abortion itself. A recapitulation of the precedents concerning the public funding of abortion will therefore be helpful at this point for providing the legal context in which the justices' discussed the abortion-funding aspects of *Webster*.

Public Funds for Abortion: Decisions of 1977–1980

In states where popular antagonism toward the Supreme Court's 1973 abortion decision was intense, legislative reaction extended beyond the overt restrictions of the sort discussed above. In addition, these states prohibited the use of state Medicaid funds for "nontherapeutic" abortions, or for abortions not "medically necessary." Statutory definition of these terms varied from state to state. (It is worth noting, however, that the Supreme Court had made clear in the 1971 case of *U. S. v. Vuitch*, described above in text for note 43, that references to the mother's "health" in such statutes would be interpreted to include mental and emotional health.)

Challenges to these refusals to fund abortions arose from two different directions. One line of attack rested on statutory interpretation, as in the case of *Beal v. Doe*.[90] Federal law establishes the Medicaid program (Title XIX of the Social Security Act), which provides federal funds for medical services to the "medically needy" (persons too poor to pay for medical care who are not already on welfare). State participation in the program is optional. But if states do participate, they must abide by any federal regulations that are part of the program. This follows from the basic principle of our legal system that federal law always overrides state law in case of a conflict.[91] This line of attack maintained that the wording of the federal Medicaid law implied that abortions had to be funded by all states participating in the Medicaid program.

The precise wording at issue was the following federal statutory requirement: "A state plan for medical assistance must . . . include *reasonable standards . . . for determining eligibility* for and *the extent of medical assistance* under the plan which . . . are consistent with the objectives of this [Title]."[92] (Emphasis added)

The wording by which the statute described its own "objective" included the phrase "to meet the costs of necessary medical services."[93] Thus, this decision hinged on whether the Supreme Court were willing to view certain abortions as "unnecessary" medical services. As of 1977 six members of the Court were. (The dissenters were Blackmun, Brennan, and Marshall. They argued that an abortion was the medically necessary service for an unwanted pregnancy.)

The particular Pennsylvania statute against which this attack was launched refused Medicaid funds to any abortions not "medically necessary," as the statute itself defined that term. "Medically necessary," as Pennsylvania viewed it, included abortions only (1) when continued pregnancy threatened the mother's health, (2) when the infant faced a probability of being born with a physical or mental deficiency, or (3) when the pregnancy resulted from rape or incest and constituted a threat to the mother's "mental or physical health." According to the Court, these three conditions were permitted within Title XIX of the Social Security Act and were not an unreasonable interpretation of federal law. (The majority also permitted other states to read the law as allowing funding for all abortions for the needy. In other words, they permitted a diversity of state approaches under this law.)

The second line of attack on state denials of abortion funding rested on the Constitution itself, using a combination of the equal protection clause and the right to privacy. This approach maintained that the right to privacy required the state to treat equally the decision to give birth and the decision to abort, because it was a right to be free of government interference in making the choice. For the state to fund one (childbirth) but not the other (abortion) was to rig the scales in the case of indigent women, thus unconstitutionally interfering with what was supposed to be an unfettered private choice.

On the same day that it handed down *Beal v. Doe*, the Supreme Court handed down two more decisions affecting the availability of abortions, and these took up challenges based on this second approach. In the first of these, *Maher v. Roe*,[94] the Court faced squarely the constitutional attack on a state's denial—Connecticut, in this case—of Medicaid funds for abortion not "medically necessary."[95] The Supreme Court had to address this equal protection argument because it had been the basis of the district court decision that pregnant indigent women needing Medicaid funds for abortions had a constitutional right to such funds. Six other lower federal courts had agreed with this reasoning of the district court in *Maher*.[96]

In sustaining the constitutional attack on Connecticut's denial of abortion funds, the district court had been acting within a complex legal environment. A substantial series of cases had announced that the Constitution forbids the government to condition the exercise of fundamental civil rights on wealth or on the payment of a fee. This rule of law had been used to strike down state laws that forbid indigents to enter the state,[97] that required even impoverished convicts to pay fees for various trial records needed to appeal their own convictions,[98] that refused to supply free attorneys to impoverished criminal defendants,[99] that imposed poll taxes on the privileges of voting,[100] that imposed a property ownership requirement on people running for public office,[101] and that required even the impoverished to pay filing fees before they could sue for divorce.[102] These cases involved, respectively, the right to travel freely among the states, the right to due process of law, the right to counsel, the right to vote and run for office, and the right to marital freedom. Although the Court had announced in the poll-tax case that "lines drawn on the basis of wealth or property, like those of race, are traditionally disfavored,"[103] it has nonetheless never invalidated a law *solely* because that law drew a line on the basis of poverty. To do so would imply that all our welfare laws and many of our tax laws are unconstitutional. And even the conditioning of certain legal procedures on the payment of a fee has not always been held unconstitutional. In 1973 the Court held that the Bankruptcy Act's requirement of a $500 filing fee was not unconstitutional because (among other reasons) bankruptcy is not a "fundamental right."[104]

Neither the combination of poverty with the fundamental right of privacy, which the *Maher* case presented, nor the equal protection reasoning of the district court persuaded the U.S. Supreme Court to rule for Susan Roe. Having just rejected the statutory attack in *Beal*, the Court rejected this constitutional attack in *Maher*. Justice Powell's basic argument for the majority was that the district court (and other courts) had misconceived the nature of the right to privacy described in *Roe v. Wade*. It was a right to be free of "government compulsion" in making certain kinds of decisions. Since this Connecticut law placed no obstacle in front of a woman who wanted an abortion, the law in no way impinged on the right of privacy. Her poverty predated the statute and was simply unaltered by it. Justice Powell went on to distinguish between "direct state interference with a protected activity" (which is generally unconstitutional) and "state encouragement of an alternate activity," for which the state has much more leeway. He concluded, "[A] State is not required to show a compelling interest for its policy choice to favor normal childbirth any more than a State must so justify its election to fund public but not private education [even though, similarly, there is a constitutionally protected right of the individual to choose to attend private school]."[105]

Finally, on the same day that it announced *Beal* and *Maher*, the Court majority, in a third case, sustained another variety of a state effort to limit the availability of abortions. St. Louis had prohibited "nontherapeutic" abortions within its two city-owned hospitals, defining "nontherapeutic" as any abortion not needed to save the mother's life or to save her from "grave physiological injury." Since this amounted to an outright governmental prohibition, although one of limited extent because private hospitals did function in St. Louis, it is somewhat surprising that the Court devoted less effort to settling this case, *Poelker v. Doe*,[106] than to either *Beal* or *Maher*. The Court issued only a brief *per curiam* opinion for this case, treating the city's decision not as a limited prohibition on abortions but rather as a refusal to provide a government subsidy (via its subsidy of the hospital facilities) for abortion services. The same three justices as in *Beal* dissented in *Maher* and *Poelker*, endorsing for the latter two the equal protection line of reasoning described above.

Even before *Beal*, *Maher*, and *Poelker* were handed down (on June 20, 1977), Congress, in an effort orchestrated by Representative Henry Hyde, had added its voice to the chorus opposing public financing of abortions. In a series of amendments to annual appropriations bills, each called a Hyde Amendment, Congress began in September 1976 to forbid the use of federal funds to reimburse the cost of abortions for Medicaid recipients, with a very narrow range of permitted exceptions. The 1977 fiscal year appropriation made an exception only for those pregnancies that endangered the life of the mother. The Hyde Amendments for 1978 and 1979 exempted abortions to end pregnancies that were the result of "promptly reported" rape or incest or that would cause "severe and long-lasting health damage" to the mother. The 1980 Hyde Amendment removed the health damage exemption but retained the exemptions for rape or incest or life-threatening pregnancies.

On September 30, 1976, the day the first Hyde Amendment was enacted, Cora McRae, a pregnant Medicaid recipient in New York, brought suit with a number of other plaintiffs to enjoin the enforcement of the funding restriction on the grounds that it was unconstitutional. The secretary of the Department of Health, Education and Welfare was joined on the defendant side by Senators James Buckley and Jesse Helms and by Representative Hyde. The district court certified the suit as a class action suit on behalf of all pregnant or potentially pregnant women eligible for Medicaid in New York State who chose to seek an abortion and all abortion service providers, and granted an injunction against enforcing the law, pending a full hearing. Then *Beal* and *Maher* were decided and the Supreme Court vacated the injunction and remanded to the district court for reconsideration in light of the reasoning in those decisions. A number of additional plaintiffs joined the first group for the reconsideration trial.

The plaintiffs argued along both statutory and constitutional lines. First, they claimed that Title XIX of the Social Security Act, even with the Hyde Amendments, still obliged the states to pay for medically necessary abortions, for they were necessary medical services within the meaning of the Act. The district court rejected this argument, and none of the Supreme Court justices quarreled with that statutory interpretation.

The plaintiffs' constitutional arguments, on the other hand, met with more success at the district court. They claimed that the Hyde Amendment violated the First Amendment clauses forbidding laws "respecting an establishment of religion," or prohibiting the free exercise of religion, and also violated the equal protection concept implied in the due process clause of the Fifth Amendment.[107] They succeeded in convincing the district court of both the free exercise and the Fifth Amendment arguments. The district court then enjoined the secretary of HEW (again) from enforcing the Hyde Amendment. The secretary appealed to the Supreme Court for a stay of the injunction pending appeal, but the Supreme Court refused to grant it. After hearing the appeal, however, in the case of *Harris v. McRae*[108] the Supreme Court did (on June 24, 1980) overturn the district court's order and permit the Hyde Amendment to take effect.[109]

The decision was 5–4, because Justice Stevens joined the *Maher* dissent group of Brennan, Marshall, and Blackmun. He made a point of arguing that there was a difference of constitutional dimension between denying a medically needed abortion, in the sense of needed for the woman's health, as this law did, and merely denying funds for nontherapeutic abortions as the laws treated in earlier decisions had done. Stevens argued that, contrary to the disclaimers of the majority, the outcome of this ordinance *was* to place a special burden on the woman who needed a therapeutic abortion. *Roe v. Wade* had established the legal principle that a woman "has a constitutional right to place a higher value on avoiding serious harm to her own health . . . than on protecting potential life" (indeed, even as to a viable fetus) and "the exercise of that right cannot provide the basis for the denial of a benefit [medically needed services] to which she would otherwise be entitled."[110]

The Court majority reiterated its reasoning of the earlier cases: This law impinged on no fundamental right, because it did not add any new obstacle that would not have been there were the government refusing to pay for all medical services. Since it impinged on no protected right, the law needed to have only some rational relation to a legitimate government interest, and protecting potential life was at least a legitimate (even if not at all stages "compelling") government interest. Encouraging childbirth, by funding it for the poor, was rationally related to the goal of protecting potential life.

After *Harris v. McRae* no major public funding issues came before the Court until *Webster v. Reproductive Health Services* in 1989, when, for the first time since 1973, a majority of the Court appeared to go on record as favoring the overruling of *Roe v. Wade*. For that reason, *Webster* appears to initiate a new phase of abortion litigation and consequently begins the next chapter.

CHAPTER 2

Current Trends
in Abortion

In a series of cases that spanned 1989–1991, the U.S. Supreme Court, which by now included three Reagan appointees—O'Connor, Scalia, and Kennedy—in addition to the original *Roe v. Wade* dissenters, White and Rehnquist, gave observers the distinct impression that *Roe v. Wade* was soon to be overruled. The case that first created this impression was *Webster v. Reproductive Health Services* (1989).[1] There Justice Scalia urged an immediate overruling of *Roe*; a three-justice (Rehnquist, White, and Kennedy) plurality opinion by Chief Justice Rehnquist argued that "the rigid trimester framework" of *Roe* had to be rejected, although the statute at issue in *Webster* did not conflict with the specific holding of *Roe*. In addition, this Rehnquist plurality opinion quoted a fifth justice, O'Connor, to the effect that the state has a compelling interest in protecting the potential life of the fetus not only after viability—contrary to *Roe*—but "*throughout* pregnancy." Justice O'Connor refused to concur with the group who quoted her, on the grounds that the rule of *Roe* did not have to be disturbed in order to uphold the statute at issue in *Webster*. Still, the *Webster* array of opinions indicated that *Roe* had five opponents and four defenders (Marshall, Brennan, Blackmun, and Stevens). Thus, it appeared that the thin 5–4 majority that had endorsed the survival of *Roe* in 1986 in *Thornburgh v. A.C.O.G.*, by 1989 had eroded (with the appointment of Anthony Kennedy) to a 4–5 minority.

This pattern appeared to shift even further against *Roe* in 1991 when Justice Brennan left the Court, to be replaced by David Souter. Justice Souter's first Supreme Court decision implicating abortion rights was *Rust v. Sullivan*[2] in 1991. At stake was a set of new federal regulations forbidding medical and other staff at federally assisted family planning clinics to discuss the abortion option with pregnant patients. The regulations made no explicit exception for abortions that might be needed to preserve a woman's health. The Supreme Court upheld these regulations in a 5–4 vote. Souter aligned with the majority, but O'Connor placed herself in dissent, on the grounds not that the choice of abortion was a fundamental right but rather that courts are obliged to construe statutes in a way that avoids serious constitutional doubts. Because these regulations imposed a "content-based restriction on speech," they raised precisely such doubts concerning the First Amendment and thus should be viewed as not permitted by the federal statute being claimed as their implicit authorization by the Reagan/Bush administrations. (The statute had been around for nearly two decades before these regulations were adopted.)

Because of the First Amendment side issue in *Rust v. Sullivan* and the absence of a direct clash with *Roe* in *Webster,* O'Connor had given no indication since her *Akron* and *Thornburgh* dissents of any change in her view, expressed there, that the reasoning of *Roe v. Wade* was "on a collision course with itself" and thus should be abandoned; or even that she in any way had altered her view, also expressed in both those cases, that a state's interest in protecting fetal life was important enough to be considered "compelling" not just after viability but also *"throughout* pregnancy." Justice Kennedy had aligned with the Rehnquist opinion in *Webster* rejecting the *Roe* framework, and again in *Rust* upholding the federal "gag rule" on abortion. The new Justice Souter had also gone along with the gag rule in *Rust.* With the addition of these to the original and still persistent *Roe* dissenters Rehnquist and White, plus the vociferously anti-*Roe* Scalia, then, by 1992 it appeared that the anti-*Roe* majority on the Supreme Court had reached the level of 6–3.

Hence it came as no small surprise to many observers in June 1992 when six justices in *Planned Parenthood v. Casey* announced *support* for the "essential holding of *Roe v. Wade."* The rest of this chapter unfolds that surprising story.

Death Knell for Roe v. Wade? Webster v. Reproductive Health Services (1989)

The *Webster* case involved a multipart anti-abortion statute from the state of Missouri, which blended funding restrictions with direct abortion regulations and with a proclamation of belief and an interpretive guideline. The belief proclamation said (in the statutory preamble), "The life of each human being begins at conception," and "unborn children have protectable interests in life, health, and well-being" (without any more concrete specification of the inter-ests). The interpretive guideline said that state laws should be interpreted "to acknowledge on behalf of the unborn child at every stage of development, all the rights, privileges and immunities available to other persons . . . of this state, *subject only to the Constitution of the United States, and decisional interpretations thereof by the U.S. Supreme Court. . . ."* (Emphasis added.) The regulation of abortion practice in the statute was a rule that before performing an abortion on a woman believed to be twenty or more weeks pregnant, the physician must ascertain whether the fetus is viable by "using and exercising that degree of care, skill, and proficiency commonly exercised by the ordinarily skillful, careful, and prudent physician" and by performing "such medical examinations and tests as are necessary to make a finding of the gestational age, weight, and lung maturity," and must record "such findings and determination of viability." Finally, the public funding restrictions had three aspects: (1) "Public facilities" (defined as facilities "owned, leased, or controlled" by the state) could not be used to perform abortions not necessary for the mother's survival; (2) public employees could not "within the scope of [their] employment" perform abortions not necessary for saving a woman's life; and (3) public funds could not be expended for "encouraging or counseling abortions."

In addition, the statute had originally prohibited public employees from doing any abortion counseling and had prohibited professional abortion counseling on the premises of legally defined "public facilities." In response to a challenge brought by a group of abortion providers that included five medical professionals employed at a state-owned hospital, the district court and the circuit court of appeals had declared these last two provisions an unconstitutional restriction of a woman's constitutional right to receive medical information needed for an informed exercise of the right to choose whether to bear a child. The state of Missouri accepted those decisions as to the last two provisions and did not appeal them to the U.S. Supreme Court.

Moreover, Missouri explained to the U.S. Supreme Court that it interpreted the prohibition on using public funds for abortion counseling to be a restriction simply on the fiscal officers of the state against spending money specifically for abortion counseling. In response to this interpretation, the attorneys for the various abortion providers withdrew their challenge to this section of the law, indicating that with this reading it no longer directly affected them. As to this single section of the law the Supreme Court managed a unanimous response: the issue was moot because the challenge had been withdrawn.

The rest of the statute, however, produced a confusing disarray on the Court: a bare majority of five (Rehnquist, White, Kennedy, O'Connor, and Scalia) concurred in the parts of the Rehnquist opinion concerning the belief declarations (and interpretive guideline) in the statute and the restrictions on the performance of abortions by on-the-job public employees and in publicly funded facilities. On the remaining piece of the statute, this majority held together on the result only: the viability testing requirement was not void.

The majority dissolved into utter ambiguity on the doctrinal issue of the decade: was *Roe v. Wade* still to be followed? One of the five, Scalia, urged an immediate overruling of it. Three of the five, Rehnquist, Kennedy, and White, ruled an immediate abandonment of what they called "key elements of the *Roe* framework—trimesters and viability." They specifically endorsed replacing these key elements with the rule that states have a compelling interest in the protection of potential life throughout pregnancy, not just after viability, and they quoted Justice O'Connor's opinions from both *Akron I* and *Thornburgh* endorsing that point. Speaking through Rehnquist, the three urged that the Court "modify and narrow *Roe*" by this new doctrine, namely, that states may regulate abortion "throughout pregnancy" to protect potential life.

The ambiguity concerning *Roe* ensued from Justice O'Connor's pointed refusal to concur in this portion of the Rehnquist opinion, which quoted her own words. She now argued instead that this Missouri statute does not conflict "in any way" with prior decisions of the Court, including *Roe v. Wade,* and that therefore the Court was behaving improperly in reconsidering *Roe* (something she had herself urged in both *Akron I* and *Thornburgh*). Her apparent waffling evidently infuriated Scalia, for not only is the tone of his opinion unusually strident, but he goes out of his way in a footnote to mock Justice O'Connor's reasoning.

Strangely enough, the dissenters, who interpret the viability-testing provision differently from the majority, would—had they agreed with the majority's reading of the statute—have upheld it as completely consistent with *Roe v. Wade.* In other words, they interpret *Roe* as less hostile to this abortion restriction than the anti-*Roe* group of Rehnquist, White, Kennedy, and Scalia. However, they believe the majority erred in reading the statute as less harsh than its language seems. While the majority believe the word "necessary" in the provision and its reference to the "prudent physician,"would preclude performance of any useless tests, the four dissenters believe (with two lower courts) that the statute requires doctors to perform certain medical tests even for cases where the doctors honestly and correctly believe the tests to be both unhelpful in determining viability and dangerous to the woman's health. On this reading, the statute turns out to be unconstitutional on the grounds of sheer irrationality. (It takes away liberty "without due process of law," since it bears no reasonable relation to any legitimate government interest.)

All four dissenters also dispute the majority's contentions concerning the declarative parts of the statute and its rules for the use of "public facilities." With the exception of Justice Stevens, however, they devote the bulk of their attention to the issue of the continued force of *Roe v. Wade.* In the complexities of arguments, counterarguments, and subarguments, the variety of opinions for *Webster* reintroduces the full range of debate over the original *Roe v. Wade* decision.

William L. Webster, Attorney General of Missouri, et al. v. Reproductive Health Services et al., 492 U.S. 490 (1989)

CHIEF JUSTICE REHNQUIST announced the judgment of the Court and delivered the opinion of the Court with respect to Parts I, II-A, II-B, and II-C, and an opinion with respect to Parts II-D and III, in which JUSTICE WHITE and JUSTICE KENNEDY join.

. . .

II

Decision of this case requires us to address four sections of the Missouri Act:

(a) the preamble; (b) the prohibition on the use of public facilities or employees to perform abortion; (c) the prohibition on public funding of abortion counseling; and (d) the requirement that physicians conduct viability tests prior to performing abortions. We address these *seriatim*.

A

The Act's preamble . . . sets forth "findings" by the Missouri legislature that "[t]he life of each human being begins at conception," and that "[u]nborn children have protectable interests in life, health, and well-being." Mo. Rev. Stat. § 1.205.1(1), (2) (1986). The Act then mandates that state laws be interpreted to provide unborn children with "all the rights, privileges, and immunities available to other persons, citizens, and residents of this state," subject to the Constitution and this Court's precedents. § 1.205.2.[4] In invalidating the preamble, the Court of Appeals relied on this Court's dictum that " 'a State may not adopt one theory of when life begins to justify its regulation of abortions.' " 851 F.2d, at 1075–76, quoting *Akron v. Akron*

Center for Reproductive Health, Inc., 462 U.S. 416, 444 (1983), in turn citing *Roe v. Wade*, 410 U.S., at 159–62. It rejected Missouri's claim that the preamble was "abortion-neutral," and "merely determine[d] when life begins in a nonabortion context, a traditional state prerogative." 851 F.2d, 'at 1076. The court thought that "[t]he only plausible inference" from the fact that "every remaining section of the bill save one regulates the performance of abortions" was that "the state intended its abortion regulations to be understood against the backdrop of its theory of life." *Ibid.*

The State contends that the preamble itself is precatory and imposes no substantive restrictions on abortions, and that appellees therefore do not have standing to challenge it. Appellees, on the other hand, insist that the preamble is an operative part of the Act intended to guide the interpretation of other provisions of the Act. They maintain, for example, that the preamble's definition of life may prevent physicians in public hospitals from dispensing certain forms of contraceptives, such as the intrauterine device.

In our view, the Court of Appeals misconceived the meaning of the *Akron* dictum, which was only that a State could not "justify" an abortion regulation otherwise invalid under *Roe v. Wade* on the ground that it embodied the State's view about when life begins. Certainly the preamble does not by its terms regulate abortion or any other

---

4. Section 1.205 provides in full:

"1. The general assembly of this state finds that: (1) The life of each human being begins at conception; (2) Unborn children have protectable interests in life, health, and well-being; (3) The natural parents of unborn children have protectable interests in the life, health, and well-being of their unborn child.

"2. Effective January 1, 1988, the laws of this state shall be interpreted and construed to acknowledge on behalf of the unborn child at every stage of development, all the rights, privileges, and immunities available to other persons, citizens, and residents of this state, subject only to the Constitution of the United States, and decisional interpretations thereof by the United States Supreme Court and specific provisions to the contrary in the statutes and constitution of this state.

"3. As used in this section, the term 'unborn children' or 'unborn child' shall include all unborn child or [*sic*] children or the offspring of human beings from the moment of conception until birth at every stage of biological development.

"4. Nothing in this section shall be interpreted as creating a cause of action against a woman for indirectly harming her unborn child by failing to properly care for herself or by failing to follow any particular program of prenatal care."

aspect of appellees' medical practice. The Court has emphasized that *Roe v. Wade* "implies no limitation on the authority of a State to make a value judgment favoring childbirth over abortion." *Maher v. Roe*, 432 U.S., at 474. The preamble can be read simply to express that sort of value judgment.

We think the extent to which the preamble's language might be used to interpret other state statutes or regulations is something that only the courts of Missouri can definitively decide. State law has offered protections to unborn children in tort and probate law, see *Roe v. Wade, supra*, at 161–62, and § 1.205.2 can be interpreted to do no more than that. What we have, then, is much the same situation that the Court confronted in *Alabama State Federation of Labor v. McAdory*, 325 U.S. 450 (1945). As in that case:

We are thus invited to pass upon the constitutional validity of a state statute which has not yet been applied or threatened to be applied by the state courts to petitioners or others in the manner anticipated. Lacking any authoritative construction of the statute by the state courts, without which no constitutional question arises, and lacking the authority to give such a controlling construction ourselves, and with a record which presents no concrete set of facts to which the statute is to be applied, the case is plainly not one to be disposed of by the declaratory judgment procedure. *Id.*, at 460.

It will be time enough for federal courts to address the meaning of the preamble should it be applied to restrict the activities of appellees in some concrete way. Until then, this Court "is not empowered to decide . . . abstract propositions, or to declare, for the government of future cases, principles or rules of law which cannot affect the result as to the thing in issue in the case before it." *Tyler v. Judges of Court of Registration*, 179 U.S.

405, 409 (1900). See also *Valley Forge Christian College v. Americans United for Separation of Church and State, Inc.*, 454 U.S. 464, 473 (1982). We therefore need not pass on the constitutionality of the Act's preamble.

B

Section 188.210 provides that "[i]t shall be unlawful for any public employee within the scope of his employment to perform or assist an abortion, not necessary to save the life of the mother," while § 188.215 makes it "unlawful for any public facility to be used for the purpose of performing or assisting an abortion not necessary to save the life of the mother."[7] The Court of Appeals held that these provisions contravened this Court's abortion decisions. 851 F.2d, at 1082–83. We take the contrary view.

As we said earlier this Term in *DeShaney v. Winnebago County Dept. of Social Services*, 489 U.S. 189, 196 (1989), "our cases have recognized that the Due Process Clauses generally confer no affirmative right to governmental aid, even where such aid may be necessary to secure life, liberty, or property interests of which the government itself may not deprive the individual." In *Maher v. Roe, supra*, the Court upheld a Connecticut welfare regulation under which Medicaid recipients received payments for medical services related to childbirth, but not for nontherapeutic abortions. The Court rejected the claim that this unequal subsidization of childbirth and abor-

7. The statue defines "public employee" to mean "any person employed by this state or any agency or political subdivison thereof." Mo. Rev. Stat. § 188.200(1) (1986). "Public facility" is defined as "any public institution, public facility, public equipment, or any physical asset owned, leased, or controlled by this state or any agency or political subdivisions thereof." § 188.200(2).

tion was impermissible under *Roe v. Wade.* As the Court put it:

> The Connecticut regulation before us is different in kind from the laws invalidated in our previous abortion decisions. The Connecticut regulation places no obstacles—absolute or otherwise—in the pregnant woman's path to an abortion. An indigent woman who desires an abortion suffers no disadvantage as a consequence of Connecticut's decision to fund childbirth; she continues as before to be dependent on private sources for the service she desires. The State may have made childbirth a more attractive alternative, thereby influencing the woman's decision, but it has imposed no restriction on access to abortions that was not already there. The indigency that may make it difficult—and in some cases, perhaps, impossible—for some women to have abortions is neither created nor in any way affected by the Connecticut regulation. 432 U.S., at 474.

Relying on *Maher,* the Court in *Poelker v. Doe,* 432 U.S. 519, 521 (1977), held that the city of St. Louis committed "no constitutional violation . . . in electing, as a policy choice, to provide publicly financed hospital services for childbirth without providing corresponding services for nontherapeutic abortions."

More recently, in *Harris v. McRae,* 448 U.S. 297 (1980), the Court upheld "the most restrictive version of the Hyde Amendment," *id.,* at 325, n. 27, which withheld from States federal funds under the Medicaid program to reimburse the costs of abortions, " 'except where the life of the mother would be endangered if the fetus were carried to term.' " *Ibid.* (quoting Pub. L. 94-439, § 209, 90 Stat. 1434). As in *Maher*

and *Poelker,* the Court required only a showing that Congress' authorization of "reimbursement for medically necessary services generally, but not for certain medically necessary abortions" was rationally related to the legitimate governmental goal of encouraging childbirth. 448 U.S., at 325.

The Court of Appeals distinguished these cases on the ground that "[t]o prevent access to a public facility does more than demonstrate a political choice in favor of childbirth; it clearly narrows and in some cases forecloses the availability of abortion to women." 851 F.2d, at 1081. The court reasoned that the ban on the use of public facilities "could prevent a woman's chosen doctor from performing an abortion because of his unprivileged status at other hospitals or because a private hospital adopted a similar anti-abortion stance." *Ibid.* It also thought that "[s]uch a rule could increase the cost of obtaining an abortion and delay the timing of it as well." *Ibid.*

We think that this analysis is much like that which we rejected in *Maher, Poelker,* and *McRae.* As in those cases, the State's decision here to use public facilities and staff to encourage childbirth over abortion "places no governmental obstacle in the path of a woman who chooses to terminate her pregnancy." *McRae,* 448 U.S., at 315. Just as Congress' refusal to fund abortions in *McRae* left "an indigent woman with at least the same range of choice in deciding whether to obtain a medically necessary abortion as she would have had if Congress had chosen to subsidize no health care costs at all," *id.,* at 317, Missouri's refusal to allow public employees to perform abortions in public hospitals leaves a pregnant woman with the same choices as if the State had chosen not to operate any public hospitals at all. The challenged provisions only restrict a woman's ability to obtain an abortion to the extent that she chooses to use a physician affiliated with a public hospital. This circumstance is more easily remedied, and thus considerably less burdensome, than indigency, which "may make it difficult—and in some cases, perhaps, impossible—for some women to have abortions" without public funding. *Maher*, 432 U.S., at 474. Having held that the State's refusal to fund abortions does not violate *Roe v. Wade*, it strains logic to reach a contrary result for the use of public facilities and employees. If the State may "make a value judgment favoring childbirth over abortion and . . . implement that judgment by the allocation of public funds," *Maher*, at 474, surely it may do so through the allocation of other public resources, such as hospitals and medical staff.

The Court of Appeals sought to distinguish our cases on the additional ground that "[t]he evidence here showed that all of the public facility's costs in providing abortion services are recouped when the patient pays." 851 F.2d, at 1083. Absent any expenditure of public funds, the court thought that Missouri was "expressing" more than "its preference for childbirth over abortions," but rather was creating an "obstacle to exercise of the right to choose an abortion [that could not] stand absent a compelling state interest." *Ibid.* We disagree.

"Constitutional concerns are greatest," we said in *Maher*, at 476, "when the State attempts to impose its will by the force of law; the State's power to encourage actions deemed to be in the public interest is necessarily far broader." Nothing in the Constitution requires States to enter or remain in the business of performing abortions. Nor, as appellees suggest, do private physicians and their patients have some kind of constitutional right of access to public facilities for the performance of abortions. Indeed, if the State does recoup all of its costs in performing abortions, and no state subsidy, direct or indirect, is available, it is difficult to see how any procreational

choice is burdened by the State's ban on the use of its facilities or employees for performing abortions.[8]

Maher, Poelker, and *McRae* all support the view that the State need not commit any resources to facilitating abortions, even if it can turn a profit by doing so. In *Poelker,* the suit was filed by an indigent who could not afford to pay for an abortion, but the ban on the performance of nontherapeutic abortions in city-owned hospitals applied whether or not the pregnant woman could pay. 432 U.S., at 520; *id.,* 524 (BRENNAN, J., dissenting). The Court emphasized that the Mayor's decision to prohibit abortions in city hospitals was "subject to public debate and approval or disapproval at the polls," and that "the Constitution does not forbid a State or city, pursuant to democratic processes, from expressing a preference for normal childbirth as St. Louis has done." *Id.,* at 521. Thus we uphold the Act's restrictions on the use of public employees and facilities for the performance or assistance of nontherapeutic abortions.

C

[Mootness discussion omitted.—Au.]

D

Section 188.029 of the Missouri Act provides:

> Before a physician performs an abortion on a woman he has reason to believe is carrying an unborn child of twenty or more weeks gestational age,

---

8. A different analysis might apply if a particular State had socialized medicine and all of its hospitals and physicians were publicly funded. This case might also be different if the State barred doctors who performed abortions in private facilities from the use of public facilities for any purpose. See *Harris v. McRae,* 448 U.S. 297, 317, n.19 (1980).

the physician shall first determine if the unborn child is viable by using and exercising that degree of care, skill, and proficiency commonly exercised by the ordinarily skillful, careful, and prudent physician engaged in similar practice under the same or similar conditions. In making this determination of viability, the physician shall perform or cause to be performed such medical examinations and tests as are necessary to make a finding of the gestational age, weight, and lung maturity of the unborn child and shall enter such findings and determination of viability in the medical record of the mother.[12]

As with the preamble, the parties disagree over the meaning of this statutory provision. The State emphasizes the language of the first sentence, which speaks in terms of the physician's determination of viability being made by the standards of ordinary skill in the medical profession. Appellees stress the language of the second sentence, which prescribes such "tests as are necessary" to make a finding of gestational age, fetal weight, and lung maturity.

The Court of Appeals read § 188.029 as requiring that after 20 weeks "doctors *must* perform tests to find gestational age, fetal weight and lung maturity." 851 F.2d, at 1075, n.5. The court indicated that the tests needed to determine fetal weight at 20 weeks are "unreliable and inaccurate" and would add $125 to $250 to the cost of an abortion. *Ibid.* It also stated that "amniocen-

12. The Act's penalty provision provides that "[a]ny person who contrary to the provisions of sections 188.010 to 188.085 knowingly performs . . . any abortion or knowingly fails to perform any action required by [these] sections . . . shall be guilty of a class A misdemeanor." Mo. Rev. Stat. § 188.075 (1986).

tesis, the only method available to determine lung maturity, is contrary to accepted medical practice until 28–30 weeks of gestation, expensive, and imposes significant health risks for both the pregnant woman and the fetus." *Ibid.*

We must first determine the meaning of § 188.029 under Missouri law. Our usual practice is to defer to the lower court's construction of a state statute, but we believe the Court of Appeals has "fallen into plain error" in this case. *Frisby v. Schultz,* 487 U.S. 474, 483 (1988); see *Brockett v. Spokane Arcades, Inc.,* 472 U.S. 491, 500, n. 9 (1985). " 'In Expounding a statute, we must not be guided by a single sentence or member of a sentence, but look to the provisions of the whole law, and to its object and policy.' " *Philbrook v. Glodgett,* 421 U.S. 707, 713 (1975), quoting *United States v. Heirs of Boisdoré,* 8 How. 113, 122 (1849). See *Chemehuevi Tribe of Indians v. FPC,* 420 U.S. 395, 402–3 (1975); *Kokoszka v. Belford,* 417 U.S. 642, 650 (1974). The Court of Appeals' interpretation also runs "afoul of the well-established principle that statutes will be interpreted to avoid constitutional difficulties." *Frisby, supra.*

We think the viability-testing provision makes sense only if the second sentence is read to require only those tests that are useful to making subsidiary findings as to viability. If we construe this provision to require a physician to perform those tests needed to make the three specified findings *in all circumstances,* including when the physician's reasonable professional judgment indicates that the tests would be irrelevant to determining viability or even dangerous to the mother and the fetus, the second sentence of § 188.029 would conflict with the first sentence's *requirement* that a physician apply his reasonable professional skill and judgment. It would also be incongruous to read this provision, especially the word "necessary,"[13] to require the performance of tests irrelevant to the expressed statutory purpose of determining viability. It thus seems clear to us that the Court of Appeals' construction of § 188.029 violates well-accepted canons of statutory interpretation used in the Missouri courts, see *State ex rel. Stern Brothers & Co. v. Stilley*, 337 S.W.2d 934, 939 (Mo. 1960) ("The basic rule of statutory construction is to first seek the legislative intention, and to effectuate it if possible, and the law favors constructions which harmonize with reason, and which tend to avoid unjust, absurd, unreasonable or confiscatory results, or oppression"); *Bell v. Mid-Century Ins. Co.*, 750 S.W.2d 708, 710 (Mo. App. 1988) ("Interpreting the phrase literally would produce an absurd result, which the Legislature is strongly presumed not to have intended"), which the dissent ignores.

The viability-testing provision of the Missouri Act is concerned with promoting the State's interest in potential human life rather than in maternal health. Section 188.029 creates what is essentially a presumption of viability at 20 weeks, which the physician must rebut with tests indicating that the fetus is not viable prior to performing an abortion. It also directs the physician's determination as to viability by specifying consideration, if feasible, of gestational age, fetal weight, and lung capacity. The District Court found that "the medical evidence is uncontradicted that a 20-week fetus is *not* viable," and that "23 ½ to 24 weeks gestation is the earliest point in pregnancy where a reasonable possibility

of viability exists." 662 F. Supp., at 420. But it also found that there may be a 4-week error in estimating gestational age, *id.*, at 421, which supports testing at 20 weeks.

In *Roe v. Wade*, the Court recognized that the State has "important and legitimate" interests in protecting maternal health and in the potentiality of human life. 410 U.S., at 162. During the second trimester, the State "may, if it chooses, regulate the abortion procedure in ways that are reasonably related to maternal health." *Id.*, at 164. After viability, when the State's interest in potential human life was held to become compelling, the State "may, if it chooses, regulate, and even proscribe, abortion except where it is necessary, in appropriate medical judgment, for the preservation of the life or health of the mother." *Id.*, at 165.[14]

In *Colautti v. Franklin, supra,* upon which appellees rely, the Court held that a Pennsylvania statute regulating the standard of care to be used by a physician

---

13. See *Black's Law Dictionary* 928 (5th ed. 1979) ("Necessary. This word must be considered in the connection in which it is used, as it is a word susceptible of various meanings. It may import absolute physical necessity or inevitability, or it may import that which is only convenient, useful, appropriate, suitable, proper, or conducive to the end sought").

14. The Court's subsequent cases have reflected this understanding. See *Colautti v. Franklin*, 439 U.S. 379, 386 (1979) (emphasis added) ("For both logical and biological reasons, we indicated in [in *Roe*] that the State's interest in the potential life of the fetus reaches the compelling point at the stage of viability. Hence, *prior to viability, the State may not seek to further this interest by directly restricting a woman's decision whether or not to terminate her pregnancy*"); *id.*, at 389 ("Viability is the critical point. And we have recognized no attempt to stretch the point of viability one way or the other"); accord *Planned Parenthood of Central Missouri v. Danforth*, 428 U.S., at 61 (State regulation designed to protect potential human life limited to period "subsequent to viability"); *Akron v. Akron Center for Reproductive Health, Inc.*, 462 U.S. 416, 428 (1983), quoting *Roe v. Wade*, 410 U.S. 113, 163 (1973) (emphasis added) (State's interest in protecting potential human life "becomes compelling *only* at viability, the point at which the fetus 'has the capability of meaningful life outside the mother's womb' ").

performing an abortion of a possibly viable fetus was void for vagueness. 439 U.S., at 390–401. But in the course of reaching that conclusion, the Court reaffirmed its earlier statement in *Planned Parenthood of Central Missouri v. Danforth*, 428 U.S. 52, 64 (1976), that " 'the determination of whether a particular fetus is viable is, and must be, a matter for the judgement of the responsible attending physician.' " 439 U.S., at 396. The dissent, at n. 6, ignores the statement in *Colautti* that "neither the legislature nor the courts may proclaim one of the elements entering into the ascertainment of viability—be it weeks of gestation or fetal weight or any other single factor—as the determinant of when the State has a compelling interest in the life or health of the fetus." 439 U.S., at 388–89. To the extent that § 188.029 regulates the method for determining viability, it undoubtedly does superimpose state regulation on the medical determination of whether a particular fetus is viable. The Court of Appeals and the District Court thought it unconstitutional for this reason. 851 F.2d, at 1074–75; 662 F. Supp., at 423. To the extent that the viability tests increase the cost of what are in fact second-trimester abortions, their validity may also be questioned under *Akron*, 462 U.S., at 434–35, where the Court held that a requirement that second trimester abortions must be performed in hospitals was invalid because it substantially increased the expense of those procedures.

We think that the doubt cast upon the Missouri statute by these cases is not so much a flaw in the statute as it is a reflection of the fact that the rigid trimester analysis of the course of a pregnancy enunciated in *Roe* has resulted in subsequent cases like *Colautti* and *Akron* making constitutional law in this area a virtual Procrustean bed. Statutes specifying elements of informed consent to be provided abortion patients, for example, were invalidated if they were thought to "structur[e] . . . the dialogue between the woman and her physician." *Thornburgh v.*

American College of Obstetricians and Gynecologists, 476 U.S. 747, 763 (1986). As the dissenters in *Thornburgh* pointed out, such a statute would have been sustained under any traditional standard of judicial review, *id.*, at 802 (WHITE, J., dissenting), or for any other surgical procedure except abortion. *Id.*, at 783 (BURGER, C. J., dissenting).

Stare decisis is a cornerstone of our legal system, but it has less power in constitutional cases, where, save for constitutional amendments, this Court is the only body able to make needed changes. See *United States v. Scott*, 437 U.S. 82, 101 (1978). We have not refrained from reconsideration of a prior construction of the Constitution that has proved "unsound in principle and unworkable in practice." *Garcia v. San Antonio Metropolitan Transit Authority*, 469 U.S. 528, 546 (1985); see *Solorio v. United States*, 483 U.S. 435, 448–50 (1987); *Erie R. Co. v. Tompkins*, 304 U.S. 64, 74–78 (1938). We think the *Roe* trimester framework falls into that category.

In the first place, the rigid *Roe* framework is hardly consistent with the notion of a Constitution cast in general terms, as ours is, and usually speaking in general principles, as ours does. The key elements of the *Roe* framework—trimesters and viability—are not found in the text of the Constitution or in any place else one would expect to find a constitutional principle. Since the bounds of the inquiry are essentially indeterminate, the result has been a web of legal rules that have become increasingly intricate, resembling a code of regulations rather than a body of constitutional doctrine.[15] As JUSTICE

15. . . . The dissent's claim, *post*, at n. 1, that the State goes too far, even under *Maher v. Roe*, 432 U.S. 464 (1977); *Poelker v. Doe*, 432 U.S. 519 (1977); and *Harris v. McRae*, 448 U.S. 297 (1980), by refusing to permit the use of public facilities, as defined in Mo. Rev. Stat. § 188.200, for the performance of abortions is another example of the fine distinctions endemic in the *Roe* framework.

WHITE has put it, the trimester framework has left this Court to serve as the country's "*ex officio* medical board with powers to approve or disapprove medical and operative practices and standards throughout the United States." *Planned Parenthood of Central Missouri v. Danforth*, 428 U.S., at 99 (opinion concurring in part and dissenting in part). Cf. *Garcia, supra*, at 547.

In the second place, we do not see why the State's interest in protecting potential human life should come into existence only at the point of viability, and that there should therefore be a rigid line allowing state regulation after viability but prohibiting it before viability. The dissenters in *Thornburgh*, writing in the context of the *Roe* trimester analysis, would have recognized this fact by posting against the "fundamental right" recognized in *Roe* the State's "compelling interest" in protecting potential human life throughout pregnancy. "[T]he State's interest, if compelling after viability, is equally compelling before viability." *Thornburgh*, 476 U.S., at 795 (WHITE, J., dissenting); see *id.*, at 828 (O'CONNOR, J., dissenting) ("State has compelling interests in ensuring maternal health and in protecting potential human life, and these interests exist 'throughout pregnancy' ") (citation omitted).

The tests that § 188.029 requires the physician to perform are designed to determine viability. The State here has chosen viability as the point at which its interest in potential human life must be safeguarded. See Mo. Rev. Stat. § 188.030 (1986) ("No abortion of a viable unborn child shall be performed unless necessary to preserve the life or health of the woman"). It is true that the tests in question increase the expense of abortion, and regulate the discretion of the physician in determining the viability of the fetus. Since the tests will undoubtedly show in many cases that the fetus is not viable, the tests will have been performed for what were in fact second-trimester

abortions. But we are satisfied that the requirement of these tests permissibly furthers the State's interest in protecting potential human life, and we therefore believe § 188.029 to be constitutional.

The dissent takes us to task for our failure to join in a "great issues" debate as to whether the Constitution includes an "unenumerated" general right to privacy as recognized in cases such as *Griswold v. Connecticut*, 381 U.S. 479 (1965), and *Roe*. But *Griswold v. Connecticut*, unlike *Roe*, did not purport to adopt a whole framework, complete with detailed rules and distinctions, to govern the cases in which the asserted liberty interest would apply. As such, it was far different from the opinion, if not the holding, of *Roe v. Wade*, which sought to establish a constitutional framework for judging state regulation of abortion during the entire term of pregnancy. That framework sought to deal with areas of medical practice traditionally subject to state regulation, and it sought to balance once and for all by reference only to the calendar the claims of the State to protect the fetus as a form of human life against the claims of a woman to decide for herself whether or not to abort a fetus she was carrying. The experience of the Court in applying *Roe v. Wade* in later cases, suggests to us that there is wisdom in not unnecessarily attempting to elaborate the abstract differences between a "fundamental right" to abortion, as the Court described it in *Akron*, 462 U.S. at 420, n. 1, a "limited fundamental constitutional right," which JUSTICE BLACKMUN's dissent today treats *Roe* as having established, or a liberty interest protected by the Due Process Clause, which we believe it to be. The Missouri testing requirement here is reasonably designed to ensure that abortions are not performed where the fetus is viable—an end which all concede is legitimate—and that is sufficient to sustain its constitutionality.

The dissent also accuses us, *inter alia*, of cowardice and illegitimacy in dealing with "the most politically divisive domestic legal issue of our time." There is no doubt that our holding today will allow some governmental regulation of abortion that would have been prohibited under the language of cases such as *Colautti v. Franklin*, 439 U.S. 379 (1979), and *Akron v. Akron Center for Reproductive Health, Inc.* But the goal of constitutional adjudication is surely not to remove inexorably "politically divisive" issues from the ambit of the legislative process, whereby the people through their elected representatives deal with matters of concern to them. The goal of constitutional adjudication is to hold true the balance between that which the Constitution puts beyond the reach of the democratic process and that which it does not. We think we have done that today. The dissent's suggestion that legislative bodies, in a Nation where more than half of our population is women, will treat our decision today as an invitation to enact abortion regulation reminiscent of the dark ages not only misreads our views but does scant justice to those who serve in such bodies and the people who elect them.

III

Both appellants and the United States as *Amicus Curiae* have urged that we overrule our decision in *Roe v. Wade*. The facts of the present case, however, differ from those at issue in *Roe*. Here, Missouri has determined that viability is the point at which its interest in potential human life must be safeguarded. In *Roe*, on the other hand, the Texas statute criminalized the performance of *all* abortions, except when the mother's life was at stake. 410 U.S., at 117–18. This case therefore affords us no occasion to revisit the holding of *Roe*, which was that the Texas statute unconstitutionally infringed the right to an abortion derived from the Due Process Clause, *id.*, at 164, and we leave it undisturbed. To the extent indicated in our opinion, we would modify and narrow *Roe* and succeeding cases.

Because none of the challenged provisions of the Missouri Act properly before us conflict with the Constitution, the judgment of the Court of Appeals is

Reversed.

JUSTICE O'CONNOR, concurring in part and concurring in the judgment.

I concur in Parts I, II-A, II-B, and II-C of the Court's opinion.

I

Nothing in the record before us or the opinions below indicates that subsections 1(1) and 1(2) of the preamble to Missouri's abortion regulation statute will affect a woman's decision to have an abortion. JUSTICE STEVENS, following appellees, suggests that the preamble may also "interfere[] with contraceptive choices," *post*, because certain contraceptive devices act on a female ovum after it has been fertilized by a male sperm. The Missouri Act defines "conception" as "the fertilization of the ovum of a female by a sperm of a male," Mo. Rev. Stat. § 188.015(3) (1986), and invests "unborn children" with "protectable interests in life, health, and well-being," Mo. Rev. Stat. § 1.205.1(2) (1986), from "the moment of conception . . . ." Mo. Rev. Stat. § 1.205.3 (1986). JUSTICE STEVENS asserts that any possible interference with a woman's right to use such post-fertilization contraceptive devices would be unconstitutional under *Griswold v. Connecticut*, 381 U.S. 479 (1965), and our subsequent contraception cases. Similarly, certain *amici* suggest that the Missouri Act's preamble may prohibit the developing technology of *in vitro* fertilization, a technique used to aid couples otherwise unable to bear children in which a number of ova are removed from the woman and fertilized by male sperm. This process often produces excess fertilized ova ("unborn children" under the Missouri Act's definition) that are discarded rather than reinserted into the woman's uterus. It may be correct that the use of postfertilization contraceptive devices is constitutionally protected by *Griswold* and its progeny but, as with a woman's abortion decision, nothing in the record or the opinions below indicates that the preamble will affect a woman's decision to practice contraception. For that matter, nothing in appellees' original complaint . . . indicates that appellees sought to enjoin potential violations of *Griswold*. Neither is there any indication of the possibility that the preamble might be applied to prohibit the performance of *in vitro* fertilization. I agree with the Court, therefore, that all of these intimations of unconstitutionality are simply too hypothetical to support the use of declaratory judgment procedures and injunctive remedies in this case.

Similarly, it seems to me to follow directly from our previous decisions concerning state or federal funding of abortions, *Harris v. McRae, Maher v. Roe*, and *Poelker v. Doe*, that appellees' facial challenge to the constitutionality of Missouri's ban on the utilization of public facilities and the participation of public employees in the performance of abortions not necessary to save the life of the mother, Mo. Rev. Stat. §§ 188.210, 188.215 (1986), cannot succeed. Given Missouri's definition of "public facility" as "any public institution, public facility, public equipment, or any physical asset owned, leased, or controlled by this state or any agency or political subdivisions thereof," Mo. Rev. Stat. § 188.200(2) (1986), there may be conceivable applications of the ban on the use of public facilities that would be unconstitutional. Appellees and *amici* suggest that the State could try to enforce the ban against private hospitals using public water and sewage lines, or against private hospitals leasing state-owned equipment

or state land. Whether some or all of these or other applications of § 188.215 would be constitutional need not be decided here. *Maher, Poelker,* and *McRae* stand for the proposition that some quite straightforward applications of the Missouri ban on the use of public facilities for performing abortions would be constitutional and that is enough to defeat appellees' assertion that the ban is facially unconstitutional. "A facial challenge to a legislative Act is, of course, the most difficult challenge to mount successfully, since the challenger must establish that no set of circumstances exists under which the Act would be valid. . . ." *United States v. Salerno,* 481 U.S. 739, 745 (1987)

. . . .

II

In its interpretation of Missouri's "determination of viability" provision, Mo. Rev. Stat. § 188.029 (1986), the plurality has proceeded in a manner unnecessary to deciding the question at hand. I agree with the plurality that it was plain error for the Court of Appeals to interpret the second sentence of Mo. Rev. Stat. § 188.029 as meaning that "doctors *must* perform tests to find gestational age, fetal weight and lung maturity." 851 F.2d, at 1075, n. 5 (emphasis in original). When read together with the first sentence of § 188.029—which requires a physician to "determine if the unborn child is viable by using and exercising that degree of care, skill, and proficiency commonly exercised by the ordinary skillful, careful, and prudent physician engaged in similar practice under the same or similar conditions"—it would be contradictory nonsense to read the second sentence as requiring a physician to perform viability examinations and tests in situations where it would be careless and imprudent to do so. The plurality is quite correct: "the viability-testing provision makes sense only if the second sentence is read to require only those tests that are useful to making subsidiary findings as to viability," and, I would add, only those examinations and tests that it would not be imprudent or careless to perform in the particular medical situation before the physician.

Unlike the plurality, I do not understand these viability testing requirements to conflict with any of the Court's past decisions concerning state regulation of abortion. Therefore, there is no necessity to accept the State's invitation to reexamine the constitutional validity of *Roe v. Wade*. Where there is no need to decide a constitutional question, it is a venerable principle of this Court's adjudicatory processes not to do so for "[t]he Court will not 'anticipate a question of constitutional law in advance of the necessity of deciding it.' " *Ashwander v. TVA*, 297 U.S. 288, 346 (1936) (Brandeis, J., concurring), quoting *Liverpool, New York and Philadelphia S.S. Co. v. Commissioners of Emigration*, 113 U.S. 33, 39 (1885). Neither will it generally "formulate a rule of constitutional law broader than is required by the precise facts to which it is to be applied." 297 U.S., at 347. Quite simply, "[i]t is not the habit of the court to decide questions of a constitutional nature unless absolutely necessary to a decision of the case." *Burton v. United States*, 196 U.S. 283, 295 (1905). The Court today has accepted the State's every interpretation of its abortion statute and has upheld, under our existing precedents, every provision of that statute which is properly before us. Precisely for this reason reconsideration of *Roe* falls not into any "good-cause exception" to this "fundamental rule of judicial restraint. . . ." *Three Affiliated Tribes of Fort Berthold Reservation v. Wold Engineering, P.C.*, 467 U.S. 138, 157 (1984). See *post* (SCALLIA, J., concurring in part and concurring in judgment). When

the constitutional invalidity of a State's abortion statute actually turns on the constitutional validity of *Roe v. Wade*, there will be time enough to reexamine *Roe*. And to do so carefully.

In assessing § 188.029 it is especially important to recognize that appellees did not appeal the District Court's ruling that the first sentence of § 188.029 is constitutional. 662 F. Supp., at 420–22. There is, accordingly, no dispute between the parties before us over the constitutionality of the "presumption of viability at 20 weeks," *ante*, created by the first sentence of § 188.029. If anything might arguably conflict with the Court's previous decisions concerning the determination of viability, I would think it is the introduction of this presumption. The plurality refers to a passage from *Planned Parenthood of Central Missouri v. Danforth*, 428 U.S. 52, 64 (1976): "The time when viability is achieved may vary with each pregnancy, and the determination of whether a particular fetus is viable is, and must be, a matter for the judgment of the responsible attending physician." The 20-week presumption of viability in the first sentence of § 188.029, it could be argued (though, I would think, unsuccessfully), restricts "the judgment of the responsible attending physician," by imposing on that physician the burden of overcoming the presumption. This presumption may be a "superimpos[ition] [of] state regulation on the medical determination of whether a particular fetus is viable," *ante*, but, if so, it is a restriction on the physician's judgment that is not before us. As the plurality properly interprets the second sentence of § 188.029, it does nothing more than delineate means by which the unchallenged 20-week presumption of viability may be overcome if those means are useful in doing so and can be prudently employed. Contrary to the plurality's suggestion, the District Court did not think the second sentence of § 188.029 unconstitutional for this reason. Rather, both the District Court and the Court of Appeals thought the second sentence to be unconstitutional precisely because they interpreted that sentence to impose state regulation on the determination of viability that it does not impose. . . .

I do not think the second sentence of § 188.029, as interpreted by the Court, imposes a degree of state regulation on the medical determination of viability that in any way conflicts with prior decisions of this Court. As the plurality recognizes, the requirement that, where not imprudent, physicians perform examinations and tests useful to making subsidiary findings to determine viability "promot[es] the State's interest in potential human life rather than in maternal health." *Ante*. No decision of this Court has held that the State may not directly promote its interest in potential life when viability is possible. Quite the contrary. In *Thornburgh v. American College of Obstetricians and Gynecologists*, 476 U.S. 747 (1986), the Court considered a constitutional challenge to a Pennsylvania statute requiring that a second physician be present during an abortion performed "when viability is possible." *Id.*, at 769–70. For guidance, the Court looked to the earlier decision in *Planned Parenthood Assn. of Kansas City, Missouri, Inc. v. Ashcroft*, 462 U.S. 476 (1983), upholding a Missouri statute requiring the presence of a second physician during an abortion performed after viability. *Id.*, at 482–86 (opinion of Powell, J.); *id.*, at 505 (opinion concurring in judgment in part and dissenting in part). The *Thornburgh* majority struck down the Pennsylvania statute merely because the statute had no exception for emergency situations and not because it found a constitutional difference between the State's promotion of its interest in potential life when viability is possible and when viability is certain. 476

U.S., at 770–71. Despite the clear recognition by the *Thornburgh* majority that the Pennsylvania and Missouri statutes differed in this respect, there is no hint in the opinion of the *Thornburgh* Court that the State's interest in potential life differs depending whether it seeks to further that interest postviability or when viability is possible. Thus, all nine Members of the *Thornburgh* Court appear to have agreed that it is not constitutionally impermissible for the State to enact regulations designed to protect the State's interest in potential life when viability is possible. See *id.*, at 811 (WHITE, J., dissenting); *id.*, at 832 (dissenting opinion). That is exactly what Missouri has done in § 188.029.

Similarly, the basis for reliance by the District Court and the Court of Appeals below on *Colautti v. Franklin*, 439 U.S. 379 (1979), disappears when § 188.029 is properly interpreted. In *Colautti* the Court observed:

> Because this point [of viability] may differ with each pregnancy, neither the legislature nor the courts may proclaim one of the elements entering into the ascertainment of viability—be it weeks of gestation or fetal weight or any other single factor—as the determinant of when the State has a compelling interest in the life or health of the fetus. Viability is the critical point. *Id.*, at 388–89.

The courts below, on the interpretation of § 188.029 rejected here, found the second sentence of that provision at odds with this passage from *Colautti*. See 851 F.2d, at 1074; 662 F. Supp., at 423. On this Court's interpretation of § 188.029 it is clear that Missouri has not substituted any of the "elements entering into the ascertainment of viability" as "the determinant of when the State has a compelling interest in the life or health of the fetus." All the second sentence of § 188.029 does is to require, when not imprudent, the performance of "those tests that are useful to making *subsidiary* findings as to viability." *Ante* (emphasis added). Thus, consistent with *Colautti,* viability remains the "critical point" under § 188.029.

Finally, and rather half-heartedly, the plurality suggests that the marginal increase in the cost of an abortion created by Missouri's viability testing provision may make § 188.029, even as interpreted, suspect under this Court's decision in *Akron,* 462 U.S., at 434–39, striking down a second-trimester hospitalization requirement. I dissented from the Court's opinion in *Akron* because it was my view that, even apart from *Roe's* trimester framework which I continue to consider problematic, see *Thornburgh,* at 828 (dissenting opinion), the *Akron* majority had distorted and misapplied its own standard for evaluating state regulation of abortion which the Court had applied with fair consistency in the past: that, previability, "a regulation imposed on a lawful abortion is not unconstitutional unless it unduly burdens the right to seek an abortion." *Akron,* at 453 (dissenting opinion).

It is clear to me that requiring the performance of examinations and tests useful to determining whether a fetus is viable, when viability is possible, and when it would not be medically imprudent to do so, does not impose an undue burden on a woman's abortion decision. On this ground alone I would reject the suggestion that § 188.029 as interpreted is unconstitutional. More to the point, however, just as I see no conflict between § 188.029 and *Colautti* or any decision of this Court concerning a State's ability to give effect to its interest in potential life, I see no conflict between § 188.029 and the Court's opinion in *Akron.* The second-trimester hospitalization requirement struck down in *Akron* imposed, in the majority's view, "a heavy, and unnecessary, burden," 462 U.S., at 438, more than doubling the cost of "women's access to a relatively inexpensive, otherwise accessible, and safe abortion procedure." *Ibid.;* see also *id.,* at 434. By contrast, the cost of examinations and tests that could usefully and prudently be performed when a woman is 20–24 weeks pregnant to determine whether the fetus is viable would only marginally, if at all, increase the cost of an abortion.... [Here O'Connor cited various briefs and medical tests to suggest that a relatively inexpensive sonogram, or even an inference from last menstrual period, could be used to determine gestational age, and then fetal weight and lung capacity could be inferred from age, because lungs "do not mature until 33–34 weeks gestation."—Au.]

Moreover, the examinations and tests required by § 188.029 are to be performed when viability is possible. This feature of § 188.029 distinguishes it from the second-trimester hospitalization requirement struck down by the *Akron* majority. As the Court recognized in *Thornburgh,* the State's compelling interest in potential life postviability renders its interest in determining the critical point of viability equally compelling. Under the Court's precedents, the same cannot be said for the *Akron* second-trimester hospitalization requirement. As I understand the Court's opinion in *Akron,* therefore, the plurality's suggestion today that *Akron* casts doubt on the validity of § 188.029, even as the Court has interpreted it, is without foundation and cannot provide a basis for reevaluating *Roe.* Accordingly, because the Court of Appeals misinterpreted Mo. Rev. Stat. § 188.029, and because, properly interpreted, § 188.029 is not inconsistent with any of this Court's prior precedents, I would reverse the decision of the Court of Appeals.

In sum, I concur in Parts I, II-A, II-B, and II-C of the Court's opinion and concur in the judgment of Part II-D.

JUSTICE SCALIA, concurring in part and concurring in the judgment.

I join Parts I, II-A, II-B, and II-C of the opinion of THE CHIEF JUSTICE. As to Part II-D, I share JUSTICE BLACKMUN's view, *post*, that it effectively would overrule *Roe v. Wade*, 410 U.S. 113 (1973). I think that should be done, but would do it more explicitly. Since today we contrive to avoid doing it, and indeed to avoid almost any decision of national import, I need not set forth my reasons, some of which have been well recited in dissents of my colleagues in other cases. See, *e.g.*, *Thornburgh v. American College of Obstetricians and Gynecologists*, 476 U.S. 747, 786–97 (1986) (WHITE, J., dissenting); *Akron v. Akron Center for Reproductive Health, Inc.*, 462 U.S. 416, 453–59 (1983) (O'CONNOR, J., dissenting); *Roe v. Wade, supra*, at 172–78 (REHNQUIST, J., dissenting); *Doe v. Bolton*, 410 U.S. 179, 221–23 (1973) (WHITE, J., dissenting).

The outcome of today's case will doubtless be heralded as a triumph of judicial statesmanship. It is not that, unless it is statesmanlike needlessly to prolong this Court's self-awarded sovereignty over a field where it has little proper business since the answers to most of the cruel questions posed are political and not juridical—a sovereignty which therefore quite properly, but to the great damage of the Court, makes it the object of the sort of organized public pressure that political institutions in a democracy ought to receive. JUSTICE O'CONNOR's assertion, that a " 'fundamental rule of judicial restraint' " requires us to avoid reconsidering *Roe*, cannot be taken seriously. By finessing *Roe* we do not, as she suggests, adhere to the strict and venerable rule that we should avoid " 'decid[ing] questions of a constitutional

nature.' " We have not disposed of this case on some statutory or procedural ground, but have decided, and could not avoid deciding, whether the Missouri statute meets the requirements of the United States Constitution. The only choice available is whether, in deciding that constitutional question, we should use *Roe v. Wade* as the benchmark, or something else. What is involved, therefore, is not the rule of avoiding constitutional issues where possible, but the quite separate principle that we will not " 'formulate a rule of constitutional law broader than is required by the precise facts to which it is to be applied.' " *Ante.* The latter is a sound general principle, but one often departed from when good reason exists. Just this Term, for example, in an opinion authored by JUSTICE O'CONNOR, despite the fact that we had already held a racially based set-aside unconstitutional because unsupported by evidence of identified discrimination, which was all that was needed to decide the case, we went on to outline the criteria for properly tailoring race-based remedies in cases where such evidence is present. *Richmond v. J. A. Croson Co.*, 488 U.S. 469, 506–08 (1989).

Also this Term, in an opinion joined by JUSTICE O'CONNOR, we announced the constitutional rule that deprivation of the right to confer with counsel during trail violates the Sixth Amendment even if no prejudice can be shown, despite our finding that there had been no such deprivation on the facts before us—which was all that was needed to decide that case. *Perry v. Leeke*, 488 U.S. 272, 278–80 (1989); see *id.*, at 285 (KENNEDY, J., concurring in part). I have not identified with certainty the first instance of our deciding a case on broader constitutional grounds than absolutely necessary, but it is assuredly no later than *Marbury v. Madison*, 1 Cranch 137 (1803), where we held that mandamus could constitutionally issue against the Secretary of State, although that was unnecessary given our holding that the law authorizing issuance of the mandamus by this Court was unconstitutional.

The Court has often spoken more broadly than needed in precisely the fashion at issue here, announcing a new rule of constitutional law when it could have reached the identical result by applying the rule thereby displaced. [Several additional examples were here described.—Au.] . . . It would be wrong, in any decision, to ignore the reality that our policy not to "formulate a rule of constitutional law broader than is required by the precise facts" has a frequently applied good-cause exception. But it seems particularly perverse to convert the policy into an absolute in the present case, in order to place beyond reach the inexpressibly "broader-than-was-required-by-the-precise-facts" structure established by *Roe v. Wade.*

The real question, then, is whether there are valid reasons to go beyond the most stingy possible holding today. It seems to me there are not only valid but compelling ones. Ordinarily, speaking no more broadly than is absolutely required avoids throwing settled law into confusion; doing so today preserves a chaos that is evident to anyone who can read and count. Alone sufficient to justify a broad holding is the fact that our retaining control, through *Roe,* of what I believe to be, and many of our citizens recognize to be, a political issue, continuously distorts the public perception of the role of this Court. We can now look forward to at least another Term with carts full of mail from the public, and streets full of demonstrators, urging us—their unelected and life-tenured judges who have been awarded those extraordinary, undemocratic characteristics precisely in order that we might follow the law despite the popular will—to follow the popular will. Indeed, I expect we can look forward to even more of that than before, given our indecisive

decision today. And if these reasons for taking the unexceptional course of reaching a broader holding are not enough, then consider the nature of the constitutional question we avoid: In most cases, we do no harm by not speaking more broadly than the decision requires. Anyone affected by the conduct that the avoided holding would have prohibited will be able to challenge it himself, and have his day in court to make the argument. Not so with respect to the harm that many States believed, pre-*Roe,* and many may continue to believe, is caused by largely unrestricted abortion. That will continue to occur if the States have the constitutional power to prohibit it, and would do so, but we skillfully avoid telling them so. Perhaps those abortions cannot constitutionally be proscribed. That is surely an arguable question, the question that reconsideration of *Roe v. Wade* entails. But what is not at all arguable, it seems to me, is that we should decide now and not insist that we be run into a corner before we grudgingly yield up our judgment. The only sound reason for the latter course is to prevent a change in the law— but to think that desirable begs the question to be decided.

It was an arguable question today whether § 188.029 of the Missouri law contravened this Court's understanding of *Roe v. Wade,** and I would have examined *Roe*

---

*That question, compared with the question whether we should reconsider and reverse *Roe,* is hardly worth a footnote, but I think JUSTICE O'CONNOR answers that incorrectly as well. In *Roe v. Wade,* 410 U.S. 113, 165–66 (1973), we said that "the physician [has the right] to administer medical treatment according to his professional judgment up to the points where important state interests provide compelling justifications for intervention." We have subsequently made clear that it is also a matter of medical judgment when viability (one of those points) is reached. "The time when viability is achieved may vary with rather than examining the contravention. Given the Court's newly contracted abstemiousness, what will it take, one must wonder, to permit us to reach that fundamental question? The result of our vote today is that we will not reconsider that prior opinion, even if most of the Justices think it is wrong, unless we have before us a statute that in fact contradicts it—and even then

---

each pregnancy, and the determination of whether a particular fetus is viable is, and must be, a matter for the judgment of the responsible attending physician." *Planned Parenthood of Central Missouri v. Danforth*, 428 U.S. 52, 64 (1976). Section 188.029 conflicts with the purpose and hence the fair import of this principle because it will sometimes require a physician to perform tests that he would not otherwise have performed to determine whether a fetus is viable. It is therefore a legislative imposition on the judgment of the physician, and one that increases the cost of an abortion.

Justice O'Connor would nevertheless uphold the law because it "does not impose an undue burden on a woman's abortion decision." This conclusion is supported by the observation that the required tests impose only a marginal cost on the abortion procedure, far less of an increase than the cost-doubling hospitalization requirement invalidated in *Akron v. Akron Center for Reproductive Health, Inc.* The fact that the challenged regulation is less costly than what we struck down in *Akron* tells us only that we cannot decide the present case on the basis of that earlier decision. It does not tell us whether the present requirement is an "undue burden," and I know of no basis for determining that this particular burden (or any other for that matter) is "due." One could with equal justification conclude that it is not. To avoid the question of *Roe v. Wade's* validity, with the attendant costs that this will have for the Court and for the principles of self-governance, on the basis of a standard that offers "no guide but the Court's own discretion," *Baldwin v. Missouri*, 281 U.S. 586, 595 (1930) (Holmes, J., dissenting), merely adds to the irrationality of what we do today.

(under our newly discovered "no-broader-than-necessary" requirement) only minor problematical aspects of *Roe* will be reconsidered, unless one expects State legislatures to adopt provisions whose compliance with *Roe* cannot even be argued with a straight face. It thus appears that the mansion of constitutionalized abortion-law, constructed overnight in *Roe v. Wade*, must be disassembled door-jamb by door-jamb, and never entirely brought down, no matter how wrong it may be.

Of the four courses we might have chosen today—to reaffirm *Roe*, to overrule it explicitly, to overrule it *sub silentio*, or to avoid the question—the last is the least responsible. On the question of the constitutionality of § 188.029, I concur in the judgment of the Court and strongly dissent from the manner in which it has been reached.

Justice Blackmun, with whom Justice Brennan and Justice Marshall join, concurring in part and dissenting in part.

Today, *Roe v. Wade*, and the fundamental constitutional right of women to decide whether to terminate a pregnancy, survive but are not secure. Although the Court extricates itself from this case without making a single, even incremental, change in the law of abortion, the plurality and

---

Similarly irrational is the new concept that Justice O'Connor introduces into the law in order to achieve her result, the notion of a State's "interest in potential life when viability is possible." Since "viability" means the mere *possibility* (not the certainty) of survivability outside the womb, "possible viability" must mean the possibility of a possibility of survivability outside-the womb. Perhaps our next opinion will expand the third trimester into the second even further, by approving state action designed to take account of "the chance of possible viability."

its progeny, holds that a State may not effectuate its compelling interest in the potential life of a viable fetus by seeking to ensure that no viable fetus is mistakenly aborted because of the inherent lack of precision in estimates of gestational age. A requirement that a physician make a finding of viability, one way or the other, for every fetus that falls within the range of possible viability does no more than preserve the State's recognized authority. Although, as the plurality correctly points out, such a testing requirement would have the effect of imposing additional costs on second-trimester abortions where the tests indicated that the fetus was not viable, these costs would be merely incidental to, and a necessary accommodation of, the State's unquestioned right to prohibit nontherapeutic abortions after the point of viability. In short, the testing provision, as construed by the plurality is consistent with the *Roe* framework and could be upheld effortlessly under current doctrine.[6]

How ironic it is, then, and disingenuous, that the plurality scolds the Court of Appeals for adopting a construction of the statute that fails to avoid constitutional difficulties. By distorting the statute, the plurality manages to avoid invalidating the testing provision on what should have been noncontroversial constitutional grounds; having done so, however, the plurality rushes headlong into a much deeper constitutional thicket, brushing past an obvious basis for upholding § 188.029 in search of a pretext for scuttling the trimester framework. Evidently, from the plurality's perspective, the real problem with the Court of Appeals' construction of § 188.029 is not that it raised a constitutional difficulty, but that it raised the wrong constitutional difficulty—one not implicating *Roe*. The plurality has remedied that, traditional canons of construction and judicial forbearance notwithstanding.

---

gerous tests. *Id.* To the extent that the plurality may be reading the provision to require tests other than those that a doctor, exercising reasonable professional judgment, would deem necessary to a finding of viability, the provision bears no rational relation to a legitimate governmental interest, and cannot stand.

6. As convincingly demonstrated by JUSTICE O'CONNOR, the cases cited by the plurality, are not to the contrary. As noted by the plurality, in both *Colautti v. Franklin*, 439 U.S. 379, 388–89 (1979), and *Planned Parenthood of Central Mo. v. Danforth*, we stressed that the determination of viability is a matter for the judgment of the responsible attending physician. But § 188.029, at least as construed by the plurality, is consistent with this requirement. The provision does nothing to remove the determination of viability from the purview of the attending physician; it merely instructs the physician to make a finding of viability using tests to

determine gestational age, weight, and lung maturity when such tests are feasible and medically appropriate.

I also see no conflict with the Court's holding in *Akron* that the State may not impose "a heavy, *and unnecessary,* burden on women's access to a relatively inexpensive, and otherwise accessible, and safe abortion procedure." 462 U.S., at 438 (emphasis added). In *Akron*, we invalidated a city ordinance requiring that all second-trimester abortions be performed in acute-care hospitals on the ground that such a requirement was not medically necessary and would double the cost of abortions. *Id.*, at 434–39. By contrast, the viability determination at issue in this case (as read by the plurality), is necessary to the effectuation of the State's compelling interest in the potential human life of viable fetuses and applies not to all second-trimester abortions, but instead only to that small percentage of abortions performed on fetuses estimated to be of more than 20 weeks gestational age.

B

Having set up the conflict between §
188.029 and the *Roe* trimester framework,
the plurality summarily discards *Roe's*
analytic core as " 'unsound in principle
and unworkable in practice.' " This is so,
the plurality claims, because the key
elements of the framework do not appear
in the text of the Constitution, because the
framework more closely resembles a regulatory code than a body of constitutional
doctrine, and because under the framework the State's interest in potential
human life is considered compelling only
after viability, when, in fact, that interest is
equally compelling throughout pregnancy.
The plurality does not bother to explain
these alleged flaws in *Roe*. Bald assertion
masquerades as reasoning. The object,
quite clearly, is not to persuade, but to
prevail.

1

The plurality opinion is far more remarkable for the arguments that it does not
advance than for those that it does. The
plurality does not even mention, much less
join, the true jurisprudential debate underlying this case: whether the Constitution
includes an "unenumerated" general right
to privacy as recognized in many of our
decisions, most notably *Griswold v. Connecticut*, and *Roe*, and, more specifically,
whether and to what extent such a right to
privacy extends to matters of childbearing
and family life, including abortion. See, *e.g.*,
Eisenstadt v. Baird, 405 U.S. 438 (1972) (contraception); *Loving v. Virginia*, 388 U.S. 1
(1967) (marriage); *Skinner v. Oklahoma ex re.
Williamson*, 316 U.S. 535 (1942) (procreation); *Pierce v. Society of Sisters*, 268 U.S.
510 (1925) (childrearing).[7] These are questions of unsurpassed significance in this
Court's interpretation of the Constitution,
and mark the battleground upon which

this case was fought, by the parties, by the
Solicitor General as *amicus* on behalf of
petitioners, and by an unprecedented number of *amici*. On these grounds, abandoned
by the plurality, the Court should decide
this case.

But rather than arguing that the text
of the Constitution makes no mention of
the right to privacy, the plurality complains that the critical elements of the *Roe*
framework—trimesters and viability—do
not appear in the Constitution and are,
therefore, somehow inconsistent with a
Constitution cast in general terms. Were

7. The plurality, ignoring all of the aforementioned cases except *Griswold*, responds that this
case does not require consideration of the
"great issues" underlying this case because
Griswold, "unlike *Roe*, did not purport to adopt
a whole framework ... to govern the cases in
which the asserted liberty interest would
apply." *Ante*. This distinction is highly ironic.
The Court in *Roe* adopted the framework of
which the plurality complains as a mechanism
necessary to give effect both to the constitutional rights of the pregnant woman and to the
State's significant interests in maternal health
and potential life. Concededly, *Griswold* does
not adopt a framework for determining the
permissible scope of state regulation of contraception. The reason is simple: in *Griswold* (and
Eisenstadt), the Court held that the challenged
statute, regulating the use of medically safe
contraception, did not properly serve *any*
significant state interest. Accordingly, the Court
had no occasion to fashion a framework to
accommodate a State's interests in regulating
contraception. Surely, the plurality is not
suggesting that it would find *Roe* unobjectionable if the Court had forgone the framework
and, as in the contraception decisions, had left
the State with little or no regulatory authority.
The plurality's focus on the framework is
merely an excuse for avoiding the real issues
embedded in this case and a mask for its
hostility to the constitutional rights that *Roe*
recognized.

this a true concern, we would have to abandon most of our constitutional jurisprudence. As the plurality well knows, or should know, the "critical elements" of countless constitutional doctrines nowhere appear in the Constitution's text. The Constitution makes no mention, for example, of the First Amendment's "actual malice" standard for proving certain libels, see *New York Times v. Sullivan*, 376 U.S. 254 (1964), or of the standard for determining when speech is obscene. See *Miller v. California*, 413 U.S. 15 (1973). Similarly, the Constitution makes no mention of the rational-basis test, or the specific verbal formulations of intermediate and strict scrutiny by which this Court evaluates claims under the Equal Protection Clause. The reason is simple. Like the *Roe* framework, these tests or standards are not, and do not purport to be, rights protected by the Constitution. Rather, they are judgemade methods for evaluating and measuring the strength and scope of constitutional rights or for balancing the constitutional rights of individuals against the competing interests of government.

With respect to the *Roe* framework, the general constitutional principle, indeed the fundamental constitutional right, for which it was developed is the right to privacy, see, *e.g.*, *Griswold v. Connecticut*, a species of "liberty" protected by the Due Process Clause, which under our past decisions safeguards the right of women to exercise some control over their own role in procreation. As we recently reaffirmed in *Thornburgh v. American College of Obstetricians and Gynecologists*, few decisions are "more basic to individual dignity and autonomy" or more appropriate to that "certain private sphere of individual liberty" that the Constitution reserves from the intrusive reach of government than the right to make the uniquely personal, intimate, and self-defining deci-

sion whether to end a pregnancy. 476 U.S., at 772. It is this general principle, the " 'moral fact that a person belongs to himself and not others nor to society as a whole,' " *id.*, at 777, n. 5 (STEVENS, J., concurring), quoting Fried, Correspondence, 6 Phil. & Pub. Aff. 288–89 (1977), that is found in the Constitution. See *Roe*, 410 U.S., at 152–53. The trimester framework simply defines and limits that right to privacy in the abortion context to accommodate, not destroy, a State's legitimate interest in protecting the health of pregnant women and in preserving potential human life. *Id.*, at 154–62. Fashioning such accommodations between individual rights and the legitimate interests of government, establishing benchmarks and standards with which to evaluate the competing claims of individuals and government, lies at the very heart of constitutional adjudication. To the extent that the trimester framework is useful in this enterprise, it is not only consistent with constitutional interpretation, but necessary to the wise and just exercise of this Court's paramount authority to define the scope of constitutional rights.

2

The plurality next alleges that the result of the trimester framework has "been a web of legal rules that have become increasingly intricate, resembling a code of regulations rather than a body of constitutional doctrine." Are these distinctions any finer, or more "regulatory," than the distinctions we have often drawn in our First Amendment jurisprudence, where, for example, we have held that a "release time" program permitting publicschool students to leave school grounds during school hours to receive religious instruction does not violate the Establishment Clause, even though a release-time program permitting religious instruction on school grounds does violate the Clause? Compare *Zorach v. Clauson*, 343 U.S. 306 (1952), with *McCollum v. Board of Education*, 333 U.S. 203 (1948). Our Fourth Amendment jurisprudence recognizes factual distinctions no less intricate. Just this Term, for example, we held that while an aerial observation from a helicopter hovering at 400 feet does not violate any reasonable expectation of privacy, such an expectation of privacy would be violated by a helicopter observation from an unusually low altitude. *Florida v. Riley*, 488 U.S. 445, 451 (1989) (O'CONNOR, J., concurring in the judgment). Similarly, in a Sixth Amendment case, the Court held that although an overnight ban on attorney-client communication violated the constitutionally guaranteed right to counsel, *Geders v. United States*, 425 U.S. 80 (1976), that right was not violated when a trial judge separated a defendant from his lawyer during a 15-minute recess after the defendant's direct testimony. *Perry v. Leeke*, 488 U.S. 272 (1989).

That numerous constitutional doctrines result in narrow differentiations between similar circumstances does not mean that this Court has abandoned adjudication in favor of regulation. Rather, these careful distinctions reflect the process of constitutional adjudication itself, which is often highly fact-specific, requiring such determinations as whether state laws are "unduly burdensome" or "reasonable" or bear a "rational" or "necessary" relation to asserted state interests. In a recent due process case, THE CHIEF JUSTICE wrote for the Court: "[M]any branches of the law abound in nice distinctions that may be troublesome but have been thought nonetheless necessary: 'I do not think we need trouble ourselves with the thought that my view depends upon differences of degree.

The whole law does so as soon as it is civilized.' " *Daniels v. Williams*, 474 U.S. 327, 334 (1986), quoting *Le Roy Fibre Co. v. Chicago, M. & St. P.R. Co.*, 232 U.S. 340, 354 (1914) (Holmes, J., partially concurring).

These "differences of degree" fully account for our holdings in *Simopoulos* and *Akron*. Those decisions rest on this Court's reasoned and accurate judgment that hospitalization and doctor-counselling requirements unduly burdened the right of women to terminate a pregnancy and were not rationally related to the State's asserted interest in the health of pregnant women, while Virginia's *substantially less restrictive* regulations were not unduly burdensome and did rationally serve the State's interest.[8] That the Court exercised its best judgment in evaluating these markedly different statutory schemes no more established the Court as an "*ex officio* medical board," than our decisions involving religion in the public schools establish the Court as a national school board, or our decisions concerning prison regulations establish the Court as a bureau of

---

8. The difference in the *Akron* and *Simopoulos* regulatory regimes is stark. The Court noted in *Akron* that the city ordinance requiring that all second-trimester abortions be performed in acute-care hospitals undoubtedly would have made the procurement of legal abortions difficult and often prohibitively expensive, thereby driving the performance of abortions back underground where they would not be subject to effective regulation. Such a requirement obviously did not further the city's asserted interest in maternal health. *Id.*, at 420, n.1. On the other hand, the Virginia law at issue in *Simopoulos*, by permitting the performance of abortions in licensed out-patient clinics as well as hospitals, did not similarly constrict the availability of legal abortions and, therefore, did not undermine its own stated purpose of protecting maternal health.

prisons. See *Thornburgh v. Abbott*, 490 U.S. 401 (1989) (adopting different standard of First Amendment review for incoming as opposed to outgoing prison mail). If, in delicate and complicated areas of constitutional law, our legal judgments "have become increasingly intricate," it is not, as the plurality contends, because we have overstepped our judicial role. Quite the opposite: the rules are intricate because we have remained conscientious in our duty to do justice carefully, especially when fundamental rights rise or fall with our decisions.

3

Finally, the plurality asserts that the trimester framework cannot stand because the State's interest in potential life is compelling throughout pregnancy, not merely after viability. The opinion contains not one word of rationale for its view of the State's interest. This "it-is-so-because-we-say-so" jurisprudence constitutes nothing other than an attempted exercise of brute force; reason, much less persuasion, has no place.

In answering the plurality's claim that the State's interest in the fetus is uniform and compelling throughout pregnancy, I cannot improve upon what JUSTICE STEVENS has written:

I should think it obvious that the State's interest in the protection of an embryo—even if that interest is defined as "protecting those who will be citizens" . . . —increases progressively and dramatically as the organism's capacity to feel pain, to experience pleasure, to survive, and to react to its surroundings increases day by day. The development of a fetus—and pregnancy itself—are not static conditions, and the assertion that the

government's interest is static simply ignores this reality. . . . [U]nless the religious view that a fetus is a "person" is adopted . . . there is a fundamental and well-recognized difference between a fetus and a human being; indeed, if there is not such a difference, the permissibility of terminating the life of a fetus could scarcely be left to the will of the state legislatures. And if distinctions may be drawn between a fetus and a human being in terms of the state interest in their protection—even though the fetus represents one of "those who will be citizens"—it seems to me quite odd to argue that distinctions may not also be drawn between the state interest in protecting the freshly fertilized egg and the state interest in protecting the 9-month-gestated, fully sentient fetus on the eve of birth. Recognition of this distinction is supported not only by logic, but also by history and by our shared experiences. *Thornburgh*, 476 U.S., at 778–79 (footnotes omitted). See also *Roe*, 410 U.S., at 129–47.

For my own part, I remain convinced, as six other Members of this Court 16 years ago were convinced, that the *Roe* framework, and the viability standard in particular, fairly, sensibly, and effectively functions to safeguard the constitutional liberties of pregnant women while recognizing and accommodating the State's interest in potential human life. The viability line reflects the biological facts and truths of fetal development; it marks that threshold moment prior to which a fetus cannot survive separate from the woman and cannot reasonably and objectively be regarded as a subject of rights or interests distinct from, or paramount to,

those of the pregnant woman. At the same
time, the viability standard takes account
of the undeniable fact that as the fetus
evolves into its postnatal form, and as it
loses its dependence on the uterine environment, the State's interest in the fetus'
potential human life, and in fostering a
regard for human life in general, becomes
compelling. As a practical matter, because
viability follows "quickening"—the point
at which a woman feels movement in her
womb—and because viability occurs no
earlier than 23 weeks gestational age, it
establishes an easily applicable standard for
regulating abortion while providing a pregnant woman ample time to exercise her
fundamental right with her responsible
physician to terminate her pregnancy.[9] Although I have stated previously for a
majority of this Court that "[c]onstitutional

9. Notably, neither the plurality nor JUSTICE
O'CONNOR advance the now-familiar catch-
phrase criticism of the Roe framework that
because the point of viability will recede with
advances in medical technology, Roe "is clearly
on a collision course with itself." See Akron, 462
U.S., at 458 (dissenting opinion). This critique
has no medical foundation. As the medical
literature and the amicus briefs filed in this case
conclusively demonstrate, "there is an 'anatom-
ic threshold' for fetal viability of about 23–24
weeks gestation." Brief for American Medical
Association, et al., as Amici Curiae 7. Prior to
that time, the crucial organs are not sufficiently
mature to provide the mutually sustaining
functions that are prerequisite to extrauterine
survival, or viability. Moreover, "no technology
exists to bridge the development gap between
the three-day embryo culture and the 24th
week of gestation." Fetal Extrauterine Survivability, Report to the New York State Task Force
on Life and Law 10 (1988). Nor does the
medical community believe that the development of any such technology is possible in the
foreseeable future. Id., at 12. In other words, the
threshold of fetal viability is, and will remain,

rights do not always have easily ascertain-
able boundaries," to seek and establish
those boundaries remains the special responsibility of this Court. Thornburgh, 476
U.S., at 771. In Roe, we discharged that
responsibility as logic and science compelled. The plurality today advances not
one reasonable argument as to why our
judgment in that case was wrong and
should be abandoned.

C

Having contrived an opportunity to
reconsider the Roe framework, and then
having discarded that framework, the
plurality finds the testing provision unobjectionable because it "permissibly furthers the State's interest in protecting
potential human life." This newly minted
standard is circular and totally meaningless. Whether a challenged abortion regulation "permissibly furthers" a legitimate
state interest is the question that courts
must answer in abortion cases, not the
standard for courts to apply. In keeping
with the rest of its opinion, the plurality
makes no attempt to explain or to justify
its new standard, either in the abstract or
as applied in this case. Nor could it. The
"permissibly furthers" standard has no
independent meaning, and consists of
nothing other than what a majority of this
Court may believe at any given moment
in any given case. The plurality's novel
test appears to be nothing more than a
dressed-up version of rational-basis review, this Court's most lenient level of
scrutiny. One thing is clear, however: were
the plurality's "permissibly furthers" stan-

no different from what it was at the time Roe was
decided. Predictions to the contrary are pure
science fiction. . . .

dard adopted by the Court, for all practical purposes, *Roe* would be overruled.[10]

The "permissibly furthers" standard completely disregards the irreducible minimum of *Roe*: the Court's recognition that a woman has a limited fundamental constitutional right to decide whether to terminate a pregnancy. That right receives no meaningful recognition in the plurality's written opinion. Since, in the plurality's view, the State's interest in potential life is compelling as of the moment of conception, and is therefore served only if abortion is abolished, every hindrance to a woman's ability to obtain an abortion must be "permissible." Indeed, the more severe the hindrance, the more effectively (and permissibly) the State's interest would be furthered. A tax on abortions or a criminal prohibition would both satisfy the plurality's standard. So, for that matter, would a requirement that a pregnant woman memorize and recite today's plurality opinion before seeking an abortion.

The plurality pretends that *Roe* survives, explaining that the facts of this case differ from those in *Roe*: here, Missouri has chosen to assert its interest in potential life only at the point of viability, whereas, in *Roe*, Texas had asserted that interest from the point of conception, criminalizing all abortions, except where the life of the mother was at stake. *Ante.* This, of course, is

10. Writing for the Court in *Akron*, Justice Powell observed the same phenomenon, though in hypothetical response to the dissent in that case: "In sum, it appears that the dissent would uphold virtually any abortion regulation under a rational-basis test. It also appears that even where heightened scrutiny is deemed appropriate, the dissent would uphold virtually any abortion-inhibiting regulation because of the State's interest in preserving potential human life.... This analysis is wholly incompatible with the existence of the fundamental right recognized in *Roe v. Wade*." 462 U.S., at 420–21, n. 1.

a distinction without a difference. The plurality repudiates every principle for which *Roe* stands; in good conscience, it cannot possibly believe that *Roe* lies "undisturbed" merely because this case does not call upon the Court to reconsider the Texas statute, or one like it. If the Constitution permits a State to enact any statute that reasonably furthers its interest in potential life, and if that interest arises as of conception, why would the Texas statute fail to pass muster? One suspects that the plurality agrees. It is impossible to read the plurality opinion and especially its final paragraph, without recognizing its implicit invitation to every State to enact more and more restrictive abortion laws, and to assert their interest in potential life as of the moment of conception. All these laws will satisfy the plurality's non-scrutiny, until sometime, a new regime of old dissenters and new appointees will declare what the plurality intends: that *Roe* is no longer good law.[11]

D

Thus, "not with a bang, but a whimper," the plurality discards a landmark case

11. The plurality claims that its treatment of *Roe*, and a woman's right to decide whether to terminate a pregnancy, "hold[s] true the balance between that which the Constitution puts beyond the reach of the democratic process and that which it does not." This is unadulterated nonsense. The plurality's balance matches a lead weight (the State's allegedly compelling interest in fetal life as of the "moment of conception") against a feather (a "liberty interest" of the pregnant woman that the plurality barely mentions, much less describes). The plurality's balance—no balance at all—places nothing, or virtually nothing, beyond the reach of the democratic process.

JUSTICE SCALIA candidly argues that this is all for the best. I cannot agree. "The very purpose of a Bill of Rights was to withdraw certain subjects from the vicissitudes of political controversy, to place them beyond the reach of majorities and of the last generation, and casts into darkness the hopes and visions of every woman in this country who had come to believe that the Constitution guaranteed her the right to exercise some control over her unique ability to bear children. The plurality does so either oblivious or insensitive to the fact that millions of women, and their families, have ordered their lives around the right to reproductive choice, and that this right has become vital to the full participation of women in the economic and political walks of American life. The plurality would clear the way once again for government to force upon women the physical labor and specific and direct medical and psychological harms that may accompany carrying a fetus to term. The plurality would clear the way again for the State to conscript a woman's body and to force upon her a "distressful life and future." *Roe,* 410 U.S., at 153.

The result, as we know from experience, see Cates & Rocket, *Illegal Abortions in the United States: 1972–1974,* 8 Family Planning Perspectives 86, 92 (1976), would be

---

officials and to establish them as legal principles to be applied by the Courts. One's right to life, liberty, and property . . . may not be submitted to vote; they depend on the outcome of no election." *West Virginia Board of Education v. Barnette,* 319 U.S. 624, 638 (1943). In a Nation that cherishes liberty, the ability of a woman to control the biological operation of her body and to determine with her responsible physician whether or not to carry a fetus to term, must fall within that limited sphere of individual autonomy that lies beyond the will or the power of any transient majority. This Court stands as the ultimate guarantor of that zone of privacy, regardless of the bitter disputes to which our decisions may give rise. In *Roe,* and our numerous cases reaffirming *Roe,* we did no more than discharge our constitutional duty.

that every year hundreds of thousands of women, in desperation, would defy the law, and place their health and safety in the unclean and unsympathetic hands of back-alley abortionists, or they would attempt to perform abortions upon themselves, with disastrous results. Every year, many women, especially poor and minority women, would die or suffer debilitating physical trauma, all in the name of enforced morality or religious dictates or lack of compassion, as it may be.

Of the aspirations and settled understandings of American women, of the inevitable and brutal consequences of what it is doing, the tough-approach plurality utters not a word. This silence is callous. It is also profoundly destructive of this Court as an institution. To overturn a constitutional decision is a rare and grave undertaking. To overturn a constitutional decision that secured a fundamental personal liberty to millions of persons would be unprecedented in our 200 years of constitutional history. Although the doctrine of *stare decisis* applies with somewhat diminished force in constitutional cases generally, even in ordinary constitutional cases "any departure from *stare decisis* demands special justification." *Arizona v. Rumsey,* 467 U.S. 203, 212 (1984). See also *Vasquez v. Hillary,* 474 U.S. 254, 266 (1986) ("the careful observer will discern that any detours from the straight path of *stare decisis* in our past have occurred for articulable reasons, and only when the Court has felt obliged 'to bring its opinions into agreement with experience and with facts newly ascertained,' " quoting *Burnet v. Coronado Oil & Gas Co.,* 285 U.S. 393, 412 (1932) (Brandeis, J., dissenting)). This requirement of justification applies with unique force where, as here, the Court's abrogation of precedent would destroy people's firm belief, based on past decisions of this Court, that they possess an unabridgeable right to undertake certain conduct.[12]

As discussed at perhaps too great length above, the plurality makes no serious attempt to carry "the heavy burden of persuading . . . that changes in society or in the law dictate" the abandonment of *Roe* and it numerous progeny, *Vasquez*, 474 U.S., at 266, much less the greater burden of explaining the abrogation of a fundamental personal freedom. Instead, the plurality pretends that it leaves *Roe* standing, and refuses even to discuss the real issue underlying this case: whether the Constitution includes an unenumerated right to privacy that encompasses a woman's right to decide whether to terminate a pregnancy. To the extent that the plurality does criticize the *Roe* framework, these criticisms are pure *ipse dixit*.

---

12. Cf. *South Carolina v. Gathers*, 490 U.S. 805, 824 (1989) (SCALIA, J., dissenting) ("the respect accorded prior decisions increases, rather than decreases, with their antiquity, as the society adjusts itself to their existence, and the surrounding law becomes premised on their validity").

Moreover, as Justice Powell wrote for the Court in *Akron*, "There are especially compelling reasons for adhering to *stare decisis* in applying the principles of *Roe v. Wade*. That case was considered with special care. It was first argued during the 1971 term, and reargued—with extensive briefing—the following Term. The decision was joined by THE CHIEF JUSTICE and six other Justices. Since *Roe* was decided in January 1973, the Court repeatedly and consistently has accepted and applied the basic principle that a woman has a fundamental right to make the highly personal choice whether or not to terminate her pregnancy." 462 U.S., at 420, n. 1. See, *e.g., Planned Parenthood of Central Mo. v. Danforth; Bellotti v. Baird*, 428 U.S. 132 (1976); *Beal v. Doe*, 432 U.S. 438 (1977); *Maher v. Roe; Colautti v. Franklin; Bellotti v. Baird*, 443 U.S. 622 (1979); *Harris v. McRae; Akron v. Akron Center for Reproductive Health, Inc. Thornburgh v. American College of Obstetricians and Gynecologists*.

This comes at a cost. The doctrine of *stare decisis* "permits society to presume that bedrock principles are founded in the law rather than in the proclivities of individuals, and thereby contributes to the integrity of our constitutional system of government, both in appearance and in fact." *Id.*, at 265–66. Today's decision involves the most politically divisive domestic legal issue of our time. By refusing to explain or to justify its proposed revolutionary revision in the law of abortion, and by refusing to abide not only by our precedents, but also by our canons for reconsidering those precedents, the plurality invites charges of cowardice and illegitimacy to our door. I cannot say that these would be undeserved.

II

For today, at least, the law of abortion stands undisturbed. For today, the women of this Nation still retain the liberty to control their destinies. But the signs are evident and very ominous, and a chill wind blows.

I dissent.

JUSTICE STEVENS, concurring in part and dissenting in part.

Having joined Part II-C of the Court's opinion, I shall not comment on § 188.205 of the Missouri statute. With respect to the challenged portions of §§ 188.210 and 188.215, I agree with JUSTICE BLACKMUN, at n. 1 (concurring in part and dissenting in part), that the record identifies a sufficient number of unconstitutional applications to support the Court of Appeals' judgment invalidating those provisions. The reasons why I would also affirm that court's invalidation of § 188.029, the viability testing provision, and §§ 1.205.1(1)(2) of the preamble,[1] require separate explanation.

I

It seems to me that in Part II-D of its opinion, the plurality strains to place a construction on § 188.029 that enables it to conclude, "[W]e would modify and narrow *Roe* and succeeding cases," *ante*. That statement is ill-advised because there is no need to modify even slightly the holdings of prior cases in order to uphold § 188.029. For the most plausible nonliteral construction, as both JUSTICE BLACKMUN, (concurring in part and dissenting in part), and JUSTICE O'CONNOR, (concurring in part and concurring in judgment), have demonstrated, is constitutional and entirely consistent with our precedents.

I am unable to accept JUSTICE O'CONNOR'S construction of the second sentence in § 188.029, however, because I believe it is foreclosed by two controlling principles of statutory interpretation. First, it is our settled practice to accept "the interpretation of state law in which the District Court and the Court of Appeals have concurred even if an examination of the state-law issue without such guidance might have justified a different conclusion." *Bishop v. Wood*, 426 U.S. 341, 346 (1976). Second, "[t]he fact that a particular application of the clear terms of a statute might be unconstitutional does not pro-

vide us with a justification for ignoring the plain meaning of the statute." *Public Citizen v. Department of Justice*, 491 U.S. 440, 481 (1989) (KENNEDY, J., concurring in judgment).[4] In this case, I agree with the Court of Appeals, 851 F.2d 1071, 1074–75 (8th Cir. 1988), and the District Court, 662 F. Supp. 407, 423 (W.D. Mo. 1987), that the meaning of the second sentence of § 188.029 is too plain to be ignored. The sentence twice uses the mandatory term "shall," and contains no qualifying language. If it is implicitly limited to tests that are useful in determining viability, it adds nothing to the requirement imposed by the preceding sentence.

My interpretation of the plain language is supported by the structure of the statute as a whole, particularly the preamble, which "finds" that life "begins at conception" and further commands that state laws shall be construed to provide the maximum protection to "the unborn child at every stage of development." I agree with the District Court that "[o]bviously, the purpose of this law is to protect the potential life of the fetus, rather than to safeguard maternal health." 662 F. Supp., at 420. A literal reading of the statute tends to accomplish that goal. Thus it is not "incongruous," *ante* to assume that the Missouri Legislature was trying to protect the potential human life of nonviable fetuses by making the abortion decision more costly.

---

1. The State prefers to refer to subsections (1) and (2) of § 1.205 as "prefatory statements with no substantive effect." Brief; see also 851 F.2d 1071, 1076 (8th Cir. 1988). It is true that § 1.205 is codified in Chapter 1, Laws in Force and Construction of Statutes, of Title I, Laws and Statutes, of the Missouri Revised Statutes, while all other provisions at issue are codified in Chapter 188, Regulation of Abortions, of Title XII, Public Health and Welfare. But because § 1.205 appeared at the beginning of House Bill No. 1596, it is entirely appropriate to consider it as a preamble relevant to those regulations.

4. We have stated that we will interpret a federal statute to avoid serious constitutional problems if "a reasonable alternative interpretation poses no constitutional question," *Gomez v. United States,* 490 U.S. 858, 864 (1989), or if "it is fairly possible to interpret the statute in a manner that renders it constitutionally valid," *Communications Workers v. Beck,* 487 U.S. 735, 762 (1988), or "unless such construction is plainly contrary to the intent of Congress." *Edward J. DeBartolo Corp. v. Florida Gulf Coast Building & Construction Trades Council,* 485 U.S. 568, 575 (1988).

On the contrary, I am satisfied that the Court of Appeals, as well as the District Court, correctly concluded that the Missouri Legislature meant exactly what it said in the second sentence of § 188.029. I am also satisfied, for the reasons stated by JUSTICE BLACKMUN, that the testing provision is manifestly unconstitutional under *Williamson v. Lee Optical Co.*, 348 U.S. 483 (1955), "irrespective of the *Roe* framework." *Ante,* (concurring in part and dissenting in part).

II

The Missouri statute defines "conception" as "the fertilization of the ovum of a female by a sperm of a male," Mo. Rev. Stat. § 188.015(3) (1986), even though standard medical texts equate "conception" with implantation in the uterus, occurring about six days after fertilization.[6] Missouri's declaration therefore implies regulation not only of previability abortions, but also of common forms of contraception such as the IUD and the morning-after pill.[7] Because the preamble, read in context, threatens serious encroachments upon the liberty of the pregnant

woman and the health professional, I am persuaded that these plaintiffs, appellees before us, have standing to challenge its constitutionality. Accord, 851 F.2d, at 1075–76.

To the extent that the Missouri statute interferes with contraceptive choices, I have no doubt that it is unconstitutional under the Court's holdings in *Griswold v. Connecticut, Eisenstadt v. Baird,*and *Carey v. Population Services International*, 431 U.S. 678 (1977). The place of *Griswold* in the mosaic of decisions defining a woman's liberty interest was accurately stated by Justice Stewart in his concurring opinion in *Roe*, 410 U.S., at 167–70:

[I]n *Griswold v. Connecticut* the Court held a Connecticut birth control law unconstitutional. In view of what had been so recently said in [*Ferguson v.*] *Skrupa,* [372 U.S. 726 (1963),] the Court's opinion in *Griswold* understandably did its best to avoid reliance on the Due Process Clause of the Fourteenth Amendment as the ground for decision. Yet, the Connecticut law did not violate any provision of the Bill of Rights, nor any other specific provision of the Constitution. So it was clear to me then, and it is equally clear to me now, that the *Griswold* decision can be rationally understood only as a holding that the Connecticut statute substantively invaded the "liberty" that is protected by the Due Process Clause of

6. The fertilized egg remains in the woman's Fallopian tube for 72 hours, then travels to the uterus' cavity, where cell division continues for another 72 hours before implantation in the uterine wall. D. Mishell & V. Davajan, *Infertility, Contraception & Reproductive Endocrinology* 109–110 (2d ed. 1986); see also Brief for Association of Reproductive Health Professionals et al. as *Amici Curiae* 31–32 (ARHP Brief) (citing *inter alia* J. Pritchard, P. MacDonald, & N. Gant, *Williams Obstetrics* 88–91 (17th ed. 1985)). "[O]nly 50 percent of fertilized ova ultimately become implanted." ARHP Brief 32, n. 25 (citing *Post Coital Contraception,* The Lancet 856 (Apr. 16, 1983)).

7. An intrauterine device, commonly called an IUD, "works primarily by preventing a fertilized egg from implanting." Burnhill, Intrauterine Contraception, in *Fertility Control* 271, 280 (S. Corson, R. Derman, & L. Tyrer eds. 1985). See also 21 CFR § 801.427, p. 32 (1988); ARHP Brief

34–35. Other contraceptive methods that may prevent implantation include "morning-after pills," high-dose estrogen pills taken after intercourse, particularly in cases of rape, ARHP Brief 33, and the French RU 486, a pill that works "during the indeterminate period between contraception and abortion," *id.*, at 37. Low-level estrogen "combined" pills—a version of the ordinary, daily ingested birth control pill—also may prevent the fertilized egg from reaching the uterine wall and implanting. *Id.*, at 35–36.

the Fourteenth Amendment. As so understood, *Griswold* stands as one in a long line of pre-*Skrupa* cases decided under the doctrine of substantive due process, and I now accept it as such.

. . .

Several decisions of this Court make clear that freedom of personal choice in matters of marriage and family life is one of the liberties protected by the Due Process Clause of the Fourteenth Amendment. *Loving v. Virginia, 388 U.S. 1, 12 [(1967)]; Griswold v. Connecticut; Pierce v. Society of Sisters; Meyer v. Nebraska.* See also *Prince v. Massachusetts,* 321 U.S. 158, 166 [(1944)]; *Skinner v. Oklahoma, 316 U.S. 535, 541 [(1942)].* As recently as last Term, in *Eisenstadt v. Baird,* 405 U.S. 438, 453, we recognized "the right of the *individual,* married or single, to be free from unwarranted governmental intrusion into matters so fundamentally affecting a person as the decision whether to bear or beget a child." That right necessarily includes the right of a woman to decide whether or not to terminate her pregnancy. "Certainly the interests of a woman in giving of her physical and emotional self during pregnancy and the interests that will be affected throughout her life by the birth and raising of a child are of a far greater degree of significance and personal intimacy than the right to send a child to private school protected in *Pierce v. Society of Sisters,* or the right to teach a foreign language protected in *Meyer v. Nebraska." Abele v. Markle,* 351 F. Supp. 224, 227 (Conn. 1972).

Clearly, therefore, the Court today is correct in holding that the right asserted by Jane Roe is embraced within the personal liberty protected by the Due Process Clause of the Fourteenth Amendment. (emphasis in original)[8]

One might argue that the *Griswold* holding applies to devices "preventing conception," 381 U.S., at 480—that is, fertilization—but not to those preventing implantation, and therefore, that *Griswold* does not protect a woman's choice to use an IUD or take a morning-after pill. There is unquestionably a theological basis for such an argument, just as there was unquestionably a theological basis for the Connecticut statute that the Court invalidated in *Griswold.* Our jurisprudence, however, has consistently required a secular basis for valid legislation. See, *e.g., Stone v. Graham,* 449 U.S. 39, 40 (1980) *(per curiam).* Because I am not aware of any secular basis for differentiating between contraceptive procedures that are effective immediately before and those that are effective immediately after fertilization, I believe it inescapably follows that the preamble to the Missouri statute is invalid under *Griswold* and its progeny.

Indeed, I am persuaded that the absence of any secular purpose for the legislative declarations that life begins at conception and that conception occurs at fertilization makes the relevant portion of the preamble invalid under the Establishment Clause of the First Amendment to the Federal Constitution. This conclusion does not, and could not, rest on the fact that the statement happens to coincide with the tenets of certain religions, see *McGowan v. Maryland,* 366 U.S. 420, 442 (1961); *Harris v. McRae,* 448 U.S. 297,

8. The contrast between Justice Stewart's careful explication that our abortion precedent flowed naturally from a stream of substantive due process cases and Justice Scalia's notion that our abortion law was "constructed overnight in *Roe v. Wade," ante* (concurring in part and concurring in judgment), is remarkable.

319–20 (1980), or on the fact that the legislators who voted to enact it may have been motivated by religious considerations, see *Washington v. Davis*, 426 U.S. 229, 253 (1976) (STEVENS, J., concurring). Rather, it rests on the fact that the preamble, an unequivocal endorsement of a religious tenet of some but by no means all Christian faiths, serves no identifiable secular purpose. That fact alone compels a conclusion that the statute violates the Establishment Clause. *Wallace v. Jaffree*, 472 U.S. 38, 56 (1985).

My concern can best be explained by reference to the position on this issue that was endorsed by St. Thomas Aquinas and widely accepted by the leaders of the Roman Catholic Church for many years. The position is summarized in a report, entitled "Catholic Teaching On Abortion," prepared by the Congressional Research Service of the Library of Congress. It states in part:

> The disagreement over the status of the unformed as against the formed fetus was crucial for Christian teaching on the soul. It was widely held that the soul was not present until the formation of the fetus 40 or 80 days after conception, for males and females respectively. Thus, abortion of the "unformed" or "inanimate" fetus (from *anima*, soul) was something less than true homicide, rather a form of anticipatory or quasi-homicide. This view received its definitive treatment in St. Thomas Aquinas and became for a time the dominant interpretation in the Latin Church.

> . . .

> For St. Thomas, as for medieval Christendom generally, there is a lapse of time—approximately 40 to 80 days—after conception and before the soul's infusion. . . . C. Whittier, Catholic Teach-

ing on Abortion: Its Origin and Later Development (May 15, 1981), reprinted in Brief for Americans United for Separation of Church and State as *Amicus Curiae* 13a, 17a (quoting St. Thomas Aquinas, *In octo libros politicorum* 7.12).

If the views of St. Thomas were held as widely today as they were in the Middle Ages, and if a state legislature were to enact a statute prefaced with a "finding" that female life begins 80 days after conception and male life begins 40 days after conception, I have no doubt that this Court would promptly conclude that such an endorsement of a particular religious tenet is violative of the Establishment Clause.

In my opinion the difference between that hypothetical statute and Missouri's preamble reflects nothing more than a difference in theological doctrine. The preamble to the Missouri statute endorses the theological position that there is the same secular interest in preserving the life of a fetus during the first 40 or 80 days of pregnancy as there is after viability—indeed, after the time when the fetus has become a "person" with legal rights protected by the Constitution.[13] To sustain that position as a matter of law, I believe Missouri has the burden of

---

13. No Member of this Court has ever questioned the holding in *Roe*, 410 U.S., at 156–59, that a fetus is not a "person" within the meaning of the Fourteenth Amendment. Even the dissenters in *Roe* implicitly endorsed that holding by arguing that state legislatures should decide whether to prohibit or to authorize abortions. See *id.*, at 177 (REHNQUIST, J., dissenting) (arguing that the Fourteenth Amendment did not "withdraw from the States the power to legislate with respect to this matter"); *Doe v. Bolton*, 410 U.S. 179, 222 (1973) (WHITE, J., dissenting jointly in *Doe* and *Roe*). By characterizing the basic question as "a political issue," see *ante*, (concurring in part and concurring in judgment), JUSTICE SCALIA likewise implicitly accepts this holding.

identifying the secular interests that differentiate the first 40 days of pregnancy from the period immediately before or after fertilization when, as *Griswold* and related cases establish, the Constitution allows the use of contraceptive procedures to prevent potential life from developing into full personhood. Focusing our attention on the first several weeks of pregnancy is especially appropriate because that is the period when the vast majority of abortions are actually performed.

As a secular matter, there is an obvious difference between the state interest in protecting the freshly fertilized egg and the state interest in protecting a 9-month-gestated, fully sentient fetus on the eve of birth. There can be no interest in protecting the newly fertilized egg from physical pain or mental anguish, because the capacity for such suffering does not yet exist; respecting a developed fetus, however, that interest is valid. In fact, if one prescinds the theological concept of ensoulment—or one accepts St. Thomas Aquinas' view that ensoulment does not occur for at least 40 days, a State has no greater secular interest in protecting the potential life of an embryo that is still "seed" than in protecting the potential life of a sperm or an unfertilized ovum.

There have been times in history when military and economic interests would have been served by an increase in population. No one argues today, however, that Missouri can assert a societal interest in increasing its population as its secular reason for fostering potential life. Indeed, our national policy, as reflected in legislation the Court upheld last Term, is to prevent the potential life that is produced by "pregnancy and childbirth among unmarried adolescents." *Bowen v. Kendrick*, 487 U.S. 589, 593 (1988). If the secular analysis were based on a strict balancing of fiscal costs and benefits, the economic costs of unlimited childbearing would outweigh those of abortion. There is, of course, an important and unquestionably valid secular interest in "protecting a young pregnant woman from the consequences of an incorrect decision," *Planned Parenthood of Central Missouri v. Danforth*, 428 U.S. 52, 102 (1976) (STEVENS, J., concurring in part and dissenting in part). Although that interest is served by a requirement that the woman receive medical and, in appropriate circumstances, parental, advice, it does not justify the state legislature's official endorsement of the theological tenet embodied in § § 1.205.1(1), (2).

The State's suggestion that the "finding" in the preamble to its abortion statute is, in effect, an amendment to its tort, property, and criminal laws is not persuasive. The Court of Appeals concluded that the preamble "is simply an impermissible state adoption of a theory of when life begins to justify its abortion regulations." 851 F.2d, at 1076. Supporting that construction is the state constitutional prohibition against legislative enactments pertaining to more than one subject matter. Mo. Const., Art. 3, § 23. Moreover, none of the tort, property, or criminal law cases cited by the State was either based on or buttressed by a theological answer to the question of when life begins. Rather, the Missouri courts, as well as a number of other state courts, had already concluded that a "fetus is a 'person,' 'minor,' or 'minor child' within the meaning of their particular wrongful death statutes." *O'Grady v. Brown*, 654 S.W.2d 904, 910 (Mo. 1983) (en banc).[15]

15. The other examples cited by the State are statutes providing that unborn children are to be treated as though born within the lifetime of the decedent, see Uniform Probate Code § 2–108 (1969), and statutes imposing criminal sanctions in the nature of manslaughter for the killing of a

Bolstering my conclusion that the preamble violates the First Amendment is the fact that the intensely divisive character of much of the national debate over the abortion issue reflects the deeply held religious convictions of many participants in the debate.[16] The Missouri Legislature

---

viable fetus or unborn quick child. See, *e.g.*, Ark. Stat. Ann. § 41–2223 (1947). None of the cited statutes included any "finding" on the theological question of when life begins.

16. No fewer than 67 religious organizations submitted their views as *amici curiae* on either side of this case. *Amicus* briefs on both sides, moreover, frankly discuss the relation between the abortion controversy and religion. See generally, *e.g.*, Brief for Agudath Israel of America as *Amicus Curiae*, Brief for Americans United for Separation of Church and State as *Amici Curiae*, Brief for Catholics for a Free Choice et al. as *Amici Curiae*, Brief for Holy Orthodox Church as *Amicus Curiae*, Brief for Lutheran Church-Missouri Synod et al. as *Amici Curiae*, Brief for Missouri Catholic Conference as *Amicus Curiae*. Cf. Burke, Religion and Politics in the United States, in *Movements and Issues in World Religions* 243, 254–56 (C. Fu & G. Spiegler eds. 1987).

may not inject its endorsement of a particular religious tradition into this debate, for "[t]he Establishment Clause does not allow public bodies to foment such disagreement." See *Allegheny County v. Greater Pittsburgh ACLU*, 492 U.S. 573, at 651 (STEVENS, J., concurring in part and dissenting in part)

In my opinion the preamble to the Missouri statute is unconstitutional for two reasons. To the extent that it has substantive impact on the freedom to use contraceptive procedures, it is inconsistent with the central holding in *Griswold*. To the extent that it merely makes "legislative findings without operative effect," as the State argues, it violates the Establishment Clause of the First Amendment. Contrary to the theological "finding" of the Missouri Legislature, a woman's constitutionally protected liberty encompasses the right to act on her own belief that—to paraphrase St. Thomas Aquinas—until a seed has acquired the powers of sensation and movement, the life of a human being has not yet begun.

CASE QUESTIONS

1. The Rehnquist opinion for the three-justice plurality urges the scrapping of "the key elements of the *Roe* framework—trimesters and viability." In addition, Justice Scalia urges an outright overruling of *Roe v. Wade*, and Justice O'Connor says she continues "to consider problematic" the "trimester framework" of *Roe*. After reading the views of these five justices in *Webster v. Reproductive Health Services*, could state legislators vote in good

conscience to adopt, say, a ban on any abortions after the first trimester of pregnancy (on the grounds that the people of that state wish to protect "potential life" from that point on)?

2. Rehnquist asserts that eliminating the trimester framework and the viability deadline on nontherapeutic abortions will not take this country back to "the dark ages" (by which he evidently means

America of 1850–1973, since under medieval Christendom—literally the Dark Ages—abortion was not a violation of any Church or state law).[3] He also asserts that the statute held unconstitutional in *Roe v. Wade* was significantly different from ones that the three-justice plurality would uphold now with their new potential-life-is-compelling-throughout-pregnancy rule. The Texas statute voided in *Roe* had banned all abortions except to save the mother's life. Does this comment on the holding of *Roe v. Wade* mean that the members of the Rehnquist plurality would still rule this Texas law unconstitutional? This plurality asserts that they "believe" abortion to be "a liberty interest protected by the due process clause" of the Constitution. Does that assertion shed any light on their possible reasons for viewing laws of the Texas type as still unconstitutional?

3. In Part I of her opinion Justice O'Connor suggests that she is reserving judgment on the question of the constitutionality of a ban on abortions at a hospital like the privately owned Truman Medical Center simply because it is built on land leased from a political subdivision of the state; she is ruling only that the ban would be constitutional as applied to state-owned (or city-owned) hospitals (like the ones in *Poelker v. Doe*). Four justices (the dissenters) argue that the ban is surely unconstitutional as applied to the Truman Medical Center. Neither the Rehnquist plurality nor Scalia speak specifically to that question. If you were director of the Truman Center, would you feel that the Court had authorized you to continue to perform abortions?

4. Justice O'Connor's reference to the rule to avoid constitutional questions where possible is an allusion to the Court's rule

that if two plausible interpretations of a statute are available, one constitutional and one not, the Court should choose the constitutional one in order to avoid "questioning" the constitutionality of the statute. This avoidance is meant to express respect for the integrity of the legislators, all of whom took an oath to uphold the Constitution. Justice Scalia *agrees* with her interpretation of the statute, and he agrees that it is not unconstitutional as so interpreted, but he believes that the statute conflicts with two later interpretations of *Roe v. Wade*—the ones in *Planned Parenthood v. Danforth* and *Akron I* (see his footnote). Instead of ruling, with the plurality, that later precedents overly rigidified *Roe*, and that its prevailing reading needs to be modified, he wants to let *Roe* stay rigid and throw it out. He gives two reasons for his hurry: (1) delay in scrapping *Roe* means delay in ending the massive lobbying of the Court that *Roe* engendered; and (2) "anyone" who is caused "harm . . . by largely unrestricted abortion" will not "be able [in a later case] to challenge it . . . and have his day in court," unlike the situation with other not-yet-ruled-upon constitutional issues. Do you agree that an end to *Roe* would end the flow of abortion cases, and attendant lobbying, to the Supreme Court? Does it seem odd that, in his second reason, Justice Scalia speaks so obliquely of the fetuses destroyed by abortion?

5. Do you agree with Justice Blackmun that the three-justice plurality "exaggerat[es] the conflict between its . . . construction [of the viability testing law] and the *Roe* trimester framework"?

6. In Section II of his partial dissent Justice Stevens describes a difference of opinion between the Missouri legislation and

"standard medical texts" on the meaning of *conception*. Medical texts now define *conception* as including implantation in the uterine wall, so that it still makes sense to use the term *contraception* to describe medications (or intrauterine devices—IUDs) that operate post-fertilization but pre-implantation. He also lists as a "method of contraception" (in footnote 7) RU-486, the drug that interrupts pregnancy if taken during the first six weeks following a woman's last menstrual period; he quotes the Association of Reproductive Health Professionals to the effect that this is "the indeterminate period between contraception and abortion." Is this phrase an example of the political distortion of language? Is any language around the abortion issue not distorted? (E.g., consider the phrase "the moment of conception." The fertilization process in fact lasts not one moment, but twenty-four hours.) Do these considerations lend credence to the view that if the Scalia-Rehnquist group develops into a solidly anti-*Roe* majority, they may have trouble drawing a clear line between the protected contraceptive freedom of *Griswold* and *Eisenstadt* and what they would treat as the unprotected practice of abortion?

Parental Notice for Minors: Hodgson v. Minnesota (1990) *and* Ohio v. Akron Center for Reproductive Health (Akron II) (1990)

The *Webster* case initiated what was to become an annual ritual for a while; from 1989 until at least 1992, the Supreme Court ended each term with a highly fragmented abortion decision. The 1989–1990 term ended with two such cases involving parental notice laws from Minnesota and Ohio, *Hodgson v. Minnesota*[4] and *Ohio v. Akron Center for Reproductive Health.*[5]

The Minnesota law said that before an unmarried, unemancipated minor could obtain an abortion not necessary to save her life either she must secure written consent from both her parents or formally declare to proper authorities that she is a victim of parental abuse, or her doctor must notify both parents and then wait forty-eight hours before performing the abortion. A second portion of the statute said that if (and only if) the first portion were declared unconstitutional, a minor seeking an abortion could bypass the other requirements by going to a court (with a right to court-appointed counsel) and convincing a judge either that she is mature enough to give informed consent or that an abortion would be in her best interest.

Five justices (Stevens, O'Connor, Brennan, Blackmun, and Marshall) ruled that the first portion of the statute was unconstitutional because it did not provide an exception for a parent not living with the child or one who was never married to the pregnant minor's mother and may not even know of the minor's existence. This failure to exempt a parent who had no contact with, or evident interest in, the pregnant minor made the statute not only "the most intrusive in the Nation"[6] but also irrational and therefore unconstitutional. Five justices (the four who had dissented to the first portion—Rehnquist, Kennedy, Scalia, and White—plus O'Connor upheld the second portion of the statute. Justice O'Connor reasoned that the opportunity for judicial bypass rendered the two-parent notice requirement not an undue burden and reasonably related to fostering the welfare of the pregnant minor.

The Ohio statute at issue in *Akron II* also fragmented the Court. It mandated that at least twenty-four hours before performing an abortion on an unemancipated, unmarried minor, the physician must notify a parent or, if the minor fears emotional or other abuse from her parents, an adult brother,sister, stepparent, or grandparent. If the minor is unwilling to notify a parent or specified parent-substitute, she may go to juvenile court and obtain a bypass order by presenting "clear and convincing evidence" either that she is mature enough to choose abortion or that abortion is in her best interest. If she has no attorney, the state will provide both an attorney and a guardian *ad litem* (i.e., for the purposes of the litigation). On this statute the Court divided 6–3 in favor of constitutionality (with Blackmun, Brennan, and Marshall dissenting), but split 5–4 over the section (V) that contained the core of the Court's reasoning. Justice Stevens abstained from concurring in that one section, apparently because he has never endorsed its "undue burden" line of reasoning. This case represents the first time that a majority managed to coalesce around the "undue burden" substitute for the original reasoning of *Roe v. Wade*, which was first proposed by Justice O'Connor in *Akron I*. This critical section of the *Akron II* decision was authored by Justice Kennedy, and it reads as follows:

> The Ohio statute, in sum, does not impose an undue, or otherwise unconstitutional, burden on a minor seeking an abortion. We believe, in addition, that the legislature acted in a rational manner in enacting H.B. 319. A free and enlightened society may decide that each of its members should attain a clearer, more tolerant understanding of the profound philosophic choices confronted by a woman who is considering whether to seek an abortion. Her decision will embrace her own destiny and personal dignity, and the origins of the other human life that lie within the embryo. The State is entitled to assume that, for most of its people, the beginnings of that understanding will be within the family, society's most intimate association. It is both rational and fair for the State to conclude that, in most instances, the family will strive to give a lonely or even terrified minor advice that is both compassionate and mature. The statute in issue here is a rational way to further those ends. It would deny all dignity to the family to say that the State cannot take this reasonable step in regulating its health professions to ensure that, in most cases, a young woman will receive guidance and understanding from a parent.[7]

Justice Scalia was now ready to articulate the foundation of his reasoning for why *Roe v. Wade* should be expressly overruled,[8] and he did so in a separate concurrence for each of these parental notice cases. This substantial excerpt from his opinion in the Minnesota case typifies both the reasoning and the tone of both his concurring opinions:

> One will search in vain the document we are supposed to be construing for text that provides the basis for the argument over these distinctions [concerning such matters as whether parental notice statutes must have a judicial bypass in order to be constitutional]; and will find in our society's tradition regarding abortion no hint that the distinctions [that divide the Court in this case] are constitutionally relevant, much less any indication how a constitutional argument about them ought to be resolved. The random and unpredictable results of our consequently unchanneled individual views make it increasingly evident, Term after Term, that the tools for this job are not to be found in the lawyer's—and hence not the judge's—workbox. I continue to dissent from this enterprise of devising an Abortion Code, and from the illusion that we have authority to do so.[9]

Freedom of Speech vs. Limits on Abortion: Rust v. Sullivan (1991)

The public funding issues with which the Court dealt in the *Webster* case reappeared with a new twist in *Rust v. Sullivan*, a case decided toward the end of the 1990–1991 term.[10] *Rust* added First Amendment, freedom of speech complications to the general question of a refusal to provide governmental funding for abortion.

In 1970 Congress had adopted Title X of the Public Service Health Act, which authorized federal subsidies to family planning clinics. Section 1008 of Title X stated, "None of the funds appropriated under this title shall be used in programs where abortion is a method of family planning."[11] Originally, in implementing the law, the secretary of Health, Education and Welfare (later entitled Health and Human Services), had adopted a regulation stating that projects receiving federal funds under Title X simply had to comply with the rule, "The project will not provide abortions as a method of family planning."[12] In February of 1988, however, the Reagan administration added a number of regulations that focused specifically on *discussing*, as contrasted with performing, abortions. These new regulations were ostensibly in furtherance of the eighteen-year-old law, which Congress had not amended. The new regulations had three elements:

First, "Title X project[s could] not provide counseling concerning the use of abortion as a method of family planning or provide referral for abortion as a method of family planning."[13] Title X projects were to provide preventive, pre-conception care and counseling but had to refer a client who was pregnant elsewhere "for appropriate prenatal and/or social services by furnishing a list of available providers that promote the welfare of the mother and unborn child."

The list could not be indirectly used to promote abortion "such as by weighing the list of referrals in favor of health care providers which perform abortions, by including on the list . . . health care providers whose principal business is the provision of abortions, by excluding available providers who do not provide abortions, or by steering clients to providers who offer abortion as a method of family planning."[14] Even if a woman specifically requested information on how to locate a medically qualified abortion provider, Title X projects were forbidden to give the information. The regulations suggested the reply, "[This] project does not consider abortion an appropriate method of family planning and therefore does not counsel or refer for abortion."[15]

Second, Title X projects were forbidden to advocate abortion in any manner, include lobbying for its legalization, or taking legal action to make abortion more widely available, or providing public speakers who would promote abortion "as a method of family planning."[16]

And third, Title X projects now had to be rendered "physically and financially separate" from facilities that did provide abortion counseling or abortion services.[17]

Before the adoption of these new regulations, agencies subsidized under Title X had understood that they might provide various reproductive health services, including counseling not only about contraception but also about the handling of unexpected pregnancies. While the agencies did not perform abortions, they understood their function to include referring a pregnant woman to a health care provider suitable to her wishes and needs. These new regulations drastically altered that counseling function.

Several family planning clinics immediately challenged the new regulations in federal courts, requesting declaratory judgments that they were unconstitutional (before the rules were allowed to go into effect), so that the clinics would not have the painful choice of either foregoing what they believed to be their, and their employees', constitutional right to freedom of speech or else foregoing the federal subsidy that enabled them to operate. Two federal circuit courts of appeal[18] did rule that the regulations were an unconstitutional infringement on the First Amendment right of freedom of speech, but a third one upheld them as not unconstitutional.[19]

The appeal of this third decision was the one the Supreme Court addressed in *Rust v. Sullivan*. President Reagan had left office by the time even the first of the appeals was decided, but President Bush kept the regulations in force, and his secretary of Health and Human Services, Louis Sullivan, was officially the other party in the case, responding to the petitioner, Dr. Irving Rust, a director of a family planning clinic. As it had in *Akron I*, *Thornburgh*, and *Webster*, the U.S. Department of Justice (presenting Sullivan's case) again asked the Supreme Court to overturn *Roe v. Wade*, but in this decision the Supreme Court ignored the issue of *Roe's* continuing validity.[20] As in *Webster* (1989) and in *Hodgson* (1990)—and despite personnel changes, Justice Souter having replaced Justice Brennan—the Supreme Court again divided 5–4 in this (1991) abortion case.

The Court addressed three separate questions challenging the executive branch regulations: (1) did they exceed the authority of the Title X statute or conflict with its intent; (2) did they violate the First Amendment rights of subsidized health care providers, such as Irving Rust; or (3) did the regulations violate the right to privacy (secured at the federal level by the Fifth Amendment due process clause) of women seeking competent pregnancy counseling at these public clinics? The majority (Rehnquist, White, Scalia, Kennedy, and Souter) answered no to each of these challenges. The dissents varied: all four answered yes on statutory invalidity of the regulations, with O'Connor and Stevens making the additional argument that the Court majority should not have proceeded to the constitutional questions; and Stevens, Blackmun, and Marshall all agreed with the two other circuit courts in the conclusion that these new regulations did violate both the First Amendment and the constitutional right to privacy. The justices' various explanations of their respective lines of reasoning follow:

Irving Rust, etc., et al., Petitioners v. Louis W. Sullivan, Secretary of Health and Human Services, 111 S. Ct. 1759 (1991)

CHIEF JUSTICE REHNQUIST delivered the opinion of the Court.

. . .

II

We begin by pointing out the posture of the cases before us. Petitioners are challenging the *facial* validity of the regulations. Thus, we are concerned only with the question whether, on their face, the regulations are both authorized by the Act, and can be construed in such a manner that they can be applied to a set of individuals without infringing upon constitutionally protected rights. Petitioners face a heavy burden in seeking to have the regulations invalidated as facially unconstitutional. "A facial challenge to a legislative Act is, of course, the most difficult challenge to mount successfully, since the challenger must establish that no set of circumstances exists under which the Act would be valid.

The fact that [the regulations] might operate unconstitutionally under some conceivable set of circumstances is insufficient to render [them] wholly invalid." *United States v. Salerno*, 481 U.S. 739, 745 (1987).

We turn first to petitioners' contention that the regulations exceed the Secretary's authority under Title X and are arbitrary and capricious. We begin with an examination of the regulations concerning abortion counseling, referral, and advocacy, which every Court of Appeals has found to be authorized by the statute, and then turn to the "program integrity requirement," with respect to which the courts below have adopted conflicting positions. We then address petitioner's claim that the regulations must be struck down because they raise a substantial constitutional question.

A

We need not dwell on the plain language of the statute because we agree with every court to have addressed the issue that the language is ambiguous. The language of § 1008—that "[n]one of the funds appropriated under this subchapter shall be used in programs where abortion is a method of family planning"—does not speak directly to the issues of counseling, referral, advocacy, or program integrity. If a statute is "silent or ambiguous with respect to the specific issue, the question for the court is whether the agency's answer is based on a permissible construction of the statute." *Chevron v. Natural Resources*, 467 U.S. 837, at 842–43.

The Secretary's construction of Title X may not be disturbed as an abuse of discretion if it reflects a plausible construction of the plain language of the statute and does not otherwise conflict with Congress' expressed intent. *Ibid.* . . .

The broad language of Title X plainly allows the Secretary's construction of the statute. By its own terms, § 1008 prohibits the use of Title X funds "in programs where abortion is a method of family planning." . . .

The District Courts and Courts of Appeals that have examined the legislative history have all found, at least with regard to the Act's counseling, referral, and advocacy provisions, that the legislative history is ambiguous with respect to Congress' intent in enacting Title X and the prohibition of § 1008. . . . We join these courts in holding that the legislative history is ambiguous and fails to shed light on relevant congressional intent. . . .

When we find, as we do here, that the legislative history is ambiguous and unenlightening on the matters with respect to which the regulations deal, we customarily defer to the expertise of the agency. Petitioners argue, however, that the regulations are entitled to little or no deference because they "reverse a longstanding agency policy that permitted nondirective counseling and referral for abortion," . . . and thus represent a

sharp break from the Secretary's prior construction of the statute. Petitioners argue that the agency's prior consistent interpretation of Section 1008 to permit nondirective counseling and to encourage coordination with local and state family planning services is entitled to substantial weight.

This Court has rejected the argument that an agency's interpretation "is not entitled to deference because it represents a sharp break with prior interpretations" of the statute in question. *Chevron*, 467 U.S., at 862. In *Chevron*, we held that a revised interpretation deserves deference because "[a]n initial agency interpretation is not instantly carved in stone" and "the agency, to engage in informed rulemaking, must consider varying interpretations and the wisdom of its policy on a continuing basis." *Id.*, at 863–64. An agency is not required to " 'establish rules of conduct to last forever,' " *Motor Vehicle Mfrs. Assn. of United States v. State Farm Mutual Automobile Ins. Co.*, 463 U.S. 29, 42 (1983), quoting *American Trucking Assns., Inc. v. Atchinson, T. & S. F. R. Co.*, 387 U.S. 397, 416 (1967); *NLRB v. Curtin Matheson Scientific, Inc.*, 494 U.S. 775 (1990), but rather "must be given ample latitude to 'adapt [its] rules and policies to the demands of changing circumstances.' " *Motor Vehicle Mfrs., supra*, at 42, quoting *Permian Basin Area Rate Cases*, 390 U.S. 747, 784 (1968).

We find that the Secretary amply justified his change of interpretation with a "reasoned analysis." *Motor Vehicle Mfrs., supra*, at 42. The Secretary explained that the regulations are a result of his determination, in the wake of the critical reports of the General Accounting Office (GAO) and the Office of the Inspector General (OIG), that prior policy failed to implement properly the statute and that it was necessary to provide "clear and operational guidance to grantees to preserve the distinction between Title X programs and abortion as a method of family planning." 53 Fed. Reg. 2923–24 (1988). He also determined that the new regulations are more in keeping with the original intent of the statute, are justified by client experience under the prior policy, and are supported by a shift in attitude against the "elimination of unborn children by abortion." We believe that these justifications are sufficient to support the Secretary's revised approach. Having concluded that the plain language and legislative history are ambiguous as to Congress' intent in enacting Title X, we must defer to the Secretary's permissible construction of the statute.

B

We turn next to the "program integrity" requirements embodied at § 59.9 of the regulations, mandating separate facilities, personnel, and records. These requirements are not inconsistent with the plain language of Title X. Petitioners contend, however, that they are based on an impermissible construction of the statute because they frustrate the clearly expressed intent of Congress that Title X programs be an integral part of a broader, comprehensive, health-care system. . . .

The Secretary defends the separation requirements of § 59.9 on the grounds that they are necessary to assure that Title X grantees apply federal funds only to federally authorized purposes and that grantees avoid creating the appearance that the government is supporting abortion-related activities. . . .

. . . Indeed, if one thing is clear from the legislative history, it is that Congress intended that Title X funds be kept separate and distinct from abortion-related activities. It is undisputed that Title X was intended to provide primarily prepregnancy preventive services. . . . Certainly the Secretary's interpretation of the statute that separate facilities are necessary, especially in

light of the express prohibition of § 1008, cannot be judged unreasonable. . . .

Petitioners also contend that the regulations must be invalidated because they raise serious questions of constitutional law. They rely on *Edward J. Debartolo Corp. v. Florida Gulf Coast Building and Construction Trades Council*, 485 U.S. 568 (1988), and *NLRB v. Catholic Bishop of Chicago*, 440 U.S. 490 (1979), which hold that "an Act of Congress ought not to be construed to violate the Constitution if any other possible construction remains available. *Id.*, at 5. Under this canon of statutory construction, "[t]he elementary rule is that every reasonable construction must be resorted to in order to *save a statute* from unconstitutionality." *Debartolo Corp., supra*, at 575 (emphasis added) *quoting Hooper v. California*, 155 U.S. 648, 657 (1895)).

The principle enunciated in *Hooper v. California, supra*, and subsequent cases, is a categorical one: "as between two possible interpretations of a statute, by one of which it would be unconstitutional and by the other valid, our plain duty is to adopt that which will save the Act." *Blodgett v. Holden*, 275 U.S. 142, 148 (1927) (opinion of Holmes, J.). This principle is based at least in part on the fact that a decision to declare an act of Congress unconstitutional "is the gravest and most delicate duty that this Court is called on to perform." *Id.* Following *Hooper, supra*, cases such as *United States v. Delaware and Hudson Co.*, 213 U.S. 366, 408, and *United States v. Jin Fuey Moy*, 241 U.S. 394, 401, developed the corollary doctrine that "[a] statute must be construed, if fairly possible, so as to avoid not only the conclusion that it is unconstitutional but also grave doubts upon that score." *Jin Fuey Moy, supra*, at 401. This canon is followed out of respect for Congress, which we assume legislates in the light of constitutional limitations. *FTC v. American Tobacco Co.*, 264 U.S. 298, 305–07 (1924). It is qualified by

the proposition that "avoidance of a difficulty will not be pressed to the point of
disingenuous evasion." *Moore Ice Cream Co.
v. Rose,* 289 U.S. 373, 379 (1933).

Here Congress forbade the use of
appropriated funds in programs where
abortion is a method of family planning. It
authorized the Secretary to promulgate regulations implementing this provision. The
extensive litigation regarding governmental
restrictions on abortion since our decision in
Roe v. Wade, 410 U.S. 113 (1973), suggests
that it was likely that any set of regulations
promulgated by the Secretary—other than
the ones in force prior to 1988 and found by
him to be relatively toothless and
ineffectual—would be challenged on constitutional grounds. While we do not think
that the constitutional arguments made by
petitioners in this case are without some
force, in Part III, infra, we hold that they do
not carry the day. Applying the canon of
construction under discussion as best we
can, we hold that the regulations promulgated by the Secretary do not raise the sort
of "grave and doubtful constitutional questions," *Delaware and Hudson Co., supra,* at
408, that would lead us to assume Congress
did not intend to authorize their issuance.
Therefore, we need not invalidate the regulations in order to save the statute from
unconstitutionality.

III

Petitioners contend that the regulations violate the First Amendment by
impermissibly discriminating based on
viewpoint because they prohibit "all discussion about abortion as a lawful option—
including counseling, referral, and the provision of neutral and accurate information
about ending a pregnancy—while compelling the clinic or counselor to provide
information that promotes continuing a
pregnancy to term." They assert that the

regulations violate the "free speech rights
of private health care organizations that
receive Title X funds, of their staff, and of
their patients" by impermissibly imposing
"viewpoint-discriminatory conditions on
government subsidies" and thus penaliz[e]
speech funded with non-Title X monies."
Id., at 13, 14, 24. Because "Title X continues
to fund speech ancillary to pregnancy testing in a manner that is not even-handed
with respect to views and information
about abortion, it invidiously discriminates
on the basis of viewpoint." Relying on
*Regan v. Taxation With Representation of
Wash.* 461 U.S. 540 (1983), and *Arkansas
Writers Project, Inc., v. Ragland,* 481 U.S. 221,
234 (1987), petitioners also assert that while
the Government may place certain conditions on the receipt of federal subsidies, it
may not "discriminate invidiously in its
subsidies in such a way as to 'ai[m] at the
suppression of dangerous ideas.'" *Regan,*
at 548 (quoting *Cammarano v. United States,*
358 U.S. 498, 513 (1959)).

There is no question but that the
statutory prohibition contained in § 1008 is
constitutional. In *Maher v. Roe,* we . . . held
that the government may "make a value
judgment favoring childbirth over abortion, and . . . implement that judgment by
the allocation of public funds." *Id.,* at 474.
Here the Government is exercising the
authority it possesses under *Maher* and
McRae to subsidize family planning services which will lead to conception and
child birth, and declining to "promote or
encourage abortion." The Government can,
without violating the Constitution, selec-
tively fund a program to encourage certain
activities it believes to be in the pubic
interest, without at the same time funding
an alternate program which seeks to deal
with the problem in another way. In so
doing, the Government has not discriminated on the basis of viewpoint; it has
merely chosen to fund one activity to the

exclusion of the other. "[A] legislature's decision not be subsidize the exercise of a fundamental right does not infringe the right." *Regan, supra,* at 549. See also, *Buckley v. Valeo,* 424 U.S. 1 (1976); *Cammarano v. United States, supra.* "A refusal to fund protected activity, without more, cannot be equated with the imposition of a 'penalty' on that activity." *McRae,* 448 U.S., at 317, n. 19. "There is a basic difference between direct state interference with a protected activity and state encouragement of an alternative activity consonant with legislative policy." *Maher,* 432 U.S., at 475.

The challenged regulations . . . are designed to ensure that the limits of the federal program are observed. The Title X program is designed not for prenatal care, but to encourage family planning. A doctor who wished to offer prenatal care to a project patient who became pregnant could properly be prohibited from doing so because such service is outside the scope of the federally funded program. The regulations prohibiting abortion counseling and referral are of the same ilk; "no funds appropriated for the project may be used in programs where abortion is a method of family planning," and a doctor employed by the project may be prohibited in the course of his project duties from counseling abortion or referring for abortion. This is not a case of the Government "suppressing a dangerous idea," but of a prohibition on a project grantee or its employees from engaging in activities outside of its scope.

To hold that the Government unconstitutionally discriminates on the basis of viewpoint when it chooses to fund a program dedicated to advance certain permissible goals, because the program in advancing those goals necessarily discourages alternate goals, would render numerous government programs constitutionally suspect. When Congress established a National Endowment for Democracy to encourage other countries to adopt democratic principles, 22 U.S.C. § 4411(b), it was not constitutionally required to fund a program to encourage competing lines of political philosophy such as Communism and Fascism. Petitioners' assertions ultimately boil down to the position that if the government chooses to subsidize one protected right, it must subsidize analogous counterpart rights. But the Court has soundly rejected that proposition. *Regan v. Taxation With Representation of Wash.; Maher v. Roe; Harris v. McRae.* Within far broader limits than petitioners are willing to concede, when the government appropriates public funds to establish a program it is entitled to define the limits of that program. . . .

Petitioners rely heavily on their claim that the regulations would not, in the circumstance of a medical emergency, permit a Title X project to refer a woman whose pregnancy places her life in imminent peril to a provider of abortions or abortion-related services. This case, of course, involves only a facial challenge to the regulations, and we do not have before us any application by the Secretary to a specific fact situation. On their face, we do not read the regulations to bar abortion referral or counseling in such circumstances. Abortion counseling as a "method of family planning" is prohibited, and it does not seem that a medically necessitated abortion in such circumstances would be the equivalent to its use as a "method of family planning." Neither § 1008 nor the specific restrictions of the regulations would apply. Moreover, the regulations themselves contemplate that a Title X project would be permitted to engage in otherwise prohibited abortion-related activity in such circumstances. Section 59.8(a)(2) provides a specific exemption for emergency care and requires Title X recipients "to refer the client immediately to an appropriate provider of emergency medical services." 42 C.F.R. 59.8(a)(2)

(1989). Section 59.5(b)(1) also requires Title X projects to provide "necessary referral to other medical facilities when medically indicated."

Petitioners also contend that the restrictions on the subsidization of abortion-related speech contained in the regulations are impermissible because they condition the receipt of a benefit, in this case Title X funding, on the relinquishment of a constitutional right, the right to engage in abortion advocacy and counseling. Relying on *Perry v. Sindermann*, 408 U.S. 593, 597 (1972), and *FCC v. League of Women Voters of Cal.* 468 U.S. 364 (1984), petitioners argue that "even though the government may deny [a] . . . benefit for any number of reasons, there are some reasons upon which the government may not rely. It may not deny a benefit to a person on a basis that infringes his constitutionally protected interests—especially, his interest in freedom of speech." *Perry, supra,* at 597.

Petitioners' reliance on these cases is unavailing, however, because here the government is not denying a benefit to anyone, but is instead simply insisting that public funds be spent for the purposes for which they were authorized. The Secretary's regulations do not force the Title X grantee to give up abortion-related speech; they merely require that the grantee keep such activities separate and distinct from Title X activities. Title X expressly distinguishes between a Title X *grantee* and a Title X *project.* The grantee, which normally is a health care organization, may receive funds from a variety of sources for a variety of purposes. The grantee receives Title X funds, however, for the specific and limited purpose of establishing and operating a Title X project. 42 U.S.C. § 300(a). The regulations govern the scope of the Title X *project's* activities, and leave the grantee unfettered in its other activities. The Title X

grantee can continue to perform abortions, provide abortion-related services, and engage in abortion advocacy; it simply is required to conduct those activities through programs that are separate and independent from the project that receives Title X funds.

In contrast, our "unconstitutional conditions" cases involve situations in which the government has placed a condition on the *recipient* of the subsidy rather than on particular program or service, thus effectively prohibiting the recipient from engaging in the protected conduct outside the scope of the federally funded program. In *FCC v. League of Women Voters of Cal.,* we invalidated a federal law providing that noncommercial television and radio stations that receive federal grants may not "engage in editorializing." Under that law, a recipient of federal funds was "barred absolutely from all editorializing" because it "is not able to segregate its activities according to the source of its funding" and thus "has no way of limiting the use of its federal funds to all noneditorializing activities." . . . We expressly recognized, however, that were Congress to permit the recipient stations to "establish 'affiliate' organizations which could then use the station's facilities to editorialize with nonfederal funds, such a statutory mechanism would plainly be valid." *Ibid.* Such a scheme would permit the station "to make known its views on matters of public importance through its nonfederally funded, editorializing affiliate without losing federal grants for its noneditorializing broadcast activities." *Ibid.* . . .

By requiring that the Title X grantee engage in abortion-related activity separately from activity receiving federal funding, Congress has, consistent with our teachings in *League of Women Voters* and *Regan,* not denied it the right to engage in abortion-related activities. Congress has merely refused to fund such activities out of the public fisc, and the Secretary has simply required a certain degree of separation from the Title X project in order to ensure the integrity of the federally funded program.

The same principles apply to petitioners' claim that the regulations abridge the free speech rights of the grantee's staff. Individuals who are voluntarily employed for a Title X project must perform their duties in accordance with the regulation's restrictions on abortion counseling and referral. The employees remain free, however, to pursue abortion-related activities when they are not acting under the auspices of the Title X project. The regulations, which govern solely the scope of the Title X project's activities, do not in any way restrict the activities of those persons acting as private individuals. The employees' freedom of expression is limited during the time that they actually work for the project; but this limitation is a consequence of their decision to accept employment in a project, the scope of which is permissibly restricted by the funding authority.

This is not to suggest that funding by the Government, even when coupled with the freedom of the fund recipients to speak outside the scope of the Government-funded project, is invariably sufficient to justify government control over the content of expression. For example, this Court has recognized that the existence of a Government "subsidy," in the form of Government-owned property, does not justify the restriction of speech in areas that have "been traditionally open to the public for expressive activity," *United States v. Kokinda,* 110 S. Ct. 3115, 3119 (1990); *Hague v. CIO,* 307 U.S. 496, 515 (1939)(opinion of Roberts, J.), or have been "expressly dedicated to speech activity." *Kokinda,* 110 S.

Ct., at 3119; *Perry Education Assn. v. Perry Local Educators' Assn.,* 460 U.S. 37, 45 (1983). Similarly, we have recognized that the university is a traditional sphere of free expression so fundamental to the functioning of our society that the Government's ability to control speech within that sphere by means of conditions attached to the expenditure of Government funds is restricted by the vagueness and overbreadth doctrines of the First Amendment, *Keyishian v. Board of Regents,* 385 U.S. 589, 603, 605–06 (1967). It could be argued by analogy that traditional relationships such as that between doctor and patient should enjoy protection under the First Amendment from government regulation, even when subsidized by the Government. We need not resolve that question here, however, because the Title X program regulations do not significantly impinge upon the doctor-patient relationship. Nothing in them requires a doctor to represent as his own any opinion that he does not in fact hold. . . . The [Title X] program does not provide post-conception medical care, and therefore a doctor's silence with regard to abortion cannot reasonably be thought to mislead a client into thinking that the doctor does not consider abortion an appropriate option for her. The doctor is always free to make clear that advice regarding abortion is simply beyond the scope of the program. In these circumstances, the general rule that the Government may choose not to subsidize speech applies with full force.

IV

We turn now to petitioners' argument that the regulations violate a woman's Fifth Amendment right to choose whether to terminate her pregnancy. We recently reaffirmed the long-recognized principle that " 'the Due Process Clauses generally confer no affirmative right to governmental aid, even where such aid may be necessary to secure life, liberty, or property interests of which the government itself may not deprive the individual.' " *Webster*, 492 U.S., at 507, quoting *Deshaney v. Winnebago County Dept. of Social Services*, 489 U.S. 189, 196 (1989). The Government has no constitutional duty to subsidize an activity merely because the activity is constitutionally protected and may validly choose to fund childbirth over abortion and " 'implement that judgment by the allocation of public funds' " for medical services relating to childbirth but not to those relating to abortion. *Webster*, at 510. The Government has no affirmative duty to "commit any resources to facilitating abortions," *Webster*, 492 U.S., at 511, and its decision to fund childbirth but not abortion "places no governmental obstacle in the path of a woman who chooses to terminate her pregnancy, but rather, by means of unequal subsidization of abortion and other medical services, encourages alternative activity deemed in the public interest." *McRae*, 448 U.S., at 315.

That the regulations do not impermissibly burden a woman's Fifth Amendment rights is evident from the line of cases beginning with *Maher* and *McRae* and culminating in our most recent decision in *Webster*. Just as Congress' refusal to fund abortions in *McRae* left "an indigent woman with at least the same range of choice in deciding whether to obtain a medically necessary abortion as she would have had if Congress had chosen to subsidize no health care costs at all," 448 U.S., at 317, and "Missouri's refusal to allow public employees to perform abortions in public hospitals leaves a pregnant woman with the same choices as if the State had chosen not to operate any public hospitals," *Webster*, at 509, Congress' refusal to fund abortion counseling and advocacy leaves a pregnant woman with the same choices as if the government had chosen not to fund family-planning services at all. The diffi-

culty that a woman encounters when a Title X project does not provide abortion counseling or referral leaves her in no different position than she would have been if the government had not enacted Title X.

In *Webster* we stated that "[h]aving held that the State's refusal [in *Maher*] to fund abortions does not violate *Roe v. Wade*, it strains logic to reach a contrary result for the use of public facilities and employees." 492 U.S., at 509–10. It similarly would strain logic, in light of the more extreme restrictions in those cases, to find that the mere decision to exclude abortion-related services from a federally funded *pre-conceptual* family planning program, is unconstitutional.

Petitioners also argue that by impermissibly infringing on the doctor/patient relationship and depriving a Title X client of information concerning abortion as a method of family planning, the regulations violate a woman's Fifth Amendment right to medical self-determination and to make informed medical decisions free of government-imposed harm. They argue that under our decisions in *Akron v. Akron Center for Reproductive Health, Inc.*, 462 U.S. 416 (1983), and *Thornburg v. American College of Obstetricians and Gynecologists*, 476 U.S. 747 (1986), the government cannot interfere with a woman's right to make an informed and voluntary choice by placing restrictions on the patient/doctor dialogue.

. . . Critical to our decisions in *Akron* and *Thornburg* to invalidate a governmental intrusion into the patient/doctor dialogue was the fact that the laws in both cases required *all* doctors within their respective jurisdictions to provide *all* pregnant patients contemplating an abortion a litany of information, regardless of whether the patient sought the information or whether the doctor thought the information necessary to the patient's decision. Under the Secretary's regulations, however, a doctor's ability to provide, and a woman's right to receive, information concerning abortion and abortion-related services outside the context of the Title X project remains unfettered. . . .

Petitioners contend, however, that most Title X clients are effectively precluded by indigency and poverty from seeing a health care provider who will provide abortion-related services. But once again, even these Title X clients are in no worse position than if Congress had never enacted Title X. . . .

The Secretary's regulations are a permissible construction of Title X and do not violate either the First or Fifth Amendments to the Constitution. Accordingly, the judgment of the Court of Appeals is

Affirmed.

JUSTICE BLACKMUN, with whom JUSTICE MARSHALL joins, with whom JUSTICE STEVENS joins as to Parts II and III, and with whom JUSTICE O'CONNOR joins as to Part I, dissenting.

Casting aside established principles of statutory construction and administrative jurisprudence, the majority in these cases today unnecessarily passes upon important questions of constitutional law. In so doing, the Court, for the first time, upholds viewpoint-based suppression of speech solely because it is imposed on those dependent upon the Government for economic support. Under essentially the same rationale, the majority upholds direct regulation of dialogue between a pregnant woman and her physician when that regulation has both the purpose and the effect of manipulating her decision as to the continuance of her pregnancy. I conclude that the Secretary's regulation of referral, advocacy, and counseling activities exceeds his statutory authority, and, also, that the Regulations violate the First and Fifth Amendments of our Constitution. Accordingly, I

dissent and would reverse the divided-vote judgment of the Court of Appeals.

I

The majority does not dispute that "[f]ederal statutes are to be so construed as to avoid serious doubt of their constitutionality." *Machinists v. Street,* 367 U.S. 740, 749 (1961). See also *Hooper v. California,* 155 U.S. 648, 657 (1895); *Crowell v. Benson,* 285 U.S. 22, 62 (1932); *United States v. Security Industrial Bank,* 459 U.S. 70, 78 (1982). Nor does the majority deny that this principle is fully applicable to cases such as the instant one, in which a plausible but constitutionally suspect statutory interpretation is embodied in an administrative regulation. See *Edward J. DeBartolo Corp. v. Florida Gulf Coast Building & Construction Trades Council,* 485 U.S. 568, 575 (1988); *NLRB v. Catholic Bishop of Chicago,* 440 U.S. 490 (1979); *Kent v. Dulles,* 357 U.S. 116, 129–130 (1957). Rather, in its zeal to address the constitutional issues, the majority sidesteps this established canon of construction with the feeble excuse that the challenged Regulations "do not raise the sort of 'grave and doubtful constitutional questions,' . . . that would lead us to assume Congress did not intend to authorize their issuance."

This facile response to the intractable problem the Court addresses today is disingenuous at best. Whether or not one believes that these Regulations are valid, it avoids reality to contend that they do not give rise to serious constitutional questions. The canon is applicable to this case not because "it is likely that [the Regulations] . . . would be challenged on constitutional grounds," but because the question squarely presented by the Regulations— the extent to which the Government may attach an otherwise unconstitutional condition to the receipt of a public benefit— implicates a troubled area of our jurisprudence in which a court ought not entangle itself unnecessarily. See, *e.g.*, Epstein, *Unconstitutional Conditions, State Power, and the Limits of Consent*, 102 Harv. L. Rev. 4, 6 (1988) (describing this problem as "the basic structural issue that for over a hundred years has bedeviled courts and commentators alike. . . ."); Sullivan, *Unconstitutional Conditions*, 102 Harv. L. Rev. 1413, 1415–16 (1989) (observing that this Court's unconstitutional conditions cases "seem a minefield to be traversed gingerly").

As is discussed in Parts II and III, the Regulations impose viewpoint-based restrictions upon protected speech and are aimed at a woman's decision whether to continue or terminate her pregnancy. In both respects, they implicate core constitutional values. This verity is evidenced by the fact that two of the three Courts of Appeals that have entertained challenges to the Regulations have invalidated them on constitutional grounds. See *Massachusetts v. Secretary of Health and Human Services*, 899 F.2d 53 (1st Cir. 1990); *Planned Parenthood Federation of America v. Sullivan*, 913 F.2d 1492 (10th Cir. 1990).

A divided panel of the Tenth Circuit found the Regulations to "fal[l] squarely within the prohibition in *Thornburgh v. American College of Obstetricians and Gynecologists*, 476 U.S. 747 (1986), and *City of Akron v. Akron Center for Reproductive Health, Inc.*, 462 U.S. 416 (1983), against intrusion into the advice a woman requests from or is given by her doctor." 913 F.2d, at 1501. The First Circuit, en banc with one judge dissenting, found the Regulations to violate both the privacy rights of Title X patients and the First Amendment rights of Title X grantees. See also *New York v. Sullivan*, 889 F.2d 401, 415 (2d Cir. 1989) (Kearse, J., dissenting in part). That a bare majority of this Court today reaches a different result does not change the fact that the constitutional questions raised by the Regulations are both grave and doubtful.

Nor is this a case in which the statutory language itself requires us to address a constitutional question. . . . The majority concedes that [it] "does not speak directly to the issues of counseling, referral, advocacy, or program integrity," and that "the legislative history is ambiguous" in this respect. Consequently, the language of § 1008 easily sustains a constitutionally trouble-free interpretation. . . . It is both logical and eminently prudent to assume that when Congress intends to press the limits of constitutionality in its enactments, it will express that intent in explicit and unambiguous terms. See Sunstein, *Law and Administration After Chevron*, 90 Colum. L. Rev. 2071, 2113 (1990) ("It is thus implausible that, after *Chevron*, agency interpretations of ambiguous statutes will prevail even if the consequence of those interpretations is to produce invalidity or to raise serious constitutional doubts").

Because I conclude that a plainly constitutional construction of § 1008 "is not only 'fairly possible' but entirely reasonable," *Machinists*, 367 U.S., at 750, I would reverse the judgment of the Court of Appeals on this ground without deciding the constitutionality of the Secretary's Regulations.

II

I also strongly disagree with the majority's disposition of petitioners' constitutional claims, and because I feel that a response thereto is indicated, I move on to that issue.

A

Until today, the Court never has upheld viewpoint-based suppression of speech simply because that suppression was a condition upon the acceptance of public funds. Whatever may be the Government's power to condition the receipt of its largess upon the relinquishment of constitutional rights, it surely does not extend to a condition that suppresses the recipient's cherished freedom of speech based solely upon the content or viewpoint of that speech. *Speiser v. Randall*, 357 U.S. 513, 518–19 (1958) ("To deny an exemption to claimants who engage in certain forms of speech is in effect to penalize them for such speech. . . . The denial is 'frankly aimed at the suppression of dangerous ideas,' " quoting *American Communications Assn. v. Douds*, 339 U.S. 382, 402 (1950)). See *Cammarano v. United States*, 358 U.S. 498, 513 (1959). See also *League of Women Voters*, 468 U.S., at 407 (REHNQUIST, J., dissenting). Cf. *Arkansas Writers' Project, Inc. v. Ragland*, 481 U.S. 221, 237 (SCALIA, J., dissenting). This rule is a sound one, for, as the Court often has noted: " 'A regulation of speech that is motivated by nothing more than a desire to curtail expression of a particular point of view on controversial issues of general interest is the purest example of a "law . . . abridging the freedom of speech, or of the press." ' " *League of Women Voters*, 468 U.S., at 383–84, quoting *Consolidated Edison Co. v. Public Service Comm'n of New York*, 447 U.S. 530, 546 (1980) (STEVENS, J., concurring in judgment). "[A]bove all else, the First Amendment means that government has no power to restrict expression because of its message, its ideas, its subject matter, or its content." *Police Department of Chicago v. Mosley*, 408 U.S. 92, 95 (1972). . . .

It cannot seriously be disputed that the counseling and referral provisions at issue in the present cases constitute content-based regulation of speech. Title X grantees may provide counseling and referral regarding any of a wide range of family planning and other topics, save abortion. Cf. *Consolidated Edison Co.*, 447 U.S., at 537 ("The First Amendment's hostility to content-based regulation extends not only to restrictions on particular viewpoints, but

also to prohibition of public discussion of an entire topic"); *Boos v. Barry*, 485 U.S. 312, 319 (1988) (opinion of O'CONNOR, J.) (same).

The Regulations are also clearly viewpoint-based. While suppressing speech favorable to abortion with one hand, the Secretary compels anti-abortion speech with the other. For example, the Department of Health and Human Services' own description of the Regulations makes plain that "Title X projects are *required* to facilitate access to prenatal care and social services, including adoption services, that might be needed by the pregnant client to promote her well-being and that of her child, while making it abundantly clear that the project is not permitted to promote abortion by facilitating access to abortion through the referral process." 53 Fed. Reg. 2927 (1988) (emphasis added).

Moreover, the Regulations command that a project refer for prenatal care each woman diagnosed as pregnant, irrespective of the woman's expressed desire to continue or terminate her pregnancy. 42 C.F.R. § 59.8(a)(2) (1990). If a client asks directly about abortion, a Title X physician or counselor is required to say, in essence, that the project does not consider abortion to be an appropriate method of family planning. § 59.8(b)(4). Both requirements are antithetical to the First Amendment. See *Wooley v. Maynard*, 430 U.S. 705, 714 (1977).

The Regulations pertaining to "advocacy" are even more explicitly viewpoint-based. These provide: "A Title X project may not *encourage, promote or advocate* abortion as a method of family planning." § 59.10 (emphasis added). They explain: "This requirement prohibits actions to *assist* women to obtain abortions or *increase* the availability or accessibility of abortion for family planning purposes." § 59.10(a) (emphasis added). The Regulations do not, however, proscribe or even regulate anti-abortion advocacy. These are clearly restrictions aimed at the suppression of "dangerous ideas."

Remarkably, the majority concludes that "the Government has not discriminated on the basis of viewpoint; it has merely chosen to fund one activity to the exclusion of another." But the majority's claim that the Regulations merely limit a Title X project's speech to preventive or preconceptional services, rings hollow in light of the broad range of non-preventive services that the Regulations authorize Title X projects to provide.[2] By refusing to fund those family-planning projects that advocate abortion *because* they advocate abortion, the Government plainly has targeted a particular viewpoint. Cf. *Ward v. Rock Against Racism*, 491 U.S. 781 (1989). The majority's reliance on the fact that the Regulations pertain solely to funding decisions simply begs the question. Clearly, there are some bases upon which government may not rest its decision to fund or not to fund. For example, the Members of the majority surely would agree that government may not base its decision to support an activity upon considerations of race. See, *e.g., Yick Wo v. Hopkins*, 118 U.S. 356 (1886). As demonstrated above, our cases make clear that ideological viewpoint is a similarly repugnant ground upon which to base funding decisions.

. . . [I]n addition to their impermissible focus upon the viewpoint of regulated speech, the provisions intrude upon a wide range of communicative conduct, including

2. In addition to requiring referral for prenatal care and adoption services, the Regulations permit general health services such as physical examinations, screening for breast cancer, treatment of gynecological problems, and treatment for sexually transmitted diseases. 53 Fed. Reg. 2927 (1988). None of the latter are strictly preventive, preconceptional services.

the very words spoken to a woman by her physician. By manipulating the content of the doctor/patient dialogue, the Regulations upheld today force each of the petitioners "to be an instrument for fostering public adherence to an ideological point of view [he or she] finds unacceptable." *Wooley v. Maynard*, 430 U.S., at 715. This type of intrusive, ideologically based regulation of speech . . . cannot be justified simply because it is a condition upon the receipt of a governmental benefit.

B

The Court concludes that the challenged Regulations do not violate the First Amendment rights of Title X staff members because any limitation of the employees' freedom of expression is simply a consequence of their decision to accept employment at a federally funded project. But it has never been sufficient to justify an otherwise unconstitutional condition upon public employment that the employee may escape the condition by relinquishing his or her job. It is beyond question "that a government may not require an individual to relinquish rights guaranteed him by the First Amendment as a condition of public employment." *Abood v. Detroit Board of Education*, 431 U.S. 209, 234 (1977), citing *Elrod v. Burns*, 427 U.S. 347, 357–60 (1976), and cases cited therein; *Perry v. Sindermann*, 408 U.S. 593 (1972); *Keyishian v. Board of Regents*, 385 U.S. 589 (1967). Nearly two decades ago, it was said:

For at least a quarter-century, this Court has made clear that even though a person has no "right" to a valuable governmental benefit and even though the government may deny him the benefit for any number of reasons, there are some reasons upon which the government may not rely. It may not deny a benefit to a person on a basis that infringes his constitutionally protected interests—especially, his interest in freedom of speech. For if the government could deny a benefit to a person because of his constitutionally protected speech or associations, his exercise of those freedoms would in effect be penalized and inhibited. This would allow the government to "produce a result which [it] could not command directly." *Perry v. Sindermann*, 408 U.S., at 597, quoting *Speiser v. Randall*, 357 U.S. 513, 526 (1958).

The majority attempts to circumvent this principle by emphasizing that Title X physicians and counselors "remain free . . . to pursue abortion-related activities when they are not acting under the auspices of the Title X project." . . . This is a dangerous proposition, and one the Court has rightly rejected in the past.

In *Abood*, it was no answer to the petitioners' claim of compelled speech as a condition upon public employment that their speech outside the workplace remained unregulated by the State. Nor was the public employee's First Amendment claim in *Rankin v. McPherson*, 483 U.S. 378 (1987), derogated because the communication that her employer sought to punish occurred during business hours. At the least, such conditions require courts to balance the speaker's interest in the message against those of government in preventing its dissemination. *Id.*, at 384; *Pickering v. Board of Education*, 391 U.S. 563, 568 (1968).

In the cases at bar, the speaker's interest in the communication is both clear and vital. In addressing the family-planning needs of their clients, the physicians and counselors who staff Title X projects seek to provide them with the full range of information and options regarding their health and re-

productive freedom. Indeed, the legitimate expectations of the patient and the ethical responsibilities of the medical profession demand no less. "The patient's right of self-decision can be effectively exercised only if the patient possesses enough information to enable an intelligent choice. . . . The physician has an ethical obligation to help the patient make choices from among the therapeutic alternatives consistent with good medical practice." Current Opinions, the Council on Ethical and Judicial Affairs of the American Medical Association ¶8.08 (1989). . . . When a client becomes pregnant, the full range of therapeutic alternatives includes the abortion option, and Title X counselors' interest in providing this information is compelling.

The Government's articulated interest in distorting the doctor/patient dialogue—ensuring that federal funds are not spent for a purpose outside the scope of the program—falls far short of that necessary to justify the suppression of truthful information and professional medical opinion regarding constitutionally protected conduct. Moreover, the offending Regulation is not narrowly tailored to serve this interest. For example, the governmental interest at stake could be served by imposing rigorous bookkeeping standards to ensure financial separation or adopting content-neutral rules for the balanced dissemination of family-planning and health information. By failing to balance or even to consider the free speech interests claimed by Title X physicians against the Government's asserted interest in suppressing the speech, the Court falters in its duty to implement the protection that the First Amendment clearly provides for this important message.

C

Finally, it is of no small significance that the speech the Secretary would suppress is truthful information regarding constitutionally protected conduct of vital importance to the listener. One can imagine no legitimate governmental interest that might be served by suppressing such information. . . .

III

By far the most disturbing aspect of today's ruling is the effect it will have on the Fifth Amendment rights of the women who, supposedly, are beneficiaries of Title X programs. The majority rejects petitioners' Fifth Amendment claims summarily. It relies primarily upon the decisions in *Harris v. McRae*, 448 U.S. 297 (1980), and *Webster v. Reproductive Health Services*, 492 U.S. 490 (1989). There were dissents in those cases, and we continue to believe that they were wrongly and unfortunately decided. Be that as it may, even if one accepts as valid the Court's theorizing in those cases, the majority's reasoning in the present cases is flawed.

Until today, the Court has allowed to stand only those restrictions upon reproductive freedom that, while limiting the availability of abortion, have left intact a woman's ability to decide without coercion whether she will continue her pregnancy to term. *Maher v. Roe*, *McRae*, and *Webster* are all to this effect. Today's decision abandons that principle, and with disastrous results.

Contrary to the majority's characterization, this is not a case in which individuals seek government aid in exercising their fundamental rights. The Fifth Amendment right asserted by petitioners is the right of a pregnant woman to be free from affirmative governmental *interference* in her decision. *Roe v. Wade* and its progeny are not so much about a medical procedure as they are about a woman's fundamental right to self-determination. Those cases serve to vindicate the idea that "liberty," if it means anything, must entail freedom from governmental domination in making the most

intimate and personal of decisions. . . . By suppressing medically pertinent information and injecting a restrictive ideological message unrelated to considerations of maternal health, the Government places formidable obstacles in the path of Title X clients' freedom of choice and thereby violates their Fifth Amendment rights.

It is crystal-clear that the aim of the challenged provisions—an aim the majority cannot escape noticing—is not simply to ensure that federal funds are not used to perform abortions, but to "reduce the incidence of abortion." 42 C.F.R. § 59.2 (1990) (in definition of "family planning"). As recounted above, the Regulations require Title X physicians and counselors to provide information pertaining only to childbirth, to refer a pregnant woman for prenatal care irrespective of her medical situation, and, upon direct inquiry, to respond that abortion is not an "appropriate method" of family planning.

The undeniable message conveyed by this forced speech, and the one that the Title X client will draw from it, is that abortion nearly always is an improper medical option. Although her physician's words, in fact, are strictly controlled by the Government and wholly unrelated to her particular medical situation, the Title X client will reasonably construe them as professional advice to forgo her right to obtain an abortion. As would most rational patients, many of these women will follow that perceived advice and carry their pregnancy to term, despite their needs to the contrary and despite the safety of the abortion procedure for the vast majority of them. Others, delayed by the Regulations' mandatory prenatal referral, will be prevented from acquiring abortions during the period in which the process is medically sound and constitutionally protected.

In view of the inevitable effect of the Regulations, the majority's conclusion that "[t]he difficulty that a woman encounters when a Title X project does not provide abortion counseling or referral leaves her in no different position than she would have been if the government had not enacted Title X," is insensitive and contrary to common human experience. Both the purpose and result of the challenged Regulations is to deny women the ability voluntarily to decide their procreative destiny. For these women, the Government will have obliterated the freedom to choose as surely as if it had banned abortions outright. The denial of this freedom is not a consequence of poverty but of the Government's ill-intentioned distortion of information it has chosen to provide.

The substantial obstacles to bodily self-determination that the Regulations impose are doubly offensive because they are effected by manipulating the very words spoken by physicians and counselors to their patients. In our society, the doctor/patient dialogue embodies a unique relationship of trust. The specialized nature of medical science and the emotional distress often attendant to health-related decisions requires that patients place their complete confidence, and often their very lives, in the hands of medical professionals. One seeks a physician's aid not only for medication or diagnosis, but also for guidance, professional judgment, and vital emotional support. Accordingly, each of us attaches profound importance and authority to the words of advice spoken by the physician.

It is for this reason that we have guarded so jealously the doctor/patient dialogue from governmental intrusion. . . .

The majority attempts to distinguish our holdings in *Akron* and *Thornburgh* on the post-hoc basis that the governmental intrusions into the doctor/patient dialogue invalidated in those cases applied to *all* physicians within a jurisdiction while the Regulations now before the Court pertain

to the narrow class of healthcare professionals employed at Title X projects. But the rights protected by the Constitution are *personal* rights. *Loving v. Virginia*, 338 U.S. 1, 12 (1967); *Shelley v. Kraemer*, 334 U.S. 1, 22 (1948). And for the individual woman, the deprivation of liberty by the Government is no less substantial because it affects few rather than many. . . .

The manipulation of the doctor/patient dialogue achieved through the Secretary's Regulations is clearly an effort "to deter a woman from making a decision that, with her physician, is hers to make." *Thornburgh*, 476 U.S., at 759. As such, it violates the Fifth Amendment.[6]

IV

In its haste further to restrict the right of every woman to control her reproductive freedom and bodily integrity, the majority disregards established principles of law and contorts this Court's decided cases to arrive at its preordained result. The majority professes to leave undisturbed the free speech protections upon which our society has come to rely, but one must wonder what force the First Amendment retains if it is read to countenance the deliberate manipulation by the Government of the dialogue between a woman and her physician. While technically

6. Significantly, the Court interprets the challenged regulations to allow a Title X project to refer a woman whose health would be seriously endangered by continued pregnancy to an abortion provider. To hold otherwise would be to adopt an interpretation that would most certainly violate a patient's right to substantive due process. See, *e.g.*, *Youngberg v. Romeo*, 457 U.S. 307 (1982); *Revere v. Massachusetts General Hospital*, 463 U.S. 239 (1983). The Solicitor General at oral argument, however, afforded the Regulations a far less charitable interpretation. See Tr. of Oral Arg. 44–47.

leaving intact the fundamental right protected by *Roe v. Wade*, the Court . . . once again has rendered the right's substance nugatory. See *Webster v. Reproductive Health Services*, 492 U.S., at 537 and 560 (opinions concurring in part and dissenting in part). . . .

JUSTICE STEVENS, dissenting.

In my opinion, the Court has not paid sufficient attention to the language of the controlling statute or to the consistent interpretation accorded the statute by the responsible cabinet officers during four different Presidencies and 18 years.

The relevant text of the "Family Planning Services and Population Research Act of 1970" has remained unchanged since its enactment. 84 Stat. 1504. The preamble to the Act states that it was passed:

> To promote public health and welfare by expanding, improving, and better coordinating the family planning services and population research activities of the Federal Government, and for other purposes. *Ibid.*

The declaration of congressional purposes emphasizes the importance of educating the public about family planning services. Thus, § 2 of the Act states, in part, that the purpose of the Act is:

> (1) to assist in making comprehensive voluntary family planning services readily available to all persons desiring such services;
>
> . . .
>
> (5) to develop and make readily available information (including educational materials) on family planning and population growth to all persons desiring such information. 42 U.S.C.

§ 300 (Congressional Declaration of Purpose).

In contrast to the statutory emphasis on making relevant information readily available to the public, the statute contains no suggestion that Congress intended to authorize the suppression or censorship of any information by any Government employee or by any grant recipient. . . . Not a word in the statute . . . authorizes the Secretary to impose any restrictions on the dissemination of truthful information or professional advice by grant recipients.

The word "prohibition" is used only once in the Act. Section 6, which adds to the Public Health Service Act the new Title X, covering the subject of population research and voluntary planning programs, includes the following provision:

> PROHIBITION OF ABORTION
> SEC. 1008. None of the funds appropriated under this title shall be used in programs where abortion is a method of family planning. 84 Stat. 1508, 42 U.S.C. § 300a–6.

Read in the context of the entire statute, this prohibition is plainly directed at conduct, rather than the dissemination of information or advice, by potential grant recipients.

The original regulations promulgated in 1971 by the Secretary of Health, Education and Welfare so interpreted the statute. This " 'contemporaneous construction of [the] statute by the men charged with the responsibility of setting its machinery in motion' " is entitled to particular respect. See *Power Reactor Development Co. v. Electrical Workers*, 367 U.S. 396, 408 (1961) (citation omitted); *Udall v. Tallman*, 380 U.S. 1, 16 (1965); *Aluminum Co. of America v. Central Lincoln Peoples' Utility District*, 467 U.S. 380, 390 (1984). The regulations described the kind of services that grant recipients had to provide in order to be eligible for federal funding, but they did not purport to regulate or restrict the kinds of advice or information that recipients might make available to their clients. Conforming to the language of the government statute, the regulations provided that "[t]he project will not *provide* abortions as a method of family planning." 42 CFR § 59.5(a)(9) (1972) (emphasis added). Like the statute itself, the regulations prohibited conduct, not speech. . . .

The entirely new approach adopted by the Secretary in 1988 was not, in my view, authorized by the statute. The new regulations did not merely reflect a change in a policy determination that the Secretary had been authorized by Congress to make. Cf. *Chevron U.S.A. Inc. v. Natural Resources Defense Counsel, Inc.*, 467 U.S. 837, 865 (1984). Rather, they represented an assumption of policymaking responsibility that Congress had not delegated to the Secretary. See *id.*, at 842–43 ("If the intent of Congress is clear, that is the end of the matter; for the court, as well as the agency, must give effect to the unambiguously expressed intent of Congress"). In a society that abhors censorship and in which policymakers have traditionally placed the highest value on the freedom to communicate, it is unrealistic to conclude that statutory authority to regulate conduct implicitly authorized the Executive to regulate speech.

Because I am convinced that the 1970 Act did not authorize the Secretary to censor the speech of grant recipients or their employees, I would hold the challenged regulations invalid and reverse the judgment of the Court of Appeals.

Even if I thought the statute were ambiguous, however, I would reach the same result for the reasons stated in JUSTICE O'CONNOR's dissenting opinion. As she also explains, if a majority of the Court had

reached this result, it would be improper to comment on the constitutional issues that the parties have debated. Because the majority has reached out to decide the constitutional questions, however, I am persuaded that JUSTICE BLACKMUN is correct in concluding that the majority's arguments merit a response. I am also persuaded that JUSTICE BLACKMUN has correctly analyzed these issues. I have therefore joined Parts II and III of his opinion.

JUSTICE O'CONNOR, dissenting.

"[W]here an otherwise acceptable construction of a statute would raise serious constitutional problems, the Court will construe the statute to avoid such problems unless such construction is plainly contrary to the intent of Congress." *Edward J. DeBartolo Corp. v. Florida Gulf Coast Building & Construction Trades Council*, 485 U.S. 568, 575 (1988). JUSTICE BLACKMUN has explained well why this long-standing canon of statutory construction applies in this case, and I join Part I of his dissent. Part II demonstrates why the challenged regulations, which constitute the Secretary's interpretation of § 1008 of the Public Health Service Act, 84 Stat. 1508, 42 U.S.C. § 300a-6, "raise serious constitutional problems": the regulations place content-based restrictions on the speech of Title X fund recipients, restrictions directed precisely at speech concerning one of "the most divisive and contentious issues that our Nation has faced in recent years."

One may well conclude, as JUSTICE BLACKMUN does in Part II, that the regulations are unconstitutional for this reason. I do not join Part II of the dissent, however, for the same reason that I do not joint Part III, in which JUSTICE BLACKMUN concludes that the regulations are unconstitutional under the Fifth Amendment. The canon of construction that JUSTICE BLACKMUN correctly applies here is grounded in large part upon our time-honored practice of not reaching constitutional questions unnecessarily. See *DeBartolo, supra,* at 575. "It is a fundamental rule of judicial restraint . . . that this Court will not reach constitutional questions in advance of the necessity of deciding them." *Three Affiliated Tribes of Fort Berthold Reservation v. Wold Engineering, P. C.,* 467 U.S. 138, 157 (1984). See also *Alexander v. Louisiana,* 405 U.S. 625, 633 (1972); *Burton v. United States,* 196 U.S. 283, 295 (1905); *Liverpool, New York, and Philadelphia S. S. Co. v. Commissioners of Emigration,* 113 U.S. 33, 39 (1885) (In the exercise of its jurisdiction to pronounce unconstitutional laws of the United States, this Court "has rigidly adhered" to the rule "never to anticipate a question of constitutional law in advance of the necessity of deciding it").

This Court acts at the limits of its power when it invalidates a law on constitutional grounds. In recognition of our place in the constitutional scheme, we must act with "great gravity and delicacy" when telling a coordinate branch that its actions are absolutely prohibited absent constitutional amendment. *Adkins v. Children's Hospital of District of Columbia,* 261 U.S. 525, 544 (1923). See also *Blodgett v. Holden,* 275 U.S. 142, 147–48 (1927) (Holmes J., concurring). In this case, we need only tell the Secretary that his regulations are not a reasonable interpretation of the statute; we need not tell Congress that it cannot pass such legislation. If we rule solely on statutory grounds, Congress retains the power to force the constitutional question by legislating more explicitly. It may instead choose to do nothing. That decision should be left to Congress; we should not tell Congress what it cannot do before it has chosen to do it. . . .

CASE QUESTIONS

1. Is it contradictory for Justice Rehnquist to claim (in Part II.A) that the new administrative regulations are justified both because they reflect the *original* intent of the statute and because "they are supported by a *shift* in attitude against the 'elimination of unborn children by abortion' "? (Emphasis added.) (On the matter of legislative intent, see "Reaction to *Rust v. Sullivan*" below.)

2. In response to the rule that an interpretation of a statute should be rejected (assuming an alternative one is available), if the interpretation raises "grave and doubtful constitutional questions," the Rehnquist groups says (in Part II) "[we are] applying the canon of construction . . . as best we can." Does that phrasing imply disapproval of the rule of construction?

3. Although the Rehnquist majority refuses to reject the administrative prohibition on abortion counseling "as a method of family planning," the group does (in Part III) reject the idea that the regulations would prohibit referral for a "medically necessitated abortion," at least where the pregnant woman's life

were in imminent peril. Does it appear from their reasoning that referral could also be given for nonemergency, but medically necessitated, abortions on the grounds that such abortions would not be a "method of family planning"?

4. Rehnquist (in Part III) points to the National Endowment for Democracy program, which propagandizes other countries on behalf of the values of liberal democracy, in order to make the point that the federal government may propagandize on one side of an issue. When tax-dollar-sponsored "encouragement" of one point of view is aimed at American citizens rather than foreigners, does this practice conflict with the spirit of the First Amendment? Does federally funded television and radio programming raise similar concerns? Would it be a violation of some part of the Constitution for the Democrat-controlled Congress to subsidize Democratic but not Republican candidates for federal office? Which part? Does the funding of pro-childbirth but not pro-abortion information present similar problems?

5. Is there a difference, from the point of view of the First Amendment, between a government decision to finance some activities and not others, and a government decision to sponsor the advocacy or recommendation of some activities and not others? May the government legitimately encourage (and not discourage) people to vote, to join the Marines, to refrain from dropping out of school, to use condoms for health purposes? If the United States had an undisputed population shortage, would the dissenters agree that it would be legitimate for the government to encourage women to have babies? (Even if many Americans strongly believed that the ethical way to deal with the shortage would be to loosen immigration restrictions?)

6. Justice Blackmun (in Part II.B) quotes the Council on Ethical and Judicial Affairs of the American Medical Association as follows: "The physician has an ethical obligation to help the patient make choices from among the therapeutic alternatives consistent with good medical practice," and he insists that lawful abortion is one such alternative. Does this rule mean that doctors with strong religious or moral scruples against helping anyone procure an abortion cannot ethically practice medicine?

Reaction to *Rust v. Sullivan*

Political reaction to *Rust v. Sullivan* came quickly. Congress promptly adopted an amendment to Title X that made explicit its intent that the full range of pregnancy counseling, including abortion referrals when desired by the pregnant patient, be permitted at funded clinics. Just as promptly, President Bush vetoed the amendment (which action allowed his regulations to stand). The Senate voted 76–26 to override the veto. But the House vote, which came in early October 1992, just one month before the 1992 elections, was 266–148, ten votes short of the two-thirds majority needed for an override. At this point, it became a matter worth speculation that would have happened had someone gone to

Court challenging the regulations as in clear contravention of Congress's current intent. But matters did not rest there.

Bush's solicitor general (the official in the Justice Department responsible for arguing the executive branch position in court cases) had argued both in his *Rust* brief and orally before the Supreme Court that the regulations did *not* permit referrals of pregnant patients for abortion even when the woman had a serious medical need for an abortion. When pressed hard, by several justices in oral argument, he had finally conceded that if the woman were in danger of dying within a matter of hours, yes, the statute did provide an exception for genuine emergencies.[21] The majority opinion in *Rust* had then strongly hinted that the Court would view with disfavor an actual application of the regulations that negatively sanctioned a doctor for giving a referral for a medically needed (as distinguished from a family-planning-method) abortion.

Probably in response to this cue from the Court, President Bush, in lieu of Congress's amendment, amended the regulations on his own, to permit physicians to refer patients for abortions that were needed to prevent serious damage to the patients' health. But his administration rushed these regulations into place (perhaps with an eye to the 1992 election) without following the detailed procedures required for new administrative regulations. As a result, the federal court for the D.C. Circuit declared the new regulations void. Since the new regulations were to have replaced the old, it now appeared that no formal regulations were in place that specified counseling policy under Title X. Before any new policy could be adopted, the voters spoke, electing Arkansas Governor Bill Clinton to replace President Bush. Clinton had made clear during the campaign that his administration would eliminate this "gag rule." Between the November defeat and his exit from office in January 1993, President Bush did not reenact the gag rule. Still, the *Rust v. Sullivan* precedent stands as the current guideline on federal government leeway in utilizing funding policy to restrict the discussion of disfavored topics.

Reprieve for Roe v. Wade: Planned Parenthood v. Casey (1992)

As the issues raised in *Rust* were wending their way through the courts, legislatures below the federal level began reacting to the Supreme Court's apparent signal in the *Webster* decision of July 1989 that five justices were now prepared to scrap *Roe v. Wade*. That signal intensified when two of the justices who had dissented in *Webster*, William Brennan and Thurgood Marshall, left the Court, to be replaced by Bush appointees David Souter and Clarence Thomas. Souter's vote in *Rust* made him appear to be the sixth anti-abortion vote on the Court—or fifth if O'Connor were abandoning the opposition to *Roe* that she had expressed in *Akron I* and *Thornburgh*. Thomas did not appear a likely supporter of

Roe, since he claimed during his 1991 Senate confirmation hearings that he had never discussed *Roe v. Wade* in his entire life. If Souter, O'Connor, and Thomas were to join Rehnquist, White, Scalia, and Kennedy (the *Webster* plurality who had argued for abandoning "the key elements of the *Roe* framework") then seven of the nine Supreme Court justices would be willing to abandon the rules established in *Roe v. Wade.*

The first legislature to respond to the apparent *Webster* invitation to contravene *Roe* was that of the territory Guam. In March of 1990, the governor of Guam signed into law a prohibition on all abortion, unless two doctors confirmed that the pregnancy threatened a woman's life or posed grave risk to her health. By January of 1991, Utah had followed suit and banned all abortions except when the circumstances involved grave danger to the woman's physical health, grave defect in the fetus, or rape or incest. (For rape or incest the abortion had to be performed during the first twenty weeks of pregnancy.) By June of 1991, Louisiana had banned all abortions except those needed to save a woman's life or to end a pregnancy that was the product of rape reported to the police within seven days or of incest reported to the police. The time limit for rape or incest victims to procure the abortion was the first thirteen weeks of pregnancy. Federal judges declared each of these laws void, on the grounds that *Roe v. Wade* had not yet been formally overruled and was thus still the law of the land. In each case, the government (state or territorial, respectively) appealed the decision.

Before any of these direct floutings of the law of *Roe v. Wade* reached the Supreme Court, the Court, to the surprise of many, shed new light on its views of *Roe v. Wade* in the June 1992 decision, *Planned Parenthood v. Casey.*[22] The *Casey* decision did not even necessitate a reconsideration of *Roe;* it involved a variety of abortion regulations but no sweeping prohibitions. But once again the executive branch requested that *Roe* be overruled, and, in contrast to its silence in *Rust v. Sullivan,* the Supreme Court decided to respond (albeit negatively) to that request.

The Court issued its *Casey* decision with striking drama, as the three pivotal justices—O'Connor, Kennedy, and Souter—announced a jointly authored, jointly signed opinion. The joint authoring of opinions is extraordinarily rare on the U.S. Supreme Court—indeed, nearly unprecedented.[23] It created an impression of unusually strong unity (at least among those three justices). The case itself produced no majority opinion. The three-justice, pivotal plurality agreed on some of the results with a four-justice group led by Rehnquist and Scalia (each of whom wrote an opinion and concurred with the other, and with whose opinions White and Thomas concurred) who were still advocating an overruling of *Roe;* and on other results, with the staunchly pro-*Roe* Justices Stevens and Blackmun (who both agreed with part but not all of the plurality opinion). The three-justice plurality staked out a position endorsing "the essential holding" of *Roe v. Wade,* but admittedly modifying some of its particulars. The reader will be able to assess the degree to which *Roe* does or does not endure after reading the *Casey* opinion of the three-justice plurality, its restatements by Stevens and Blackmun, and its critiques by Rehnquist and Scalia.

The specific issues addressed in *Casey* concern the constitutionality of a variety of abortion regulations adopted by the state of Pennsylvania (whose governor, Robert Casey, appears in the case title). The regulations (the lengthy list of which took up several pages of the Court opinion) essentially required the following:

1. Except in the case of medical emergency, a woman must provide written "informed consent" at least twenty-four hours before an abortion. Informed consent means that a physician has told the woman the probable gestational age of the fetus; the proposed abortion procedure and "those risks and alternatives to the procedure ... that a reasonable patient would consider material to the decision whether or not to undergo the abortion" (unless the physician "reasonably believe[s] that furnishing the information would ... result [] in a severely adverse effect on the physical or mental health of the patient"); and the medical risks associated with continuing the pregnancy to term. In addition, the woman must be informed by a counselor that free printed materials are available that describe fetal development and list agencies that offer alternatives to abortion; that medical assistance benefits for pregnancy and childbirth and neonatal care may be available, as explained further in the printed materials; and that the father of the "unborn child" is liable to assist in its support, even if he offered to pay for the abortion. The last point need not be mentioned to victims of rape.

2. An unemancipated minor must obtain the "informed consent" (as described above) of a parent or guardian, or go to court and obtain an order either that the abortion is in her best interest or that she is mature enough to make her own decision.

3. A married woman seeking abortion of a fetus fathered by her husband— except in the case of medical emergency—must provide the physician with a signed statement indicating either that her husband has been notified of the pending abortion or (a) that she is unable to locate him, (b) that the fetus resulted from spousal sexual assault, or (c) that she fears bodily injury if she notifies him.

4. Facilities providing abortions that receive public funds must file publicly available reports indicating who owns the facility, and how many abortions— broken down by trimester of pregnancy—are performed there each quarter year. Abortion providers must also file confidential reports specifying the names of the person performing the abortion, and the referring physician and data on the woman receiving the abortion: name, age, county of residence, number of previous pregnancies, type of procedure used, and nature of medical complications. If a medical emergency necessitated the abortion, the physician must specify the grounds for that judgment and, if her husband were not notified, the grounds for that decision as well.

The federal district court had obliged Planned Parenthood's request for a declaratory judgment that all of these provisions were "on their face" unconstitutional because they violated a strict reading of the rules established in *Roe v. Wade* (using reasoning very similar to that in Justice Blackmun's partially dissenting opinion below). The circuit court of appeals decided that the prevailing rule of law since *Akron II* and *Hodgson* was an "undue burden" test grafted on to the basic framework of *Roe*.[24] Applying this test, the circuit court upheld all of these provisions except husband notification. The U.S. Supreme Court, with varying groups of justices dissenting on particular results, affirmed the judgment of the court of appeals. The issues of *Casey* engendered the following several opinions at the Supreme Court level.

Planned Parenthood v. Casey, 112 S. Ct. 2791 (1992)

JUSTICE O'CONNOR, JUSTICE KENNEDY, and JUSTICE SOUTER announced the judgment of the Court and delivered the opinion of the Court with respect to Parts I, II, III, V-A, V-C, and VI; an opinion with respect to Part V-E, in which JUSTICE STEVENS joins; and an opinion with respect to Parts IV, I-B, and V-D.

I

Liberty finds no refuge in a jurisprudence of doubt. Yet 19 years after our holding that the Constitution protects a woman's right to terminate her pregnancy in its early stages, *Roe v. Wade*, that definition of liberty is still questioned. Joining the respondents as *amicus curiae*, the United States, as it has done in five other cases in the last decade, again asks us to overrule *Roe*.

At issue in these cases are five provisions of the Pennsylvania Abortion Control Act of 1982 as amended in 1988 and 1989. 18 Pa. Cons. Stat. §§ 3203–3220 (1990). . . . [Here followed a summary of the Act.–Au.]

The Court of Appeals found it necessary to follow an elaborate course of reasoning even to identify the first premise to use to determine whether the statute enacted by Pennsylvania meets constitutional standards. See 947 F.2d, at 687–98. And at oral argument in this Court, the attorney for the parties challenging the statute took the position that none of the enactments can be upheld without overruling *Roe v. Wade*. We disagree with that analysis; but we acknowledge that our decisions after *Roe* cast doubt upon the meaning and reach of its holding. Further, the CHIEF JUSTICE admits that he would overrule the central holding of *Roe* and adopt the rational relationship test as the sole criterion of constitutionality. State and federal courts as well as legislatures throughout the Union must have guidance as they seek to address this subject in conformance with the Constitution. Given these premises, we find it imperative to review once more the principles that define the rights of the woman and the legitimate authority of the State respecting the termination of pregnancies by abortion procedures.

After considering the fundamental constitutional questions resolved by *Roe*, principles of institutional integrity, and the rule of *stare decisis*, we are led to conclude this: the essential holding of *Roe v. Wade* should be retained and once again reaffirmed.

It must be stated at the outset and with clarity that *Roe*'s essential holding, the holding we reaffirm, has three parts. First is a recognition of the right of the woman to choose to have an abortion before viability and to obtain it without undue interference from the State. Before viability, the State's interests are not strong enough to support a prohibition of abortion or the imposition of a substantial obstacle to the woman's effective right to elect the procedure. Second is a confirmation of the State's power to restrict abortions after fetal viability, if the law contains exceptions for pregnancies which endanger a woman's life or health. And third is the principle that the State has legitimate interests from the outset of the pregnancy in protecting the health of the woman and the life of the fetus that may become a child. These principles do not contradict one another; and we adhere to each.

II

Constitutional protection of the woman's decision to terminate her pregnancy derives from the Due Process Clause of the Fourteenth Amendment. . . . The controlling word in the case before us is "liberty." Although a literal reading of the Clause might suggest that it governs only the procedures by which a State may deprive persons of liberty, for at least 105 years, at least since *Mugler v. Kansas,* 123 U.S. 623, 660–61 (1887), the Clause has been understood to contain a substantive component as well, one "barring certain government actions regardless of the fairness of the procedures used to implement them." *Daniels v. Williams,* 474 U.S. 327, 331 (1986). As Justice Brandeis (joined by Justice Holmes) observed, "[d]espite arguments to the contrary which had seemed to me persuasive, it is settled that the due process clause of the Fourteenth Amendment applies to matters of substantive law as well as to matters of procedure. Thus all funda-

mental rights comprised within the term liberty are protected by the Federal Constitution from invasion by the States." *Whitney v. California,* 274 U.S. 357, 373 (1927) (Brandeis, J., concurring). . . .

The most familiar of the substantive liberties protected by the Fourteenth Amendment are those recognized by the Bill of Rights. We have held that the Due Process Clause of the Fourteenth Amendment incorporates most of the Bill of Rights against the States. See, *e.g., Duncan v. Louisiana,* 391 U.S. 145, 147–48 (1968). It is tempting, as a means of curbing the discretion of federal judges, to suppose that liberty encompasses no more than those rights already guaranteed to the individual against federal interference by the express provisions of the first eight amendments to the Constitution. See *Adamson v. California,* 332 U.S. 46, 68–92 (1947) (Black, J., dissenting). But of course this Court has never accepted that view.

It is also tempting, for the same reason, to suppose that the Due Process Clause protects only those practices, defined at the most specific level, that were protected against government interference by other rules of law when the Fourteenth Amendment was ratified. See *Michael H. v. Gerald D.,* 491 U.S. 110, 127–28, n.6 (1989) (opinion of SCALIA, J.). But such a view would be inconsistent with our law. It is a promise of the Constitution that there is a realm of personal liberty which the government may not enter. We have vindicated this principle before. Marriage is mentioned nowhere in the Bill of Rights and interracial marriage was illegal in most States in the 19th century, but the Court was no doubt correct in finding it to be an aspect of liberty protected against state interference by the substantive component of the Due Process Clause in *Loving v. Virginia,* 388 U.S. 1, 12 (1967) (relying, in an opinion for eight Justices, on the Due Process Clause). . . .

Neither the Bill of Rights nor the specific practices of States at the time of the adoption of the Fourteenth Amendment marks the outer limits of the substantive sphere of liberty which the Fourteenth Amendment protects. See U.S. Const., Amend. 9. As the second Justice Harlan recognized:

[T]he full scope of the liberty guaranteed by the Due Process Clause cannot be found in or limited by the precise terms of the specific guarantees elsewhere provided in the Constitution. This 'liberty' is not a series of isolated points pricked out in terms of the taking of property; the freedom of speech, press, and religion; the right to keep and bear arms; the freedom from unreasonable searches and seizures; and so on. It is a rational continuum which, broadly speaking, includes a freedom from all substantial arbitrary impositions and purposeless restraints, ... and which also recognizes, what a reasonable and sensitive judgment must, that certain interests require particularly careful scrutiny of the state needs asserted to justify their abridgement. *Poe v. Ullman,* 367 U.S. 497, at 543 (Harlan, J., dissenting from dismissal on jurisdictional grounds).

... It is settled now, as it was when the Court heard arguments in *Roe v. Wade,* that the Constitution places limits on a State's right to interfere with a person's most basic decisions about family and parenthood, see *Carey v. Population Services International; Moore v. East Cleveland,* 431 U.S. 494 (1977); *Eisenstadt v. Baird; Loving v. Virginia; Griswold v. Connecticut, Skinner v. Oklahoma ex rel. Williamson; Pierce v. Society of Sisters; Meyer v. Nebraska,* as well as bodily integrity. See, *e.g., Washington v. Harper,* 494 U.S. 210, 221–22 (1990); *Winston v. Lee,* 470 U.S. 753 (1985); *Rochin v. California,* 342 U.S. 165 (1952).

The inescapable fact is that adjudication of substantive due process claims may call upon the Court in interpreting the Constitution to exercise that same capacity which by tradition courts always have exercised: reasoned judgment. Its boundaries are not susceptible of expression as a simple rule. That does not mean we are free to invalidate state policy choices with which we disagree; yet neither does it permit us to shrink from the duties of our office. As Justice Harlan observed:

[T]hrough the course of this Court's decisions it has represented the balance which our Nation, built upon postulates of respect for the liberty of the individual, has struck between that liberty and the demands of organized society.... The balance of which I speak is the balance struck by this country, having regard to what history teaches are the traditions from which it developed as well as the traditions from which it broke. That tradition is a living thing. A decision of this Court which radically departs from it could not long survive, while a decision which builds on what has survived is likely to be sound.... *Poe v. Ullman,* 367 U.S., at 542 (Harlan, J., dissenting ...)

...

Men and women of good conscience can disagree, and we suppose some always shall disagree, about the profound moral and spiritual implications of terminating a pregnancy, even in its earliest stage. Some of us as individuals find abortion offensive to our most basic principles of morality, but that cannot control our decision. Our obligation is to define the liberty of all, not to mandate our own moral code. The underlying constitutional issue is whether the State can resolve these philosophic questions in such a definitive way that a woman lacks all choice in the matter, except perhaps in those rare circumstances in which the pregnancy is itself a danger to her own life or health, or is the result of rape or incest. . . .

Our law affords constitutional protection to personal decisions relating to marriage, procreation, contraception, family relationships, child rearing, and education. *Carey v. Population Services International*, 431 U.S., at 685. Our cases recognize "the right of the *individual*, married or single, to be free from unwarranted governmental intrusion into matters so fundamentally affecting a person as the decision whether to bear or beget a child." *Eisenstadt v. Baird*, at 453 (emphasis in original). Our precedents "have respected the private realm of family life which the state cannot enter." *Prince v. Massachusetts*, 321 U.S. 158, 166 (1944). These matters, involving the most intimate and personal choices a person may make in a lifetime, choices central to personal dignity and autonomy, are central to the liberty protected by the Fourteenth Amendment. At the heart of liberty is the right to define one's own concept of existence, of meaning, of the universe, and of the mystery of human life. Beliefs about these matters could not define the attributes of personhood were they formed under compulsion of the State.

These considerations begin our analysis of the woman's interest in terminating her pregnancy but cannot end it, for this reason: though the abortion decision may originate within the zone of conscience and belief, it is more than a philosophic exercise. Abortion is a unique act. It is an act fraught with consequences for others: for the woman who must live with the implications of her decision; for the persons who perform and assist in the procedure; for the spouse, family, and society which must confront the knowledge that these procedures exist, procedures some deem nothing short of an act of violence against innocent human life; and, depending on one's beliefs, for the life or potential life that is aborted. Though abortion is conduct, it does not follow that the State is entitled to proscribe it in all instances. That is because the liberty of the woman is at stake in a sense unique to the human condition and so unique to the law. The mother who carries a child to full term is subject to anxieties, to physical constraints, to pain that only she must bear. That these sacrifices have from the beginning of the human race been endured by woman with a pride that ennobles her in the eyes of others and gives to the infant a bond of love cannot alone be grounds for the State to insist she make the sacrifice. Her suffering is too intimate and personal for the State to insist, without more, upon its own vision of the woman's role, however dominant that vision has been in the course of our history and our culture. The destiny of the woman must be shaped to a large extent on her own conception of her spiritual imperatives and her place in society.

It should be recognized, moreover, that in some critical respects the abortion decision is of the same character as the decision to use contraception, to which *Griswold v. Connecticut, Eisenstadt v. Baird*, and *Carey v. Population Services International*, afford constitutional protection. We have no doubt as to the correctness of those decisions. They support the reasoning in *Roe* relating to the woman's liberty because they involve personal decisions concerning not only the meaning of procreation but also human responsibility and respect for it. . . . The same concerns are present when the woman confronts the reality that, perhaps despite her attempts to avoid it, she has become pregnant.

It was this dimension of personal liberty that *Roe* sought to protect, and its holding invoked the reasoning and the tradition of the precedents we have discussed, granting protection to substantive liberties of the person. *Roe* was, of course, an extension of those cases and, as the decision itself indicated, the separate States could act in some degree to further their own legitimate interests in protecting pre-natal life. The extent to which the legislatures of the States might act to outweigh the interests of the woman in choosing to terminate her pregnancy was a subject of debate both in *Roe* itself and in decisions following it.

... [T]he reservations any of us may have in reaffirming the central holding of *Roe* are outweighed by the explication of individual liberty we have given combined with the force of *stare decisis*. We turn now to that doctrine.

III

A

The obligation to follow precedent begins with necessity, and a contrary necessity marks its outer limit. With Cardozo, we recognize that no judicial system could do society's work if it eyed each issue afresh in every case that raised it. See B. Cardozo, *The Nature of the Judicial Process* 149 (1921). Indeed, the very concept of the rule of law underlying our own Constitution requires such continuity over time that a respect for precedent is, by definition, indispensable. At the other extreme, a different necessity would make itself felt if a prior judicial ruling should come to be seen so clearly as error that its enforcement was for that very reason doomed.

Even when the decision to overrule a prior case is not, as in the rare, latter instance, virtually foreordained, it is common wisdom that the rule of *stare decisis* is not an "inexorable command," and certainly it is not such in every constitutional case, see *Burnet v. Coronado Oil Gas Co.*, 285 U.S. 393, 405–11 (1932) (Brandeis, J., dissenting).

Rather, when this Court reexamines a prior holding, its judgment is customarily informed by a series of prudential and pragmatic considerations designed to test the consistency of overruling a prior. decision with a ideal of the rule of law, and to gauge the respective costs of reaffirming and overruling a prior case. Thus, for example, we may ask whether the rule has proved to be intolerable simply in defying practical workability, *Swift & Co. v. Wickham*, 382 U.S. 111, 116 (1965); whether the rule is subject to a kind of reliance that would lend a special hardship to the consequences of overruling and add inequity to the cost of repudiation, *e.g., United States v. Title Ins. & Trust Co.*, 265 U.S. 472, 486 (1924); whether related principles of law have so far developed as to have left the old rule no more than a remnant of abandoned doctrine, see *Patterson v. McLean Credit Union*, 491 U.S. 164, 173–74 (1989); or whether facts have so changed or come to be seen so differently, as to have robbed the old rule of significant application or justification, *e.g., Burnet, supra*, at 412 (Brandeis, J., dissenting).

So in this case we may inquire whether *Roe*'s central rule has been found unworkable; whether the rule's limitation on state power could be removed without serious inequity to those who have relied upon it or significant damage to the stability of the society governed by the rule in question; whether the law's growth in the intervening years has left *Roe*'s central rule a doctrinal anachronism discounted by society; and whether *Roe*'s premises of fact have so far changed in the ensuing two decades as to render its central holding somehow irrelevant or unjustifiable in dealing with the issue it addressed.

1

Although *Roe* has engendered opposition, it has in no sense proven "unworkable," representing as it does a simple limitation beyond which a state law is unenforceable....

2

The inquiry into reliance counts the cost of a rule's repudiation as it would fall on those who have relied reasonably on the rule's continued application.

. . .[F]or two decades of economic and social developments, people have organized intimate relationships and made choices that define their views of themselves and their places in society, in reliance on the availability of abortion in the event that contraception should fail. The ability of women to participate equally in the economic and social life of the Nation has been facilitated by their ability to control their reproductive lives. See, *e.g.*, R. Petchesky, *Abortion and Woman's Choice* 109, 133, n.7 (rev. ed. 1990). The Constitution serves human values, and while the effect of reliance on *Roe* cannot be exactly measured, neither can the certain cost of overruling *Roe* for people who have ordered their thinking and living around that case be dismissed.

3

No evolution of legal principle has left *Roe*'s doctrinal footings weaker than they were in 1973. No development of constitutional law since the case was decided has implicitly or explicitly left *Roe* behind as a mere survivor of obsolete constitutional thinking.

It will be recognized, of course, that *Roe* stands at an intersection of two lines of decisions, but in whichever doctrinal category one reads the case, the result for present purposes will be the same. The *Roe* Court itself placed its holding in the succession of cases most prominently exemplified by *Griswold v. Connecticut*, see *Roe*, 410 U.S, at 152–53. When it is so seen, *Roe* is clearly in no jeopardy, since subsequent constitutional developments have neither disturbed, nor do they threaten to diminish, the scope of recognized protection accorded to the liberty relating to intimate relationships, the family, and decisions about whether or not to beget or bear a child.

Roe, however, may be seen not only as an exemplar of *Griswold* liberty but as a rule (whether or not mistaken) of personal autonomy and bodily integrity, with doctrinal affinity to cases recognizing limits on governmental power to mandate medical treatment or to bar its rejection. If so, our cases since *Roe* accord with *Roe*'s view that a State's interest in the protection of life falls short of justifying any plenary override of individual liberty claims. *Cruzan v. Director, Missouri Dept. of Health*, 497 U.S. 261, 278 (1990); Cf., *e.g.*, *Riggins v. Nevada*, 504 U.S. ——, —— (1992); *Washington v. Harper*, 494 U.S. 210 (1990); see also, *e.g.*, *Rochin v. California*, 342 U.S. 165 (1952); *Jacobson v. Massachusetts*, 197 U.S. 11, 24–30 (1905).

Finally, one could classify *Roe* as *sui generis*. If the case is so viewed, then there clearly has been no erosion of its central determination. The original holding resting on the concurrence of seven Members of the Court in 1973 was expressly affirmed by a majority of six in 1983, see *Akron v. Akron Center for Reproductive Health, Inc.*, 462 U.S. 416 (1983) (*Akron I*), and by a majority of five in 1986, see *Thornburgh v. American College of Obstetricians and Gynecologists*, expressing adherence to the constitutional ruling despite legislative efforts in some States to test its limits. More recently, in *Webster v. Reproductive Health Services*, although two of the present authors questioned the trimester framework in a way consistent with our judgment today, see *id.*, at 518 (Rehnquist C. J., joined by White, and Kennedy, JJ.); *id.*, at 529 (O'Connor, J., concurring in part and concurring in judgment), a majority of the Court either decided to reaffirm or declined to address the constitutional validity of the central holding of *Roe*. See *Webster*, 492 U.S., at 521 (REHNQUIST, C. J., joined by WHITE and KENNEDY, JJ.); *id.*, at 525–26 (O'CONNOR, J., concurring in part and concurring in judgment); *id.*, at 537, 553 (BLACKMUN, J., joined by BRENNAN and MARSHALL, JJ., concurring in part and dissenting in part); *id.*, at 561–63 (STEVENS, J., concurring in part and dissenting in part).

Nor will courts building upon *Roe* be likely to hand down erroneous decisions as a consequence. Even on the assumption that the central holding of *Roe* was in error, that error would go only to the strength of the state interest in fetal protection, not to the recognition afforded by the Constitution to the woman's liberty.

The soundness of this prong of the *Roe* analysis is apparent from a consideration of the alternative. If indeed the woman's interest in deciding whether to bear and beget a child had not been recognized as in *Roe*, the State might as readily restrict a woman's right to choose to carry a pregnancy to term as to terminate it, to further asserted state interests in population control, or eugenics, for example. Yet *Roe* has been sensibly relied upon to counter any such suggestions. *E.g., Arnold v. Board of Education of Escambia County, Ala.*, 880 F.2d 305, 311 (11th Cir. 1989) (relying upon *Roe* and concluding that government officials violate the Constitution by coercing a minor to have an abortion); *Avery v. County of Burke*, 660 F.2d 111, 115 (4th Cir. 1981) ([condemning] county agency inducing teenage girl to undergo unwanted sterilization on the basis of misrepresentation that she had sickle cell trait); see also *In re Quinlan*, 70 N.J. 10, 355 A.2d 647, cert. denied *sub nom. Garger v. New Jersey*, 429 U.S. 922 (1976) (relying on *Roe* in finding a right to terminate medical treatment). In any event, because *Roe*'s scope is confined by the fact of its concern with postconcep-

tion potential life, a concern otherwise likely to be implicated only by some forms of contraception protected independently under *Griswold* and later cases, any error in *Roe* is unlikely to have serious ramifications in future cases.

4

We have seen how time has overtaken some of *Roe*'s factual assumptions: advances in maternal health care allow for abortions safe to the mother later in pregnancy than was true in 1973, see *Akron I*, at 429, n. 11, and advances in neonatal care have advanced viability to a point somewhat earlier. Compare *Roe*, 410 U.S., at 160, with *Webster*, at 515–16 (opinion of REHNQUIST, C.J.); see *Akron I*, at 457, and n.5 (O'CONNOR, J., dissenting). But these facts go only to the scheme of time limits on the realization of competing interests, and the divergences from the factual premises of 1973 have no bearing on the validity of *Roe*'s central holding, that viability marks the earliest point at which the State's interest in fetal life is constitutionally adequate to justify a legislative ban on nontherapeutic abortions. ... Whenever it may occur, the attainment of viability may continue to serve as the critical fact, just as it has done since *Roe* was decided....

5

The sum of the precedential inquiry to this point shows *Roe*'s underpinnings unweakened in any way affecting its central holding. While it has engendered disapproval, it has not been unworkable. An entire generation has come to age free to assume *Roe*'s concept of liberty in defining the capacity of women to act in society, and to make reproductive decisions; [nor have the other conditions that call for overruling been met.] ... Within the bounds of normal *stare decisis* analysis, then, and subject to the considerations on which it customarily turns, the stronger argument is for affirming *Roe*'s central holding, with whatever degree of personal reluctance any of us may have, not for overruling it.

B

In a less significant case, *stare decisis* analysis could, and would, stop at the point we have reached. But the sustained and widespread debate *Roe* has provoked calls for some comparison between that case and others of comparable dimension that have responded to national controversies and taken on the impress of the controversies addressed.

The first example is that line of cases identified with *Lochner v. New York*, 198 U.S. 45 (1905), which imposed substantive limitations on legislation limiting economic autonomy in favor of health and welfare regulation, adopting, in Justice Holmes' view, the theory of *laissez-faire*. *Id.*, at 75 (Holmes, J., dissenting). The *Lochner* decisions were exemplified by *Adkins v. Children's Hospital of D.C.*, 261 U.S. 525 (1923), in which this Court held it to be an infringement of constitutionally protected liberty of contract to require the employers of adult women to satisfy minimum wage standards. Fourteen years later, *West Coast Hotel Co. v. Parrish*, 300 U.S. 379 (1937), signalled the demise of *Lochner* by overruling *Adkins*. In the meantime, the Depression had come and, with it, the lesson that seemed unmistakable to most people by 1937, that the interpretation of contractual freedom protected in *Adkins* rested on fundamentally false factual assumptions about the capacity of a relatively unregulated market to satisfy minimal levels of human welfare. See *West Coast Hotel Co., supra*, at 399. . . . [T]he clear demonstration that the facts of economic life were different from those previously assumed warranted the repudiation of the old law.

The second comparison that 20th century history invites is with the cases employing the separate-but-equal rule for applying the Fourteenth Amendment's equal protection guarantee. They began with *Plessy v. Ferguson*, 163 U.S. 537 (1896), holding that legislatively mandated racial segregation in public transportation works no denial of equal protection, rejecting the argument that racial separation enforced by the legal machinery of American society treats the black race as inferior. The *Plessy* Court considered "the underlying fallacy of the plantiff's argument to consist in the assumption that the enforced separation of the two races stamps the colored race with a badge of inferiority. If this be so, it is not by reason of anything found in the act, but solely because the colored race chooses to put that construction upon it." *Id.*, at·551. Whether, as a matter of historical fact, the Justices in the *Plessy* majority believed this or not, see *id.*, at 557, 562 (Harlan, J., dissenting), this understanding of the implication of segregation was the stated justification for the Court's opinion. But this understanding of the facts and the rule it was stated to justify were repudiated in *Brown v. Board of Education*, 347 U.S. 483 (1954). . . .

The Court in *Brown* addressed these facts . . . by observing that whatever may have been the understanding in *Plessy*'s time of the power of segregation to stigmatize those who were segregated with a "badge of inferiority," it was clear by 1954 that legally sanctioned segregation had just such an effect, to the point that racially separate public educational facilities were deemed inherently unequal. 374 U.S., at 494–95. Society's understanding of the facts upon which a constitutional ruling was sought in 1954 was thus fundamentally different from the basis claimed for the decision in 1896. While we think *Plessy* was wrong the day it was decided, see *Plessy, supra,* at 552–64 (Harlan, J., dissenting), we must also recognize that the *Plessy* Court's explanation for its decision was so clearly at odds with the facts apparent to the Court in 1954 that the decision to reexamine *Plessy* was on this ground alone not only justified but required.

West Coast Hotel and *Brown* each rested on facts, or an understanding of facts, changed from those which furnished the claimed justifications for the earlier constitutional resolutions. ... As the decisions were thus comprehensible they were also defensible, not merely as the victories of one doctrinal school over another by dint of numbers (victories though they were), but as applications of constitutional principle to facts as they had not been seen by the Court before. In constitutional adjudication as elsewhere in life, changed circumstances may impose new obligations, and the thoughtful part of the Nation could accept each decision to overrule a prior case as a response to the Court's constitutional duty.

Because the case before us presents no such occasion it could be seen as no such response. Because neither the factual underpinnings of *Roe*'s central holding nor our understanding of it has changed (and because no other indication of weakened precedent has been shown) the Court could not pretend to be reexamining the prior law with any justification beyond a present doctrinal disposition to come out differently from the Court of 1973. To overrule prior law for no other reason than that would run counter to the view repeated in our cases, that a decision to overrule should rest on some special reason over and above the belief that a prior case was wrongly decided. See, *e.g., Mitchell v. W. T. Grant,* 416 U.S. 600, 636 (1974) (Stewart, J., dissenting) ("A basic change in the law

upon a ground no firmer than a change in our membership invites the popular misconception that this institution is little different from the two political branches of the Government. ...")

C

... [O]verruling *Roe*'s central holding would not only reach an unjustifiable result under principles of *stare decisis,* but would seriously weaken the Court's capacity to exercise the judicial power and to function as the Supreme Court of a Nation dedicated to the rule of law. To understand why this would be so it is necessary to understand the source of this Court's authority, the conditions necessary for its preservation, and its relationship to the country's understanding of itself as a constitutional Republic.

... The Court's power lies ... in its legitimacy, a product of substance and perception that shows itself in the people's acceptance of the Judiciary as fit to determine what the Nation's law means and to declare what it demands.

The underlying substance of this legitimacy is of course the warrant for the Court's decisions in the Constitution and the lesser sources of legal principle on which the Court draws. That substance is expressed in the Court's opinions, and our contemporary understanding is such that a decision without principled justification would be no judicial act at all. But even when justification is furnished by apposite legal principle, something more is required. ... The Court must take care to speak and act in ways that allow people to accept its decisions on the terms the Court claims for them, as grounded truly in principle, not as compromises with social and political pressures having, as such, no bearing on the principled choices that the Court is obliged to make. Thus, the Court's legitimacy depends on making legally principled decisions under circumstances in which their principled character is sufficiently plausible to be accepted by the Nation.

The need for principled action to be perceived as such is implicated to some degree whenever this, or any other appellate court, overrules a prior case. This is not to say, of course, that this Court cannot give a perfectly satisfactory explanation in most cases. . . .

In two circumstances, however, the Court would almost certainly fail to receive the benefit of the doubt in overruling prior cases. There is, first, a point beyond which frequent overruling would overtax the country's belief in the Court's good faith. Despite the variety of reasons that may inform and justify a decision to overrule, we cannot forget that such a decision is usually perceived (and perceived correctly) as, at the least, a statement that a prior decision was wrong. There is a limit to the amount of error that can plausibly be imputed to prior courts. If that limit should be exceeded, disturbance of prior rulings would be taken as evidence that justifiable reexamination of principle had given way to drives for particular results in the short term. The legitimacy of the Court would fade with the frequency of its vacillation.

That first circumstance can be described as hypothetical; the second is to the point here and now. Where, in the performance of its judicial duties, the Court decides a case in such a way as to resolve the sort of intensely divisive controversy reflected in *Roe* and those rare, comparable cases, its decision has a dimension that the resolution of the normal case does not carry. It is the dimension present whenever the Court's interpretation of the Constitution calls the contending sides of a national controversy to end their national division by accepting a common mandate rooted in the Constitution.

The Court is not asked to do this very often, having thus addressed the Nation only twice in our lifetime, in the decisions of *Brown* and *Roe*. But when the Court does act in this way, its decision requires an equally rare precedential force to counter the inevitable efforts to overturn it and to thwart its implementation. Some of those efforts may be mere unprincipled emotional reactions; others may proceed from principles worthy of profound respect. But whatever the premises of opposition may be, only the most convincing justification under accepted standards of precedent could suffice to demonstrate that a later decision overruling the first was anything but a surrender to political pressure, and an unjustified repudiation of the principle on which the Court staked its authority in the first instance. So to overrule under fire in the absence of the most compelling reason to reexamine a watershed decision would subvert the Court's legitimacy beyond any serious question. Cf. *Brown v. Board of Education, 349 U.S. 294, 300 (1955)* (*Brown II*) ("[I]t should go without saying that the vitality of th[e] constitutional principles [announced in *Brown v. Board of Education, 347 U.S. 483 (1954)*,] cannot be allowed to yield simply because of disagreement with them").

The country's loss of confidence in the judiciary would be underscored by an equally certain and equally reasonable condemnation for another failing in overruling unnecessarily and under pressure. Some cost will be paid by anyone who approves or implements a constitutional decision where it is unpopular. . . . The price may be criticism or ostracism, or it may be violence. An extra price will be paid by those who themselves disapprove of the decision's results when viewed outside of constitutional terms, but who nevertheless struggle to accept it, because they respect the rule of law. To all those who will be so tested by following, the Court implicitly undertakes to remain steadfast, lest in the end a price be paid for nothing. The promise of constancy, once given, binds its maker for as long as the power to stand by the decision survives and the understanding of the issue has not changed so fundamentally as to render the commitment obsolete. From the obligation of this promise this Court cannot and should not assume any exemption when duty requires it to decide a case in conformance with the Constitution. A willing breach of it would be nothing less than a breach of faith, and no Court that broke its faith with the people could sensibly expect credit for principle in the decision by which it did that.

. . . If the Court's legitimacy should be undermined. then, so would the country be in its very ability to see itself through its constitutional ideals. The Court's concern with legitimacy is not for the sake of the Court but for the sake of the Nation to which it is responsible.

. . . A decision to overrule *Roe's* essential holding under the existing circumstances would address error, if error there was, at the cost of both profound and unnecessary damage to the Court's legitimacy, and to the Nation's commitment to the rule of law. It is therefore imperative to adhere to the essence of *Roe's* original decision, and we do so today.

IV

From what we have said so far it follows that it is a constitutional liberty of the woman to have some freedom to terminate her pregnancy. We conclude that the basic decision in *Roe* was based on a constitutional analysis which we cannot now repudiate. The woman's liberty is not so unlimited, however, that from the outset the State cannot show its concern for the life of the unborn, and at a later point in fetal development the State's interest in life

has sufficient force so that the right of the woman to terminate the pregnancy can be restricted.

That brings us, of course, to the point where much criticism has been directed at *Roe*, a criticism that always inheres when the Court draws a specific rule from what in the Constitution is but a general standard. We conclude, however, that the urgent claims of the woman to retain the ultimate control over her destiny and her body, claims implicit in the meaning of liberty, require us to perform that function. Liberty must not be extinguished for want of a line that is clear. And it falls to us to give some real substance to the woman's liberty to determine whether to carry her pregnancy to full term.

We conclude the line should be drawn at viability, so that before that time the woman has a right to choose to terminate her pregnancy. We adhere to this principle for two reasons. First, as we have said, is the doctrine of *stare decisis*. Any judicial act of line-drawing may seem somewhat arbitrary, but *Roe* was a reasoned statement, elaborated with great care. We have twice reaffirmed it in the face of great opposition. See *Thornburgh v. American College of Obstetricians & Gynecologists*, 476 U.S., at 759; *Akron I*, 462 U.S., at 419–20. Although we must overrule those parts of *Thornburgh* and *Akron I* which, in our view, are inconsistent with *Roe's* statement that the State has a legitimate interest in promoting the life or potential life of the unborn the central premise of those cases represents an unbroken commitment by this Court to the essential holding of *Roe*. It is that premise which we reaffirm today.

The second reason is that the concept of viability, as we noted in *Roe*, is the time at which there is a realistic possibility of maintaining and nourishing a life outside the womb, so that the independent existence of the second life can in reason and all fairness be the object of state protection that now overrides the rights of the woman. See *Roe v. Wade*, 410 U.S., at 163. Consistent with other constitutional norms, legislatures may draw lines which appear arbitrary without the necessity of offering a justification. But courts may not. We must justify the lines we draw. And there is no line other than viability which is more workable. To be sure, as we have said, there may be some medical developments that affect the precise point of viability, but this is an imprecision within tolerable limits given that the medical community and all those who must apply its discoveries will continue to explore the matter. The viability line also has, as a practical matter, an element of fairness. In some broad sense it might be said that a woman who fails to act before viability has consented to the State's intervention on behalf of the developing child.

The woman's right to terminate her pregnancy before viability is the most central principle of *Roe v. Wade*. It is a rule of law and a component of liberty we cannot renounce.

On the other side of the equation is the interest of the State in the protection of potential life. The *Roe* Court recognized the State's "important and legitimate interest in protecting the potentiality of human life." *Roe, supra,* at 162. The weight to be given this state interest, not the strength of the woman's interest, was the difficult question faced in *Roe*. We do not need to say whether each of us, had we been Members of the Court when the valuation of the State interest came before it as an original matter, would have concluded, as the *Roe* Court did, that its weight is insufficient to justify a ban on abortions prior to viability even when it is subject to certain exceptions. The matter is not before us in the first instance, and coming as it does after nearly 20 years of litigation in *Roe's* wake we are

satisfied that the immediate question is not the soundness of *Roe's* resolution of the issue, but the precedential force that must be accorded to its holding. And we have concluded that the essential holding of *Roe* should be reaffirmed.

Yet it must be remembered that *Roe v. Wade* speaks with clarity in establishing not only the woman's liberty but also the State's "important and legitimate interest in potential life." *Roe,* at 163. That portion of the decision in *Roe* has been given too little acknowledgement and implementation by the Court in its subsequent cases. Those cases decided that any regulation touching upon the abortion decision must survive strict scrutiny, to be sustained only if drawn in narrow terms to further a compelling state interest. See, *e.g., Akron I,* at 427. Not all of the cases decided under that formulation can be reconciled with the holding in *Roe* itself that the State has legitimate interests in the health of the woman and in protecting the potential life within her. In resolving this tension, we choose to rely upon *Roe,* as against the later cases.

Roe established a trimester framework to govern abortion regulations. Under this elaborate but rigid construct, almost no regulation at all is permitted during the first trimester of pregnancy; regulations designed to protect the woman's health, but not to further the State's interest in potential life, are permitted during the second trimester; and during the third trimester, when the fetus is viable, prohibitions are permitted provided the life or health of the mother is not at stake. *Roe v. Wade,* at 163–66. Most of our cases since *Roe* have involved the application of rules derived from the trimester framework. See, *e.g., Thornburgh v. American College of Obstetricians and Gynecologists; Akron I.*

. . . We do not agree, however, that the trimester approach is necessary.

Though the woman has a right to choose to terminate or continue her pregnancy before viability, it does not at all follow that the State is prohibited from taking steps to ensure that this choice is thoughtful and informed. Even in the earliest stages of pregnancy, the State may enact rules and regulations designed to encourage her to know that there are philosophic and social arguments of great weight that can be brought to bear in favor of continuing the pregnancy to full term and that there are procedures and institutions to allow adoption of unwanted children as well as a certain degree of state assistance if the mother chooses to raise the child herself. " '[T]he Constitution does not forbid a State or city, pursuant to democratic processes, from expressing a preference for normal childbirth.' " *Webster v. Reproductive Health Services*, 492 U.S., at 511 (opinion of the Court) (quoting *Poelker v. Doe*, 432 U.S. 519, 521 (1977)). It follows that States are free to enact laws to provide a reasonable framework for a woman to make a decision that has such profound and lasting meaning. This, too, we find consistent with *Roe's* central premises, and indeed the inevitable consequence of our holding that the State has an interest in protecting the life of the unborn.

We reject the trimester framework, which we do not consider to be part of the essential holding of *Roe*. See *Webster v. Reproductive Health Services*, at 518 (opinion of REHNQUIST, C.J.); *id.*, at 529 (O'CONNOR, J., concurring in part and concurring in judgment) (describing the trimester framework as "problematic"). Measures aimed at ensuring that a woman's choice contemplates the consequences for the fetus do not necessarily interfere with the right recognized in *Roe*, although those measures have been found to be inconsistent with the rigid trimester framework announced in that

case. A logical reading of the central holding in *Roe* itself, and a necessary reconciliation of the liberty of the woman and the interest of the State in promoting prenatal life, require, in our view, that we abandon the trimester framework as a rigid prohibition on all previability regulation aimed at the protection of fetal life. The trimester framework suffers from these basic flaws: in its formulation it misconceives the nature of the pregnant woman's interest; and in practice it undervalues the State's interest in potential life, as recognized in *Roe*.

As our jurisprudence relating to all liberties save perhaps abortion has recognized, not every law which makes a right more difficult to exercise is, *ipso facto*, an infringement of that right. An example clarifies the point. We have held that not every ballot access limitation amounts to an infringement of the right to vote. Rather, the States are granted substantial flexibility in establishing the framework within which voters choose the candidates for whom they wish to vote. *Anderson v. Celebrezze*, 460 U.S. 780, 788 (1983); *Norman v. Reed*, 502 U.S. —— (1992).

The abortion right is similar. Numerous forms of state regulation might have the incidental effect of increasing the cost or decreasing the availability of medial care, whether for abortion or any other medical procedure. The fact that a law which serves a valid purpose, one not designed to strike at the right itself, has the incidental effect of making it more difficult or more expensive to procure an abortion cannot be enough to invalidate it. Only where state regulation imposes an undue burden on a woman's ability to make this decision does the power of the State reach into the heart of the liberty protected by the Due Process Clause. See *Hodgson v. Minnesota*, 497 U.S. 417, 458–59 (1990) (O'CONNOR, J., concurring in part and concurring in judgment in part); *Ohio v. Akron Center for Reproductive Health,* 497 U.S. 502, —— (1990) (*Akron II*) (opinion of KENNEDY, J.) *Webster v. Reproductive Health Services,* at 530 (O'Connor, J., concurring in part and concurring in judgment); *Thornburgh v. American College of Obstetricians and Gynecologists,* 476 U.S., at 828 (O'CONNOR, J., dissenting); *Simopoulos v. Virginia,* 462 U.S. 506, 520 (1983) (O'CONNOR, J., concurring in part and concurring in judgment); *Planned Parenthood Assn. of Kansas City v. Ashcroft,* 462 U.S. 476, 505 (1983) (O'CONNOR, J., concurring in judgment in part and dissenting in part); *Akron I,* 462 U.S., at 464 (O'CONNOR, J., joined by WHITE and REHNQUIST, JJ., dissenting); *Bellotti v. Baird,* 428 U.S. 132, 147 (1976) (*Bellotti I*).

For the most part, the Court's early abortion cases adhered to this view. In *Maher v. Roe,* 432 U.S. 464, 473–74 (1977), the Court explained: "*Roe* did not declare an unqualified 'constitutional right to an abortion,' as the District Court seemed to think. Rather, the right protects the woman from unduly burdensome interference with her freedom to decide whether to terminate her pregnancy." See also *Doe v. Bolton,* 410 U.S. 179, 198 (1973) ("[T]he interposition of the hospital abortion committee is unduly restrictive of the patient's rights"); *Bellotti I, supra,* at 147 (State may not "impose undue burdens upon a minor capable of giving an informed consent"); *Harris v. McRae,* 448 U.S. 297, 314 (1980)

... [D]espite the protestations contained in the original *Roe* opinion to the effect that the Court was not recognizing an absolute right, 410 U.S., at 154–55, the Court's experience applying the trimester framework has led to the striking down of some abortion regulations which in no real sense deprived women of the ultimate decision. Those decisions went too far because the right recognized by *Roe* is a right "to be free from unwarranted governmental intrusion into matters so fundamentally

affecting a person as the decision whether to bear or beget a child." *Eisenstadt v. Baird,* 405 U.S., at 453. Not all governmental intrusion is of necessity unwarranted; and that brings us to the other basic flaw in the trimester framework: even in *Roe's* terms, in practice it undervalues the State's interest in the potential life within the woman.

... Before viability, *Roe* and subsequent cases treat all governmental attempts to influence a woman's decision on behalf of the potential life within her as unwarranted. This treatment is, in our judgment, incompatible with the recognition that there is a substantial state interest in potential life throughout pregnancy. Cf. *Webster,* 492 U.S., at 519 (opinion of REHNQUIST, C.J.); *Akron I,* at 461 (O'CONNOR, J., dissenting).

The very notion that the State has a substantial interest in potential life leads to the conclusion that not all regulations must be deemed unwarranted. Not all burdens on the right to decide whether to terminate a pregnancy will be undue. In our view, the undue burden standard is the appropriate means of reconciling the State's interest with the woman's constitutionally protected liberty.

The concept of an undue burden has been utilized by the Court as well as individual members of the Court, including two of us, in ways that could be considered inconsistent. See, *e.g., Hodgson v. Minnesota,* 497 U.S., at —— (O'CONNOR, J., concurring in part and concurring in judgment); *Akron II,* 497 U.S., at——(opinion of KENNEDY, J.); *Thornburgh v. American College of Obstetricians and Gynecologists,* 476 U.S., at 828–29 (O'CONNOR, J., dissenting); *Akron I,* at 461–66 (O'CONNOR, J., dissenting); *Harris v. McRae,* at 314; *Maher v. Roe,* at 473; *Beal v. Doe,* 432 U.S. 438, 446 (1977); *Bellotti I,* at 147. Because we set forth a standard of general application to which we intend to adhere, it is important to clarify what is meant by an undue burden.

A finding of an undue burden is a shorthand for the conclusion that a state regulation has the purpose or effect of placing a substantial obstacle in the path of a woman seeking an abortion of a nonviable fetus. A statute with this purpose is invalid because the means chosen by the State to further the interest in potential life must be calculated to inform the woman's free choice, not hinder it. And a statute which, while furthering the interest in potential life or some other valid state interest, has the effect of placing a substantial obstacle in the path of a woman's choice cannot be considered a permissible means of serving its legitimate ends. To the extent that the opinions of the Court or of individual Justices use the undue burden standard in a manner that is inconsistent with this analysis, we set out what in our view should be the controlling standard. . . . In our considered judgment, an undue burden is an unconstitutional burden. See *Akron II, supra*, at —— (opinion of KENNEDY, J.). Understood another way, we answer the question, left open in previous opinions discussing the undue burden formulation, whether a law designed to further the State's interest in fetal life which imposes an undue burden on the woman's decision before fetal viability could be constitutional. See, *e.g., Akron I*, at 462–63 (O'CONNOR, J., dissenting). The answer is no. . . . Regulations which do no more than create a structural mechanism by which the State, or the parent or guardian of a minor, may express profound respect for the life of the unborn are permitted, if they are not a substantial obstacle to the woman's exercise of the right to choose. Unless it has that effect on her right of choice, a state measure designed to persuade her to choose childbirth over abortion will be upheld if reasonably related to that goal. Regulations designed to foster the health of a woman seeking an abortion

are valid if they do not constitute an undue burden.

Even when jurists reason from shared premises, some disagreement is inevitable. Compare *Hodgson*, 497 U.S., at —— (opinion of KENNEDY, J.) with *id.*, at —— (O'CONNOR, J., concurring in part and concurring in judgment in part). That is to be expected in the application of any legal standard which must accommodate life's complexity. We do not expect it to be otherwise with respect to the undue burden standard. We give this summary:

(a) To protect the central right recognized by *Roe v. Wade* while at the same time accommodating the State's profound interest in potential life, we will employ the undue burden analysis as explained in this opinion. An undue burden exists, and therefore a provision of law is invalid, if its purpose or effect is to place a substantial obstacle in the path of a woman seeking an abortion before the fetus attains viability.

(b) We reject the rigid trimester framework of *Roe v. Wade*. To promote the State's profound interest in potential life, throughout pregnancy the State may take measures to ensure that the woman's choice is informed, and measures designed to advance this interest will not be invalidated as long as their purpose is to persuade the woman to choose childbirth over abortion. These measures must not be an undue burden on the right.

(c) As with any medical procedure, the State may enact regulations to further the health or safety of a woman seeking an abortion. Unnecessary health regulations that have the purpose or effect of presenting a substantial obstacle to a woman seeking an abortion impose an undue burden on the right.

(d) Our adoption of the undue burden analysis does not disturb the central holding of *Roe v. Wade*, and we reaffirm that holding. Regardless of whether exceptions are made for particular circumstances, a State may not prohibit any woman from making the ultimate decision to terminate her pregnancy before viability.

(e) We also reaffirm *Roe's* holding that "subsequent to viability, the State in promoting its interest in the potentiality of human life may, if it chooses, regulate, and even proscribe, abortion except where it is necessary, in appropriate medical judgment, for the preservation of the life or health of the mother." *Roe v. Wade,* 410 U.S., at 164–65.

These principles control our assessment of the Pennsylvania statute, and we now turn to the issue of the validity of its challenged provisions.

V

The Court of Appeals applied what it believed to be the undue burden standard and upheld each of the provisions except for the husband notification requirement. We agree generally with this conclusion, but refine the undue burden analysis in accordance with the principles articulated above. We now consider the separate statutory sections at issue.

A

[We follow the Circuit Court in construing the statutory definition of "medical emergency" so that it is constitutional.]

B

We next consider the informed consent requirement. 18 Pa. Cons. Stat. Ann. § 3205. . . .

Our prior decisions establish that as with any medical procedure, the State may require a woman to give her written informed consent to an abortion. See *Planned Parenthood of Central Mo. v. Danforth,* 428 U.S., at 67. In this respect, the statute is unexceptional. Petitioners challenge the statute's definition of informed consent be-

cause it includes the provision of specific information by the doctor and the mandatory 24-hour waiting period. The conclusions reached by a majority of the Justices in the separate opinions filed today and the undue burden standard adopted in this opinion require us to overrule in part some of the Court's past decisions, decisions driven by the trimester framework's prohibition of all previability regulations designed to further the State's interest in fetal life.

In *Akron I,* 462 U.S. 416 (1983), we invalidated an ordinance which required that a woman seeking an abortion be provided by her physician with specific information "designed to influence the woman's informed choice between abortion or childbirth." *Id.,* at 444. As we later described the *Akron I* holding in *Thornburgh v. American College of Obstetricians and Gynecologists,* 476 U.S., at 762, there were two purported flaws in the Akron ordinance: the information was designed to dissuade the woman from having an abortion and the ordinance imposed "a rigid requirement that a specific body of information be given in all cases, irrespective of the particular needs of the patient. . . ." *Ibid.*

To the extent *Akron I* and *Thornburgh* find a constitutional violation when the government requires, as it does here, the giving of truthful, nonmisleading information about the nature of the procedure, the attendant health risks and those of childbirth, and the "probable gestational age" of the fetus, those cases go too far, are inconsistent with *Roe's* acknowledgment of an important interest in potential life, and are overruled. This is clear even on the very terms of *Akron I* and *Thornburgh.* Those decisions, along with *Danforth,* recognize a substantial government interest justifying a requirement that a woman be apprised of the health risks of abortion and childbirth. . . . In attempting to ensure that a woman apprehend the full consequences of her decision, the State furthers the legitimate purpose of reducing the risk that a woman may elect an abortion, only to discover later, with devastating psychological consequences, that her decision was not fully informed. If the information the State requires to be made available to the woman is truthful and not misleading, the requirement may be permissible.

We also see no reason why the State may not require doctors to inform a woman seeking an abortion of the availability of materials relating to the consequences to the fetus, even when those consequences have no direct relation to her health. An example illustrates the point. We would think it constitutional for the State to require that in order for there to be informed consent to a kidney transplant operation the recipient must be supplied with information about risks to the donor as well as risks to himself or herself. . . . We conclude, however, that informed choice need not be defined in such narrow terms that all considerations of the effect on the fetus are made irrelevant. . . . [W]e depart from the holdings of *Akron I* and *Thornburgh* to the extent that we permit a State to further its legitimate goal of protecting the life of the unborn by enacting legislation aimed at ensuring a decision that is mature and informed, even when in so doing the State expresses a preference for childbirth over abortion. In short, requiring that the woman be informed of the availability of information relating to fetal development and the assistance available should she decide to carry the pregnancy to full term is a reasonable measure to insure an informed choice, one which might cause the woman to choose childbirth over abortion. This requirement cannot be considered a substantial obstacle to obtaining an abortion, and, it follows, there is no undue burden.

Our prior cases also suggest that the "straitjacket," *Thornburgh*, at 762 (quoting *Danforth*, at 67, n. 8), of particular information which must be given in each case interferes with a constitutional right of privacy between a pregnant woman and her physician. As a preliminary matter, it is worth noting that the statute now before us does not require a physician to comply with the informed consent provisions "if he or she can demonstrate by a preponderance of the evidence, that he or she reasonably believed that furnishing the information would have resulted in a severely adverse effect on the physical or mental health of the patient." 18 Pa. Cons. Stat. § 3205 (1990). In this respect, the statute does not prevent the physician from exercising his or her medical judgment.

. . . [A] requirement that a doctor give a woman certain information as part of obtaining her consent to an abortion is, for constitutional purposes, no different from a requirement that a doctor give certain specific information about any medical procedure.

. . . [T]he practice of medicine [is] subject to reasonable licensing and regulation by the State. Cf. *Whalen v. Roe*, 429 U.S. 589, 603 (1977). We see no constitutional infirmity in the requirement that the physician provide the information mandated by the State here.

The Pennsylvania statute also requires us to reconsider the holding in *Akron I* that the State may not require that a physician, as opposed to a qualified assistant, provide information relevant to a woman's informed consent. 462 U.S., at 448. Since there is no evidence on this record that requiring a doctor to give the information as provided by the statute would amount in practical terms to a substantial obstacle to a woman seeking an abortion, we conclude that it is not an undue burden. Our cases reflect the fact that the Constitution gives the States broad latitude to decide that particular functions may be performed only by licensed professionals, even if an objective assessment might suggest that those same tasks could be performed by others. See *Williamson v. Lee Optical of Oklahoma, Inc.*, 348 U.S. 483 (1955). Thus, we uphold the provision. . . .

Our analysis of Pennsylvania's 24-hour waiting period between the provision of the information deemed necessary to informed consent and the performance of an abortion under the undue burden standard requires us to reconsider the premise behind the decision in *Akron I* invalidating a parallel requirement. In *Akron I* we said: "Nor are we convinced that the State's legitimate concern that the woman's decision be informed is reasonably served by requiring a 24-hour delay as a matter of course." 462 U.S., at 450. We consider that conclusion to be wrong. The idea that important decisions will be more informed and deliberate if they follow some period of reflection does not strike us as unreasonable, particularly where the statute directs that important information become part of the background of the decision. The statute, as construed by the Court of Appeals, permits avoidance of the waiting period in the event of a medical emergency and the record evidence shows that in the vast majority of cases, a 24-hour delay does not create any appreciable health risk. In theory, at least, the waiting period is a reasonable measure to implement the State's interest in protecting the life of the unborn, a measure that does not amount to an undue burden.

Whether the mandatory 24-hour waiting period is nonetheless invalid because in practice it is a substantial obstacle to a woman's choice to terminate her pregnancy is a closer question. The findings of fact by the District Court indicate that because of the distances many women must travel to reach an abortion provider, the practical effect will often be a delay of much more than a day because the waiting period requires that a woman seeking an abortion make at least two visits to the doctor. The District Court also found that in many instances this will increase the exposure of women seeking abortions to "the harassment and hostility of anti-abortion protestors demonstrating outside a clinic." 744 F. Supp., at 1351. . . .

These findings are troubling in some respects, but they do not demonstrate that the waiting period constitutes an undue burden. We do not doubt that, as the District Court held, the waiting period has the effect of "increasing the cost and risk of delay of abortions," *id.*, at 1378, but . . . we cannot say that the waiting period imposes a real health risk.

We also disagree with the District Court's conclusion that the "particularly burdensome" effects of the waiting period on some women require its invalidation. A particular burden is not of necessity a substantial obstacle. Whether a burden falls on a particular group is a distinct inquiry from whether it is a substantial obstacle even as to the women in that group. And the District Court did not conclude that the waiting period is such an obstacle even for the women who are most burdened by it. Hence, on the record before us, and in the context of this facial challenge, we are not convinced that the 24-hour waiting period constitutes an undue burden.

. . . [T]he right protected by *Roe* is a right to decide to terminate a pregnancy free of undue interference by the State. Because the informed consent requirement facilitates the wise exercise of that right it cannot be classified as an interference with the right *Roe* protects. The informed consent requirement is not an undue burden on that right.

C

Section 3209 of Pennsylvania's abortion law provides, except in cases of medical emergency, that no physician shall perform an abortion on a married woman without receiving a signed statement from the woman that she has notified her spouse that she is about to undergo an abortion [or that she fits into one of the statute's exceptions.] . . .

The District Court heard the testimony of numerous expert witnesses, and made detailed findings of fact regarding the effect of this statute. These included:

273. The vast majority of women consult their husbands prior to deciding to terminate their pregnancy. . . .

. . .

279. The "bodily injury" exception could not be invoked by a married woman whose husband, if notified, would, in her reasonable belief, threaten to (a) publicize her intent to have an abortion to family, friends or acquaintances; (b) retaliate against her in future child custody or divorce proceedings; (c) inflict psychological intimidation or emotional harm upon her, her children or other persons; (d) inflict bodily harm on other persons such as children, family members or other loved ones; or (e) use his control over finances to deprive of necessary monies for herself or her children. . . .

. . .

281. Studies reveal that family violence occurs in two million families in the United States. This figure, however, is a conservative one that substantially understates (because battering is usually not reported until it reaches life-threatening proportions) the actual number of families affected by domestic violence. In fact, researchers estimate that one of every two women will be battered at some time in their life. . . .

282. A wife may not elect to notify her husband of her intention to have an abortion for a variety of reasons, including the husband's illness, concern about her own health, the imminent failure of the marriage, or the husband's absolute opposition to the abortion. . . .

. . .

288. In a domestic abuse situation, it is common for the battering husband to also abuse the children in an attempt to coerce the wife. . . .

289. Mere notification of pregnancy is frequently a flashpoint for battering and violence within the family. The number of battering incidents is high during pregnancy. . . .

290. Secrecy typically shrouds abusive families. Family members are instructed not to tell anyone, especially police or doctors, about the abuse and violence. Battering husbands often threaten their wives or her children with further abuse if she tells an outsider of the violence and tells her that nobody will believe her. A battered woman, therefore, is highly unlikely to disclose the violence against her for fear of retaliation by the abuser. . . . 744 F. Supp., at 1360–62.

These findings are supported by studies of domestic violence. . . . According to the AMA, "[r]esearchers on family violence agree that the true incidence of partner

violence is probably ... four million severely assaulted women per year. Studies
suggest that from one-fifth to one-third of
all women will be physically assaulted by a
partner or ex-partner during their lifetime." AMA Council on Scientific Affairs,
Violence Against Women 7 (1991). Thus on an
average day in the United States, nearly
11,000 women are severely assaulted by
their male partners.

Other studies fill in the rest of this
troubling picture. Physical violence is only
the most visible form of abuse. Psychological abuse, particularly forced social and
economic isolation of women, is also
common. L. Walker, *The Battered Woman
Syndrome* 27–28 (1984). ... Thirty percent
of female homicide victims are killed by
their male partners. *Domestic Violence:
Terrorism in the Home. Hearing before the
Subcommittee on Children, Family, Drugs and
Alcoholism of the Senate Committee on Labor
and Human Resources,* 101st Cong., 2d
Sess., 3 (1990).

This information and the District
Court's findings reinforce what common
sense would suggest. In well-functioning
marriages, spouses discuss important intimate decisions such as whether to bear a
child. But there are millions of women in
this country who are the victims of regular
physical and psychological abuse at the
hands of their husbands. Should these
women become pregnant, they may have
very good reasons for not wishing to inform their husbands of their decision to
obtain an abortion. ... Many may have a
reasonable fear that notifying their husbands will provoke further instances of
child abuse; these women are not exempt
from § 3209's notification requirement.
Many may fear devastating forms of psychological abuse from their husbands,
including verbal harassment, threats of future violence, the destruction of posses-
sions, physical confinement to the home,

the withdrawal of financial support, or the
disclosure of the abortion to family and
friends. These methods of psychological
abuse may act as even more of a deterrent
to notification than the possibility of physical violence, but women who are the victims of the abuse are not exempt from
§ 3209's notification requirement. And
many women who are pregnant as a result
of sexual assaults by their husbands will be
unable to avail themselves of the exception
for spousal sexual assault, § 3209(b)(3), because the exception requires that the
woman have notified law enforcement authorities within 90 days of the assault, and
her husband will be notified of her report
once an investigation begins. § 3128(c). ...

The spousal notification requirement is
thus likely to prevent a significant number
of women from obtaining an abortion. It
does not merely make abortions a little
more difficult or expensive to obtain; for
many women, it will impose a substantial
obstacle. We must not blind ourselves to
the fact that the significant number of
women who fear for their safety and the
safety of their children are likely to be
deterred from procuring an abortion as
surely as if the Commonwealth had outlawed abortion in all cases.

... Respondents argue that since some
of these women will be able to notify their
husbands without adverse consequences or
will qualify for one of the exceptions, the
statute affects fewer than one percent of
women seeking abortions. For this reason,
it is asserted, the statute cannot be invalid
on its face. We disagree. ...

The analysis does not end with the one
percent of women upon whom the statute
operates; it begins there. ... The proper
focus of constitutional inquiry is the group
whom the law is a restriction, not the
group for whom the law is irrelevant. ...
[The target of section 3209] is married
women seeking abortions who do not wish

to notify their husbands of their intentions and who do not qualify for one of the statutory exceptions to the notice requirement. The unfortunate yet persisting conditions we document above will mean that in a large fraction of the cases in which § 3209 is relevant, it will operate as a substantial obstacle to a woman's choice to undergo an abortion. It is an undue burden, and therefore invalid.

This conclusion is in no way inconsistent with our decisions upholding parental notification or consent requirements. See, e.g., *Akron II*, 497 U.S., at ——; *Bellotti v. Baird*, 443 U.S. 622 (1979) (*Bellotti II*); *Planned Parenthood of Central Mo. v. Danforth*, 428 U.S., at 74. Those enactments, and our judgment that they are constitutional, are based on the quite reasonable assumption that minors will benefit from consultation with their parents and that children will often not realize that their parents have their best interests at heart. We cannot adopt a parallel assumption about adult women.

We recognize that a husband has a "deep and proper concern and interest . . . in his wife's pregnancy and in the growth and development of the fetus she is carrying." *Danforth, supra*, at 69. With regard to the children he has fathered and raised, the Court has recognized his "cognizable and substantial" interest in their custody. *Stanley v. Illinois*, 405 U.S. 645, 651–52 (1972); see also *Quilloin v. Walcott*, 434 U.S. 246 (1978); *Caban v. Mohammed*, 441 U.S. 380 (1979); *Lehr v. Robertson*, 463 U.S. 248 (1983). If this case concerned a State's ability to require the mother to notify the father before taking some action with respect to a living child raised by both, therefore, it would be reasonable to conclude as a general matter that the father's interest in the welfare of the child and the mother's interest are equal.

Before birth, however, the issue takes on a very different cast. It is an inescapable biological fact that state regulation with respect to the child a woman is carrying will have a far greater impact on the mother's liberty than on the father's. The effect of state regulation on a woman's protected liberty is doubly deserving of scrutiny in such a case, as the State has touched not only upon the private sphere of the family but upon the very bodily integrity of the pregnant woman. Cf. *Cruzan v. Director, Missouri Dept. of Health*, 497 U.S., at 281. The Court has held that "when the wife and the husband disagree on this decision, the view of only one of the two marriage partners can prevail. Inasmuch as it is the woman who physically bears the child and who is the more directly and immediately affected by the pregnancy, as between the two, the balance weighs in her favor." *Danforth, supra*, at 71. This conclusion rests upon the basic nature of marriage and the nature of our Constitution: "[T]he marital couple is not an independent entity with a mind and heart of its own, but an association of two individuals each with a separate intellectual and emotional makeup. If the right of privacy means anything, it is the right of the *individual*, married or single, to be free from unwarranted governmental intrusion into matters so fundamentally affecting a person as the decision whether to bear or beget a child." *Eisenstadt v. Baird*, 405 U.S., at 453 (emphasis in original). . . .

There was a time, not so long ago, when a different understanding of the family and of the Constitution prevailed. . . . Only one generation has passed since this Court observed that "woman is still regarded as the center of home and family life," with attendant "special responsibilities" that precluded full and independent legal status under the Constitution. *Hoyt v. Florida*, 368 U.S. 57, 62 (1961). These views, of course, are no longer consistent with our understanding of the family, the individual, or the Constitution.

In keeping with our rejection of the common-law understanding of a woman's role within the family, the Court held in *Danforth* that the Constitution does not permit a State to require a married woman to obtain her husband's consent before undergoing an abortion. 428 U.S., at 69. The principles that guided the Court in *Danforth* should be our guides today. For the great many women who are victims of abuse inflicted by their husbands, or whose children are the victims of such abuse, a spousal notice requirement enables the husband to wield an effective veto over his wife's decision. . . .

. . . If a husband's interest in the potential life of the child outweighs a wife's liberty, the State could require a married woman to notify her husband before she uses a postfertilization contraceptive. Perhaps next in line would be a statute requiring pregnant married women to notify their husbands before engaging in conduct causing risks to the fetus. After all, if the husband's interest in the fetus' safety is a sufficient predicate for state regulation, the State could reasonably conclude that pregnant wives should notify their husbands before drinking alcohol or smoking. Perhaps married women should notify their husbands before using contraceptives or before undergoing any type of surgery that may have complications affecting the husband's interest in his wife's reproductive organs. And if a husband's interest justifies notice in any of these cases, one might reasonably argue that it justifies exactly what the *Danforth* Court held it did not justify—a requirement of the husband's consent as well. A State may not give to a man the kind of dominion over his wife that parents exercise over their children.

Section 3209 embodies a view of marriage . . . repugnant to our present understanding of marriage and of the nature of the rights secured by the Constitution. Women do not lose their constitutionally protected liberty when they marry. . . . Section 3209 is invalid.

D

[As to parental consent w]e have been over most of this ground before. Our cases establish, and we reaffirm today, that a State may require a minor seeking an abortion to obtain the consent of a parent or guardian, provided that there is an adequate judicial bypass procedure. See, *e.g.,* *Akron II,* 497 U.S., at ——; *Hodgson,* 497 U.S., at ——; *Akron I,* at 440; *Bellotti II,* at 643–44 (plurality opinion). Under these precedents, in our view, the one-parent consent requirement and judicial bypass procedure are constitutional. . . .

E

[Here appeared a summary of the reporting requirements.—Au.] In *Danforth,* 428 U.S., at 80, we held that recordkeeping and reporting provisions "that are reasonably directed to the preservation of maternal health and that properly respect a patient's confidentiality and privacy are permissible." We think that under this standard, all provisions at issue here except that relating to spousal notice are constitutional. Although they do not relate to the State's interest in informing the woman's choice, they do relate to health. The collection of information with respect to actual patients is a vital element of medical research, and so it cannot be said that the requirements serve no purpose other than to make abortions more difficult. Nor do we find that the requirements impose a substantial obstacle to a woman's choice. At most they might increase the cost of some abortions by a slight amount. While at some point increased cost could become a substantial obstacle, there is no such showing on the record before us. . . .

VI

Our Constitution is a covenant running from the first generation of Americans to us and then to future generations. It is a coherent succession. Each generation must learn anew that the Constitution's written terms embody ideas and aspirations that must survive more ages than one. We accept our responsibility not to retreat from interpreting the full meaning of the covenant in light of all of our precedents. We invoke it once again to define the freedom guaranteed by the Constitution's own promise, the promise of liberty.

. . .

The judgment [of the Circuit Court] is affirmed. . . .

JUSTICE STEVENS, concurring in part and dissenting in part.

The portions of the Court's opinion that I have joined are more important than those with which I disagree. I shall therefore first comment on significant areas of agreement, and then explain the limited character of my disagreement.

I

The Court is unquestionably correct in concluding that the doctrine of *stare decisis* has controlling significance in a case of this kind, notwithstanding an individual justice's concerns about the merits.[1] The cen-

tral holding of *Roe v. Wade,* has been a "part of our law" for almost two decades. *Planned Parenthood of Central Mo. v. Danforth,* 428 U.S. 52, 101 (1976) (STEVENS, J., concurring in part and dissenting in part). It was a natural sequel to the protection of individual liberty established in *Griswold v. Connecticut.* See also *Carey v. Population Services Int'l,* 431 U.S. 678, 687, 702 (1977) (WHITE, J., concurring in part and concurring in result). The societal costs of overruling *Roe* at this late date would be enormous. *Roe* is an integral part of a correct understanding of both the concept of liberty and the basic equality of men and women. . . .

I also accept what is implicit in the Court's analysis, namely, a reaffirmation of *Roe*'s explanation of *why* the State's obligation to protect the life or health of the mother must take precedence over any duty to the unborn. The Court in *Roe* carefully considered, and rejected, the State's argument "that the fetus is a 'person' within the language and meaning of the Fourteenth Amendment." 410 U.S., at 156. After analyzing the usage of "person" in the Constitution, the Court concluded that that word "has application only postnatally." *Id.,* at 157. Commenting on the contingent property interests of the unborn that are generally represented by guardians ad litem, the Court noted: "Perfection of the interests involved, again, has generally been contingent upon live birth. In short, the unborn have never been recognized in the law as persons in the whole sense." *Id.,* at 162. Accordingly, an abortion is not "the

---

1. It is sometimes useful to view the issue of *stare decisis* from a historical perspective. In the last nineteen years, fifteen Justices have confronted the basic issue presented in *Roe.* Of those, eleven have voted as the majority does

today: Chief Justice Burger, Justices Douglas, Brennan, Stewart, Marshall, and Powell, and JUSTICES BLACKMUN, O'CONNOR, KENNEDY, SOUTER, and myself. Only four—all of whom happen to be on the Court today—have reached the opposite conclusion.

termination of life entitled to Fourteenth Amendment protection." *Id.,* at 159. From this holding, there was no dissent, see *id.,* at 173; indeed, no member of the Court has ever questioned this fundamental proposition. Thus, as a matter of federal constitutional law, a developing organism that is not yet a "person" does not have what is sometimes described as a "right to life." This has been and, by the Court's holding today, remains a fundamental premise of our constitutional law governing reproductive autonomy.

II

My disagreement with the joint opinion begins with its understanding of the trimester framework established in *Roe.* Contrary to the suggestion of the joint opinion, it is not a "contradiction" to recognize that the State may have a legitimate interest in potential human life and, at the same time, to conclude that that interest does not justify the regulation of abortion before viability (although other interests, such as maternal health, may). The fact that the State's interest is legitimate does not tell us when, if ever, that interest outweighs the pregnant woman's interest in personal liberty. It is appropriate, therefore, to consider more carefully the nature of the interests at stake. . . .

Identifying the State's interests—which the States rarely articulate with any precision—makes clear that the interest in protecting potential life is not grounded in the Constitution. It is, instead, an indirect interest supported by both humanitarian and pragmatic concerns. Many of our citizens believe that any abortion reflects an unacceptable disrespect for potential human life and that the performance of more than a million abortions each year is intolerable; many find third-trimester abortions performed when the fetus is approaching personhood particularly offensive. The

State has a legitimate interest in minimizing such offense. The State may also have a broader interest in expanding the population, believing society would benefit from the services of additional productive citizens—or that the potential human lives might include the occasional Mozart or Curie. These are the kinds of concerns that comprise the State's interest in potential human life.

Weighing the State's interest in potential life and the woman's liberty interest, I agree with the joint opinion that the State may " 'expres[s] a preference for normal childbirth,' " that the State may take steps to ensure that a woman's choice "is thoughtful and informed," and that "States are free to enact laws to provide a reasonable framework for a woman to make a decision that has such profound and lasting meaning." Serious questions arise, however, when a State attempts to "persuade the woman to choose childbirth over abortion." Decisional autonomy must limit the State's power to inject into a woman's most personal deliberations its own views of what is best. The State may promote its preferences by funding childbirth, by creating and maintaining alternatives to abortion, and by espousing the virtues of family; but it must respect the individual's freedom to make such judgments.

In my opinion, the principles established in [a] long line of cases and the wisdom reflected in Justice Powell's opinion for the Court in *Akron* (and followed by the Court just six years ago in *Thornburgh*) should govern our decision today. Under these principles, §§ 3205(a)(2)(i)-(iii) of the Pennsylvania statute are unconstitutional. Those sections require a physician or counselor to provide the woman with a range of materials clearly designed to persuade her to choose not to undergo the abortion. While the State is free, pursuant to § 3208 of the Pennsylvania law, to produce and disseminate such material, the State may not inject such information into the woman's deliberations just as she is weighing such an important choice.

Under this same analysis, §§ 3205(a)(1)(i) and (iii) of the Pennsylvania statute are constitutional. Those sections, which require the physician to inform a woman of the nature and risks of the abortion procedure and the medical risks of carrying to term, are neutral requirements comparable to those imposed in other medical procedures. . . .

III

The 24-hour waiting period required by §§ 3205(a)(1)-(2) of the Pennsylvania statute raises even more serious concerns. . . .

. . . [I]t can . . . be argued that the 24-hour delay furthers the State's interest in ensuring that the woman's decision is informed and thoughtful. But there is no evidence that the mandated delay benefits women or that it is necessary to enable the physician to convey any relevant information to the patient. The mandatory delay thus appears to rest on outmoded and unacceptable assumptions about the decisionmaking capacity of women. While there are well-established and consistently maintained reasons for the State to view with skepticism the ability of minors to make decisions, see *Hodgson v. Minnesota*, 497 U.S. 417, 449 (1990), none of those reasons applies to an adult woman's decisionmaking ability. Just as we have left behind the belief that a woman must consult her husband before undertaking serious matters, so we must reject the notion that a woman is less capable of deciding matters of gravity. . . .

No person undertakes such a decision lightly—and States may not presume that a woman has failed to reflect adequately merely because her conclusion differs from the State's preference. . . .

IV

In my opinion, a correct application of the "undue burden" standard leads to the same conclusion concerning the constitutionality of these requirements. A state-imposed burden on the exercise of a constitutional right is measured both by its effects and by its character: A burden may be "undue" either because the burden is too severe or because it lacks a legitimate, rational justification.[6]

The counseling provisions are similarly infirm. Whenever government commands private citizens to speak or to listen, careful review of the justification for that command is particularly appropriate. In this case, the Pennsylvania statute directs that counselors provide women seeking abortions with information concerning alternatives to abortion, the availability of medical assistance benefits, and the possibility of child-support payments. §§ 3205(a)(2)(i)-(iii). The statute requires that this information be given to *all* women seeking abortions, including those for whom such information is clearly useless, such as those who are married, those who have undergone the procedure in the past and are fully aware of the options, and

6. The meaning of any legal standard can only be understood by reviewing the actual cases in which it is applied. For that reason, I discount both JUSTICE SCALIA's comments on past descriptions of the standard, and the attempt to give it crystal clarity in the joint opinion. The several opinions supporting the judgment in *Griswold v. Connecticut* are less illuminating than the central holding of the case, which appears to have passed the test of time. The future may also demonstrate that a standard that analyzes both the severity of a regulatory burden and the legitimacy of its justification will provide a fully adequate framework for the review of abortion legislation even if the contours of the standard are not authoritatively articulated in any single opinion.

those who are fully convinced that abortion is their only reasonable option. Moreover, the statute requires physicians to inform all of their patients of "the probable gestational age of the unborn child." § 3205(a)(1)(ii). This information is of little decisional value in most cases, because 90 percent of all abortions are performed during the first trimester when fetal age has less relevance than when the fetus nears viability. Nor can the information required by the statute be justified as relevant to any "philosophic" or "social" argument either favoring or disfavoring the abortion decision in a particular case. In light of all of these facts, I conclude that the information requirements in § 3205(a)(1)(ii) and §§ 3205(a)(2)(i)-(iii) do not serve a useful purpose and thus constitute an unnecessary—and therefore undue—burden on the woman's constitutional liberty to decide to terminate her pregnancy.

Accordingly, while I disagree with Parts IV, V-B, and V-D of the joint opinion,[8] I join the remainder of the Court's opinion.

JUSTICE BLACKMUN, concurring in part, concurring in the judgment in part, and dissenting in part.

I join parts, I, II, III, V-A, V-C, and VI of the joint opinion of JUSTICES O'CONNOR, KENNEDY, and SOUTER.

Three years ago, in *Webster v. Reproductive Health Serv.*, four Members of this Court appeared poised to "cas[t] into darkness the hopes and visions of every women in this country" who had come to believe that the Constitution guaranteed her the right to

8. Although I agree that a parental-consent requirement (with the appropriate bypass) is constitutional, I do not join Part V-D of the joint opinion because its approval of Pennsylvania's informed parental-consent requirement is based on the reasons given in Part V-B, with which I disagree.

reproductive choice. *Id.*, at 557 (BLACKMUN, J., dissenting). See *id.*, at 499 (opinion of REHNQUIST, C.J.); *id.*, at 532 (opinion of SCALIA, J.). All that remained between the promise of *Roe* and the darkness of the plurality was a single, flickering flame. Decisions since *Webster* gave little reason to hope that this flame would cast much light. See, *e.g., Ohio v. Akron Center for Reproductive Health*, 497 U.S. 502, 524 (1990) (opinion of BLACKMUN, J.). But now, just when so many expected the darkness to fall, the flame has grown bright.

I do not underestimate the significance of today's joint opinion. Yet I remain steadfast in my belief that the right to reproductive choice is entitled to the full protection afforded by this Court before *Webster*. And I fear for the darkness as four Justices anxiously await the single vote necessary to extinguish the light.

I

Make no mistake, the joint opinion of JUSTICES O'CONNOR, KENNEDY, and SOUTER is an act of personal courage and constitutional principle. In contrast to previous decisions in which JUSTICES O'CONNOR and KENNEDY postponed reconsideration of *Roe v. Wade*, the authors of the joint opinion today join JUSTICE STEVENS and me in concluding that "the essential holding of *Roe* should be retained and once again reaffirmed." In brief, five Members of this Court today recognize that "the Constitution protects a woman's right to terminate her pregnancy in its early stages."

A fervent view of individual liberty and the force of *stare decisis* have led the Court to this conclusion.

In striking down the Pennsylvania statute's spousal notification requirement, the Court has established a framework for evaluating abortion regulations that responds to the social context of women facing issues of reproductive choice. In determining the burden imposed by the challenged regulation, the Court inquires whether the regulation's *"purpose or effect* is to place a substantial obstacle in the path of a woman seeking an abortion before the fetus attains viability." (emphasis added). The Court reaffirms: "The proper focus of constitutional inquiry is the group for whom the law is a restriction, not the group for whom the law is irrelevant." . . . And in applying its test, the Court remains sensitive to the unique role of women in the decision-making process. . . .

Lastly, while I believe that the joint opinion errs in failing to invalidate the other regulations, I am pleased that the joint opinion has not ruled out the possibility that these regulations may be shown to impose an unconstitutional burden. . . . I am confident that in the future evidence will be produced to show that "in a large fraction of the cases in which [these regulations are] relevant, [they] will operate as a substantial obstacle to a woman's choice to undergo an abortion."

II

Today, no less than yesterday, the Constitution and decisions of this Court require that a State's abortion restrictions be subjected to the strictest of judicial scrutiny. Our precedents and the joint opinion's principles require us to subject all non-*de minimis* abortion regulations to strict scrutiny. Under this standard, the Pennsylvania statute's provisions requiring content-based counseling, a 24-hour delay, informed parental consent, and reporting of abortion-related information must be invalidated.

A

State restrictions on abortion violate a woman's right of privacy in two ways. First, compelled continuation of a pregnancy infringes upon a woman's right to bodily integrity by imposing substantial physical intrusions and significant risks of physical harm. . . . See, *e.g., Winston v. Lee,* 470 U.S. 753 (1985) (invalidating surgical removal of bullet from murder suspect); *Rochin v. California,* 342 U.S. 165 (1952) (invalidating stomach-pumping).[3]

Further, when the State restricts a woman's right to terminate her pregnancy, it deprives a woman of the right to make her own decision about reproduction and family planning—critical life choices that this Court long has deemed central to the right to privacy. The decision to terminate or continue a pregnancy has no less an impact on a woman's life than decisions about contraception or marriage. 410 U.S., at 153. . . .

B

The Court has held that limitations on the right of privacy are permissible only if they survive "strict" constitutional scrutiny— that is, only if the governmental entity imposing the restriction can demonstrate that the limitation is both necessary and narrowly tailored to serve a compelling governmental interest. *Griswold v. Connecticut,* 381 U.S. 479, 485 (1965). We have applied this principle specifically in the context of abortion regulations. *Roe v. Wade,* 410 U.S., at 155. . . . *Roe* identified two relevant State interests: "an interest in preserving and protecting the health of the pregnant woman" and an interest in "protecting the potentiality of human life." 410 U.S., at 162. With respect to the State's interest in the health of the mother, "the 'compelling' point

3. As the joint opinion acknowledges, this Court has recognized the vital liberty interest of persons in refusing unwanted medical treatment. *Cruzan v. Director, Missouri Dept. of Health,* 497 U.S. 261 (1990). Just as the Due Process Clause protects the deeply personal decision of the individual to *refuse* medical treatment, it also must protect the deeply personal decision to *obtain* medical treatment, including a woman's decision to terminate a pregnancy.

... is at approximately the end of the first trimester," because it is at that point that the mortality rate in abortion approaches that in childbirth. *Roe*, 410 U.S., at 163. With respect to the State's interest in potential life, "the 'compelling' point is at viability," because it is at that point that the fetus "presumably has the capability of meaningful life outside the mother's womb." *Ibid.* In order to fulfill the requirement of narrow tailoring, "the State is obligated to make a reasonable effort to limit the effect of its regulations to the period in the trimester during which its health interest will be furthered." *Akron*, 462 U.S., at 434.

In my view, application of this analytical framework is no less warranted than when it was approved by seven Members of this Court in *Roe.* . . . No majority of this Court has ever agreed upon an alternative approach. The factual premises of the trimester framework have not been undermined, see *Webster*, 492 U.S., at 553 (BLACKMUN, J., dissenting), and the *Roe* framework is far more administrable, and far less manipulable, than the "undue burden" standard adopted by the joint opinion.

Roe's requirement of strict scrutiny as implemented through a trimester framework should not be disturbed. No other approach has gained a majority, and no other is more protective of the woman's fundamental right. Lastly, no other approach properly accommodates the woman's constitutional right with the State's legitimate interests.

C

Application of the strict scrutiny standard results in the invalidation of all the challenged provisions. . . .

This Court has upheld informed and written consent requirements only where the State has demonstrated that they genuinely further important health-related state concerns. See *Danforth*, 428 U.S., at 65–67.

Measured against these principles, some aspects of the Pennsylvania informed-consent scheme are unconstitutional. While it is unobjectionable for the Commonwealth to require that the patient be informed of the nature of the procedure, the health risks of the abortion and of childbirth, and the probable gestational age of the unborn child, compare §§ 3205(a)(i)-(iii) with *Akron*, 462 U.S., at 446, n. 37, I remain unconvinced that there is a vital state need for insisting that the information be provided by a physician rather than a counselor. *Id.*, at 448. The District Court found that the physician-only requirement necessarily would increase costs to the plaintiff-clinics, costs that undoubtedly would be passed on to patients. And because trained women counselors are often more understanding than physicians, and generally have more time to spend with patients, the physician-only disclosure requirement is not narrowly tailored to serve the Commonwealth's interest in protecting maternal health.

Sections 3205(a)(2)(i)-(iii) of the Act further requires that the physician or a qualified non-physician inform the woman that printed materials are available from the Commonwealth that describe the fetus and provide information about medical assistance for childbirth, information about child support from the father, and a list of agencies offering . . . adoption and other services as alternatives to abortion. *Thornburgh* invalidated biased patient-counseling requirements virtually identical to the one at issue here. What we said of those requirements fully applies in this case:

> the listing of agencies in the printed Pennsylvania form presents serious problems; it contains names of agencies that well may be out of step with the needs of the particular woman and

thus places the physician in an awkward position and infringes upon his or her professional responsibilities. Forcing the physician or counselor to present the materials and the list to the woman makes him or her in effect an agent of the State in treating the woman and places his or her imprimatur upon both the materials and the list. All this is, or comes close to being, state medicine imposed upon the woman, not the professional medical guidance she seeks, and it officially structures—as it obviously was intended to do—the dialogue between the woman and her physician. Much of this . . ., for many patients, would be irrelevant and inappropriate. For a patient with a life-threatening pregnancy, the "information" in its very rendition may be cruel as well as destructive of the physician-patient relationship. . . . 476 U.S., at 763.

"This type of compelled information is the antithesis of informed consent," *id.*, at 764. . . .[7]

7. While I do not agree with the joint opinion's conclusion that these provisions should be upheld, the joint opinion has remained faithful to principles this Court previously has announced in examining counseling provisions. For example, the joint opinion concludes that the "information the State requires to be made available to the woman" must be "truthful and not misleading." Because the State's information must be "calculated to inform the woman's free choice, not hinder it," the measures must be designed to ensure that a woman's choice is "mature and informed," not intimidated, imposed, or impelled. To this end, when the State requires the provision of certain information, the State may not alter the *manner* of presentation in order to inflict "psychological abuse," designed to shock or unnerve a woman seeking to exercise her liberty right. This, for example, would appear to preclude a State from requiring a woman to view

The 24-hour waiting period following the provision of the foregoing information is also clearly unconstitutional. The District Court found that the mandatory 24-hour delay could lead to delays in excess of 24 hours, thus increasing health risks, and that it would require two visits to the abortion provider, thereby increasing travel time, exposure to further harassment, and financial cost. Finally, the District Court found that the requirement would pose especially significant burdens on women living in rural areas and those women that have difficulty explaining their whereabouts. In *Akron* this Court invalidated a similarly arbitrary or inflexible waiting period because, as here, it furthered no legitimate state interest.

As JUSTICE STEVENS insightfully concludes, the mandatory delay rests either on outmoded or unacceptable assumptions about the decisionmaking capacity of women or the belief that the decision to terminate the pregnancy is presumptively wrong. . . .

Finally, the Pennsylvania statute requires every facility performing abortions to report its activities to the Commonwealth. Pennsylvania contends that this requirement is valid under *Danforth*, in which this Court held that recordkeeping and reporting requirements that are reasonably directed to the preservation of

graphic literature or films detailing the performance of an abortion operation. Just as a visual preview of an operation to remove an appendix plays no part in a physician's securing informed consent to an appendectomy, a preview of scenes appurtenant to any major medical intrusion into the human body does not constructively inform the decision of a woman of the State's interest in the preservation of the woman's health or demonstrate the State's "profound respect for the potential life she carries within her."

maternal health and that properly respect a patient's confidentiality are permissible. 428 U.S., at 79–81. The Commonwealth attempts to justify its required reports on the ground that the public has a right to know how its tax dollars are spent. A regulation designed to inform the public about public expenditures does not further the Commonwealth's interest in protecting maternal health. Accordingly, such a regulation cannot justify a legally significant burden on a woman's right to obtain an abortion.

The confidential reports . . . may seem valid, given the State's interest in maternal health and enforcement of the Act. The District Court found, however, that, notwithstanding the confidentiality protections, many physicians, particularly those who have previously discontinued performing abortions because of harassment, would refuse to refer patients to abortion clinics if their names were to appear on these reports.

The Commonwealth has failed to show that the name of the referring physician either adds to the pool of scientific knowledge concerning abortion or is reasonably related to the Commonwealth's interest in maternal health. I therefore agree with the District Court's conclusion that the confidential reporting requirements are unconstitutional insofar as they require the name of the referring physician and the basis for his or her medical judgment.

. . . I would affirm the judgment [of the District Court and reverse the judgment of the Circuit Court of Appeals.]

III

. . . If there is much reason to applaud the advances made by the joint opinion today, there is far more to fear from THE CHIEF JUSTICE's opinion.

THE CHIEF JUSTICE's criticism of *Roe* follows from his stunted conception of individual liberty. While recognizing that the Due Process Clause protects more than simple physical liberty, he then goes on to construe this Court's personal-liberty cases as establishing only a laundry list of particular rights, rather than a principled account of how these particular rights are grounded in a more general right of privacy. This constricted view is reinforced by THE CHIEF JUSTICE's exclusive reliance on tradition as a source of fundamental rights. He argues that the record in favor of a right to abortion is no stronger than the record in *Michael H. v. Gerald D.*, 491 U.S. 110 (1989), where the plurality found no fundamental right to visitation privileges by an adulterous father, or in *Bowers v. Hardwick*, 478 U.S. 186 (1986), where the Court found no fundamental right to engage in homosexual sodomy, or in a case involving the "firing of a gun . . . into another person's body." In THE CHIEF JUSTICE's world, a woman considering whether to terminate a pregnancy is entitled to no more protection than adulterers, murderers, and so-called "sexual deviates." Given THE CHIEF JUSTICE's exclusive reliance on tradition, people using contraceptives seem the next likely candidate for his list of outcasts.

Even more shocking than THE CHIEF JUSTICE's cramped notion of individual liberty is his complete omission of any discussion of the effects that compelled childbirth and motherhood have on women's lives. The only expression of concern with women's health is purely instrumental—for THE CHIEF JUSTICE, only women's *psychological* health is a concern, and only to the extent that he assumes that every woman who decides to have an abortion does so without serious consideration of the moral implications of their decision. In short, THE CHIEF JUSTICE's view of the State's compelling interest in maternal health has less to do with health than it does with compelling women to be maternal.

Nor does THE CHIEF JUSTICE give any serious consideration to the doctrine of *stare decisis.*" For THE CHIEF JUSTICE, the facts that gave rise to *Roe* are surprisingly simple: "women become pregnant, there is a point somewhere, depending on medical technology, where a fetus becomes viable, and women give birth to children." This characterization of the issue thus allows THE CHIEF JUSTICE quickly to discard the joint opinion's reliance argument by asserting that "reproductive planning could take . . . virtually immediate account of a decision overruling *Roe.*"

THE CHIEF JUSTICE's narrow conception of individual liberty and *stare decisis* leads him to propose the same standard of review proposed by the plurality in *Webster*. "States may regulate abortion procedures in ways rationally related to a legitimate state interest. *Williamson v. Lee Optical Co.,* 348 U.S. 483, 491 (1955); cf. *Stanley v. Illinois,* 405 U.S. 645, 651–53 (1972)." THE CHIEF JUSTICE then further weakens the test by providing an insurmountable requirement for facial challenges: petitioners must "show that no set of circumstances exists under which the [provision] would be valid." In short, in his view, petitioners must prove that the statute cannot constitutionally be applied to *anyone*. Finally, in applying his standard to the spousal-notification provision, THE CHIEF JUSTICE contends that the record lacks any "hard evidence" to support the joint opinion's contention that a "large fraction" of women who prefer not to notify their husbands involve situations of battered women and unreported spousal assault. *Post,* at n. 2. Yet throughout the explication of his standard, THE CHIEF JUSTICE never explains what hard evidence is, how large a fraction is required, or how a battered women is supposed to pursue an as-applied challenge.

Under his standard, States can ban abortion if that ban is rationally related to a legitimate state interest—a standard which the United States calls "deferential, but not toothless." Yet when pressed at oral argument to describe the teeth, the best protection that the Solicitor General could offer to women was that a prohibition, enforced by criminal penalties, *with no exception for the life of the mother,* "could raise very serious questions." Perhaps, the Solicitor General offered, the failure to include an exemption for the life of the mother would be "arbitrary and capricious." If, as THE CHIEF JUSTICE contends, the undue burden test is made out of whole cloth, the so-called "arbitrary and capricious" limit is the Solicitor General's "new clothes."

Even if it is somehow "irrational" for a State to require a woman to risk her life for her child, what protection is offered for women who become pregnant through rape or incest? Is there anything arbitrary or capricious about a State's prohibiting the sins of the father from being visited upon his offspring?[12]

12. JUSTICE SCALIA urges the Court to "get out of this area" and leave questions regarding abortion entirely to the States. Putting aside the fact that what he advocates is nothing short of an abdication by the Court of its constitutional responsibilities, JUSTICE SCALIA is uncharacteristically naive if he thinks that overruling *Roe* and holding that restrictions on a woman's right to an abortion are subject only to rational-basis review will enable the Court henceforth to avoid reviewing abortion-related issues. State efforts to regulate and prohibit abortion in a post-*Roe* world undoubtedly would raise a host of distinct and important constitutional questions meriting review by this Court. For example, does the Eighth Amendment impose any limits on the degree or kind of punishment a State can inflict upon physicians who perform, or women who undergo, abortions? What effect would differences among States in their approaches to abortion have on a woman's right to engage in interstate travel? Does the First Amendment permit States that choose not to criminalize abortion to ban all advertising providing information about where and how to obtain abortions?

But, we are reassured, there is always the protection of the democratic process. While there is much to be praised about our democracy, our country since its founding has recognized that there are certain fundamental liberties that are not to be left to the whims of an election. A woman's right to reproductive choice is one of those fundamental liberties. Accordingly, that liberty need not seek refuge at the ballot box.

IV

In one sense, the Court's approach is worlds apart from that of THE CHIEF JUSTICE and JUSTICE SCALIA. And yet, in another sense, the distance between the two approaches is short—the distance is but a single vote.

I am 83 years old. I cannot remain on this Court forever, and when I do step down, the confirmation process for my successor well may focus on the issue before us today. That, I regret, may be exactly where the choice between the two worlds will be made.

CHIEF JUSTICE REHNQUIST, with whom JUSTICE WHITE, JUSTICE SCALIA, and JUSTICE THOMAS join, concurring in the judgment in part and dissenting in part.

The joint opinion, following its newly-minted variation on *stare decisis,* retains the outer shell of *Roe v. Wade,* but beats a wholesale retreat from the substance of that case. We believe that *Roe* was wrongly decided, and that it can and should be overruled consistently with our traditional approach to *stare decisis* in constitutional cases. We would adopt the approach of the plurality in *Webster v. Reproductive Health Services* and uphold the challenged provisions of the Pennsylvania statute in their entirety.

I

In ruling on this case below, the Court of Appeals for the Third Circuit . . . directed its attention to the question of the standard of review for abortion regulations. In attempting to settle on the correct standard, however, the court confronted the confused state of this Court's abortion jurisprudence. After considering the several opinions in *Webster v. Reproductive Health Services* and *Hodgson v. Minnesota,* 497 U.S. 417 (1990), the Court of Appeals concluded that JUSTICE O'CONNOR's "undue burden" test was controlling, as that was the narrowest ground on which we had upheld recent abortion regulations. 947 F.2d, at 693–97 (" 'When a fragmented court decides a case and no single rationale explaining the result enjoys the assent of five Justices, the holding of the Court may be viewed as that position taken by those Members who concurred in the judgments on the narrowest grounds' " (quoting *Marks v. United States,* 430 U.S. 188, 193 (1977) (internal quotation marks omitted)). Applying this standard, the Court of Appeals upheld all of the challenged regulations except the one requiring a woman to notify her spouse of an intended abortion.

. . . We agree with the Court of Appeals that our decision in *Roe* is not directly implicated by the Pennsylvania statute, which does not prohibit, but simply regulates, abortion. But, as the Court of Appeals found, the state of our post-*Roe* decisional law dealing with the regulation of abortion is confusing and uncertain, indicating that a reexamination of that line of cases is in order. Unfortunately for those who must apply this Court's decisions, the reexamination undertaken today leaves the Court no less divided than beforehand. Although they reject the trimester framework that formed the underpinning of *Roe,* JUSTICES O'CONNOR, KENNEDY, and SOUTER adopt a revised undue burden standard to analyze the challenged regulations. We conclude, however, that such an outcome is an unjustified constitutional compromise, one which leaves the Court in a position to closely scrutinize all types of abortion regulations despite the fact that it lacks the power to do so under the Constitution.

. . .

Dissents in [cases since *Roe*] expressed the view that the Court was expanding upon *Roe* in imposing ever greater restrictions on the States. See *Thornburgh v. American College of Obstetricians and Gynecologists*, 476 U.S., at 783 (BURGER, C.J., dissenting) ("The extent to which the Court has departed from the limitations expressed in *Roe* is readily apparent"); *id.*, at 814 (WHITE, J., dissenting) ("[T]he majority indiscriminately strikes down statutory provisions that in no way contravene the right recognized in *Roe*"). And, when confronted with State regulations of this type in past years, the Court has become increasingly more divided: the three most recent abortion cases have not commanded a Court opinion. See *Ohio v. Akron Center for Reproductive Health*, 497 U.S. 502 (1990); *Hodgson v. Minnesota*, 497 U.S. 417 (1990); *Webster v. Reproductive Health Services*.

The task of the Court of Appeals in the present case was obviously complicated by this confusion and uncertainty. Following *Marks v. United States*, 430 U.S. 188 (1977), it concluded that in light of *Webster* and *Hodgson*, the strict scrutiny standard enunciated in *Roe* was no longer applicable, and that the "undue burden" standard adopted by JUSTICE O'CONNOR was the governing principle. This state of confusion and disagreement warrants reexamination of the "fundamental right" accorded to a woman's decision to abort a fetus in *Roe*, with its concomitant requirement that any state regulation of abortion survive "strict scrutiny." See *Payne v. Tennessee*, 501 U.S.——, ——, —— (1991) (observing that reexamination of constitutional decisions is appropriate when those decisions have generated uncertainty

and failed to provide clear guidance, because "correction through legislative action is practically impossible" (internal quotation marks omitted)); *Garcia v. San Antonio Metropolitan Transit Authority*, 469 U.S. 528, 546–47, 557 (1985).

We have held that a liberty interest protected under the Due Process Clause of the Fourteenth Amendment will be deemed fundamental if it is "implicit in the concept of ordered liberty." *Palko v. Connecticut*, 302 U.S. 319, 325 (1937). Three years earlier, in *Snyder v. Massachusetts*, 291 U.S. 97 (1934), we referred to a "principle of justice so rooted in the traditions and conscience of our people as to be ranked as fundamental." *Id.*, at 105; see also *Michael H. v. Gerald D.*, 491 U.S. 110, 122 (1989) (plurality opinion) (citing the language from *Snyder*). These expressions are admittedly not precise, but our decisions implementing this notion of "fundamental" rights do not afford any more elaborate basis on which to base such a classification.

In construing the phrase "liberty" incorporated in the Due Process Clause of the Fourteenth Amendment, we have recognized that its meaning extends beyond freedom from physical restraint. In *Pierce v. Society of Sisters*, we held that it included a parent's right to send a child to private school; in *Meyer v. Nebraska*, we held that it included a right to teach a foreign language in a parochial school. Building on these cases, we have held that that the term "liberty" includes a right to marry, *Loving v. Virginia*; right to procreate, *Skinner v. Oklahoma ex rel. Williamson*; and a right to use contraceptives. *Griswold v. Connecticut*; *Eisenstadt v. Baird*. But a reading of these opinions makes clear that they do not endorse any all-encompassing "right of privacy."

In *Roe v. Wade*, the Court recognized a "guarantee of personal privacy" which "is broad enough to encompass a woman's decision whether or not to terminate her pregnancy." 410 U.S., at 152–53. We are now of the view that, in terming this right fundamental, the Court in *Roe* read the earlier opinions upon which it based its decision much too broadly. Unlike marriage, procreation and contraception, abortion "involves the purposeful termination of potential life." *Harris v. McRae*, 448 U.S. 297, 325 (1980). . . . One cannot ignore the fact that a woman is not isolated in her pregnancy, and that the decision to abort necessarily involves the destruction of a fetus. See *Michael H. v. Gerald D.*, at 124, n.4 (To look "at the act which is assertedly the subject of a liberty interest in isolation from its effect upon other people [is] like inquiring whether there is a liberty interest in firing a gun where the case at hand happens to involve its discharge into another person's body").

Nor do the historical traditions of the American people support the view that the right to terminate one's pregnancy is "fundamental." The common law which we inherited from England made abortion after "quickening" an offense. At the time of the adoption of the Fourteenth Amendment, statutory prohibitions or restrictions on abortion were commonplace; in 1868, at least 28 of the then-37 States and 8 Territories had statutes banning or limiting abortion. J. Mohr, *Abortion in America* 200 (1978). By the turn of the century virtually every State had a law prohibiting or restricting abortion on its books. . . . [I]n 1973 when *Roe* was decided, an overwhelming majority of the States prohibited abortion unless necessary to preserve the life or health of the mother. *Roe v. Wade*, 410 U.S., at 139–40; *id.*, at 176–77, n.2 (REHNQUIST, J., dissenting). On this record, it can scarcely be said that any deeply rooted tradition of relatively unrestricted abortion in our history supported the classification of the right to abortion as "fundamental" under the Due Process Clause of the Fourteenth Amendment.

We think, therefore, both in view of this history and of our decided cases dealing with substantive liberty under the Due Process Clause, that the Court was mistaken in *Roe* when it classified a woman's decision to terminate her pregnancy as a "fundamental right" that could be abridged only in a manner which withstood "strict scrutiny." . . .

We believe that the sort of constitutionally imposed abortion code of the type illustrated by our decisions following *Roe* is inconsistent "with the notion of a Constitution cast in general terms, as ours is, and usually speaking in general principles, as ours does." *Webster v. Reproductive Health Services*, 492 U.S., at 518 (plurality opinion). The Court in *Roe* reached too far when it analogized the right to abort a fetus to the rights involved in *Pierce, Meyer, Loving,* and *Griswold,* and thereby deemed the right to abortion fundamental.

II

. . . *Roe* analyzed abortion regulation under a rigid trimester framework, a framework which has guided this Court's decisionmaking for 19 years. The joint opinion rejects that framework.

Stare decisis is defined in *Black's Law Dictionary* as meaning "to abide by, or adhere to, decided cases." *Black's Law Dictionary* 1406 (6th ed. 1990). Whatever the "central holding" of *Roe* that is left after the joint opinion finishes dissecting it is surely not the result of that principle. While purporting to adhere to precedent, the joint opinion instead revises it. *Roe* continues to exist, but only in the way a storefront on a western movie set exists: a mere facade to give the illusion of reality. Decisions following *Roe,* such as *Akron v. Akron Center for Reproductive Health, Inc.,* 462 U.S. 416 (1983), and *Thornburgh v. American College of Obstetricians and Gynecologists,* are frankly overruled in part under the "undue burden" standard expounded in the joint opinion.

In our view, authentic principles of *stare decisis* do not require that any portion of the reasoning in *Roe* be kept intact. "*Stare decisis* is not . . . a universal, inexorable command," especially in cases involving the interpretation of the Federal Constitution. *Burnet v. Coronado Oil & Gas Co.,* 285 U.S. 393, 405 (1932) (Brandeis, J., dissenting). Erroneous decisions in such constitutional cases are uniquely durable, because correction through legislative action, save for constitutional amendment, is impossible. It is therefore our duty to reconsider constitutional interpretations that "depar[t] from a proper understanding" of the Constitution. *Garcia v. San Antonio Metropolitan Transit Authority,* 469 U.S., at 557; see *United States v. Scott,* 437 U.S. 82, 101 (1978) (" '[I]n cases involving the Federal Constitution, . . . [t]he Court bows to the lessons of experience and the force of better reasoning, recognizing that the process of trial and error, so fruitful in the physical sciences, is appropriate also in the judicial function.' " (quoting *Burnet v. Coronado Oil & Gas Co., supra,* at 406–8 (Brandeis, J., dissenting))); *Smith v. Allwright,* 321 U.S. 649, 665 (1944). Our constitutional watch does not cease merely because we have spoken before on an issue; when it becomes clear that a prior constitutional interpretation is unsound we are obliged to reexamine the question. See, *e.g., West Virginia State Bd. of Education v. Barnette,* 319 U.S. 624, 642 (1943); *Erie R. Co. v. Tompkins,* 304 U.S. 64, 74–78 (1938).

The joint opinion discusses several *stare decisis* factors which, it asserts, point toward retaining a portion of *Roe.* Two of these factors are that the main "factual underpinning" of *Roe* has remained the same, and that its doctrinal foundation is no weaker now than it was in 1973. Of course, what might be called the basic facts which gave rise to *Roe* have remained the same—women become pregnant, there is a point somewhere, depending on medical technology, where a fetus becomes viable, and women give birth to children. But this is only to say that the same facts which gave rise to *Roe* will continue to give rise to similar cases. It is not a reason, in and of itself, why those cases must be decided in the same incorrect manner as was the first case to deal with the question. And surely there is no requirement, in considering whether to depart from *stare decisis* in a constitutional case, that a decision be more wrong now than it was at the time it was rendered. If that were true, the most outlandish constitutional decision could survive forever, based simply on the fact that it was no more outlandish later than it was when originally rendered.

Nor does the joint opinion faithfully follow this alleged requirement. The opinion frankly concludes that *Roe* and its progeny were wrong in failing to recognize that the State's interests in maternal health and in the protection of the unborn human life exist throughout pregnancy. But there is no indication that these components of *Roe* are any more incorrect at this juncture than they were at its inception.

The joint opinion also points to the reliance interests involved in this context in its effort to explain why precedent must be followed for precedent's sake. Certainly it is true that where reliance is truly at issue, as in the case of judicial decisions that have formed the basis for private decisions, "[c]onsiderations in favor of *stare decisis* are at their acme." *Payne v. Tennessee,* 501 U.S., at—— But, as the joint opinion apparently agrees, any traditional notion of reliance is not applicable here. The Court today cuts back on the protection afforded by *Roe,* and no one claims that this action defeats any reliance interest in the disavowed trimester framework. Similarly, reliance interests would not be diminished were the Court to go further and acknowledge the full error of *Roe*, as "reproductive planning could take virtually immediate account of" this action.

The joint opinion thus turns to what can only be described as an unconventional—and unconvincing—notion of reliance, a view based on the surmise that the availability of abortion since *Roe* has led to "two decades of economic and social developments" that would be undercut if the error of *Roe* were recognized. The joint opinion's assertion of this fact is undeveloped and totally conclusory. In fact, one can not be sure to what economic and social developments the opinion is referring. Surely it is dubious to suggest that women have reached their "places in society" in reliance upon *Roe*, rather than as a result of their determination to obtain higher education and compete with men in the job market, and of society's increasing recognition of their ability to fill positions that were previously thought to be reserved only for men.

In the end, having failed to put forth any evidence to prove any true reliance, the joint opinion's argument is based solely on generalized assertions about the national psyche, on a belief that the people of this country have grown accustomed to the *Roe* decision over the last 19 years and have "ordered their thinking and living around" it. As an initial matter, one might inquire how the joint opinion can view the "central holding" of *Roe* as so deeply rooted in our constitutional culture, when it so casually uproots and disposes of that same decision's trimester framework. Furthermore, at various points in the past, the same could have been said about this Court's erroneous decisions that the Constitution allowed "separate but equal" treatment of minorities, see *Plessy v. Ferguson*, 163 U.S. 537 (1896), or that "liberty" under the Due Process Clause protected "freedom of contract." See *Adkins v. Children's Hospital of*

D.C., 261 U.S. 525 (1923); *Lochner v. New York*, 198 U.S. 45 (1905). The "separate but equal" doctrine lasted 58 years after *Plessy*, and *Lochner's* protection of contractual freedom lasted 32 years. However, the simple fact that a generation or more had grown used to these major decisions did not prevent the Court from correcting its errors in those cases, nor should it prevent us from correctly interpreting the Constitution here. See *Brown v. Board of Education*, 347 U.S. 483 (1954) (rejecting the "separate but equal" doctrine); *West Coast Hotel Co. v. Parrish*, 300 U.S. 379 (1937) (overruling *Adkins v. Children's Hospital, supra,* in upholding Washington's minimum wage law).

Apparently realizing that conventional *stare decisis* principles do not support its position, the joint opinion advances a belief that retaining a portion of *Roe* is necessary to protect the "legitimacy" of this Court. Because the Court must take care to render decisions "grounded truly in principle," and not simply as political and social compromises, the joint opinion properly declares it to be this Court's duty to ignore the public criticism and protest that may arise as a result of a decision. Few would quarrel with this statement, although it may be doubted that Members of this Court, holding their tenure as they do during constitutional "good behavior," are at all likely to be intimidated by such public protests.

But the joint opinion goes on to state that when the Court "resolve[s] the sort of intensely divisive controversy reflected in *Roe* and those rare, comparable cases," its decision is exempt from reconsideration under established principles of *stare decisis* in constitutional cases. This is so, the joint opinion contends, because in those "intensely divisive" cases the Court has "call[ed] the contending sides of a national controversy to end their national division by accepting a common mandate rooted in the Constitution," and must therefore take special care not to be perceived as "surrender[ing] to political pressure" and continued opposition. This is a truly novel principle, one which is contrary to both the Court's historical practice and to the Court's traditional willingness to tolerate criticism of its opinions. Under this principle, when the Court has ruled on a divisive issue, it is apparently prevented from overruling that decision for the sole reason that it was incorrect, *unless opposition to the original decision has died away.*

The first difficulty with this principle lies in its assumption that cases which are "intensely divisive" can be readily distinguished from those that are not. The question of whether a particular issue is "intensely divisive" enough to qualify for special protection is entirely subjective and dependent on the individual assumptions of the members of this Court. In addition, because the Court's duty is to ignore public opinion and criticism on issues that come before it, its members are in perhaps the worst position to judge whether a decision divides the Nation deeply enough to justify such uncommon protection. Although many of the Court's decisions divide the populace to a large degree, we have not previously on that account shied away from applying normal rules of *stare decisis* when urged to reconsider earlier decisions. . . .

. . . In terms of public protest, however, *Roe,* so far as we know, was unique. But just as the Court should not respond to that sort of protest by retreating from the decision simply to allay the concerns of the protesters, it should likewise not respond by determining to adhere to the decision at all costs lest it *seem* to be retreating under fire. Public protests should not alter the normal application of *stare decisis,* lest perfectly lawful protest activity be penalized by the Court itself. . . .

The joint opinion agrees that the Court's statute would have been seriously damaged if in *Brown* and *West Coast Hotel* it had dug in its heels and refused to apply normal principles of *stare decisis* to the earlier decisions. But the opinion contends that the Court was entitled to overrule *Plessy* and *Lochner* in those cases, despite the existence of opposition to the original decisions, only because both the Nation and the Court had learned new lessons in the interim. This is at best a feebly supported, *post hoc* rationalization for those decisions. . . .

When the Court finally recognized its error in *West Coast Hotel,* it did not engage in the *post hoc* rationalization that the joint opinion attributes to it today; it did not state that *Lochner* had been based on an economic view that had fallen into disfavor, and that it therefore should be overruled. Chief Justice Hughes in his opinion for the Court simply recognized what Justice Holmes had previously recognized in his *Lochner* dissent, that "[t]he Constitution does not speak of freedom of contract." *West Coast Hotel Co. v. Parrish,* 300 U.S., at 391. . . .

The joint opinion also agrees that the Court acted properly in rejecting the doctrine of "separate but equal" in *Brown.* . . . To us, adherence to *Roe* today under the guise of "legitimacy" would seem to resemble more closely adherence to *Plessy* on the same ground. Fortunately, the Court did not choose that option in *Brown,* and instead frankly repudiated *Plessy.* The joint opinion concludes that such repudiation was justified only because of newly discovered evidence that segregation had the effect of treating one race as inferior to another. . . . It is clear that the same arguments made before the Court in *Brown* were made in *Plessy* as well. The Court in *Brown* simply recognized, as Justice Harlan had recognized beforehand, that the Fourteenth

Amendment does not permit racial segregation. The rule of *Brown* is not tied to popular opinion about the evils of segregation; it is a judgment that the Equal Protection Clause does not permit racial segregation, no matter whether the public might come to believe that it is beneficial. On that ground it stands, and on that ground alone the Court was justified in properly concluding that the *Plessy* Court had erred.

There is also a suggestion in the joint opinion that the propriety of overruling a "divisive" decision depends in part on whether "most people" would now agree that it should be overruled. Either the demise of opposition or its progression to substantial popular agreement apparently is required to allow the Court to reconsider a divisive decision. How such agreement would be ascertained, short of a public opinion poll, the joint opinion does not say. But surely even the suggestion is totally at war with the idea of "legitimacy" in whose name it is invoked. The Judicial Branch derives its legitimacy, not from following public opinion, but from deciding by its best lights whether legislative enactments of the popular branches of Government comport with the Constitution. The doctrine of *stare decisis* is an adjunct of this duty, and should be no more subject to the vagaries of public opinion than is the basic judicial task.

There are other reasons why the joint opinion's discussion of legitimacy is unconvincing as well. In assuming that the Court is perceived as "surrender[ing] to political pressure" when it overrules a controversial decision, the joint opinion forgets that there are two sides to any controversy. The joint opinion asserts that, in order to protect its legitimacy, the Court must refrain from overruling a controversial decision lest it be viewed as favoring those who oppose the decision. But a decision to *adhere* to prior precedent is subject to the

same criticism, for in such a case one can easily argue that the Court is responding to those who have demonstrated in favor of the original decision.

Roe is not this Court's only decision to generate conflict. Our decisions in some recent capital cases, and in *Bowers v. Hardwick*, 478 U.S. 186 (1986), have also engendered demonstrations in opposition. The joint opinion's message to such protesters appears to be that they must cease their activities in order to serve their cause, because their protests will only cement in place a decision which by normal standards of *stare decisis* should be reconsidered.... Strong and often misguided criticism of a decision should not render the decision immune from reconsideration, lest a fetish for legitimacy penalize freedom of expression.

The end result of the joint opinion's paeans of praise for legitimacy is the enunciation of a brand new standard for evaluating state regulation of a woman's right to abortion—the "undue burden" standard. As indicated above, *Roe v. Wade* adopted a "fundamental right" standard under which state regulations could survive only if they met the requirement of "strict scrutiny." While we disagree with that standard, it at least had a recognized basis in constitutional law at the time *Roe* was decided. The same cannot be said for the "undue burden" standard, which is created largely out of whole cloth by the authors of the joint opinion. It is a standard which even today does not command the support of a majority of this Court. And it will not, we believe, result in the sort of "simple limitation," easily applied, which the joint opinion anticipates. In sum, it is a standard which is not built to last.

In evaluating abortion regulations under that standard, judges will have to decide whether they place a "substantial obstacle" in the path of a woman seeking an abortion. In that this standard is based even more on a judge's subjective determinations than was the trimester framework, the standard will do nothing to prevent "judges from roaming at large in the constitutional field" guided only by their personal views. *Griswold v. Connecticut*, 381 U.S., at 502 (Harlan, J., concurring in judgment). Because the undue burden standard is plucked from nowhere, the question of what is a "substantial obstacle" to abortion will undoubtedly engender a variety of conflicting views. For example, in the very matter before us now, the authors of the joint opinion would uphold Pennsylvania's 24-hour waiting period, concluding that a "particular burden" on some women is not a substantial obstacle. But the authors would at the same time strike down Pennsylvania's spousal notice provision, after finding that in a "large fraction" of cases the provision will be a substantial obstacle. And, while the authors conclude that the informed consent provisions do not constitute an "undue burden," JUSTICE STEVENS would hold that they do.

... The "undue burden" inquiry does not in any way supply the distinction between parental consent and spousal consent which the joint opinion adopts. Despite the efforts of the joint opinion, the undue burden standard presents nothing more workable than the trimester framework which it discards today. Under the guise of the Constitution, this Court will still impart its own preferences on the States in the form of a complex abortion code.

The sum of the joint opinion's labors in the name of *stare decisis* and "legitimacy" is this: *Roe v. Wade* stands as a sort of judicial Potemkin Village, which may be pointed out to passers by as a monument to the importance of adhering to precedent. But behind the facade, an entirely new method of analysis, without any roots in constitutional law, is imported to decide the constitutionality of state laws regulating abortion. Neither *stare decisis* nor "legitimacy" are truly served by such an effort.

We have stated above our belief that the Constitution does not subject state abortion regulations to heightened scrutiny. Accordingly, we think that the correct analysis is that set forth by the plurality opinion in *Webster*. A woman's interest in having an abortion is a form of liberty protected by the Due Process Clause, but States may regulate abortion procedures in ways rationally related to a legitimate state interest. *Williamson v. Lee Optical of Okla., Inc.*, 348 U.S. 483, 491 (1955); cf. *Stanley v. Illinois*, 405 U.S. 645, 651–53 (1972). With this rule in mind, we examine each of the challenged provisions.

III

A

[Here followed a summary of informed consent provisions of Section 3205—Au.] . . .

We conclude that this provision of the statute is rationally related to the State's interest in assuring that a woman's consent to an abortion be a fully informed decision. . . . [As to the specific information required to be delivered by the physician,] we agree with the Court of Appeals that a State "may rationally decide that physicians are better qualified than counselors to impart this information and answer questions about the medical aspects of the available alternatives." 947 F.2d, at 704. [As to the printed material,] [w]e conclude that this required presentation of "balanced information" is rationally related to the State's legitimate interest in ensuring that the woman's consent is truly informed, *Thornburgh v. American College of Obstetricians and Gynecologists*, 476 U.S., at 830 (O'CONNOR, J., dissenting), and in addition furthers the State's interest in preserving unborn life. . . .

[As to the 24-hour waiting period,] [w]e are of the view that, in providing time for reflection and reconsideration, the waiting period helps ensure that a woman's decision to abort is a well-considered one, and reasonably furthers the State's legitimate interest in maternal health and in the unborn life of the fetus. . . .

B

[We find the parental consent with judicial bypass option a "rational and fair" way to further the "strong and legitimate" state interest in the "welfare of young citizens."] . . .

C

. . . [As to the spousal notice provision, petitioners contend] that the real effect of such a notice requirement is to give the power to husbands to veto a woman's abortion choice. The District Court indeed found that the notification provision created a risk that some woman who would otherwise have an abortion will be prevented from having one. 947 F.2d, at 712. For example, petitioners argue, many notified husbands will prevent abortions through physical force, psychological coercion, and other types of threats. But Pennsylvania has incorporated exceptions in the notice provision in an attempt to deal with these problems. For instance, a woman need not notify her husband if the pregnancy is result of a reported sexual assault, or if she has reason to believe that she would suffer bodily injury as a result of the notification. 18 Pa. Cons. Stat. § 3209(b) (1990). Furthermore, because this is a facial challenge to the Act, it is insufficient for petitioners to show that the notification provision "might operate unconstitutionally under some conceivable set of circumstances." *United States v. Salerno*, 481 U.S. 739, 745 (1987). Thus, it is not enough for petitioners to show that, in some "worst-case" circumstances, the notice provision will operate as a grant of veto power to husbands. *Ohio v. Akron Center for Reproductive Health*, 497 U.S., at 514. Because they are making a facial challenge to the provision, they must "show that no ,set of circumstances exists under which the [provision] would be valid." *Ibid.* (internal quotation marks omitted). This they have failed to do.[2]

The question before us is therefore whether the spousal notification requirement rationally furthers any legitimate

2. The joint opinion of JUSTICES O'CONNOR, KENNEDY, AND SOUTER appears to ignore this point in concluding that the spousal notice provision imposes an undue burden on the abortion decision. In most instances the notification requirement operates without difficulty. As the District Court found, the vast majority of wives seeking abortions notify and consult with their husbands, and thus suffer no burden as a result of the provision. 744 F. Supp. 1323, 1360 (E.D. Pa. 1990). In other instances where a woman does not want to notify her husband, the Act provides exceptions. For example, notification is not required if the husband is not the father, if the pregnancy is the result of a reported spousal sexual assault, or if the woman fears bodily injury as a result of notifying her husband. Thus, in these instances as well, the notification provision imposes no obstacle to the abortion decision.

The joint opinion puts to one side these situations where the regulation imposes no obstacle at all, and instead focuses on the group of married women who would not otherwise notify their husbands and who do not qualify for one of the exceptions. . . . The joint opinion concentrates on the situations involving battered women and unreported spousal assault, and assumes, without any support in the record, that these instances constitute a "large fraction" of those cases in which women prefer not to notify their husbands (and do not qualify for an exception). This assumption is not based on any hard evidence, however. . . .

state interests. We conclude that it does. First, a husband's interests in procreation within marriage and in the potential life of his unborn child are certainly substantial ones. See *Planned Parenthood of Central Mo. v. Danforth*, 428 U.S., at 69 ("We are not unaware of the deep and proper concern and interest that a devoted and protective husband has in his wife's pregnancy and in the growth and development of the fetus she is carrying"); *id.*, at 93 (WHITE, J., concurring in part and dissenting in part); *Skinner v. Oklahoma ex rel. Williamson*, 316 U.S., at 541. The State itself has legitimate interests both in protecting these interests of the father and in protecting the potential life of the fetus, and the spousal notification requirement is reasonably related to advancing those state interests. By providing that a husband will usually know of his spouse's intent to have an abortion, the provision makes it more likely that the husband will participate in deciding the fate of his unborn child, a possibility that might otherwise have been denied him. This participation might in some cases result in a decision to proceed with the pregnancy. As Judge Alito observed in his dissent below, "[t]he Pennsylvania legislature could have rationally believed that some married women are initially inclined to obtain an abortion without their husbands' knowledge because of perceived problems—such as economic constraints, future plans, or the husbands' previously expressed opposition—that may be obviated by discussion prior to the abortion." 947 F.2d, at 726 (Alito, J., concurring in part and dissenting in part).

The State also has a legitimate interest in promoting "the integrity of the marital relationship." 18 Pa. Cons. Stat. § 3209(a) (1990). This Court has previously recognized "the importance of the marital relationship in our society." *Planned Parenthood of Central Mo. v. Danforth*, at 69. In our view, the spousal notice requirement is a rational

attempt by the State to improve truthful communication between spouses and encourage collaborative decisionmaking, and thereby fosters marital integrity. See *Labine v. Vincent*, 401 U.S. 532, 538 (1971) ("[T]he power to make rules to establish, protect, and strengthen family life" is committed to the state legislatures). Petitioners argue that the notification requirement does not further any such interest; they assert that the majority of wives already notify their husbands of their abortion decisions, and the remainder have excellent reasons for keeping their decisions a secret. In the first case, they argue, the law is unnecessary, and in the second case it will only serve to foster marital discord and threats of harm. Thus, petitioners see the law as a totally irrational means of furthering whatever legitimate interest the State might have. But, in our view, it is unrealistic to assume that every husband-wife relationship is either (1) so perfect that this type of truthful and important communication will take place as a matter of course, or (2) so imperfect that, upon notice, the husband will react selfishly, violently, or contrary to the best interests of his wife. See *Planned Parenthood of Central Mo. v. Danforth*, at 103–4 (STEVENS, J., concurring in part and dissenting in part) (making a similar point in the context of a parental consent statute). The spousal notice provision will admittedly be unnecessary in some circumstances, and possibly harmful in others, but "the existence of particular cases in which a feature of a statute performs no function (or is even counterproductive) ordinarily does not render the statute unconstitutional or even constitutionally suspect." *Thornburgh v. American College of Obstetricians and Gynecologists*, 476 U.S., at 800 (WHITE, J., dissenting). The Pennsylvania Legislature was in a position to weigh the likely benefits of the provision against its likely adverse effects, and presumably concluded, on balance, that the provision would be beneficial. Whether this was a wise decision or not, we cannot say that it was irrational. We therefore conclude that the spousal notice provision comports with the Constitution.

D

The Act also imposes various reporting requirements. [A summary of them followed.–Au.] . . . [The confidential reports] rationally further the State's legitimate interests in advancing the state of medical knowledge concerning maternal health and prenatal life, in gathering statistical information with respect to patients, and in ensuring compliance with other provisions of the Act.

. . . Petitioners . . . contend, however, that the forced public disclosure of the information given by facilities receiving public funds serves no legitimate state interest. We disagree. Records relating to the expenditure of public funds are generally available to the public under Pennsylvania law. See Pa. Stat. Ann., Tit. 65, §§ 66.1, 66.2 (Purdon 1959 and Supp. 1991–1992). As the Court of Appeals observed, "[w]hen a state provides money to a private commercial enterprise, there is a legitimate public interest in informing taxpayers who the funds are benefiting and what services the funds are supporting." 947 F.2d, at 718. These reporting requirements rationally further this legitimate state interest.

E

[We agree with the Circuit Court's interpretation of the medical emergency definition as constitutional.]

IV

For the reasons stated, we therefore would hold that each of the challenged provisions of the Pennsylvania statute is consistent with the Constitution. It bears emphasis that our conclusion in this regard

does not carry with it any necessary approval of these regulations. . . . [T]heir wisdom as a matter of public policy is for the people of Pennsylvania to decide.

JUSTICE SCALIA, with whom THE CHIEF JUSTICE, JUSTICE WHITE, and JUSTICE THOMAS join, concurring in the judgment in part and dissenting in part.

My views on this matter are unchanged from those I set forth in my separate opinions in *Webster v. Reproductive Health Services,* 492 U.S. 490, 532, (1989) (SCALIA, J., concurring in part and concurring in judgment), and *Ohio v. Akron Center for Reproductive Health,* 497 U.S. 502, 520 (1990) (*Akron II*) (SCALIA, J., concurring). The States may, if they wish, permit abortion-on-demand, but the Constitution does not *require* them to do so. The permissibility of abortion, and the limitations upon it, are to be resolved like most important questions in our democracy: by citizens trying to persuade one another and then voting. . . . Laws against bigamy, for example—which entire societies of reasonable people disagree with—intrude upon men and women's liberty to marry and live with one another. But bigamy happens not to be a liberty specially "protected" by the Constitution.

That is, quite simply, the issue in this case: not whether the power of a woman to abort her unborn child is a "liberty" in the absolute sense; or even whether it is a liberty of great importance to many women. Of course it is both. The issue is whether it is a liberty protected by the Constitution of the United States. I am sure it is not. I reach that conclusion . . . for the same reason I reach the conclusion that bigamy is not constitutionally protected— because of two simple facts: (1) the Constitution says absolutely nothing about it, and (2) the longstanding traditions of

American society have permitted it to be legally proscribed.[1] *Akron II,* at 520 (SCALIA, J., concurring). . . .

. . . But the Court does not wish to be fettered by any such limitations on its preferences. The Court's statement that it is "tempting" to acknowledge the authoritativeness of tradition in order to "cur[b] the discretion of federal judges," is of course rhetoric rather than reality; no government official is "tempted" to place restraints upon his own freedom of action, which is why Lord Acton did not say "Power tends to purify." The Court's temptation is in the quite opposite and more natural direction—towards systematically eliminating checks upon its own power; and it succumbs.

Beyond that brief summary of the essence of my position, I will not swell the United States Reports with repetition of what I have said before; and applying the rational basis test, I would uphold the Pennsylvania statute in its entirety. I must, however, respond to a few of the more outrageous arguments in today's opinion,

---

1. The Court's suggestion that adherence to tradition would require us to uphold laws against interracial marriage is entirely wrong. Any tradition in that case was contradicted by a text—an Equal Protection Clause that explicitly establishes racial equality as a constitutional value. See *Loving v. Virginia,* 388 U.S. 1, 9 (1967). The enterprise launched in *Roe,* by contrast, sought to *establish*—in the teeth of a clear, contrary tradition—a value found nowhere in the constitutional text.

There is, of course, no comparable tradition barring recognition of a "liberty interest" in carrying one's child to term free from state efforts to kill it. For that reason, it does not follow that the Constitution does not protect childbirth simply because it does not protect abortion. The Court's contention that the only way to protect childbirth is to protect abortion shows the utter bankruptcy of constitutional analysis deprived of tradition as a validating factor.

which it is beyond human nature to leave unanswered. I shall discuss each of them under a quotation from the Court's opinion to which they pertain.

"The inescapable fact is that adjudication of substantive due process claims may call upon the Court in interpreting the Constitution to exercise that same capacity which by tradition courts always have exercised: reasoned judgment."

. . . But "reasoned judgment" does not begin by begging the question, as *Roe* and subsequent cases unquestionably did by assuming that what the State is protecting is the mere "potentiality of human life." See, *e.g., Roe, supra,* at 162. . . . The whole argument of abortion opponents is that what the Court calls the fetus and what others call the unborn child *is a human life.* Thus, whatever answer *Roe* came up with after conducting its "balancing" is bound to be wrong, unless it is correct that the human fetus is in some critical sense merely potentially human. There is of course no way to determine that as a legal matter; it is in fact a value judgment. Some societies have considered newborn children not yet human, or the incompetent elderly no longer so.

The authors of the joint opinion, of course, do not squarely contend that *Roe v. Wade* was a *correct* application of "reasoned judgment"; merely that it must be followed, because of *stare decisis.* But in their exhaustive discussion of all the factors that go into the determination of when *stare decisis* should be observed and when disregarded, they never mention "how wrong was the decision on its face?" Surely, if "[t]he Court's power lies . . . in its legitimacy, a product of substance and perception," the "substance" part of the equation demands that plain error be acknowledged and eliminated. *Roe* was plainly wrong—

even on the Court's methodology of "reasoned judgment," and even more so (of course) if the proper criteria of text and tradition are applied.

. . . [A]fter more than 19 years of effort by some of the brightest (and most determined) legal minds in the country, after more than 10 cases upholding abortion rights in this Court, and after dozens upon dozens of *amicus* briefs submitted in this and other cases, the best the Court can do to explain how it is that the word "liberty" *must* be thought to include the right to destroy human fetuses is to rattle off a collection of adjectives that simply decorate a value judgment and conceal a political choice. The right to abort, we are told, inheres in "liberty" because it is among "a person's most basic decision"; it involves a "most intimate and personal choic[e]"; it is "central to personal dignity and autonomy"; it "originate[s] within the zone of conscience and belief"; it is "too intimate and personal" for state interference. . . . But it is obvious to anyone applying "reasoned judgment" that the same adjectives can be applied to many forms of conduct that this Court (including one of the Justices in today's majority, see *Bowers v. Hardwick*, 478 U.S. 186 (1986)) has held are *not* entitled to constitutional protection—because, like abortion, they are forms of conduct that have long been criminalized in American society. Those adjectives might be applied, for example, to homosexual sodomy, polygamy, adult incest, and suicide, all of which are equally "intimate" and "deep[ly] personal" decisions involving "personal autonomy and bodily integrity," and all of which can constitutionally be proscribed because it is our unquestionable constitutional tradition that they are proscribable. It is not reasoned judgment that supports the Court's decision; only personal predilection. . . .

"Liberty finds no refuge in a jurisprudence of doubt."

. . . The shortcomings of *Roe* did not include lack of clarity: Virtually all regulation of abortion before the third trimester was invalid. But to come across this phrase in the joint opinion—which calls upon federal district judges to apply an "undue burden" standard as doubtful in application as it is unprincipled in origin—is really more than one should have to bear. . . .

The joint opinion explains that a state regulation imposes an "undue burden" if it "has the purpose or effect of placing a substantial obstacle in the path of a woman seeking an abortion of a nonviable fetus." An obstacle is "substantial," we are told, if it is "calculated[,] [not] to inform the woman's free choice, [but to] hinder it."[4] This

4. The joint opinion further asserts that a law imposing an undue burden on abortion decisions is not a "permissible" means of serving "legitimate" state interests. This description of the undue burden standard in terms more commonly associated with the rational-basis test will come as a surprise even to those who have followed closely our wanderings in this forsaken wilderness. See, *e.g.*, *Akron I*, at 463 (O'CONNOR, J., dissenting) ("The 'undue burden' . . . represents the required threshold inquiry that must be conducted before this Court can require a State to justify its legislative actions under the exacting 'compelling state interest' standard"); see also *Hodgson v. Minnesota*, 497 U.S. 417,—— (1990) (O'CONNOR, J., concurring in part and concurring in judgment in part); *Thornburgh v. American College of Obstetricians and Gynecologists*, 476 U.S. 747, 828 (1986) (O'CONNOR, J., dissenting). This confusing equation of the two standards is apparently designed to explain how one of the Justices who joined the plurality opinion in *Webster v. Reproductive Health Services*, which adopted the rational basis test, could join an opinion expressly adopting the undue burden test. See *id.*, at 520 (rejecting the view that abortion is a

latter statement cannot possibly mean what it says. *Any* regulation of abortion that is intended to advance what the joint opinion concedes is the State's "substantial" interest in protecting unborn life will be "calculated [to] hinder" a decision to have an abortion. It thus seems more accurate to say that the joint opinion would uphold abortion regulations only if they do not *unduly* hinder the woman's decision. That, of course, brings us right back to square one: Defining an "undue burden" as an "undue hindrance" (or a "substantial obstacle") hardly "clarifies" the test. . . .

———

"fundamental right," instead inquiring whether a law regulating the woman's "liberty interest" in abortion is "reasonably designed" to further "legitimate" state ends). The same motive also apparently underlies the joint opinion's erroneous citation of the plurality opinion in *Ohio v. Akron Center for Reproductive Health,* 497 U.S. 502,——— (1990) (*Akron II*) (opinion of KENNEDY, J.), as applying the undue burden test. See *ante,* (using this citation to support the proposition that "two of us"—*i. e.,* two of the authors of the joint opinion—have previously applied this test). In fact, *Akron II* does not mention the undue burden standard until the conclusion of the opinion, when it states that the statute at issue "does not impose an undue, *or otherwise unconstitutional,* burden." 497 U.S., at 519 (emphasis added). I fail to see how anyone can think that saying a statute does not impose an unconstitutional burden under *any* standard, including the undue burden test, amounts to adopting the undue burden test as the *exclusive* standard. The Court's citation of *Hodgson* as reflecting JUSTICE KENNEDY's and JUSTICE O'CONNOR's "shared premises," is similarly inexplicable, since the word "undue" was never even used in the former's opinion in that case. I joined JUSTICE KENNEDY's opinions in both *Hodgson* and *Akron II*; I should be grateful, I suppose, that the joint opinion does not claim that I, too, have adopted the undue burden test.

. . . I agree, indeed I have forcefully urged, that a law of general applicability which places only an incidental burden on a fundamental right does not infringe that right, see *R. A. V. v. St. Paul,* 505 U.S. ——, ——(1992); *Employment Division, Dept. of Human Resources of Ore. v. Smith,* 494 U.S. 872, 878–882 (1990), but that principle does not establish the quite different (and quite dangerous) proposition that a law which *directly* regulates a fundamental right will not be found to violate the Constitution unless it imposes an "undue burden." It is that, of course, which is at issue here: Pennsylvania has *consciously and directly* regulated conduct that our cases have held is constitutionally protected. The appropriate analogy, therefore, is that of a state law requiring purchasers of religious books to endure a 24-hour waiting period, or to pay a nominal additional tax of 1 cent. The joint opinion cannot possibly be correct in suggesting that we would uphold such legislation on the ground that it does not impose a "substantial obstacle" to the exercise of First Amendment rights. The "undue burden" standard is not at all the generally applicable principle the joint opinion pretends it to be; rather, it is a unique concept created specially for this case, to preserve some judicial foothold in this ill-gotten territory. . . .

. . . JUSTICE O'CONNOR has also abandoned (again without explanation) the view she expressed in *Planned Parenthood Assn. of Kansas City, Mo., Inc. v. Ashcroft,* 462 U.S. 476 (1983) (dissenting opinion), that a medical regulation which imposes an "undue burden" could nevertheless be upheld if it "reasonably relate[s] to the preservation and protection of maternal health," *id.,* at 505 (citation and internal quotation marks omitted). In today's version, even health measures will be upheld only "*if they do not constitute an undue burden,*" ante (emphasis added). Gone too is Justice O'Connor's statement that "the State possesses *compelling* interests in the protection of potential human life ... throughout pregnancy," *Akron I*, at 461 (emphasis added); see also *Ashcroft, supra*, at 505 (O'Connor, J., concurring in judgment in part and dissenting in part); *Thornburgh*, at 828 (O'Connor, J., dissenting); instead, the State's interest in unborn human life is stealthily downgraded to a merely "substantial" or "profound" interest. (That had to be done, of course, since designating the interest as "compelling" throughout pregnancy would have been, shall we say, a "substantial obstacle" to the joint opinion's determined effort to reaffirm what it views as the "central holding" of *Roe*. See *Akron I*, 462 U.S., at 420, n.1.) And "viability" is no longer the "arbitrary" dividing line previously decried by Justice O'Connor in *Akron I, id.*, at 461; the Court now announces that "the attainment of viability may continue to serve as the critical fact." It is difficult to maintain the illusion that we are interpreting a Constitution rather than inventing one, when we amend its provisions so breezily.

[I turn now to the plurality's application of its "undue burden" standard.] ...

I do not, of course, have any objection to the notion that, in applying legal principles, one should rely only upon the facts that are contained in the record or that are properly subject to judicial notice. But what is remarkable about the joint opinion's fact-intensive analysis is that it does not result in any measurable clarification of the "undue burden" standard. Rather, the approach of the joint opinion is, for the most part, simply to highlight certain facts in the record that apparently strike the three Justices as particularly significant in establishing (or refuting) the existence of an undue burden; after describing these facts, the opinion then simply announces that the provision either does or does not impose a "substantial obstacle" or an "undue burden." We do not know whether the same conclusions could have been reached on a different record, or in what respects the record would have had to differ before an opposite conclusion would have been appropriate. The inherently standardless nature of this inquiry invites the district judge to give effect to his personal preferences about abortion.

To the extent I can discern *any* meaningful content in the "undue burden" standard as applied in the joint opinion, it appears to be that a State may not regulate abortion in such a way as to reduce significantly its incidence. ... Thus, despite flowery rhetoric about the State's "substantial" and "profound" interest in "potential human life," and criticism of *Roe* for undervaluing that interest, the joint opinion permits the State to pursue that interest only so long as it is not too successful. As Justice Blackmun recognizes (with evident hope), the "undue burden" standard may ultimately require the invalidation of each provision upheld today if it can be shown, on a better record, that the State is too effectively "express[ing] a preference for childbirth over abortion." Reason finds no refuge in this jurisprudence of confusion.

"While we appreciate the weight of the arguments ... that *Roe* should be overruled, the reservations any of us may have in reaffirming the central holding of *Roe* are outweighed by the explication of individual liberty we have given combined with the force of *stare decisis*."

The Court's reliance upon *stare decisis* can best be described as contrived. ...

I am certainly not in a good position to dispute that the Court *has saved* the "central holding" of *Roe*, since to do that effectively I would have to know what the

Court has saved, which in turn would require me to understand (as I do not) what the "undue burden" test means. I must confess, however, that I have always thought, and I think a lot of other people have always thought, that the arbitrary trimester framework, which the Court today discards, was quite as central to *Roe* as the arbitrary viability test, which the Court today retains. . . .

"Where, in the performance of its judicial duties, the Court decides a case in such a way as to resolve the sort of intensely divisive controversy reflected in *Roe* . . . its decision has a dimension that the resolution of the normal case does not carry. It is the dimension present whenever the Court's interpretation of the Constitution calls the contending sides of a national controversy to end their national division by accepting a common mandate rooted in the Constitution."

The Court's description of the place of *Roe* in the social history of the United States is unrecognizable. Not only did *Roe* not, as the Court suggests, *resolve* the deeply divisive issue of abortion; it did more than anything else to nourish it, by elevating it to the national level where it is infinitely more difficult to resolve. National politics were not plagued by abortion protests, national abortion lobbying, or abortion marches on Congress, before *Roe v. Wade* was decided. Profound disagreement existed among our citizens over the issue—as it does over other issues, such as the death penalty—but that disagreement was being worked out at the state level. As with many other issues, the division of sentiment within each State was not as closely balanced as it was among the population of the Nation as a whole, meaning not only that more people would be satisfied with the results of state-by-state resolution, but also that those results would be

more stable. Pre-*Roe*, moreover, political compromise was possible.

Roe's mandate for abortion-on-demand destroyed the compromises of the past, rendered compromise impossible for the future, and required the entire issue to be resolved uniformly, at the national level. At the same time, *Roe* created a vast new class of abortion consumers and abortion proponents by eliminating the moral opprobrium that had attached to the act. ("If the Constitution *guarantees* abortion, how can it be bad?"—not an accurate line of thought, but a natural one.) Many favor all of those developments, and it is not for me to say that they are wrong. But to portray *Roe* as the statesmanlike "settlement" of a divisive issue, a jurisprudential Peace of Westphalia that is worth preserving, is nothing less than Orwellian. *Roe* fanned into life an issue that has inflamed our national politics in general, and has obscured with its smoke the selection of Justices to this Court in particular, ever since. And by keeping us in the abortion-umpiring business, it is the perpetuation of that disruption, rather than of any *pax Roeana*, that the Court's new majority decrees.

"[T]o overrule under fire . . . would subvert the Court's legitimacy. . . .

"To all those who will be . . . tested by following, the Court implicitly undertakes to remain steadfast. . . . The promise of constancy, once given, binds its maker for as long as the power to stand by the decision survives and . . . the commitment [is not] obsolete. . . ."

The Imperial Judiciary lives. . . .
. . . [C]ompare this ecstasy of a Supreme Court in which there is, especially on controversial matters, no shadow of change or hint of alteration ("There is a limit to the amount of error that can plausibly be imputed to prior courts"), with the more democratic views of a more humble man:

[T]he candid citizen must confess that if the policy of the Government upon vital questions affecting the whole people is to be irrevocably fixed by decisions of the Supreme Court, ... the people will have ceased to be their own rulers, having to that extent practically resigned their Government into the hands of that eminent tribunal. A. Lincoln, First Inaugural Address (Mar. 4, 1861), reprinted in *Inaugural Addresses of the Presidents of the United States*, S. Doc. No. 101–10, p. 139 (1989).

It is particularly difficult, in the circumstances of the present decision, to sit still for the Court's lengthy lecture upon the virtues of "constancy," of "remain[ing] steadfast," of adhering to "principle." Among the five Justices who purportedly adhere to *Roe*, at most three agree upon the *principle* that constitutes adherence (the joint opinion's "undue burden" standard)—and that principle is inconsistent with *Roe*, see 410 U.S., at 154–56.[7] To make matters worse, two of the three, in order thus to remain steadfast, had to abandon previously stated positions. See n.4 *supra*. It is beyond me how the Court expects these accommodations to be accepted "as grounded truly in principle, not as compromises with social and political pressures having, as such, no bearing on the principled choices that the Court is obliged to make." ...

7. JUSTICE BLACKMUN's effort to preserve as much of *Roe* as possible leads him to read the joint opinion as more "constan[t]" and "steadfast" than can be believed. He contends that the joint opinion's "undue burden" standard requires the application of strict scrutiny to "all non-*de minimis*" abortion regulations, but that could only be true if a "substantial obstacle" (joint opinion) were the same thing as a non-*de minimis* obstacle—which it plainly is not.

I cannot agree with, indeed I am appalled by, the Court's suggestion that the decision whether to stand by an erroneous constitutional decision must be strongly influenced—*against* overruling, no less—by the substantial and continuing public opposition the decision has generated. ...

But whether it would "subvert the Court's legitimacy" or not, the notion that we would decide a case differently from the way we otherwise would have in order to show that we can stand firm against public disapproval is frightening. It is a bad enough idea, even in the head of someone like me, who believes that the text of the Constitution, and our traditions, say what they say and there is no fiddling with them. But when it is in the mind of a Court that believes the Constitution has an evolving meaning; that the Ninth Amendment's reference to "othe[r]" rights is not a disclaimer, but a charter for action; and that the function of this Court is to "speak before all others for [the people's] constitutional ideals" unrestrained by meaningful text or tradition—then the notion that the Court must adhere to a decision for as long as the decision faces "great opposition" and the Court is "under fire" acquires a character of almost czarist arrogance. We are offended by these marchers who descend upon us, every year on the anniversary of *Roe*, to protest our saying that the Constitution requires what our society has never thought the Constitution requires. These people who refuse to be "tested by following" must be taught a lesson. We have no Cossacks, but at least we can stubbornly refuse to abandon an erroneous opinion that we might otherwise change—to show how little they intimidate us.

Of course, as THE CHIEF JUSTICE points out, we have been subjected to what the Court calls "political pressure" by *both* sides of this issue. Maybe today's decision *not* to overrule *Roe* will be seen as buckling to pressure from *that* direction. Instead of engaging in the hopeless task of predicting public perception—a job not for lawyers but for political campaign managers—the Justices should do what is *legally* right by asking two questions: (1) Was *Roe* correctly decided? (2) Has *Roe* succeeded in producing a settled body of law? If the answer to both questions is no, *Roe* should undoubtedly be overruled.

In truth, I am as distressed as the Court is—and expressed my distress several years ago, see *Webster,* 492 U.S., at 535—about the "political pressure" directed to the Court: the marches, the mail, the protests aimed at inducing us to change our opinions. How upsetting it is, that so many of our citizens (good people, not lawless ones, on both sides of this abortion issue, and on various sides of other issues as well) think that we Justices should properly take into account their views, as though we were engaged not in ascertaining an objective law but in determining some kind of social consensus. The Court would profit, I think, from giving less attention to the *fact* of this distressing phenomenon, and more attention to the *cause* of it. That cause permeates today's opinion: a new mode of constitutional adjudication that relies not upon text and traditional practice to determine the law, but upon what the Court calls "reasoned judgment," which turns out to be nothing but philosophical predilection and moral intuition. . . .

. . . As long as this Court thought (and the people thought) that we Justices were doing essentially lawyers' work up here—reading text and discerning our society's traditional understanding of that text—the public pretty much left us alone. Texts and traditions are facts to study, not convictions to demonstrate about. But if in reality our process of constitutional adjudication consists primarily of making *value judgments;* if

we can ignore a long and clear tradition clarifying an ambiguous text, as we did, for example, five days ago in declaring unconstitutional invocations and benedictions at public-high-school graduation ceremonies, *Lee v. Weisman,* 505 U.S.—— (1992); if, as I say, our pronouncement of constitutional law rests primarily on value judgments, then a free and intelligent people's attitude towards us can be expected to be (*ought* to be) quite different. The people know that their value judgments are quite as good as those taught in any law school—maybe better. If, indeed, the "liberties" protected by the Constitution are, as the Court says, undefined and unbounded, then the people *should* demonstrate, to protest that we do not implement *their* values instead of *ours.* Not only that, but confirmation hearings for new Justices *should* deteriorate into question-and-answer sessions in which Senators go through a list of their constituents' most favored and most disfavored alleged constitutional rights, and seek the nominee's commitment to support or oppose them. . . .

There is a poignant aspect to today's opinion. Its length, and what might be called its epic tone, suggest that its authors believe they are bringing to an end a troublesome era in the history of our Nation and of our Court. "It is the dimension" of authority, they say, to "cal[l] the contending sides of national controversy to end their national division by accepting a common mandate rooted in the Constitution." . . .

It is no more realistic for us in this case, than it was for [the author of the *Dred Scott* decision] to think that an issue of the sort they both involved—an issue involving life and death, freedom and subjugation—can be "speedily and finally settled" by the Supreme Court. . . . Quite to the contrary, by foreclosing all democratic outlet for the deep passions this issue arouses, by banishing the issue from the political forum that gives all participants, even the losers, the satisfaction of a fair hearing and an honest fight, by continuing the imposition of a rigid national rule instead of allowing for regional differences,

the Court merely prolongs and intensifies the anguish.

We should get out of this area, where we have no right to be, and where we do neither ourselves nor the country any good by remaining.

CASE QUESTIONS

1. In Section II the plurality opinion describes the abortion decision as "fraught with consequences for others," but in section III.A.3 it says that "any error in *Roe* is unlikely to have serious ramifications in future cases." Can both be true?

2. In Section V.E the plurality opinion upholds all of the statutory reporting requirements (both those for public records and those that remain confidential) because they further "medical research" and thereby, women's health. How would medical research be fostered by putting on the public record the names of owners of those abortion clinics that receive state funds? Both Justice Blackmun and Justice Rehnquist identify the purpose of this reporting requirement as letting taxpayers keep track of where their money is going. Why does the plurality seem to avoid this conclusion? Might they have viewed this government interest as not "compelling"? (Consider in this light article I, section 9, clause 7 of the U.S. Constitution.)

3. Justice Stevens asserts (in Section II of his opinion) that it is constitutional for Pennsylvania to "produce and disseminate" printed material such as the kind at issue here but it is unconstitutional

for the state to ordain that women contemplating abortion be told of the availability of this printed material. What in the Constitution convinces him that disseminating to the general public is acceptable but to particular groups at particular times is not acceptable?

4. Justice Stevens (in Section IV) insists that information as to gestational age of the fetus is not "justified as relevant to any 'philosophic' or 'social' argument . . . favoring or disfavoring the abortion decision." Is gestational age really separate from viability, on which Stevens hinges his own "philosophic or social argument" concerning the point at which legislation may interfere with the private freedom to choose abortion?

5. Is Justice Stevens being overly optimistic in asserting (in Section III) that no woman "undertakes [an abortion] decision lightly"?

6. Justice Blackmun rejects the state's claim that it is necessary for the physician (as contrasted with a counselor) to explain to the patient the risks associated both with continued pregnancy and with the abortion technique being considered. In upholding the claim, the

Rehnquist group made the point that the physician is better qualified than non-medical personnel to answer any questions the patient may have about the risks that are being explained. Does Justice Blackmun answer that argument?

7. Justice Blackmun praises the plurality for their acknowledgment that our Constitution places certain "fundamental liberties" beyond the reach of majorities hostile to them. Does either Blackmun or the plurality explain what guidelines they employ to decide which liberties are or are not "fundamental" for Americans?

In explaining his own guideline for that question, Justice Scalia itemizes the constitutional text and tradition. He justifies going against the tradition forbidding interracial marriage, because, he says, the (textual) equal protection clause "explicitly establishes racial equality as a constitutional value" (footnote 1). (Note that the word *race* is not "explicit" in the equal protection clause.) However, he opposes the Court's recent decision that official school prayers at graduation ceremonies of state-run high schools violate the First Amendment ban on any "law respecting an establishment of religion."[25] Despite the explicitness of the establishment clause, Justice Scalia calls it an "ambiguous text" which was "clarif[ied]" by the "clear tradition" of the graduation prayers. Is the equal protection clause really less ambiguous than the establishment clause or the antimiscegenation tradition any less clear than the prayer tradition?

8. Both Rehnquist (in Section II) and Scalia express concern about the plurality's new rule that those "watershed" decisions of the Court that are the most "intensely divisive" should be overruled only when the Court has "the most compelling reason" to do so, in order to avoid the appearance of "overruling under fire." The Rehnquist/Scalia concern is that this rule runs afoul of the First Amendment rights of people who wish to protest the decision: the more they protest, the more the decision will appear "divisive," so the new rule looks like a threat that the decision will be maintained as a kind of punishment for the protest. (It is perhaps worth noting that in 1992 the Court was facing a case that dealt with the punishment of violent protests at abortion clinics,[26] so the question of abortion protests was highly salient for the justices.) Should the plurality's reasoning have been more attentive to this First Amendment concern?

9. When Justice Rehnquist states (in Section I) that abortion is a "liberty interest protected under the Due Process Clause," which may be restricted whenever the state has a rational basis for doing so, he is saying that abortion is protected *not* as a fundamental right but only as much as any other liberty, such as, say walking down the street or driving an automobile. On the other hand, the Rehnquist group continues to view contraception as a fundamental right. Abortion, Rehnquist says, is different because it "involves the purposeful termination of potential life." When an IUD or a birth-control pill causes a fertilized egg to fail to nest in the uterine wall, is this, too, a "purposeful termination of potential life"? Does the Rehnquist opinion mean that only pre-fertilization birth-control techniques are now protected by the Constitution? Would this be a strange principle of constitutional law?

10. Consider Justice Scalia's footnote 4. Is he persuasive in his suggestion that the meaning of the "undue burden" test has changed dramatically over the ten years that it has been discussed on the Court?

11. Justice Scalia argues that a larger number of people would be content with abortion policy if it were allowed to vary from state to state. Is he correct? Could the same argument be made about the meaning of, say an "unreasonable search and seizure" or what is a "law respecting an establishment of religion"? Both of these clauses, and most other parts of the Bill of Rights, have been applied to state governments, nationwide, through the due process clause of the Fourteenth Amendment. Would there be a greater number of contented Americans if state variation on all these matters were allowed?

12. Who is the proper group to consider in assessing the constitutionality of the spousal notice provision—married pregnant women in general, the vast majority of whom would discuss any consideration of abortion with their husbands; or only those married pregnant women who feel burdened by the law, in which group a large fraction will experience the law as an "effective veto"?

13. In the sixth to the last paragraph of his opinion, Justice Scalia poses two questions to guide a conscientious judge considering whether to overrule a precedent, and suggests that if the answer to *both* is no, it should be overruled. What if a judge thinks the answer for *Roe* is no for the first question (whether it was correctly decided) but yes for the second question (whether it produced settled law)?

Follow-up to *Casey*

Within months, the Supreme Court clarified the import of the *Casey* precedent by refusing to review three federal circuit court decisions. While the Court never explains in writing its refusal to grant review, and may have any number of reasons for one, certain inferences may sometimes plausibly be drawn. For instance, in the first of these actions, on November 30, 1992, the Court let stand a ruling that the Guam statute described above (in the introduction to the *Casey* case) was unconstitutional on the grounds that it clashed directly with *Roe v. Wade*. Three justices—Scalia, Rehnquist, and White—dissented, with the latter two joining in Scalia's argument that the Court should consider whether, instead of declaring the entire statue void, the lower court should instead have tried to uphold it as constitutional in part, because it would be constitutional if applied only to viable fetuses.[27] One cannot know why Clarence Thomas, who had concurred with them in *Casey*, left their ranks this time. Perhaps he simply saw no point in reviewing the decision if five other justices were going to vote to affirm anyway.) But one can know, at least, that not as many as five justices were so troubled by the voiding of the Guam law that they were moved to overrule it. Had they wanted to uphold laws of the Guam type—sweeping prohibitions of abortion that did not respect the viability threshold—this case presented an opportunity to do so.

In March 1993, the Supreme Court ratified the implicit message of the Guam refusal, declining to hear the appeal of the invalidation of Louisiana's abortion prohibition.[28] To this refusal, no one recorded a dissent. On the other side of the abortion policy scale, just one week after the Guam denial, the Supreme Court refused, without dissent, to review a decision upholding a statute of the state of Mississippi that was virtually identical to the one the Supreme Court upheld in *Casey*.[29] Pro-choice attorneys had hoped that a fact-based argument emphasizing how different Pennsylvania is from Mississippi, where approximately 50 percent of women live more than 100 miles from an abortion clinic, would convince the Court that a twenty-four-hour waiting period in the southern state in fact amounted to an undue burden, because it often necessitated either a second, arduous journey or the extra cost of an overnight stay. One difficulty with their argument was that they were asking for a declaratory judgment that the law was unconstitutional "on its face." Such a declaration is supposed to rest on the premise that there are no circumstances where the law can be applied constitutionally. This law obviously did not place such an extra burden on women living near the clinics. Thus, while the Court officially left open in *Casey* the possibility that attorneys might be able to demonstrate circumstances where a twenty-four-hour waiting period is unconstitutional, the justices evidently are willing to be so convinced only with regard to particular applications of the law, not with a declaratory judgment *before* the law is ever applied.

CHAPTER 3

Parenthood and Privacy: Contemporary Applications

The earliest cases that served as direct precedents for the right of procreative privacy were two cases in the 1920s (*Meyer v. Nebraska*[1] and *Pierce v. Society*[2]), which invoked a fundamental right of parents "to direct the upbringing and education of children under their control."[3] Like other fundamental rights, this one too was restrictable to the degree necessitated by any compelling governmental interest. And early on, the Supreme Court had specified that society's obligation to protect the welfare of children (since they are relatively helpless against parental mistreatment) was one such compelling interest.[4]

The recent cases presented in this chapter depict the courts coping with conflicts between the right of parental privacy and a variety of alleged compelling interests. The first, *In re A.C.*, shows a conflict between, on the one hand, parental privacy, strengthened by the additional privacy interest in bodily integrity, and on the other hand, society's interest in the welfare of a not-yet-born child (i.e., a very late term fetus, who was planned and desired by both parents as a child to be born).

The second section of the chapter presents a number of custody disputes that center on conflicts with parental privacy rights. The Baby M. case presents a conflict between a mother's fundamental right of custody and a father's right to enforce the obligations of a contract (that she abandon this right). (See Article I, section 10, clause 1, of the Constitution for a reference to the obligation of contracts under state law.) The case of *Michael H. v. Gerald D.* presents a conflict between, in a sense, the right of family privacy and the right of parental privacy. The *Mississippi Choctaw* case presents a conflict between the right of Native American tribes to preserve tribal survival and the right of individual Native Americans to control their own child's upbringing. The abstract assertion that the right of parental privacy is fundamental is not adequate for resolving any of these difficult conflicts. The specific resolutions arrived at by the judges confronting these difficult questions are described and discussed in the rest of this chapter.

152

Coerced Caesareans: In re A.C. (1990)

The right to privacy has applications beyond the contexts of abortion and contraception, and one of its dimensions is the right to bodily integrity. This right to bodily integrity has not always prevailed in cases where it competed with other interests. For instance, early in the century, the Supreme Court upheld the power of the state to compel even unwilling persons to get a smallpox vaccination.[5] In that case the interest in protecting public health outweighed the right of bodily integrity. But typically the right is respected; persons with religious objections to direly needed medicine or surgery are not forced to accept either, despite the general public policy against suicide.

In a parallel way, the right of parental control combines with the child's right of bodily integrity to require in normal circumstances parental consent for a medically needed intrusion upon the body of a child. The state does intervene (against the fundamental right of parental control), however, to protect children who need such things as surgery or a blood transfusion when the parents, who normally have to give consent, object to such life-saving measures on religious grounds. This exception is founded on the societal obligation to protect the welfare of children.

The principles from these two lines of cases can come into conflict on the site of the body of a (willingly) pregnant woman when her fetus needs some medical intervention to which the mother is opposed. In certain prominent cases, appellate courts have ordered life-saving blood transfusions for a fetus against the wishes of a pregnant woman.[6] The question of a coerced caesarean delivery greatly intensifies this conflict. The woman's right to bodily integrity would seem to preclude the government's power to coerce her to permit the massive surgical intrusion of a caesarean delivery. On the other hand, the state's policy to protect children against abusive or destructive decisions of their parents would seem to call for protection of a near-term, viable fetus, especially in cases where the parents did not opt for abortion and fully intend for the child to be born.

One case presenting these clashing principles was fraught with so much melodrama that the story was later adapted for an episode of the television series *L.A. Law*. As a binding precedent it had a small reach geographically, having been decided by the D.C. Court of Appeals (similar to a state court of appeals, but situated in the District of Columbia) in 1990. The issues in the case were so compelling, however, that several national-level interest groups participated in writing briefs, including the American Medical Association, the American College of Obstetricians and Gynecologists,[7] the National Organization for Women, the American Civil Liberties Union, Americans United for Life, and the United States Catholic Conference.

In the circumstances of the case, *In re A.C.*,[8] A.C. was twenty-six and a half weeks pregnant and had had cancer for several years. At the critical point in her story, doctors diagnosed her as having only twenty-four to forty-eight hours left to live, and her fetus, if delivered immediately, as having a 50 to 60 percent chance of survival and a less than 20 percent chance of substantial impairment. With each passing hour the fetal chances of survival dwindled and likelihood of substantial impairment increased. Two hearings were held to determine the wishes of A.C. concerning caesarean delivery. During the first, convened at the hospital in response to the hospital's request for a declaratory judgment on how to proceed, her doctors testified that earlier they had discussed caesarean delivery with A.C. as an option for a twenty-eight-week fetus and that she had clearly consented to it, if it would enhance fetal survival, even if for her it would be "a terminal event." Her mother claimed that these earlier discussions should be discounted because A.C. never understood that caesarean surgery might cause her to die before she could hold her baby. Her husband was too distraught to testify. One doctor testified that he had heard A.C. say nothing to indicate that she would refuse permission for the caesarean. Another doctor testified that in the earlier discussions of a caesarean A.C. had never seriously considered the possibility that she might not survive the operation. In response to a judicial query whether A.C. could be questioned at that moment about her wishes, her doctors testified that A.C. was at that time heavily sedated—too sedated for her consent to count as "informed consent" for legal purposes—and that any reduction in her sedation to intensify her level of consciousness would hasten her death.

After this hearing the trial court entered findings to the effect that one could not clearly know the views of A.C., that the state has an important and legitimate interest in protecting the potentiality of life in the viable fetus, that the operation "may very well" hasten the death of A.C., and that any delay would greatly increase risk to the fetus. Relying on a precedent, *In re Madyun*,[9] the court then ordered the surgery.

A.C.'s doctors went to her bedside and informed her of the court order. One of them explained the situation, including the point that a caesarean was the fetus's only chance for survival, and asked if she would agree to the operation. She said yes. He asked if she understood that she might not survive the procedure. She said yes again. He then repeated both questions and asked if she understood them and she again said yes. He reported her responses in his testimony when the court reconvened later in the day. The court recommended moving the hearing to A.C.'s bedside, but the doctors prevailed against that idea. Instead, two doctors and A.C.'s mother and husband went to her bedside to confirm her consent. In response to similar questions but, as the doctors described it, "flanked by a weeping husband and mother," A.C. now said of the procedure, "I don't want it done. I don't want it done." Both doctors testified that her level of sedation had worn off enough by this time that she was conscious of what she was hearing and saying but that the circumstances—intensive care intubation, the presence of profusely distraught family members, and the stress of the situation—made informed consent impossible. The court ruled that A.C.'s intent was "still not clear" and again ordered the surgery. A request for a stay to the appeals court was denied, and the surgery took place. A few hours later the baby died, and two days later A.C. died of cancer.

A.C.'s estate sued the hospital. Meanwhile, the hospital asked the appeals court for a declaratory judgment, so that it would have guidance for future, similar cases. The appeals court accepted the hospital's request, explaining that this was one of those situations "capable of repetition but [if mootness rules were strictly applied] evading review." The court of appeals produced a 7–1 decision critical of the trial court's approach to the case. Both the majority and the dissenting lines of reasoning follow.

In re A.C., 573 A.2d 1235 (D.C. App. 1990)

JOHN A. TERRY, Associate Judge:

. . .

A. Informed Consent and Bodily Integrity

From a recent national survey, it appears that over the five years preceding the survey there were thirty-six attempts to override maternal refusals of proposed medical treatment, and that in fifteen instances where court orders were sought to authorize caesarean interventions, thirteen such orders were granted. *Obstetrical Interventions*, 316 New Eng. J. Med. at 1192–93. *Compare* Goldberg, *Medical Choices During Pregnancy: Whose Decision Is It Anyway?*, 41 Rutgers L. Rev. 591, 609 (1989) (finding twelve such cases). Nevertheless, there is only one published decision from an appellate court that deals with the question of when, or even whether, a court may order a caesarean section: *Jefferson v. Griffin Spalding County Hospital Authority*, 274 S.E.2d 457 (1981).

Jefferson is of limited relevance, if any at all, to the present case. In *Jefferson* there was a competent refusal by the mother to undergo the proposed surgery, but the ev-

idence showed that performance of the caesarean was in the medical interests of both the mother and the fetus.[7] In the instant case, by contrast, the evidence is unclear as to whether A.C. was competent when she mouthed her apparent refusal of the caesarean ("I don't want it done"), and it was generally assumed that while the surgery would most likely be highly beneficial to the fetus, it would be dangerous for the mother. . . . The procedure may well have been against A.C.'s medical interest, but if she was competent and given the choice, she may well have consented to an

7. Because the patient in *Jefferson* had a placenta previa which blocked the birth canal, doctors estimated that without caesarean intervention there was a ninety-nine percent chance that her full-term fetus would perish and a fifty percent chance that the mother would die as well. The mother was unquestionably competent to make her own treatment decisions, but refused a caesarean because of her religious beliefs. A trial court gave custody of the fetus to state human resources officials and ordered a caesarean section; the Georgia Supreme Court denied the parents' motion for a stay.

operation of significant risk to herself in order to maximize her fetus' chance for survival. From the evidence, however, we simply cannot tell whether she would have consented or not.

Thus our analysis of this case begins with the tenet common to all medical treatment cases: that any person has the right to make an informed choice, if competent to do so, to accept or forego medical treatment. The doctrine of informed consent, based on this principle and rooted in the concept of bodily integrity, is ingrained in our common law. Under the doctrine of informed consent, a physician must inform the patient, "at a minimum," of "the nature of the proposed treatment, any alternative treatment procedures, and the nature and degree of risks and benefits inherent in undergoing and in abstaining from the proposed treatment." *Crain v. Allison,* 443 A.2d 558, 561–62 (D.C. 1982). To protect the right of every person to bodily integrity, courts uniformly hold that a surgeon who performs an operation without the patient's consent may be guilty of a battery, *Canterbury v. Spence,* 464 F.2d 772, 783, or that if the surgeon obtains an insufficiently informed consent, he or she may be liable for negligence. *Crain v. Allison,* 443 A.2d at 561–62. Furthermore, the right to informed consent "also encompasses a right to informed refusal." *In re Conroy,* 486 A.2d 1209, 1222 (1985).

In the same vein, courts do not compel one person to permit a significant intrusion upon his or her bodily integrity for the benefit of another person's health.*See, e.g., Bonner v. Moran,* 126 F.2d 121, 122 (1941) (parental consent required for skin graft from fifteen-year-old for benefit of cousin who had been severely burned); *McFall v. Shimp,* 10 Pa.D. & C.3d 90 (Allegheny County Ct. 1978). In *McFall* the court refused to order Shimp to donate bone marrow which was necessary to save the life of his cousin, McFall.... Even though Shimp's refusal would mean death for McFall, the court would not order Shimp to allow his body to be invaded. It has been suggested that fetal cases are different because a woman who "has chosen to lend her body to bring [a] child into the world" has an enhanced duty to assure the welfare of the fetus, sufficient even to require her to undergo caesarean surgery. Surely, however, a fetus cannot have rights in this respect superior to those of a person who has already been born.[8]

This court has recognized as well that, above and beyond common law protections, the right to accept or forego medical treatment is of constitutional magnitude. *See In re Bryant,* 542 A.2d 1216, 1218 (D.C. 1988); *In re Boyd,* 403 A.2d 744, 748 (D.C. 1979); *In re Osborne,* 294 A.2d 372 (D.C. 1972). Other courts also have found a basis in the Constitution for refusing medical treatment. [Citations omitted.—Au.]

Decisions of the Supreme Court, while not explicitly recognizing a right to bodily integrity, seem to assume that individuals have the right, depending on the circumstances, to accept or refuse medical treatment or other bodily invasion. *See, e.g.,*

8. There are also practical consequences to consider. What if A.C. had refused to comply with a court order that she submit to a caesarean? Under the circumstances, she obviously could not have been held in civil contempt and imprisoned or required to pay a daily fine until compliance. Enforcement could be accomplished only through physical force or its equivalent. A.C. would have to be fastened with restraints to the operating table, or perhaps involuntarily rendered unconscious by forcibly injecting her with an anesthetic, and then subjected to unwanted major surgery. Such actions would surely give one pause in a civilized society, especially when A.C. had done no wrong. *Cf. Rochin v. California,* 342 U.S. 165, 169 (1952).

Winston v. Lee, 470 U.S. 753 (1985); *Schmerber v. California,* 384 U.S. 757 (1966); *Rochin v. California, supra,* note 8; *cf. Union Pacific Ry v. Botsford,* 141 U.S. 250, 251 (1891) ("No right is held more sacred, or is more carefully guarded, *by the common law,* than the right of every individual to the possession and control of his own person, free from all restraint or interference of others, unless by clear and unquestionable authority of law" (emphasis added)). In *Winston v. Lee* a robbery suspect challenged the state's right to compel him to submit to surgery for the removal of a bullet which was lodged in a muscle in his chest. The Court noted that the proposed surgery, which would require a general anesthetic, "would be an 'extensive' intrusion on respondent's personal privacy and bodily integrity" and a "virtually total divestment of respondent's ordinary control over surgical probing beneath his skin," 470 U.S. at 764–65, and held that, without the patient-suspect's consent, the surgery was constitutionally impermissible. Nevertheless, even in recognizing a right to refuse medical treatment or state-imposed surgery, neither *Winston* nor any other Supreme Court decision holds that this right of refusal is absolute. Rather, in discussing the constitutional "reasonableness of surgical intrusions beneath the skin," the Court said in *Winston* that the Fourth Amendment "neither forbids nor permits all such intrusions. . . ." *Id.* at 760 (citing *Schmerber v. California); see also Jacobson v. Massachusetts,* 197 U.S. 11 (1905).[9]

This court and others, while recognizing the right to accept or reject medical

9. We think it appropriate here to reiterate that this case is not about abortion. . . . The issue presented in this case is not whether A.C. (or any woman) should have a child but, rather, who should decide how that child should be delivered. That decision involves the right of A.C. (or any woman) to accept or forego medical treatment. . . .

treatment, have consistently held that the right is not absolute. . . . In some cases, especially those involving life-or-death situations or incompetent patients, the courts have recognized four countervailing interests that may involve the state as *parens patriae:* preserving life, preventing suicide, maintaining the ethical integrity of the medical profession, and protecting third parties. Neither the prevention of suicide[12] nor the integrity of the medical profession has any bearing on this case. Further, the state's interest in preserving life must be truly compelling to justify overriding a competent person's right to refuse medical treatment. This is equally true for incompetent patients, who have just as much right as competent patients to have their decisions made while competent respected, even in a substituted judgment framework.

In those rare cases in which a patient's right to decide her own course of treatment has been judicially overridden, courts have usually acted to vindicate the state's interest in protecting third parties, even if in fetal state. *See Jefferson v. Griffin Spalding County Hospital Authority, supra* (ordering that caesarean section be performed on a woman in her thirty-ninth week of pregnancy to save both the mother and the fetus); *Raleigh Fitkin-Paul Morgan Memorial Hospital v. Anderson* 201 A.2d 537 (ordering blood transfusions over the objection of a Jehovah's Witness, in her thirty-second week of pregnancy, to save her life and that of the fetus), *cert. denied,* 377 U.S. 985 (1964); *In re Jamaica Hospital,* 491 N.Y.S.2d 898 (Sup.Ct.1985) (ordering the transfusion of blood to a Jehovah's Witness eighteen weeks pregnant, who objected on religious grounds, and finding that

12. Courts have uniformly drawn a distinction between affirmatively acting to commit suicide and merely allowing one's body to follow its natural course without treatment. . . .

the state's interest in the not-yet-viable fetus outweighed the patient's interests); *Crouse Irving Memorial Hospital, Inc. v. Paddock*, 485 N.Y.S.2d 443 (Sup.Ct.1985) (ordering transfusions as necessary over religious objections to save the mother and a fetus that was to be prematurely delivered); *cf. In re President & Directors of Georgetown College, Inc.*, 331 F.2d 1000, 1008, *cert. denied*, 377 U.S. 978 (1964) (ordering a transfusion, *inter alia*, because of a mother's parental duty to her living minor children). *But see Taft v. Taft*, 446 N.E.2d 395 (1983) (vacating an order which required a woman in her fourth month of pregnancy to undergo a "purse-string" operation, on the ground that there were no compelling circumstances to justify overriding her religious objections and her constitutional right of privacy).

What we distill from the cases discussed in this section is that every person has the right, under the common law and the Constitution, to accept or refuse medical treatment. This right of bodily integrity belongs equally to persons who are competent and persons who are not. Further, it matters not what the quality of a patient's life may be; the right of bodily integrity is not extinguished simply because someone is ill, or even at death's door. To protect that right against intrusion by others—family members, doctors, hospitals, or anyone else, however well-intentioned—we hold that a court must determine the patient's wishes by any means available, and must abide by those wishes unless there are truly extraordinary or compelling reasons to override them. When the patient is incompetent, or when the court is unable to determine competency, the substituted judgment procedure must be followed.

From the record before us, we simply cannot tell whether A.C. was ever competent, after being sedated, to make an informed decision one way or the other regarding the proposed caesarean section. The trial court

never made any finding about A.C.'s competency to decide. Undoubtedly, during most of the proceedings below, A.C. was incompetent to make a treatment decision. . . .

We think it is incumbent on any trial judge in a case like this, unless it is impossible to do so, to ascertain whether a patient is competent to make her own medical decisions. Whenever possible, the judge should personally attempt to speak with the patient and ascertain her wishes directly, rather than relying exclusively on hearsay evidence, even from doctors. . . . We have no reason to believe that, if competent, A.C. would or would not have refused consent to a caesarean. We hold, however, that without a competent refusal from A.C. to go forward with the surgery, and without a finding through substituted judgment that A.C. would not have consented to the surgery, it was error for the trial court to proceed to a balancing analysis, weighing the rights of A.C. against the interests of the state.

There are two additional arguments against overriding A.C.'s objections to caesarean surgery. First, as the American Public Health Association cogently states in its *amicus curiae* brief:

Rather than protecting the health of women and children, court-ordered caesareans erode the element of trust that permits a pregnant woman to communicate to her physician—without fear of reprisal—all information relevant to her proper diagnosis and treatment. An even more serious consequence of court-ordered intervention is that it drives women at high risk of complications during pregnancy and childbirth out of the health care system to avoid coerced treatment.

Second, and even more compellingly, any judicial proceeding in a case such as this will ordinarily take place—like the one before us here—under time constraints so pressing that it is difficult or impossible for the mother to communicate adequately with counsel, or for counsel to organize an effective factual and legal presentation in defense of her liberty and privacy interests and bodily integrity. Any intrusion implicating such basic values ought not to be lightly undertaken when the mother not only is precluded from conducting pre-trial discovery (to which she would be entitled as a matter of course in any controversy over even a modest amount of money) but also is in no position to prepare meaningfully for trial. . . .

In this case A.C.'s court-appointed attorney was unable even to meet with his client before the hearing. By the time the case was heard, A.C.'s condition did not allow her to be present, nor was it reasonably possible for the judge to hear from her directly. The factual record, moreover, was significantly flawed because A.C.'s medical records were not before the court. . . . Finally, the time for legal preparation was so minimal that neither the court nor counsel mentioned the doctrine of substituted judgment, which—with benefit of briefs, oral arguments, and above all, time—we now deem critical to the outcome of this case. We cannot be at all certain that the trial judge would have reached the same decision if . . . there had been enough time for him to consider and reflect on these matters as a judge optimally should do.

B. Substituted Judgment

In the previous section we discussed the right of an individual to accept or reject medical treatment. We concluded that if a patient is competent and has made an informed decision regarding the course of her medical treatment, that decision will control in virtually all cases. Sometimes, however, as our analysis presupposes here, a once competent patient will be unable to

render an informed decision. In such a case, we hold that the court must make a substituted judgment on behalf of the patient, based on all the evidence. This means that the duty of the court, "as surrogate for the incompetent, is to determine as best it can what choice that individual, if competent, would make with respect to medical procedures." *In re Boyd*, 403 A.2d at 750.

Under the substituted judgment procedure, the court as decision-maker must "substitute itself as nearly as may be for the incompetent, and . . . act upon the same motives and considerations as would have moved her. . . ." *City Bank Farmers Trust Co. v. McGowan*, 323 U.S. 594, 599 (1945).

We have found no reported opinion applying the substituted judgment procedure to the case of an incompetent pregnant patient whose own life may be shortened by a caesarean section, and whose unborn child's chances of survival may hang on the court's decision. Despite this precedential void, we conclude that substituted judgment is the best procedure to follow in such a case because it most clearly respects the right of the patient to bodily integrity. Thus we reaffirm our holding in *In re Boyd*, in which we discussed how a substituted judgment should be made when a patient, although incompetent, has previously expressed objections to treatment, and we observe that many of the factors found relevant to discerning the patient's choice in *Boyd* are relevant here.

We begin with the proposition that the substituted judgment inquiry is primarily a subjective one: as nearly as possible, the court must ascertain what the patient would do if competent. *In re Boyd*, 403 A.2d at 750. . . .

Because it is the patient's decisional rights which the substituted judgment inquiry seeks to protect, courts are in accord that the greatest weight should be given to the previously expressed wishes of the patient. This includes prior statements, either written or oral, even though the treatment alternatives at hand may not have been addressed. The court should also consider previous decisions of the patient concerning medical treatment, especially when there may be a discernibly consistent pattern of conduct or of thought. . . . Thus in a case such as this it would be highly relevant that A.C. had consented to intrusive and dangerous surgeries in the past, and that she chose to become pregnant and to protect her pregnancy by seeking treatment at the hospital's high-risk pregnancy clinic. It would also be relevant that she accepted a plan of treatment which contemplated caesarean intervention at the twenty-eighth week of pregnancy, even though the possibility of a caesarean during the twenty-sixth week was apparently unforeseen. On the other hand, A.C. agreed to a plan of palliative treatment which posed a greater danger to the fetus than would have been necessary if she were unconcerned about her own continuing care. Further, when A.C. was informed of the fatal nature of her illness, she was equivocal about her desire to have the baby.

Courts in substituted judgment cases have also acknowledged the importance of probing the patient's value system as an aid in discerning what the patient would choose. We agree with this approach. Most people do not foresee what calamities may befall them; much less do they consider, or even think about, treatment alternatives in varying situations. The court in a substituted judgment case, therefore, should pay special attention to the known values and goals of the incapacitated patient, and should strive, if possible, to extrapolate from those values and goals what the patient's decision would be.

Although treating physicians may be an invaluable source of such information about a patient, the family will often be the best source. . . . Family members or other loved ones will usually be in the best position to say what the patient would do if competent. The court should be mindful, however, that while in the majority of cases family members will have the best interests of the patient in mind, sometimes family members will rely on their own judgments or predilections rather than serving as conduits for expressing the patient's wishes. This is why the court should endeavor, whenever possible, to make an in-person appraisal "of the patient's personal desires and ability for rational choice. . . ."*In re Osborne*, 294 A.2d at 374. . . .

In short, to determine the subjective desires of the patient, the court must consider the totality of the evidence, focusing particularly on written or oral directions concerning treatment to family, friends, and health-care professionals. The court should also take into account the patient's past decisions regarding medical treatment, and attempt to ascertain from what is known about the patient's value system, goals, and desires what the patient would decide if competent.

After considering [all these] . . . the court may supplement its knowledge about the patient by determining what most persons would likely do in a similar situation. When the patient is pregnant, however, she may not be concerned exclusively with her own welfare. Thus it is proper for the court, in a case such as this, to weigh (along with all the other factors) the mother's prognosis, the viability of the fetus, the probable result of treatment or non-treatment for both mother and fetus, and the mother's likely interest in avoiding impairment for her child together with her own instincts for survival.

Additionally, the court should consider the context in which prior declarations, treatment decisions, and expressions of personal values were made, including whether statements were made casually or after contemplation, or in accordance with deeply held beliefs. Finally, in making a substituted judgment, the court should become as informed about the patient's condition, prognosis, and treatment options as one would expect any patient to become before making a treatment decision. Obviously, the weight accorded to all of these factors will vary from case to case.

C. The Trial Court's Ruling

In this case there is an understandable paucity of factual findings, which necessarily limits our review. The trial court, faced with an issue affecting life and death, was forced to make a decision with almost no time for deliberation. Nevertheless, after reviewing the transcript of the hearing and the court's oral findings, it is clear to us that the trial court did not follow the substituted judgment procedure. On the contrary, ... [i]nstead, the court undertook to balance the state's and L.M.C.'s interests in surgical intervention against A.C.'s perceived interest in not having the caesarean performed.

After A.C. was informed of the court's decision, she consented to the caesarean; moments later, however, she withdrew her consent. The trial court did not then make a finding as to whether A.C. was competent to make the medical decision or whether she had made an informed decision one way or the other. Nor did the court then make a substituted judgment for A.C. Instead, the court said that it was "still not clear what her intent is" and again ordered the caesarean.

It is that order which we must now set aside. What a trial court must do in a case such as this is to determine, if possible, whether the patient is capable of making an informed decision about the course of her medical treatment. If she is, and if she makes such a decision, her wishes will control in virtually all cases. If the court finds that the patient is incapable of mak-

ing an informed consent (and thus incompetent), then the court must make a substituted judgment. Again, in virtually all cases the decision of the patient, albeit discerned through the mechanism of substituted judgment, will control. We do not quite foreclose the possibility that a conflicting state interest may be so compelling that the patient's wishes must yield,[22] but we anticipate that such cases will be extremely rare and truly exceptional. This is not such a case.

Having said that, we go no further. We need not decide whether, or in what circumstances, the state's interests can ever prevail over the interests of a pregnant patient. We emphasize, nevertheless, that it would be an extraordinary case indeed in which a court might ever be justified in overriding the patient's wishes and authorizing a major surgical procedure such as a caesarean section.... Indeed, some may doubt that there could ever be a situation extraordinary or compelling enough to justify a massive intrusion into a person's body, such as a caesarean section, against that person's will. Whether such a situation may someday present itself is a question that we need not strive to answer here. We see no need to reach out and decide an issue that is not presented on the record before us; this case is difficult enough as it is. We think it sufficient for now to chart the course for future cases resembling this one, and to express the hope that we shall not be presented with a case in the foreseeable future that requires us to sail off the chart into the unknown....

JAMES A. BELSON, Associate Judge, concurring in part and dissenting in part:

---

22. Absolutes like "never" should generally be avoided because "the future may bring scenarios which prudence counsels our not resolving anticipatorily." *Florida Star v. B.J.F.*, 491 U.S. 524, 532 (1989).

I agree with much of the majority opinion, but I disagree with its ultimate ruling that the trial court's order must be set aside, and with the narrow view it takes of the state's interest in preserving life and the unborn child's interest in life.

More specifically, I agree with the guidance the opinion affords trial judges as to how to approach a case like this, first determining the mother's competency to make an informed decision whether to have a caesarean delivery and, if the mother is not competent, then making a substituted judgment for the mother. I also agree that, with respect to surgical procedures, the pregnant woman's wishes, either as stated expressly or as discerned through substituted judgment, should ordinarily be respected and carried out unless there are compelling reasons to override them.

I disagree, however, with the majority's holding that the trial judge erred in failing to determine competency. I think it quite clear from the record that Judge Sullivan found A.C. incompetent. . . . I submit that the most reasonable reading of the record is that the judge found her incompetent when he stated:"The Court is of the view that it does not clearly know what [A.C.'s] present views are with respect to the issue of whether or not the child should live or die." A short time later, after hearing testimony about the sedated A.C.'s apparent reaction to the court's decision regarding surgery, the trial judge said: "The Court is still not clear what her intent is." . . . It is clear that the trial judge, at the very least, made a finding that was, under the majority's explanation of appropriate procedures, sufficient to move the inquiry forward to the substituted judgment stage. . . .

Another aspect of the majority opinion deserves comment. Having determined that the trial court must be reversed, the majority goes on to opine, in dictum, that this particular case is not one of those "extremely rare and truly exceptional" cases in which a patient's wishes regarding the proposed medical treatment can be overruled by reason of a compelling state interest (here, the interest in protecting the life of the viable unborn child). This is dictum because, as the majority points out, "[w]e have no reason to believe that, if competent, A.C. would or would not have refused consent to a caesarean."[2] . . .

I think it appropriate, nevertheless, to state my disagreement with the very limited view the majority opinion takes of the circumstances in which the interests of a viable unborn child can afford such compelling reasons. The state's interest in preserving human life and the viable unborn child's interest in survival are entitled, I think, to more weight than I find them assigned by the majority when it states that "in virtually all cases the decision of the patient . . . will control." I would hold that in those instances, fortunately rare, in which the viable unborn child's interest in living and the state's parallel interest in protecting human life come into conflict with the mother's decision to forgo a procedure such as a caesarean section, a balancing should be struck in which the unborn child's and the state's interests are entitled to substantial weight.

It was acknowledged in *Roe v. Wade,* 410 U.S. 113 (1973), that the state's interest in potential human life becomes compelling at the point of viability. Even before viability, the state has an "important and legitimate interest in protecting the potentiality of human life." *Id.* at 162. When approximately the third trimester of pregnancy is reached (roughly the time of via-

2. In view of this statement, I find puzzling the majority's discussion of "two additional arguments against overriding A.C.'s objections to caesarean surgery." No such objections were found to exist.

bility, although with advances in medical science the time of viability is being reached sooner and sooner), the state's interest becomes sufficiently compelling to justify what otherwise would be unduly burdensome state interference with the woman's constitutionally protected privacy interest. Once that stage is reached, the state "may, if it chooses, regulate, and even proscribe, abortion except where it is necessary, in appropriate medical judgment, for the preservation of the life or health of the mother." *Roe*, 410 U.S. at 165. In addressing this issue, it is important to emphasize, as does the majority opinion, that this case is not about abortion, majority opinion at n. 9;[3] we are not discussing whether a woman has the legal right to terminate her pregnancy in its early stages. Rather, we are dealing with the situation that exists when a woman has carried an unborn child to viability. When the unborn child reaches the state of viability, the child becomes a party whose interests must be considered. *See* King, *The Juridical Status of the Fetus: A Proposal for Legal Protection of the Unborn*, 77 Mich. L. Rev. 1647, 1687 (1979) (viability, not birth, the determinative moment in development for purpose of determining when fetus is entitled to legal protection).

3. The majority opinion, however, oversimplifies matters when it states, n. 9: "[T]he issue presented in this case is not whether A.C. (or any woman) should have a child but, rather, who should decide how that child should be delivered." The cruel realities of the situation made the issue far more difficult. It could better be stated as whether the unborn child should face a greatly reduced chance of survival upon *post mortem* delivery occasioned by a decision to forgo a caesarean procedure or whether, instead, the child should be afforded a probability of living as a result of a surgical procedure that involved both some risk to A.C. and an invasion of her bodily integrity.

Turning to the rights of the child, tort law has long recognized the right of a living child to recover for injuries suffered when she was a viable unborn child. *See Bonbrest v. Kotz*, 65 F. Supp. 138 (D.D.C. 1946). . . .

Bonbrest proved to be a landmark case. In *Greater Southeast Hospital v. Williams*, 482 A.2d 394 (D.C. 1984), this court noted that "every jurisdiction in the United States has followed *Bonbrest* in recognizing a cause of action for prenatal injury, at least when the injury is to a viable infant later born alive." *Id.* at 396. We went on to hold in *Greater Southeast Hospital* that a viable unborn child *is a person* within the coverage of the wrongful death statute, D.C.Code § 16-2701 (1981). . . .

The holdings in *Bonbrest* and *Greater Southeast Hospital* establish that for purposes that are, at least, relevant to this case, a viable unborn child is a *person* at common law who has legal rights that are entitled to the protection of the courts. In a case like the one before us, the unborn child is a patient of both the hospital and any treating physician, and the hospital or physician may be liable to the child for the child's prenatal injury or death if caused by their negligence. . . .

. . . [T]he already recognized rights and interests mentioned above are sufficient to indicate the need for a balancing process in which the rights of the viable unborn child are assigned substantial weight. . . .

The balancing test should be applied in instances in which women become pregnant and carry an unborn child to the point of viability. This is not an unreasonable classification because, I submit, a woman who carries a child to viability is in fact a member of a unique category of persons. Her circumstances differ fundamentally from those of other potential patients for medical procedures that will aid another person, for example, a potential donor of bone marrow for transplant. This is so because she has undertaken to bear another human being, and has carried an unborn child to viability. Another unique feature of the situation we address arises from the singular nature of the dependency of the unborn child upon the mother. A woman carrying a viable unborn child is not in the same category as a relative, friend, or stranger called upon to donate bone marrow or an organ for transplant. Rather, the expectant mother has placed herself in a special class of persons who are bringing another person into existence, and upon whom that other person's life is totally dependent. Also, uniquely, the viable unborn child is literally captive within the mother's body. No other potential beneficiary of a surgical procedure on another is in that position.

For all of these reasons, a balancing becomes appropriate in those few cases where the interests we are discussing come into conflict. To so state is in no sense to fail to recognize the extremely strong interest of each individual person, including of course the expectant mother, in her bodily integrity, her privacy, and, where involved, her religious beliefs.

Thus, I cannot agree with the conclusion of the majority opinion that while we "do not quite foreclose the possibility that a conflicting state interest may be so compelling that the patient's wishes must yield ... we anticipate that such cases will be extremely rare and truly exceptional." While it is, fortunately, true that such cases will be rare in the sense that such conflicts between mother and viable unborn child are rare,[7] I cannot agree that in cases where a viable unborn child is in the picture, it

would be extremely rare, within that universe, to require that the mother accede to the vital needs of the viable unborn child[8]. ...

I next address the sensitive question of how to balance the competing rights and interests of the viable unborn child and the state against those of the rare expectant mother who elects not to have a caesarean section necessary to save the life of her child. The indisputable view that a woman carrying a viable child has an extremely strong interest in her own life, health, bodily integrity, privacy, and religious beliefs necessarily requires that her election be given correspondingly great weight in the balancing process. In a case, however, where the court in an exercise of a substituted judgment has concluded that the patient would probably opt against a caesarean section, the court should vary the weight to be given this factor in proportion

---

7. The majority opinion at n. 21 quotes Opinion No. 55 of the Ethics Committee of the American College of Obstetricians and Gynecologists as follows: "[t]he welfare of the fetus is of the utmost importance to the majority of women; thus only rarely will a conflict arise." Another observer described the attitude of most expectant mothers more graphically: "The vast majority of women will accept significant risk, pain, and inconvenience to give their babies the best chance possible. One obstetrician who performs innovative fetal surgery stated that most of the women he sees 'would cut off their heads to save their babies.' " Rhoden, *The Judge in the Delivery Room: The Emergence of Court-Ordered Cesareans*, 74 Calif. L. Rev. 1951, 1959 (1986).

8. To the contrary, it appears that a majority of courts faced with this issue have found that the state's compelling interest in protection of the unborn child should prevail. *See* Noble-Allgire, *Court-Ordered Cesarean Sections*, 10 J. Legal Med. 211, 236 (1989). I add that in mapping this uncharted area of the law, we can draw lines, and a line I would draw would be to preclude the use of physical force to perform an operation. The force of the court order itself as well as the use of the contempt power would, I think, be adequate in most cases. *See id.* at 243.

to the confidence the court has in the accuracy of its conclusion. Thus, in a case where the indicia of the incompetent patient's judgment are equivocal, the court should accord this factor correspondingly less weight. The appropriate weight to be given other factors will have to be worked out by the development of law in this area, and cannot be prescribed in a single court opinion [but the mother's above-mentioned strong interests would certainly] ... deserve inclusion in the balancing process.

On the other side of the analysis, it is appropriate to look to the relative likelihood of the unborn child's survival....

The child's interest in being born with as little impairment as possible should also be considered. This may weigh in favor of a delivery sooner rather than later. The most important factor on this side of the scale, however, is life itself, because the viable unborn child that dies because of the mother's refusal to have a caesarean delivery is deprived, entirely and irrevocably, of the life on which the child was about to embark....

... I think this court cannot on this record hold that the trial judge abused his discretion in striking the balance he did....

CASE QUESTIONS

1. The judges in this case all agree that when a patient is unable to give informed consent to a needed medical procedure, the judicial technique of substituted judgment should be applied. They also all agree that when a patient gives "informed refusal" to surgery, only the most compelling of interests can ever override such a refusal. The judges differ among themselves over how compelling is the societal interest in protecting the survival of a viable fetus (one whom the mother never wished to abort and to whom the mother wishes to give birth). The dissenter argues that the strong interest in fetal survival should be taken seriously and is enough to justify the judicial order in the circumstances of this case (where the mother's objections were, at best, uncertain). The majority disagrees and says, further, that if the mother's refusal is clear, then her wishes may "virtually" never be overridden; any exception would be

"truly rare." They refuse to describe the possible exception. Does either side really give adequate guidance for future cases? Is such guidance possible?

2. Do you believe that a judge constructing a "substituted judgment" in a situation where the evidence of the woman's wishes is truly ambiguous will really be able to separate his or her own views of right and wrong from what the patient would want?

3. Compare footnote 8 of the majority opinion to footnote 8 of the dissent. Does the dissenter's guideline precluding the use of governmental force to compel surgery amount to an invitation to civil disobedience on the part of refusers? Is the judge not promising in advance that if the patient cares enough to resist, then the government will oblige? Does this guideline amount to discrimination against the unconscious (who are unable to resist)?

4. The dissenter sees the legal position regarding a compelled caesarean for a woman who decides to carry a fetus past the point of viability as different from the position of other persons who might be called upon to take medical risks for others, such as organ donors. Do you agree?

5. Is the degree of bodily intrusion (and commensurate health risk) so much greater for a caesarean delivery than for a blood transfusion that different rules should apply? Does this decision imply disapproval of coerced blood transfusions also?

6. This case pits risk to a mother's health against fetal survival. A number of other recent cases have pitted the personal freedom of pregnant women against fetal well-being: many of these have involved cocaine addicts who were prosecuted after childbirth for having harmed the newborn (e.g., by "delivering" drugs through the umbilical cord), or who were incarcerated before birth in order to protect the fetus from the cocaine habit. At what point, if any, should the societal duty to protect helpless children justify restricting the freedom of a pregnant woman? What of the pregnant woman who enjoys having a few drinks, and thus is willing to expose her fetus to an increased risk of incurring fetal alcohol syndrome? Do pregnant women have any less right to basic liberty than other Americans?

Child Custody

A dimension of the right of privacy that is noted in court opinions even more often than the right of bodily integrity is the right to "the care and custody" of one's children. The Supreme Court first discussed this fundamental right in what was essentially an equal protection context. In *Stanley v. Illinois* (1972) the state tried to deprive a man (Stanley) of legal custody of his own children for the sole reason that the children's mother died. For years Stanley had lived with his children and their mother but had never married the mother. When the mother died, the state refused to recognize him as their lawful father and tried to take the children. Stanley took his case to the Supreme Court, arguing that the law that would allow a divorced father in his situation to keep his own children and would allow the same to a never-married mother of children whose father had died denied him equal protection of the law by treating him differently from these similarly situated persons. The U.S. Supreme Court agreed and in its written opinion created the rule that "the interest of a parent in the companionship, care, custody, and management of his or her children" is so fundamental that it is constitutionally protected under the due process clause.[10] Since *Stanley*, the Supreme Court has had a number of occasions to apply the constitutional right of parental custody, typically in situations involving unwed fathers who were contesting some legal preference for the mother.[11]

In recent years, however, the kinds of parental rights cases coming before appellate courts have become more variegated. One new sort of case involves conflicts resulting from new reproductive technologies. The most celebrated of these, *Baby M*, involved an attempt by a woman to regain maternal rights over, and legal custody of, a baby to whom she had given birth pursuant to a so-called surrogate mother contract. The state supreme court opinion appears below.

Another new issue, this one at the U.S. Supreme Court level, concerned a child custody conflict among the parties in a romantic triangle: a still-married woman, her husband, and the woman's extramarital paramour, who had fathered her child while she was married. This case, *Michael H. v. Gerald D.*, is the next one presented in this section.

The last of the child custody issues dealt with in this section concerned the conflict between the power of Indian tribal governments and the personal rights of tribal Indians, in *Mississippi Choctaw Indians v. Holyfield*. The case involved two tribal, reservation Indians who tried to give up their twins for adoption off the reservation, to non-Indians. While the first two cases in this section present a conflict between mothers' rights and fathers' rights, this one presents a conflict between mothers' (combined with fathers') rights and government. The outcome of the case indicates, as will become evident, that however much the Constitution may protect the right of a parent in general to control the "care and custody" of her child, if the parent is an Indian living on a reservation and trying to give the child up for adoption, she does not seem to have that right to the degree that the rest of the population does.

Surrogate Mothers: The *Baby M* Case (1988)

Like *A.C.*, the coerced caesarean case discussed above, *Baby M* had only a small geographic reach as a binding precedent—the state of New Jersey—yet it presented such compelling issues that it attracted amicus curiae (friend of the court) briefs from a number of prominent national organizations (e.g., the American Adoption Congress, the National Emergency Civil Liberties Union, the Eagle Forum, the Catholic League for Religious and Civil Rights) and even prominent, interested persons (e.g., authors Betty Friedan and Gloria Steinem). Unlike *A.C.*, it concerned not a brief and intensely private episode, but a drawn-out, public melodrama. Thus, it also attracted weeks of national media attention.

Prior to this New Jersey Supreme Court decision, a number of other state courts had dealt with the legality of so-called surrogacy contracts—i.e., contracts between a man and a woman not married to each other that stipulate a sum of money to be paid to the woman in exchange for her conceiving, by artificial insemination, bearing his child, and then agreeing to a termination of her own maternal rights so that his wife can adopt the baby. Courts in both New York[12] and Kentucky[13] had ruled that such contracts did not violate existing laws that prohibited baby-selling, or the payment of excessive fees in connection with adoption. Both courts stated that if the legislature wished to prohibit for-pay surrogacy contracts, it would have to do so explicitly. By contrast, the Michigan Supreme Court had ruled that state laws against excessive fees in connection with an adoption forbade a man to pay a woman for conceiving and bearing his child and for transferring the child to him and his wife.[14] All of these cases differed from the *Baby M* case in that they involved three willing parties—the husband, the wife, and the mother—and a challenge by government officials to the exchange of money.

The *Baby M* case began when the previously willing party, Mary Beth Whitehead, turned unwilling. Under a contract set up February of 1985 with her husband, Richard Whitehead, and with William Stern (and with regard to his wife, Elizabeth Stern), Mary Beth Whitehead agreed to conceive a child through artificial insemination using Stern's sperm, carry the child, deliver it at birth to the Sterns, and then do whatever was necessary to terminate her parental rights so that Mrs. Stern could adopt the baby. The Sterns agreed to pay nothing if the pregnancy did not proceed past four months, to pay $1,000 if the child were stillborn, and to pay $10,000 upon completion of Mrs. Whitehead's surrender of custody and termination of parental rights. (Stern also paid $7,500 to the Infertility Center of New York for arrangements in connection with the surrogacy contract.)

The motives of the parties were described in court as follows: Mrs. Stern had been diagnosed as possibly having multiple sclerosis and therefore feared serious risk to her health if she became pregnant. Mr. Stern wanted to continue his biological bloodline because most of his family had been destroyed in the Holocaust and he was the only survivor. Mrs. Whitehead's motives were that she wanted to give another couple "the gift of life" and also that her own family (she had two children with Mr. Whitehead) needed the $10,000.

On March 27, 1986, a baby was born to Mary Beth Whitehead, and on March 30 she delivered it to the Sterns, who took it home and named it Melissa. By this time Mrs. Whitehead had already cried when the Sterns mentioned naming the baby and expressed uncertainty about giving up the child. On March 31, she went to the Sterns' home and told them that she had become unable to eat, sleep, or concentrate on anything other than her need to have the baby back. She said she could not survive without the baby and that she had to have her, even if just for a week, after which she would return her. Fearing a potential suicide, the Sterns did relinquish the baby upon a promise of her return one week hence.

Mrs. Whitehead refused to return the baby and fled the state when Mr. Stern obtained a court order for custody of the child. She hid out with the baby in Florida until the Florida police tracked her down and enforced a second custody order that Stern had obtained from the Florida judiciary. From time to time during Mrs. Whitehead's fugitive sojourn in Florida, she would telephone the

Sterns and plead her case, eventually turning to a variety of desperate threats (she would kill herself, kill the child, or falsely accuse William Stern of having sexually molested her other daughter). After the child was back in New Jersey, the trial court ruled that the surrogacy contract was enforceable; ordered termination of Whitehead's parental rights; granted sole custody to William Stern; and then, after a few minutes of testimony from Mrs. Stern, ordered that Mrs. Stern be allowed to adopt Melissa, her husband's daughter. Mary Beth Whitehead appealed the decision to the New Jersey Supreme Court, which handed down the following decision in February 1988, by which time Baby M was almost two years old.

In the Matter of Baby M, 537 A.2d 1227 (N.J. 1988)

CHIEF JUSTICE ROBERT N. WILENTZ:

. . .

II
Invalidity and Unenforceability of Surrogacy Contract

We have concluded that this surrogacy contract is invalid. Our conclusion has two bases: direct conflict with existing statutes and conflict with the public policies of this State, as expressed in its statutory and decisional law. . . .

A. Conflict with Statutory Provisions

The surrogacy contract conflicts with: (1) laws prohibiting the use of money in connection with adoptions; (2) laws requiring proof of parental unfitness or abandonment before termination of parental rights is ordered or an adoption is granted; and (3) laws that make surrender of custody and consent to adoption revocable in private placement adoptions.

(1) Our law prohibits paying or accepting money in connection with any placement of a child for adoption. . . . Excepted are fees of an approved agency . . . and certain expenses in connection with childbirth. . . .

Considerable care was taken in this case to structure the surrogacy arrange-ment so as not to violate this prohibition. The arrangement was structured as follows: the adopting parent, Mrs. Stern, was not a party to the surrogacy contract; the money paid to Mrs. Whitehead was stated to be for her services—not for the adoption; the sole purpose of the contract was stated as being that "of giving a child to William Stern, its natural and biological father"; the money was purported to be "compensation for services and expenses and in no way . . . a fee for termination of parental rights or a payment in exchange for consent to surrender a child for adoption"; the fee to the Infertility Center ($7,500) was stated to be for legal representation, advice, administrative work, and other "services." Nevertheless, it seems clear that the money was paid and accepted in connection with an adoption. . . .

. . . The surrogacy agreement requires Mrs. Whitehead to surrender Baby M for the purposes of adoption. The agreement notes that Mr. *and Mrs.* Stern wanted to have a child, and provides that the child be "placed" with Mrs. Stern in the event Mr. Stern dies before the child is born. The payment of the $10,000 occurs only on surrender of custody of the child and "completion of the duties and obligations" of Mrs. Whitehead, including termination of her parental rights to facilitate adoption by Mrs. Stern. As for the contention that the Sterns are paying only for services and not for an adoption, we need note only that they would pay nothing in the event the child died before the fourth month of pregnancy, and only $1,000 if the child were stillborn, even though the "services" had been fully rendered. . . .

Mr. Stern knew he was paying for the adoption of a child; Mrs. Whitehead knew she was accepting money so that a child might be adopted; the Infertility Center knew that it was being paid for assisting in the adoption of a child. The actions of all three worked to frustrate the goals of the statute. It strains credulity to claim that these arrangements, touted by those in the surrogacy business as an attractive alternative to the usual route leading to an adoption, really amount to something other than a private placement adoption for money.

. . . The evils inherent in baby-bartering are loathsome for a myriad of reasons. The child is sold without regard for whether the purchasers will be suitable parents. . . . The natural mother does not receive the benefit of counseling and guidance to assist her in making a decision that may affect her for a lifetime. In fact, the monetary incentive to sell her child may, depending on her financial circumstances, make her decision less voluntary. . . .

. . . The negative consequences of baby-buying are potentially present in the surrogacy context, especially the potential for placing and adopting a child without regard to the interest of the child or the natural mother.

(2) The termination of Mrs. Whitehead's parental rights, called for by the surrogacy contract . . . fails to comply with the stringent requirements of New Jersey law. Our law, recognizing the finality of any termination of parental rights, provides

for such termination only where there has been a voluntary surrender of a child to an approved agency or to the Division of Youth and Family Services [DYFS] . . . or where there has been a showing of parental abandonment or unfitness. . . .

. . . Our statutes, and the cases interpreting them, leave no doubt that where there has been no written surrender to an approved agency or to DYFS, termination of parental rights will not be granted in this state absent a very strong showing of abandonment or neglect. . . . It is clear that a "best interests" determination is never sufficient to terminate parental rights; the statutory criteria must be proved.

In this case a termination of parental rights was obtained not by proving the statutory prerequisites but by claiming the benefit of contractual provisions. From all that has been stated above, it is clear that a contractual agreement to abandon one's parental rights, or not to contest a termination action, will not be enforced in our courts. . . .

Since the termination was invalid, it follows, as noted above, that adoption of Melissa by Mrs. Stern could not properly be granted.

(3) The provision in the surrogacy contract stating that Mary Beth Whitehead agrees to "surrender custody . . . and terminate all parental rights" contains no clause giving her a right to rescind. It is intended to be an irrevocable consent to surrender the child for adoption. . . .

. . . Such a provision, however, making irrevocable the natural mother's consent to surrender custody of her child in a private placement adoption, clearly conflicts with New Jersey law. . . .

. . . Not only do the form and substance of the consent in the surrogacy contract fail to meet statutory requirements, but the surrender of custody is made to a private party. It is not made, as the statute requires, either to an approved agency or to DYFS. . . . The legislative goal is furthered by regulations requiring approved agencies, prior to accepting irrevocable consents, to provide advice and counseling to women, making it more likely that they fully understand and appreciate the consequences of their acts.

. . . The provision in the surrogacy contract, agreed to before conception, requiring the natural mother to surrender custody of the child without any right of revocation is one more indication of the essential nature of this transaction: the creation of a contractual system of termination and adoption designed to circumvent our statutes.

B. Public Policy Considerations

The surrogacy contract's invalidity, resulting from its direct conflict with the above statutory provisions, is further underlined when its goals and means are measured against New Jersey's public policy. The contract's basic premise that the natural parents can decide in advance of birth which one is to have custody of the child, bears no relationship to the settled law that the child's best interests shall determine custody. . . .

The surrogacy contract guarantees permanent separation of the child from one of its natural parents. Our policy, however, has long been that to the extent possible, children should remain with and be brought up by both of their natural parents. . . .

The surrogacy contract violates the policy of this State that the rights of natural parents are equal concerning their child. . . . The whole purpose and effect of the surrogacy contract was to give the father the exclusive right to the child by destroying the rights of the mother.

The policies expressed in our comprehensive laws governing consent to the surrender of a child, discussed *supra*, stand in stark contrast to the surrogacy contract and what it implies. Here there is no counseling, independent or otherwise, of the natural mother, no evaluation, no warning.

Mrs. Whitehead was examined and psychologically evaluated, but if it was for her benefit, the record does not disclose that fact. . . . It is apparent that the profit motive got the better of the Infertility Center. Although the evaluation was made, it was not put to any use, and understandably so, for the psychologist warned that Mrs. Whitehead demonstrated certain traits that might make surrender of the child difficult and that there should be further inquiry into this issue in connection with her surrogacy. To inquire further, however, might have jeopardized the Infertility Center's fee. The record indicates that neither Mrs. Whitehead nor the Sterns were ever told of this fact, a fact that might have ended their surrogacy arrangement.

Under the contract, the natural mother is irrevocably committed before she knows the strength of her bond with her child. She never makes a totally voluntary, informed decision, for quite clearly any decision prior to the baby's birth is, in the most important sense, uninformed, and any decision after that, compelled by a pre-existing contractual commitment, the threat of a lawsuit, and the inducement of a $10,000 payment, is less than totally voluntary. Her interests are of little concern to those who controlled this transaction.

Worst of all, however, is the contract's total disregard of the best interests of the child. There is not the slightest suggestion that any inquiry will be made at any time to determine the fitness of the Sterns as custodial parents, of Mrs. Stern as an adoptive parent, their superiority to Mrs. Whitehead, or the effect on the child of not living with her natural mother.

This is the sale of a child, or, at the very least, the sale of a mother's right to her child, the only mitigating factor being that one of the purchasers is the father. Almost every evil that prompted the prohibition on the payment of money in connection with adoptions exists here.

The differences between an adoption and a surrogacy contract should be noted, since it is asserted that the use of money in connection with surrogacy does not pose the risks found where money buys an adoption.

First, and perhaps most important, all parties concede that it is unlikely that surrogacy will survive without money. Despite the alleged selfless motivation of surrogate mothers, if there is no payment, there will be no surrogates, or very few. That conclusion contrasts with adoption. . . .

Second, the use of money in adoptions does not *produce* the problem—conception occurs, and usually the birth itself, before illicit funds are offered. With surrogacy, the "problem," if one views it as such, consisting of the purchase of a woman's procreative capacity, at the risk of her life, is caused by and originates with the offer of money.

Third, with the law prohibiting the use of money in connection with adoptions, the built-in financial pressure of the unwanted pregnancy and the consequent support obligation do not lead the mother to the highest paying, ill-suited, adoptive parents. She is just as well-off surrendering the child to an approved agency. In surrogacy, the highest bidders will presumably become the adoptive parents regardless of suitability, so long as payment of money is permitted.

Fourth, the mother's consent to surrender her child in adoptions is revocable, even after surrender of the child, unless it be to an approved agency, where by regulation there are protections against an ill-advised surrender. In surrogacy, consent occurs so early that no amount of advice would satisfy the potential mother's need, yet the consent is irrevocable.

The main difference, that the unwanted pregnancy is unintended while the situation of the surrogate mother is voluntary and intended, is really not significant. . . . On reflection . . . it appears that the essential evil is the same, taking advantage of a woman's circumstances (the unwanted pregnancy or the need for money) in order to take away her child, the difference being one of degree.

In the scheme contemplated by the surrogacy contract in this case, a middle man, propelled by profit, promotes the sale. Whatever idealism may have motivated any of the participants, the profit motive predominates, permeates, and ultimately governs the transaction. The demand for children is great and the supply small. The availability of contraception, abortion, and the greater willingness of single mothers to bring up their children has led to a shortage of babies offered for adoption. . . . The situation is ripe for the entry of the middleman who will bring some equilibrium into the market by increasing the supply through the use of money.

Intimated, but disputed, is the assertion that surrogacy will be used for the benefit of the rich at the expense of the poor. . . .

In any event, even in this case one should not pretend that disparate wealth does not play a part simply because the contrast is not the dramatic "rich versus poor." At the time of trial, the Whiteheads' net assets were probably negative—Mrs. Whitehead's own sister was foreclosing on a second mortgage. Their income derived from Mr. Whitehead's labors. Mrs. Whitehead is a homemaker, having previously held part-time jobs. The Sterns are both professionals, she a medical doctor, he a biochemist. Their combined income when both were working was about $89,500 a year and their assets sufficient to pay for the surrogacy contract arrangements.

The point is made that Mrs. Whitehead *agreed* to the surrogacy arrangement, supposedly fully understanding the consequences. Putting aside the issue of how compelling her need for money may have been, and how significant her understanding of the consequences, we suggest that her consent is irrelevant. There are, in a civilized society, some things that money cannot buy. In America, we decided long ago that merely because conduct purchased by money was "voluntary" did not mean that it was good or beyond regulation and prohibition. *West Coast Hotel Co. v. Parrish*, 300 U.S. 379 (1937). Employers can no longer buy labor at the lowest price they can bargain for, even though that labor is "voluntary," 29 U.S.C. § 206 (1982), or buy women's labor for less money than paid to men for the same job, 29 U.S.C. § 206(d), or purchase the agreement of children to perform oppressive labor, 29 U.S.C. § 212, or purchase the agreement of workers to subject themselves to unsafe or unhealthful working conditions, 29 U.S.C. §§ 651 to 678. (Occupational Safety and Health Act of 1970). There are, in short, values that society deems more important than granting to wealth whatever it can buy, be it labor, love, or life. Whether this principle recommends prohibition of surrogacy, which presumably sometimes results in great satisfaction to all of the parties, is not for us to say. We note here only that, under existing law, the fact that Mrs. Whitehead "agreed" to the arrangement is not dispositive.

The long-term effects of surrogacy contracts are not known, but feared—the impact on the child who learns her life was bought, that she is the offspring of someone who gave birth to her only to obtain money; the impact on the natural mother as the full weight of her isolation is felt along with the full reality of the sale of her body and her child; the impact on the natural father and adoptive mother once they realize the consequences of their conduct. . . .

The surrogacy contract is based on principles that are directly contrary to the objectives of our laws.[10] It guarantees the separation of a child from its mother; it looks to adoption regardless of suitability; it totally ignores the child; it takes the child from the mother regardless of her wishes and her maternal fitness; and it does all of this, it accomplishes all of its goals, through the use of money.

Beyond that is the potential degradation of some women that may result from this arrangement. In many cases, of course, surrogacy may bring satisfaction, not only to the infertile couple, but to the surrogate mother herself. The fact, however, that many women may not perceive surrogacy negatively but rather see it as an opportunity does not diminish its potential for devastation to other women.

10. We note the argument of the Sterns that the sperm donor section of our Parentage Act, N.J.S.A. 9:17–38 to –59, implies a legislative policy that would lead to approval of this surrogacy contract. Where a married woman is artificially inseminated by another with her husband's consent, the Parentage Act creates a parent-child relationship between the husband and the resulting child. N.J.S.A. 9:17–44. The Parentage Act's silence, however, with respect to surrogacy, rather than supporting, defeats any contention that surrogacy should receive treatment parallel to the sperm donor artificial insemination situation. In the latter case the statute expressly transfers parental rights from the biological father, *i.e.*, the sperm donor, to the mother's husband. *Ibid.* Our Legislature could not possibly have intended any other arrangement to have the consequence of transferring parental rights without legislative authorization when it had concluded that legislation was necessary to accomplish that result in the sperm donor artificial insemination context.

In sum, the harmful consequences of this surrogacy arrangement appear to us all too palpable. In New Jersey the surrogate mother's agreement to sell her child is void. Its irrevocability infects the entire contract, as does the money that purports to buy it.

III
Termination

Nothing in this record justifies a finding that would allow a court to terminate Mary Beth Whitehead's parental rights under the statutory standard. It is not simply that obviously there was no "intentional abandonment or very substantial neglect of parental duties . . ." quite the contrary, but furthermore that the trial court never found Mrs. Whitehead an unfit mother and indeed affirmatively stated that Mary Beth Whitehead had been a good mother to her other children. 525 A.2d 1128.

IV
Constitutional Issues

Both parties argue that the Constitutions—state and federal—mandate approval of their basic claims. The source of their constitutional arguments is essentially the same: the right of privacy, the right to procreate, the right to the companionship of one's child, those rights flowing either directly from the fourteenth amendment or by its incorporation of the Bill of Rights, or from the ninth amendment, or through the penumbra surrounding all of the Bill of Rights. They are the rights of personal intimacy, of marriage, of sex, of family, of procreation. Whatever their source, it is clear that they are fundamental rights protected by both the federal and state Constitutions. *Lehr v. Robertson,* 463 U.S. 248 (1983); *Santosky v. Kramer,* 455 U.S. 745 (1982); *Zablocki v. Redhail,* 434 U.S. 374 (1978); *Quilloin v. Walcott,* 434 U.S. 246 (1978); *Carey v. Population Servs. Int'l,* 431 U.S. 678 (1977); *Roe v. Wade; Stanley v. Illinois,* 405 U.S. 645 (1972); *Griswold v. Connecticut; Skinner v.*

Oklahoma; Meyer v. Nebraska. The right asserted by the Sterns is the right of procreation; that asserted by Mary Beth Whitehead is the right to the companionship of her child. We find that the right of procreation does not extend as far as claimed by the Sterns. As for the right asserted by Mrs. Whitehead, since we uphold it on other grounds (*i.e.,* we have restored her as mother and recognized her right, limited by the child's best interests, to her companionship), we need not decide that constitutional issue, and for reasons set forth below, we should not.

The right to procreate, as protected by the Constitution, has been ruled on directly only once by the United States Supreme Court. *See Skinner v. Oklahoma,* (forced sterilization of habitual criminals violates equal protection clause of fourteenth amendment). Although *Griswold v. Connecticut* is obviously of a similar class, strictly speaking it involves the right *not* to procreate. The right to procreate very simply is the right to have natural children, whether through sexual intercourse or artificial insemination. It is no more than that. Mr. Stern has not been deprived of that right. Through artificial insemination of Mrs. Whitehead, Baby M is his child. The custody, care, companionship, and nurturing that follow birth are not parts of the right to procreation; they are rights that may also be constitutionally protected, but that involve many considerations other than the right of procreation. To assert that Mr. Stern's right of procreation gives him the right to the custody of Baby M would be to assert that Mrs. Whitehead's right of procreation does *not* give her the right to the custody of Baby M; it would be to assert that the constitutional right of procreation includes within it a constitutionally protected contractual right to destroy someone else's right of procreation.

We conclude that the right of procreation is best understood and protected if confined to its essentials, and that when dealing with rights concerning the resulting child, different interests come into play. There is nothing in our culture or society that even begins to suggest a fundamental right on the part of the father to the custody of the child as part of his right to procreate when opposed by the claim of the mother to the same child. We therefore disagree with the trial court: there is no constitutional basis whatsoever requiring that Mr. Stern's claim to the custody of Baby M be sustained. Our conclusion may thus be understood as illustrating that a person's rights of privacy and self-determination are qualified by the effect on innocent third persons of the exercise of those rights.

Mr. Stern also contends that he has been denied equal protection of the laws by the State's statute granting full parental rights to a husband in relation to the child produced, with his consent, by the union of his wife with a sperm donor. N.J.S.A. 9:17–44. The claim really is that of Mrs. Stern. It is that she is in precisely the same position as the husband in the statute: she is presumably infertile, as is the husband in the statute; her spouse by agreement with a third party procreates with the understanding that the child will be the couple's child. The alleged unequal protection is that the understanding is honored in the statute when the husband is the infertile party, but no similar understanding is honored when it is the wife who is infertile.

It is quite obvious that the situations are not parallel. A sperm donor simply cannot be equated with a surrogate mother. The State has more than a sufficient basis to distinguish the two situations—even if the only difference is between the time it takes to provide sperm for artificial insemination and the time invested in a nine-month pregnancy—so as to justify automatically divesting the sperm donor of his parental rights without automatically divesting a surrogate mother. Some basis for an equal

protection argument might exist if Mary Beth Whitehead had contributed her egg to be implanted, fertilized or otherwise, in Mrs. Stern, resulting in the latter's pregnancy. That is not the case here, however.

Mrs. Whitehead, on the other hand, asserts a claim that falls within the scope of a recognized fundamental interest protected by the Constitution. As a mother, she claims the right to the companionship of her child. This is a fundamental interest, constitutionally protected. Furthermore, it was taken away from her by the action of the court below. Whether that action under these circumstances would constitute a constitutional deprivation, however, we need not and do not decide. By virtue of our decision Mrs. Whitehead's constitutional complaint—that her parental rights have been unconstitutionally terminated—is moot. We have decided that both the statutes and public policy of this state require that that termination be voided and that her parental rights be restored. It therefore becomes unnecessary to decide whether that same result would be required by virtue of the federal or state Constitutions. Refraining from deciding such constitutional issues avoids further complexities involving the full extent of a parent's right of companionship,[14] or questions involving the fourteenth amendment.[15]

14. This fundamental right is not absolute. The parent-child biological relationship, by itself, does not create a protected interest in the absence of a demonstrated commitment to the responsibilities of parenthood; a natural parent who does not come forward and seek a role in the child's life has no constitutionally protected relationship. *Lehr v. Robertson*, 463 U.S. at 258–62; *Quilloin v. Walcott*, 434 U.S. at 254–55. The right is not absolute in another sense, for it is also well settled that if the state's interest is sufficient the right may be regulated, restricted, and on occasion terminated. *See Santosky v. Kramer, supra.*

15. Were we to find such a constitutional determination necessary, we would be faced

Having held the contract invalid and having found no other grounds for the termination of Mrs. Whitehead's parental rights, we find that nothing remains of her constitutional claim. . . .[16]

----

with the question of whether it was state action—essential in triggering the fourteenth amendment—that deprived her of that right, i.e., whether the judicial decision enforcing the surrogacy contract should be considered "state action" within the scope of the fourteenth amendment. *See Shelley v. Kraemer*, 334 U.S. 1 (1948); Cherminsky, *Rethinking State Action*, 80 Nw.U.L.Rev. 503 (1985).

16. If the Legislature were to enact a statute providing for enforcement of surrogacy agreements, the validity of such a statute might depend on the strength of the state interest in making it more likely that infertile couples will be able to adopt children. As a value, it is obvious that the interest is strong; but if, as plaintiffs assert, ten to fifteen percent of all couples are infertile, the interest is of enormous strength. This figure is given both by counsel for the Sterns and by the trial court, 217 N.J.Super. at 331, 525 A.2d 1128. We have been unable to find reliable confirmation of this statistic, however, and we are not confident of its accuracy. We note that at least one source asserts that in 1982, the rate of married couples who were both childless and infertile was only 5.8%. B. Wattenberg, *The Birth Dearth* 125 (1987).

On such quantitative differences, constitutional validity can depend, where the statute in question is justified as serving a compelling state interest. The quality of the interference with the parents' right of companionship bears on these issues: if a statute, like the surrogacy contract before us, made the consent given prior to conception irrevocable, it might be regarded as a greater interference with the fundamental right than a statute that gave that effect only to a consent executed, for instance, more than six months after the child's birth. There is an entire spectrum of circumstances that strengthen and weaken the fundamental right involved, and a similar spectrum of state

V
Custody

Having decided that the surrogacy contract is illegal and unenforceable, we now must decide the custody question without regard to the provisions of the surrogacy contract that would give Mr. Stern sole and permanent custody. . . .

We are not concerned at this point with the question of termination of parental rights, either those of Mrs. Whitehead or of Mr. Stern. As noted in various places in this opinion, such termination, in the absence of abandonment or a valid surrender, generally depends on a showing that the particular parent is unfit. . . . [N]o serious contention is made in this case that either is unfit. The issue here is which life would be better *for Baby M, one with primary custody in the Whiteheads or one with primary custody in the Sterns.* . . .

Our custody conclusion is based on strongly persuasive testimony contrasting both the family life of the Whiteheads and the Sterns and the personalities and characters of the individuals. The stability of

----

interests that justify or do not justify particular restrictions on that right. We do not believe it would be wise for this Court to attempt to identify various combinations of circumstances and interests, and attempt to indicate which combinations might and which might not constitutionally permit termination of parental rights.

We will say this much, however: a parent's fundamental right to the companionship of one's child can be significantly eroded by that parent's consent to the surrender of that child. That surrender, if voluntarily and knowingly made, may reduce the strength of that fundamental right to the point where a statute awarding custody and all parental rights to an adoptive couple, especially one that includes a parent of the child, would be valid.

the Whitehead family life was doubtful at the time of trial. Their finances were in serious trouble ... Mr. Whitehead's employment, though relatively steady, was always at risk because of his alcoholism, a condition that he seems not to have been able to confront effectively. . . . Mrs. Whitehead had not worked for quite some time, her last two employments having been part-time. One of the Whiteheads' positive attributes was their ability to bring up two children, and apparently well, even in so vulnerable a household. Yet substantial question was raised even about that aspect of their home life. . . . Her inconsistent stories about various things engendered grave doubts about her ability to explain honestly and sensitively to Baby M—and at the right time—the nature of her origin. . . .

The Sterns have no other children, but all indications are that their household and their personalities promise a much more likely foundation for Melissa to grow and thrive. There *is* a track record of sorts—during the one-and-a-half years of custody Baby M has done very well, and the relationship between both Mr. and Mrs. Stern and the baby has become very strong. The household is stable, and likely to remain so. Their finances are more than adequate, their circle of friends supportive, and their marriage happy. Most important, they are loving, giving, nurturing, and open-minded people. . . .

Based on all of this we have concluded, independent of the trial court's identical conclusion, that Melissa's best interests call for custody in the Sterns.

VI
Visitation

Our reversal of the trial court's order . . . requires delineation of Mrs. Whitehead's rights to visitation. It is apparent to us that this factually sensitive issue, which was never addressed below, should not be determined *de novo* by this Court. We therefore remand the visitation issue to [a new judge on] the trial court for an abbreviated hearing and determination . . .

CASE QUESTIONS

1. What exactly is the societal harm in allowing adoptive parents to pay a birth mother for her child? Does New Jersey Chief Justice Wilentz convince you that this was a "baby-selling" contract rather than a contract for services rendered? Can a father somehow "buy" his own child?

   If this is more sensibly viewed as a contract for services rendered, might the state nonetheless forbid it, just as it forbids prostitution? Is payment for the use of a uterus (and "donation" of an egg) significantly different from payment for the use of a vagina? If it is unconscionable for the state to allow payment for these services, should the state not also forbid payment to sperm "donors," as well as egg "donors"? Are donations of sperm and eggs, for pay, different in significant respects from selling one's parental rights to an actual child?

2. Should the right to privacy cover the right to exchange money for procreative services? Does the very exchange of money take the transaction out of the

realm of the private and put it in the realm of the public? Would it be consistent with the Constitution for a state to ban the payment of money for abortion services? If a state were to set a minimum fee for surrogacy contracts in order to prevent economic exploitation of poor women, say, at $25,000, might someone who wanted to negotiate a contract for less—say, $22,000—plausibly claim an infringement of the right to privacy?

Should the right to privacy mean that parenthood is so fundamental that mothers may not divest themselves of parental rights in advance of childbirth, and even after that must be given a substantial waiting period for further reflection?

3. Suppose that in the judge's consideration of the custody issue, the two families had seemed approximately equal in quality of temperament, sensitivity to children's needs, and emotional and financial stability. (And suppose further that the two families were intensely hostile to each other, as these had become, so that joint custody was out of the question.) Would it be appropriate for the judge to count against the mother her written agreement to give up all right to her child? To give the mother an automatic preference as a way of diminishing the incentives for fathers to hire "surrogate mothers" in the future?

In a society where female full-time wage-earners average seventy-one cents for every dollar earned on average by male full-time workers,[15] is it unconstitutionally discriminatory for judges awarding custody in divorce suits to consider the issue of "financial stability"? Is it unfair to the child not to consider it?

Adulterous Fathers: *Michael H. v. Gerald D.* (1989)

In June of 1989 the U.S. Supreme Court issued its opinion concerning another child custody dispute, also one with a high level of drama, but drama perhaps more typical of television soap operas than of stories about law, whether fictional or newsworthy. The case, *Michael H. v. Gerald D.*, presented a dispute over fathers' rights that involved a mother who at the time of conception and birth and thereafter was wed to someone other than the child's father.[16] California, like the other states, treats the mother's husband, in general, as the legal father of all children born into the marriage. The statutory exceptions follow:

> Except as provided [here] the issue of a wife cohabiting with her husband, who is not impotent or sterile, is conclusively presumed to be a child of the marriage.... The notice of a motion for blood tests [to determine paternity] ... may be raised by the husband not later than two years from the child's date of birth ... [or] by the mother of the child [under the same deadline] if the child's biological father has filed an affidavit with the Court acknowledging paternity.... (Calif. Evid. Code Ann. Sec. 621.)

Michael H., informed by Carole, the mother (who was married to Gerald D.), that he, Michael, was the father of Victoria, the child—information confirmed by blood tests with 98 percent accuracy—challenged the constitutionality of this statute, asking that he be declared the legal (or one of the two legal) father(s) of Victoria and be accorded visitation rights as such.

Justice Scalia (an Italian Catholic in his early fifties), writing for a plurality of four (who with Stevens's vote produced a majority upholding the law), began his opinion with the statement, "The facts of this case are, we must hope, extraordinary." Justice Brennan (an Irish Catholic in his eighties) concluded his dissent with the remark that "the situation confronting us here . . . repeat[s] itself every day in every corner of the country." Here follows the story whose typicalness is being so bluntly disputed:

Carole (an "international model") and Gerald D. (a "top executive in a French oil company") were married in 1976 and established a home in Los Angeles. In the summer of 1978 Carole began an affair with Michael H., a neighbor. Carole gave birth to Victoria in May 1981. Gerald was listed on the birth certificate as the father, but soon after the birth Carole confided to Michael that she believed him to be the father. For the first three years of Victoria's life, her mother lived with her in the following circumstances: May–October 1981, with husband Gerald (in October, Gerald left for New York, for business; in late October Carole and Michael had blood tests confirming his paternity); January 1982–March 1982, in Michael's home in St. Thomas (his primary business home); March 1982–autumn 1982, with Scott (a third man) in California; periods in spring and summer of 1982, with husband Gerald in New York City and on vacation in Europe; fall 1982–March 1983, with Scott in California; March 1983–July 1983 with husband Gerald in New York City; August 1983–April 1984, with Michael in Los Angeles (in Carole's apartment) whenever Michael was not in St. Thomas (in April 1984 Carole signed a stipulation that Michael was Victoria's father, but she moved out on him in May and ordered her lawyers not to file the stipulation); June 1984–1989, with husband Gerald, having reconciled with him, in New York (and opposed to visits by Michael).

During 1983–1984, before the case reached the Supreme Court, a number of motions and cross-motions were filed: Michael asked for filiation hearings to establish his paternity and a right to regular visitation; Carole in some motions supported his request and in others turned against him. Eventually, in October 1984, the husband Gerald had moved for a summary judgment denying Michael's request, since under California law, he, Gerald, was Victoria's father. Meanwhile a court-appointed guardian *ad litem* for the daughter, Victoria, had filed a request that if Victoria had more than one "psychological or de facto father," she should be allowed "to maintain her filial relationship with all its attendant rights, duties, and obligations, with both" fathers. For the duration of the litigation at the trial court level, pursuant to a recommendation from a court-appointed psychologist, the court ordered limited visitation rights between Michael and Victoria. In January 1985, the trial court granted Gerald's summary judgment, rejecting Michael and Victoria's argument[17] for the unconstitutionality of the statute declaring Gerald to be Victoria's father. The judge ruled further that visitation would not be permitted pending the appeal (which visitation the judge was statutorily authorized to allow to any person "having a reasonable interest in the welfare of [a] child"). The judge claimed that "the integrity of the family unit" of Victoria would be "impugned" by further visitation. Michael's and Victoria's lawyers appealed, alleging that this outcome violated constitutional rights of both procedural and substantive due process. In addition to its denial of the procedural right to a hearing to demonstrate paternity, Michael claimed that this ruling transgressed the substance of his constitutional right to the care and companionship of his child. The California Court of Appeals affirmed, and the California Supreme Court refused to hear the case. The U.S. Supreme Court then took the appeal, and by the time it decided the case Victoria was already eight years old. (At the U.S. Supreme Court, the lawyers also challenged the statutes on equal protection grounds, but Michael's lawyer had failed to raise that issue below, so the Supreme Court, as is standard, refused to address it.)[18]

The Supreme Court's resolution of this dispute is difficult to summarize because the justices disagreed among themselves even over what were the issues of the case. Scalia, Rehnquist, O'Connor, and Kennedy believed that Michael was claiming a constitution right "to be declared *the* father of Victoria" and to obtain thereby parental rights. They ruled that a man in Michael's situation has no such fundamental constitutional right. Justice Stevens concurred in the judgment, stating that this is no constitutional right in the abstract to have paternity merely declared. On the other hand, he believed that since California law did provide for a court to establish visitation rights for *any* person "having an interest in the welfare of the child" when the court believed such visits would serve the best interests of the child, "Michael was given a fair opportunity to show that he is Victoria's natural father, that he developed a relationship with her, and that her interests would be served by . . . visitation." Thus, Stevens believed that Michael *had been* accorded his "constitutional right to try to convince a trial judge that Victoria's best interest would be served by granting him visitation rights."

The dissenters (Brennan, Blackmun, Marshall, and White) agreed with Stevens that the issue in the case was a procedural one—the right to a hearing as to parental visitation rights—but they disagreed with his conclusion that California law honored this right by merely allowing others "interested in the welfare of the child" to be accorded, at the discretion of the judge, visitation rights. They believed that Michael had a constitutional right to an opportunity to establish his fatherhood in court because an official declaration of paternity would have a substantial impact on the visitation decision.

The five-justice majority in *Michael H.* broke ranks over a lengthy footnote (footnote 6), in which Scalia tried to limit the right to privacy to what were, in effect, relations within the nuclear family (whether *de jure* or *de facto*). Thus he viewed the issue as whether the Constitution specifically protects *adulterous* fatherhood (and answered no), whereas the dissenters focused on parenthood as such. Both O'Connor and Kennedy, as well as Stevens and the dissenters, noted that Scalia's approach was inconsistent with precedents such as *Eisenstadt v. Baird.* Excerpts from this multiplicity of opinions follow.

Michael H. v. Gerald D., 491 U.S. 110 (1989)

JUSTICE SCALIA announced announced the judgment of the Court and delivered an opinion, in which THE CHIEF JUSTICE joins, and in all but note 6 of which JUSTICE O'CONNOR and JUSTICE KENNEDY join.

I

The facts of this case are, we must hope, extraordinary.... [Here followed the facts.—Au.]

. . .

III

... California law, like nature itself, makes no provision for dual fatherhood. Michael was seeking to be declared *the* father of Victoria. The immediate benefit he evidently sought to obtain from that status was visitation rights. See Cal.Civ.Code Ann. § 4601 (West 1983) (parent has statutory right to visitation "unless it is shown that such visitation would be detrimental to the best interests of the child"). But if Michael were successful in being declared the father, other rights would follow—most importantly, the right to be considered as the parent who should have custody....

Michael raises two related challenges to the constitutionality of § 621. First, he asserts that requirements of procedural due process prevent the State from terminating his liberty interest in his relationship with

his child without affording him an opportunity to demonstrate his paternity in an evidentiary hearing. We believe this claim derives from a fundamental misconception of the nature of the California statute. While § 621 is phrased in terms of a presumption, that rule of evidence is the implementation of a substantive rule of law. California declares it to be, except in limited circumstances, *irrelevant* for paternity purposes whether a child conceived during and born into an existing marriage was begotten by someone other than the husband and had a prior relationship with him. As the Court of Appeal phrased it:

> "The conclusive presumption is actually a substantive rule of law based upon a determination by the Legislature as a matter of overriding social policy, that given a certain relationship between the husband and wife, the husband is to be held responsible for the child, and that the integrity of the family unit should not be impugned." 191 Cal. App. 3d, at 1005, 236 Cal. Rptr., at 816....

Of course the conclusive presumption not only expresses the State's substantive policy but also furthers it, excluding inquiries into the child's paternity that would be destructive of family integrity and privacy.[1]

This Court has struck down as illegitimate certain "irrebuttable presumptions." See, *e.g., Stanley v. Illinois*, 405 U.S. 645 (1972). . . . Those holdings did not, however, rest upon *procedural* due process. A conclusive presumption does, of course, foreclose the person against whom it is invoked from demonstrating, in a particularized proceeding, that applying the presumption to him will in fact not further the lawful governmental policy the presumption is designed to effectuate. But the same can be said of any legal rule that establishes general classifications, whether framed in terms of a presumption or not . . . We therefore reject Michael's procedural due process challenge and proceed to his substantive claim.

Michael contends as a matter of substantive due process that because he has established a parental relationship with Victoria, protection of Gerald's and Carole's marital union is an insufficient state interest to support termination of that relationship. This argument is, of course, predicated on the assertion that Michael has a constitutionally protected liberty interest in his relationship with Victoria.

It is an established part of our constitutional jurisprudence that the term "liberty" in the Due Process Clause extends beyond freedom from physical restraint. See, *e.g., Pierce v. Society of Sisters; Meyer v. Nebraska*. Without that core textual mean-

ing as a limitation, defining the scope of the Due Process Clause "has at times been a treacherous field for this Court," giving "reason for concern lest the only limits to . . . judicial intervention become the predilections of those who happen at the time to be Members of this Court." *Moore v. East Cleveland*, 431 U.S. 494, 502 (1977). The need for restraint has been cogently expressed by Justice White:

> That the Court has ample precedent for the creation of new constitutional rights should not lead it to repeat the process at will. The Judiciary, including this Court, is the most vulnerable and comes nearest to illegitimacy when it deals with judge-made constitutional law having little or no cognizable roots in the language or even the design of the Constitution. Realizing that the present construction of the Due Process Clause represents a major judicial gloss on its terms, as well as on the anticipation of the Framers . . ., the Court should be extremely reluctant to breathe still further substantive content into the Due Process Clause so as to strike down legislation adopted by a State or city to promote its welfare. Whenever the Judiciary does so, it unavoidably pre-empts for itself another part of the governance of the country without express constitutional authority. *Moore, supra*, at 544 (dissenting opinion).

In an attempt to limit and guide interpretation of the Clause, we have insisted not merely that the interest denominated as a "liberty" be "fundamental" (a concept that, in isolation, is hard to objectify), but also that it be an interest traditionally protected by our society.[2] As we have put it,

---

1. In those circumstances in which California allows a natural father to rebut the presumption of legitimacy of a child born to a married woman, *e.g.*, where the husband is impotent or sterile, or where the husband and wife have not been cohabiting, it is more likely that the husband already knows the child is not his, and thus less likely that the paternity hearing will disrupt an otherwise harmonious and apparently exclusive marital relationship.

2. We do not understand what JUSTICE BRENNAN has in mind [when he says] . . . our practice of

the Due Process Clause affords only those protections "so rooted in the traditions and conscience of our people as to be ranked as fundamental." *Snyder v. Massachussetts*, 291 U.S. 97, 105 (1934) . . .

This insistence that the asserted liberty interest be rooted in history and tradition is evident, as elsewhere, in our cases according constitutional protection to certain parental rights. Michael reads the landmark case of *Stanley v. Illinois*, and the subsequent cases of *Quilloin v. Walcott*, *Caban v. Mohammed*, and *Lehr v. Robertson*, as establishing that a liberty interest is created by biological fatherhood plus an established parental relationship—factors that exist in the present case as well. We think that distorts the rationale of those cases. As we view them, they rest not upon such isolated factors but upon the historic respect—indeed, sanctity would not be too strong a term—traditionally accorded to the relationships that develop within the unitary family.[3] In *Stanley*, for example, we forbade the destruction of such a family when, upon the death of the mother,

the state had sought to remove children from the custody of a father who had lived with and supported them and their mother for 18 years. As Justice Powell stated for the plurality in *Moore v. East Cleveland, supra*, 431 U.S., at 503:

> Our decisions establish that the Constitution protects the sanctity of the family precisely because the institution of the family is deeply rooted in this Nation's history and tradition.

Thus, the legal issue in the present case reduces to whether the relationship between persons in the situation of Michael and Victoria has been treated as a protected family unit under the historic practices of our society, or whether on any other basis it has been accorded special protection. We think it impossible to find that it has. In fact, quite to the contrary, our traditions have protected the marital family (Gerald, Carole, and the child they acknowledge to be theirs) against the sort of claim Michael asserts.[4]

---

limiting the Due Process Clause to traditionally protected interests turns the clause "into a redundancy." Its purpose is to prevent future generations from lightly casting aside important traditional values—not to enable this Court to invent new ones.

3. JUSTICE BRENNAN asserts that only "a pinched conception of 'the family'" would exclude Michael, Carole and Victoria from protection. We disagree. The family unit accorded traditional respect in our society, which we have referred to as the "unitary family," is typified, of course, by the marital family, but also includes the household of unmarried parents and their children. Perhaps the concept can be expanded even beyond this, but it will bear no resemblance to traditionally respected relationships—and will thus cease to have any constitutional significance—if it is stretched so far as to include the relationship established between a married

woman, her lover and their child, during a three-month sojourn in St. Thomas, or during a subsequent 8-month period when, if he happened to be in Los Angeles, he stayed with her and the child.

4. JUSTICE BRENNAN insists that in determining whether a liberty interest exists we must look at Michael's relationship with Victoria in isolation, without reference to the circumstance that Victoria's mother was married to someone else when the child was conceived, and that that woman and her husband wish to raise the child as their own. We cannot imagine what compels this strange procedure of looking at the act which is assertedly the subject of a liberty interest in isolation from its effect upon other people—rather like inquiring whether there is a liberty interest in firing a gun where the case at hand happens to involve its discharge into another person's body. . . .

The presumption of legitimacy was a fundamental principle of the common law. H. Nicholas, *Adulturine Bastardy* 1 (1836). Traditionally, that presumption could be rebutted only by proof that a husband was incapable of procreation or had had no access to his wife during the relevant period. *Id.,* at 9–10 (citing Bracton, *De Legibus et Consuetudinibus Angliae*, bk. i, ch. 9, p. 6; bk. ii, ch. 29, p. 63, ch. 32, p. 70 (1569)). . . .

We have found nothing in the older sources, nor in the older cases, addressing specifically the power of the natural father to assert parental rights over a child born into a woman's existing marriage with another man. Since it is Michael's burden to establish that such a power (at least where the natural father has established a relationship with the child) is so deeply embedded within our traditions as to be a fundamental right, the lack of evidence alone might defeat his case. But the evidence shows that even in modern times—when, as we have noted, the rigid protection of the marital family has in other respects been relaxed—the ability of a person in Michael's position to claim paternity has not been generally acknowledged.

Moreover, even if it were clear that one in Michael's position generally possesses, and has generally always possessed, standing to challenge the marital child's legitimacy, that would still not establish Michael's case. As noted earlier, what is at issue here is not entitlement to a state pronouncement that Victoria was begotten by Michael. It is no conceivable denial of constitutional right for a State to decline to declare facts unless some legal consequence hinges upon the requested declaration. What Michael asserts here is a right to have himself declared the natural father *and thereby to obtain parental prerogatives.* What he must establish, therefore, is not

that our society has traditionally allowed a natural father in his circumstances to establish paternity, but that it has traditionally accorded such a father parental rights, or at least has not traditionally denied them. . . . What counts is whether the States in fact award substantive parental rights to the natural father of a child conceived within and born into an extant marital union that wishes to embrace the child. We are not aware of a single case, old or new, that has done so. This is not the stuff of which fundamental rights qualifying as liberty interests are made.[6]

---

6. JUSTICE BRENNAN criticizes our methodology in using historical traditions specifically relating to the rights of an adulterous natural father, rather than inquiring more generally "whether parenthood is an interest that historically has received our attention and protection." There seems to us no basis for the contention that this methodology is "nove[l]." . . .

Though the dissent has no basis for the level of generality it would select, we do: We refer to the most specific level at which a relevant tradition protecting, or denying protection to, the asserted right can be identified. If, for example, there were no societal tradition, either way, regarding the rights of the natural father of a child adulterously conceived, we would have to consult, and (if possible) reason from, the traditions regarding natural fathers in general. But there is such a more specific tradition, and it unqualifiedly denies protection to such a parent.

One would think that JUSTICE BRENNAN would appreciate the value of consulting the most specific tradition available, since he acknowledges that "[e]ven if we can agree . . . that 'family' and 'parenthood' are part of the good life, it is absurd to assume that we can agree on the content of those terms and destructive to pretend that we do." Because such general traditions provide such imprecise guidance, they permit judges to dictate rather than discern the society's views. The need, if arbitrary decision-making is to be avoided, to adopt the most specific tradition as the point of reference—or at least to announce,

... In accord with our traditions, a limit is also imposed by the circumstance that the mother is, at the time of the child's conception and birth, married to and co-habitating with another man, both of whom wish to raise the child as the off-spring of their union. It is a question of legislative policy and not constitutional law whether California will allow the pre-sumed parenthood of a couple desiring to retain a child conceived within and born into their marriage to be rebutted.

We do not accept JUSTICE BRENNAN'S crit-icism that this result "squashes" the liberty that consists of "the freedom not to con-form." ... If Michael has a "freedom not to conform" (whatever that means), Gerald must equivalently have a "freedom to con-form." One of them will pay a price for asserting that "freedom"—Michael by be-ing unable to act as father of the child he has adulterously begotten, or Gerald by being unable to preserve the integrity of the traditional family unit he and Victoria have established. ...

---

as JUSTICE BRENNAN declines to do, some other criterion for selecting among the innumerable relevant traditions that could be consulted—is well enough exemplified by the fact that in the present case JUSTICE BRENNAN'S opinion and JUSTICE O'CONNOR'S opinion, which disapproves this foot-note, *both* appeal to tradition, but on the basis of the tradition they select reach opposite results. Although assuredly having the virtue (if it be that) of leaving judges free to decide as they think best when the unanticipated occurs, a rule of law that binds neither by text nor by any particular, identifiable tradition, is no rule of law at all.

Finally, we may note that this analysis is not inconsistent with the result in cases such as *Gris-wold v. Connecticut,* or *Eisenstadt v. Baird* None of those cases acknowledged a longstanding and still extant societal tradition withholding the very right pronounced to be the subject of a liberty interest and then rejected it. ...

The judgment of the California Court of Appeal is

Affirmed.

JUSTICE O'CONNOR, with whom JUSTICE KENNEDY joins, concurring in part.

I concur in all but footnote 6 of JUSTICE SCALIA'S opinion. This footnote sketches a mode of historical analysis to be used when identifying liberty interests protected by the Due Process Clause of the Fourteenth Amendment that may be somewhat inconsis-tent with our past decisions in this area. See *Griswold v. Connecticut, Eisenstadt v. Baird.* On occasion the Court has characterized relevant traditions protecting asserted rights at levels of generality that might not be "the most spe-cific level" available. *Ante,* at n. 6. See *Loving v. Virginia,* 388 U.S. 1, 12 (1967); *Turner v. Safley,* 482 U.S. 78 (1987). ... I would not foreclose the unanticipated by the prior imposition of a single mode of historical analysis.

JUSTICE STEVENS, concurring in the judg-ment.

As I understand this case, it raises two different questions about the validity of California's statutory scheme. First, is Cal. Evid. Code Ann. § 621 (West Supp. 1989) unconstitutional because it prevents Michael and Victoria from obtaining a judi-cial determination that he is her biological father—even if no legal rights would be affected by that determination? Second, does the California statute deny appellants a fair opportunity to prove that Victoria's best interests would be served by granting Michael visitation rights?

On the first issue I agree with JUSTICE SCALIA that the Federal Constitution im-poses no obligation upon a State to "de-clare facts unless some legal consequence hinges upon the requested declaration." ...

On the second issue I do not agree with JUSTICE SCALIA's analysis. He seems to reject the possibility that a natural father might ever have a constitutionally protected interest in his relationship with a child whose mother was married to and cohabiting with another man at the time of the child's conception and birth. I think cases like *Stanley v. Illinois* and *Caban v. Mohammed* demonstrate that enduring "family" relationships may develop in unconventional settings. I therefore would not foreclose the possibility that a constitutionally protected relationship between a natural father and his child might exist in a case like this. Indeed, I am willing to assume for the purpose of deciding this case that Michael's relationship with Victoria is strong enough to give him a constitutional right to try to convince a trial judge that Victoria's best interest would be served by granting him visitation rights. I am satisfied, however, that the California statute, as applied in this case, gave him that opportunity.

Section 4601 of the California Civil Code Annotated (West Supp. 1989) provides:

[R]easonable visitation rights [shall be awarded] to a parent unless it is shown that the visitation would be detrimental to the best interests of the child. In the discretion of the court, reasonable visitation rights may be granted *to any other person having an interest in the welfare of the child.* (Emphasis added.)

The presumption established by § 621 denied Michael the benefit of the first sentence of § 4601 because, as a matter of law, he is not a "parent." It does not, however, prevent him from proving that he is an "other person having an interest in the welfare of the child." On its face, therefore, the statute plainly gave the trial judge the authority to grant Michael "reasonable visitation rights."

I recognize that my colleagues have interpreted § 621 as creating an absolute bar that would prevent a California trial judge from regarding the natural father as either a "parent" within the meaning of the first sentence of § 4601 *or* as "any other person" within the meaning of the second sentence. That is not only an unnatural reading of the statute's plain language, but it is also not consistent with the California courts' reading of the statute. [Discussion of California cases followed.—Au.] . . .

[The trial judge found] that "the existence of two (2) 'fathers' as male authority figures will confuse the child and be counter-productive to her best interests." In its opinion, the Court of Appeal also concluded that Michael "is not entitled to rights of visitation under section 4601."

Under the circumstances of the case before us, Michael was given a fair opportunity to show that he is Victoria's natural father, that he had developed a relationship with her, and that her interests would be served by granting him visitation rights. On the other hand, the record also shows that after its rather shaky start, the marriage between Carole and Gerald developed a stability that now provides Victoria with a loving and harmonious family home. In the circumstances of this case, I find nothing fundamentally unfair about the exercise of a judge's discretion that, in the end, allows the mother to decide whether her child's best interest would be served by allowing the natural father visitation privileges. Because I am convinced that the trial judge had the authority under state law both to hear Michael's plea for visitation rights and to grant him such rights if Victoria's best interests so warranted, I am satisfied that the California statutory scheme is consistent with the Due Process Clause of the Fourteenth Amendment.

I therefore concur in the Court's judgment of affirmance.

JUSTICE BRENNAN, with whom JUSTICE MARSHALL and JUSTICE BLACKMUN join, dissenting.

In a case that has yielded so many opinions as has this one, it is fruitful to begin by emphasizing the common ground shared by a majority of this Court. Five Members of the Court refuse to foreclose "the possibility that a natural father might ever have a constitutionally protected interest in his relationship with a child whose mother was married to and cohabiting with another man at the time of the child's conception and birth." (STEVENS, J., concurring in judgment). Five Justices agree that the flaw inhering in a conclusive presumption that terminates a constitutionally protected interest without any hearing whatsoever is a *procedural* one. (WHITE, J., dissenting); (STEVENS, J., concurring in judgment). Four Members of the Court agree that Michael H. has a liberty interest in his relationship with Victoria, (WHITE, J., dissenting), and one assumes for purposes of this case that he does, see (STEVENS, J., concurring in judgment).

In contrast, only two Members of the Court fully endorse JUSTICE SCALIA's view of the proper method of analyzing questions arising under the Due Process Clause. (O'CONNOR, J., concurring in part). Nevertheless, because the plurality opinion's exclusively historical analysis portends a significant and unfortunate departure from our prior cases and from sound constitutional decisionmaking, I devote a substantial portion of my discussion to it.

I

Once we recognized that the "liberty" protected by the Due Process Clause of the Fourteenth Amendment encompasses more than freedom from bodily restraint, today's plurality opinion emphasizes, the concept was cut loose from one natural limitation on its meaning. This innovation paved the way, so the plurality hints, for judges to substitute their own preferences for those of elected officials. Dissatisfied with this supposedly unbridled and uncertain state of affairs, the plurality casts about for another limitation on the concept of liberty.

It finds this limitation in "tradition." Apparently oblivious to the fact that this concept can be as malleable and as elusive as "liberty" itself, the plurality pretends that tradition places a discernible border around the Constitution. The pretense is seductive; it would be comforting to believe that a search for "tradition" involves nothing more idiosyncratic or complicated than poring through dusty volumes on American history.... Indeed, wherever I would begin to look for an interest "deeply rooted in the country's traditions," one thing is certain: I would not stop (as does the plurality) at Bracton, or Blackstone, or Kent, or even the American Law Reports in conducting my search. Because reasonable people can disagree about the content of particular traditions, and because they can disagree even about which traditions are relevant to the definition of "liberty," the plurality has not found the objective boundary that it seeks.

Even if we could agree, moreover, on the content and significance of particular traditions, we still would be forced to identify the point at which a tradition becomes firm enough to be relevant to our definition of liberty and the moment at which it becomes too obsolete to be relevant any longer. The plurality supplies no objective means by which we might make these determinations. Indeed, as soon as the plurality sees signs that the tradition upon which it bases its decision (the laws denying putative fathers like Michael standing to assert paternity) is crumbling, it shifts ground and says that the case has nothing to do with that tradition, after all. "What is at issue here," the plurality asserts after canvassing the law on paternity suits, "is not entitlement to a state pronouncement that Victoria was begotten by Michael." But that is precisely what is at issue here, and the plurality's last-minute denial of this fact dramatically illustrates the subjectivity of its own analysis.

It is ironic that an approach so utterly dependent on tradition is so indifferent to our precedents. . . .

It is not that tradition has been irrelevant to our prior decisions. Throughout our decisionmaking in this important area runs the theme that certain interests and practices—freedom from physical restraint, marriage, childbearing, childrearing, and others—form the core of our definition of "liberty." Our solicitude for these interests is partly the result of the fact that the Due Process Clause would seem an empty promise if it did not protect them, and partly the result of the historical and traditional importance of these interests in our society. . . .

Today's plurality, however, does not ask whether parenthood is an interest that historically has received our attention and protection; the answer to that question is too clear for dispute. Instead, the plurality asks whether the specific variety of parenthood under consideration—a natural father's relationship with a child whose mother is married to another man—has enjoyed such protection.

If we had looked to tradition with such specificity in past cases, many a decision would have reached a different result. [Here Brennan reviewed *Eisenstadt, Griswold, Stanley* and others.—Au.] . . .

The plurality's interpretive method is more than novel; it is misguided. It ignores

the good reasons for limiting the role of "tradition" in interpreting the Constitution's deliberately capacious language. In the plurality's constitutional universe, we may not take notice of the fact that the original reasons for the conclusive presumption of paternity are out of place in a world in which blood tests can prove virtually beyond a shadow of a doubt who sired a particular child and in which the fact of illegitimacy no longer plays the burdensome and stigmatizing role it once did. Nor, in the plurality's world, may we deny "tradition" its full scope by pointing out that the rationale for the conventional rule has changed over the years, . . . to ask whether the basis for that rule—which is the true reflection of the values undergirding it—has changed too often or too recently to call the rule embodying that rationale a "tradition." Moreover, by describing the decisive question as whether Michael and Victoria's interest is one that has been "traditionally *protected by* our society," (emphasis added), rather than one that society traditionally has thought important (with or without protecting it), and by suggesting that our sole function is to *"discern the society's views,"* ante, at n. 6 (emphasis added), the plurality acts as if the only purpose of the Due Process Clause is to confirm the importance of interests already protected by a majority of the States. Transforming the protection afforded by the Due Process Clause into a redundancy mocks those who, with care and purpose, wrote the Fourteenth Amendment. . . .

The document that the plurality construes today is unfamiliar to me. It is not the living charter that I have taken to be our Constitution; it is instead a stagnant, archaic, hidebound document steeped in the prejudices and superstitions of a time long past. *This* Constitution does not recognize that times change, does not see that sometimes a practice or rule outlives its foundations. I cannot accept an interpretive method that does such violence to the charter that I am bound by oath to uphold.

II

... [W]e confront an interest—that of a parent and child in their relationship with each other—that was among the first that this Court acknowledged in its cases defining the "liberty" protected by the Constitution, see, e.g., Meyer v. Nebraska, Skinner v. Oklahoma, Prince v. Massachusetts, 321 U.S. 158, 166, (1944), and I think I am safe in saying that no one doubts the wisdom or validity of those decisions. Where the interest under consideration is a parent-child relationship, we need not ask, over and over again, whether that interest is one that society traditionally protects. . . .

The . . . approach—commanded by our prior cases and by common sense—is to ask whether the specific parent-child relationship under consideration is close enough to the interests that we already have protected to be deemed an aspect of "liberty" as well. On the facts before us, therefore, the question is . . . whether the relationship under consideration is sufficiently substantial to qualify as a liberty interest under our prior cases.

On four prior occasions, we have considered whether unwed fathers have a constitutionally protected interest in their relationships with their children. See Stanley v. Illinois; Quilloin v. Walcott, 434 U.S. 246 (1978); Caban v. Mohammed, 441 U.S. 380 (1979); and Lehr v. Robertson, 463 U.S. 248 (1983). Though different in factual and legal circumstances, these cases have produced a unifying theme: although an unwed father's biological link to his child does not, in and of itself, guarantee him a constitutional stake in his relationship with that child, such a link combined with a substantial parent-child relationship will

do so. "When an unwed father demonstrates a full commitment to the responsibilities of parenthood by 'com[ing] forward to participate in the rearing of his child,' . . . his interest in personal contact with his child acquires substantial protection under the Due Process Clause. At that point it may be said that he 'act[s] as a father toward his children.' " Lehr v. Robertson, at 261, quoting Caban v. Mohammed, 441 U.S., at 392, 389, n. 7. This commitment is why Mr. Stanley and Mr. Caban won; why Mr. Quilloin and Mr. Lehr lost; and why Michael H. should prevail today. Michael H. is almost certainly Victoria D.'s natural father, has lived with her as her father, has contributed to her support, and has from the beginning sought to strengthen and maintain his relationship with her. . . .

The evidence is undisputed that Michael, Victoria, and Carole did live together as a family; that is, they shared the same household, Victoria called Michael "Daddy," Michael contributed to Victoria's support, and he is eager to continue his relationship with her. Yet they are not, in the plurality's view, a "unitary family," whereas Gerald, Carole, and Victoria do compose such a family. The only difference between these two sets of relationships, however, is the fact of marriage. . . . However, the very premise of Stanley and the cases following it is that marriage is not decisive in answering the question whether the Constitution protects the parental relationship under consideration. These cases are, after all, important precisely because they involve the rights of unwed fathers. It is important to remember, moreover, that in Quilloin, Caban, and Lehr, the putative father's demands would have disrupted a "unitary family" as the plurality defines it; in each case, the husband of the child's mother sought to adopt the child over the objections of the natural father.

Significantly, our decisions in those cases in no way relied on the need to protect the marital family. Hence the plurality's claim that *Stanley, Quilloin, Caban,* and *Lehr* were about the "unitary family," as that family is defined by today's plurality, is surprising indeed. . . .

. . . In announcing that what matters is not the father's ability to claim paternity, but his ability to obtain "substantive parental rights," the plurality turns procedural due process upside down. Michael's challenge in this Court does not depend on his ability ultimately to obtain visitation rights; it would be strange indeed if, before one could be granted a hearing, one were required to prove that one would prevail on the merits. The point of procedural due process is to give the litigant a fair chance at prevailing, not to ensure a particular substantive outcome. . . .[5]

III

. . . California's interest, minute in comparison with a father's interest in his relationship with his child, cannot justify its refusal to hear Michael out on his claim that he is Victoria's father.

A

We must first understand the nature of the challenged statute: it is a law that stubbornly insists that Gerald is Victoria's father, in the face of evidence showing a 98 percent probability that her father is Michael.[6] What Michael wants is a chance

to show that he is Victoria's father. By depriving him of this opportunity, California prevents Michael from taking advantage of the best-interest standard embodied in § 4601 of California's Civil Code, which directs that *parents* be given visitation rights unless "the visitation would be detrimental to the best interests of the child." Cal. Civ. Code Ann. § 4601.

. . . When, as a result of § 621, a putative father may not establish his paternity, neither may he obtain discretionary visitation rights as a "nonparent" under § 4601. JUSTICE STEVENS' assertion to the contrary is mere wishful thinking. . . .

[Here followed a discussion of California cases.—Au.]

. . . [I]n the case before us, the court's finding that "the existence of two 'fathers' as male authority figures will confuse the child and be counterproductive to her best interests," is not an evaluation of the relationship between Michael and Victoria, but a restatement of the policies underlying § 621 itself. It may well be that the California courts' interpretation of § 4601 as precluding visitation rights for a putative father is "an unnatural reading" of that provision, but it is not for us to decide what California's statute means.

Section 621 as construed by the California courts thus cuts off the relationship between Michael and Victoria—a liberty interest protected by the Due Process Clause—without affording the least bit of process. . . .

B

The question before us, therefore, is whether California has an interest so powerful that it justifies granting Michael *no*

---

5. One need only look as far as *Quilloin v. Walcott,* 434 U.S., at 255 to understand why an unwed father might lose for reasons having nothing to do with his own relationship with the child: there, we approved the use of a "best interest" standard, rather than an "unfitness" standard, for an unwed father who objected to the adoption of his child by another man.

6. JUSTICE STEVENS' claim that "Michael was given a fair opportunity to show that he is

Victoria's natural father," ignores the fact that this case is before us precisely because California law refuses to allow men like Michael such an opportunity.

hearing before terminating his parental rights. . . .

. . . Gerald D. explains that § 621 promotes marriage, maintains the relationship between the child and presumed father, and protects the integrity and privacy of the matrimonial family. . . . [But a]dmittedly, § 621 does not foreclose inquiry into the husband's fertility or virility—matters that are ordinarily thought of as the couple's private business. In this day and age, however, proving paternity by asking intimate and detailed questions about a couple's relationship would be decidedly anachronistic. Who on earth would choose this method of establishing fatherhood when blood tests prove it with far more certainty and far less fuss? The State's purported interest in protecting matrimonial privacy thus does not measure up to Michael and Victoria's interest in maintaining their relationship with each other.

Make no mistake: to say that the State must provide Michael with a hearing to prove his paternity is not to express any opinion of the ultimate state of affairs between Michael and Victoria and Carole and Gerald. In order to change the current situation among these people, Michael first must convince a court that he is Victoria's father, and even if he is able to do this, he will be denied visitation rights if that would be in Victoria's best interests. See Cal. Civ. Code Ann. § 4601 (West Supp.1989). It is elementary that a determination that a State must afford procedures before it terminates a given right is not a prediction about the end result of those procedures.

IV

The atmosphere surrounding today's decision is one of make-believe. Beginning with the suggestion that the situation confronting us here does not repeat itself every day in every corner of the country, moving on to the claim that it is tradition alone that supplies the details of the liberty that the Constitution protects, and passing finally to the notion that the Court always has recognized a cramped vision of "the family," today's decision lets stand California's pronouncement that Michael—whom blood tests show to a 98 percent probability to be Victoria's father—is not Victoria's father. When and if the Court awakes to reality, it will find a world very different from the one it expects.

JUSTICE WHITE, with whom JUSTICE BRENNAN joins, dissenting.

. . .

I

Like JUSTICES BRENNAN, MARSHALL, BLACKMUN and STEVENS, I do not agree with the plurality opinion's conclusion that a natural father can never "have a constitutionally protected interest in his relationship with a child whose mother was married to and cohabiting with another man at the time of the child's conception and birth." (STEVENS, J., concurring in judgment). Prior cases here have recognized the liberty interest of a father in his relationship with his child. In none of these cases did we indicate that the fathers' rights were dependent on the marital status of the mother or biological father. The basic principle enunciated in the Court's unwed father cases is that an unwed father who has demonstrated a sufficient commitment to his paternity by way of personal, financial, or custodial responsibilities has a protected liberty interest in a relationship with his child. . . .

In the case now before us, Michael H. is not a father unwilling to assume his responsibilities as a parent. To the contrary, he is a father who has asserted his interests in raising and providing for his child since the very time of the child's birth. In contrast to the father in *Lehr*, Michael H. had begun to develop a relationship with his daughter. There is no dispute on this point. Michael contributed to the child's support. Michael and Victoria lived together (albeit intermittently, given Carole's itinerant lifestyle.) There is a personal and emotional relationship between Michael and Victoria, who grew up calling him "Daddy." Michael H. held Victoria out as his daughter and contributed to the child's financial support. . . . "When an unwed father demonstrates a full commitment to the responsibilities of parenthood by 'com[ing] forward to participate in the rearing of his child,' *Caban*, 441 U.S., at 392, his interest in personal contact with his child acquires substantial protection under the Due Process Clause." *Lehr*, 463 U.S., at 261. The facts in this case satisfy the *Lehr* criteria, which focused on the relationship between father and child, not on the relationship between father and mother. Under *Lehr* a "mere biological relationship" is not enough, but in light of Carole's vicissitudes, what more could Michael H. have done? It is clear enough that Michael H. . . . has a liberty interest entitled to protection under the Due Process Clause of the Fourteenth Amendment.

II

California plainly denies Michael this protection, by refusing him the opportunity to rebut the State's presumption that the mother's husband is the father of the child. California law not only deprives Michael H. of a legal parent-child relationship with his daughter Victoria but even denies him the opportunity to introduce blood-test evidence to rebut the demonstrable fiction that Gerald is Victoria's father. . . .

The interest in protecting a child from the social stigma of illegitimacy lacks any real connection to the facts of a case where a father is seeking to establish, rather than repudiate, paternity. . . . It may be true that a child conceived in an extra-marital relationship would be considered a "bastard" in the literal sense of the word, but whatever stigma remains in today's society is far less compelling in the context of a child of a married mother, especially when there is a father asserting paternity and seeking a relationship with his child. It is hardly rare in this world of divorce and remarriage for a child to live with the "father" to whom her mother is married, and still have a relationship with her biological father.

The State's professed interest in the preservation of the existing marital unit is a more significant concern. To be sure, the intrusion of an outsider asserting that he is the father of a child whom the husband believes to be his own would be disruptive to say the least. On the facts of this case, however, Gerald was well aware of the liaison between Carole and Michael. . . .

. . . I fail to see the fairness in the process established by the State of California and endorsed by the Court today.

. . . I respectfully dissent.

CASE QUESTIONS

1. Had Carole been the unmarried person and Michael married to another woman, Carole's parental rights would have been unquestioned by the law. With the

situation reversed (i.e., Michael the un-married one) Michael's parental rights are utterly negated by the law. Should this be viewed as unjustified sex dis-crimination and thus a violation of "equal protection of the laws," or rather as a necessary accommodation to natu-ral differences in the birth process and thus justified as serving important gov-ernmental interests?

Under this statute, either partner of the marital couple could mount a legal challenge to "their" child's paternity (al-though if it were the woman, her chal-lenge had to be accompanied by that of her extramarital partner), but the extra-marital biological father had no legal right to bring such a challenge on his own. Does this pattern violate equal pro-tection in that is discriminates to an unconstitutional degree between the married and the unmarried?

2. Is this case best understood as present-ing a conflict between the familial di-mension of the right to privacy of the marital couple, and parental dimension of the right to privacy of the biological father? Is such a conflict better left to legislatures or courts for resolution?

3. Justice Stevens interprets California's section 4601 as authorizing a judge to grant persons in Michael H.'s situation visitation rights if the child's best interest warrants it. (This is a standard similar to that typically applied to noncustodial

divorced fathers.) Four justices (in dissent) argue that Stevens misinterprets the stat-ute, that in fact it denies visitation rights to persons in Michael's situation, and that, as thus (correctly) interpreted, the statute is unconstitutional. Does this combination of five votes mean that in the future, to honor the Constitution, California must interpret section 4601 as Justice Stevens has done?

4. Justice Scalia refers snidely to "the rela-tionship established between a married woman, her lover and their child, during a three-month sojourn in St. Thomas, or during a subsequent 8-month period when, if he happened to be in Los Ange-les, he stayed with her and the child." As Justice White describes this father-daughter relationship, the father had lived with his daughter, contributed to her support, held himself out as her fa-ther, and was known to her as "Daddy." Is this dramatic difference in describing the same situation more a manifestation of idiosyncratic judicial psychology than of legal analysis?

5. Justice White poses the question, "[I]n light of Carole's vicissitudes, what more could Michael H. have done?" Is it wrong to let Michael's constitutional rights turn on "Carole's vicissitudes"? If Gerald and Carole were suddenly to die without a will, would Michael have any legal claim to custody or guardianship? Is his lack of claim a problem?

Native Americans and Familial Privacy: *Mississippi Choctaw Indians v. Holyfield* (1989)

The parental rights cases that have come to the Supreme Court since *Stanley v. Illinois* have typically involved a desire to retain custody or to retain at least enough of parental rights to have visiting privileges. They have also typically occurred in an adoption context. Mr. Stanley's children might have been adopted by strangers had he lost custody of them; Mr. Caban, Mr. Quilloin, and Mr. Lehr each was attempting to block adoption of his offspring by the man who had married the child's mother after the child's birth.[19] The *Mississippi Choctaw* case also involves an adoption context, but presents a situation where the mother and father are trying to give up custody in circumstances of their own choosing.[20] They were challenged in this attempt by their tribal government, and the Supreme Court ruled that federal law gives the tribe rather than the parents control over this custody decision. As in *Baby M*, the legal conflict is settled officially by reference to a statute[21] but constitutional questions are lurking beneath the surface.

Unlike the *Baby M* case, however, the justices here are silent about those questions. This silence is perhaps explainable by the anomalous constitutional status of Native Americans residing on reservations. The various tribal governments predated the American Constitution and did not ratify it as their official government. Thus, the Bill of Rights, as such, does not describe the relation between tribal governments and tribe members. The U.S. government, however, intervened in 1968 to give the basic civil liberties set forth in that part of the Constitution to Native Americans by means of a federal law, the Indian Civil Rights Act.[22] This law essentially listed virtually all the protections of the Bill of Rights and accorded them to American Indians with respect to their tribal government on the reservation. The only noteworthy omissions from the statutory list are freedom from established religion (the First Amendment) and the reference to the taking of "life" in the due process clause (Fifth Amendment). Thus tribal governments are explicitly forbidden to take "liberty or property without due process of law."

The right of parents to the "care, custody and management" of their children (*Stanley*) or "to direct the upbringing of children under their control" (*Pierce v. Society of Sisters*) is a right that the Supreme Court inferred from the command (in the due process clauses of the Fifth and Fourteenth amendments) that government shall not take "liberty ... without due process of law." Thus, it would seem that the 1968 act did confer upon Indians the same fundamental rights to parental privacy that other Americans have.

The Indian Civil Rights Act of 1968, however, is not mentioned in the decision of *Mississippi Choctaw Indians v. Holyfield*. Instead the justices limit their discussion to the meaning of the Indian Child Welfare Act (ICWA) of 1978. In this sense, the constitutional rights[23] implied in the Civil Rights Act are merely lurking in the background of this case. In any event, the Court's resolution of the case, enabling tribal governments to forbid parents to direct the custody of their children toward certain kinds of parents (i.e., non-Indian), would seem to be of dubious constitutionality outside the Indian context. In other words, if a pregnant Anglo woman were to travel out of her home state to give up her child for adoption in the second state because she preferred its adoption procedures, her rights of parental privacy would seem to permit her that option. The comparable right to travel two hundred miles away from her reservation in order to give up her twins for adoption to non-Indians was denied to J.B. (and to her companion, the twins' father, W.J.) by the U.S. Supreme Court in this case.[24]

The ICWA established tribal court jurisdiction over adoptive and foster care placement of Indian children and established a preference for Indian parents as against non-Indian parents, and tribal over nontribal, for those placements. For Indians living off a reservation, a tribal court is permitted to take jurisdiction away from a state court in a proceeding for either foster care or adoptive placement of the Indian child, "absent objection by either parent."

In the Choctaw case both parents (unwed reservation Indians) had traveled two hundred miles from the reservation so that their twins would be born outside tribal jurisdiction. The parents then intentionally placed the babies for adoption in a non-Indian home. Three years later the tribal court intervened and voided the Mississippi adoption order, claiming that its own jurisdiction followed the parents and covered their children. The chancery court, which had first placed the children, overruled the tribal court on the grounds that the twins, in accord with the wishes of their biological parents, had been born off the reservation and had been promptly placed for adoption. The court thus ruled that the twins had never been under the jurisdiction of the tribal court. The Mississippi Supreme Court had affirmed,[25] and the tribal government had then appealed to the U.S. Supreme Court.

The Court majority of six upheld the tribe's reading of the statute. The dissenters (Stevens, Rehnquist, and Kennedy) insisted that the statute was meant to inhibit state removal of children *against* the will of their Indian parents, not to thwart the will of the parents. The majority argued that the statute aimed at preserving specifically *tribal* rights over Indian children. Neither group made any reference to any fundamental constitutional right of either the Indian or the adoptive parents, the Holyfields, who for years had been under the impression they had had full parental rights to these twins. No one on the Court raised the question whether this statute denied to Indian mothers and fathers constitutional rights that could not be denied to other Americans.

Excerpts from the justices' opinion follow.

Mississippi Band of Choctaw Indians v. Holyfield, 490 U.S. 30 (1989)

JUSTICE BRENNAN delivered the opinion of the Court.

This appeal requires us to construe the provisions of the Indian Child Welfare Act that establish exclusive tribal jurisdiction over child custody proceedings involving Indian children domiciled on the tribe's reservation.

I

A

The Indian Child Welfare Act of 1978 (ICWA), 92 Stat. 3069, 25 U.S.C. §§ 1901–1963, was the product of rising concern in the mid-1970's over the consequences to Indian children, Indian families, and Indian tribes of abusive child welfare practices that resulted in the separation of large numbers of Indian children from their families and tribes through adoption or foster care placement, usually in non-Indian homes. Senate oversight hearings in 1974 yielded numerous examples, statistical data, and expert testimony documenting what one witness called "the wholesale removal of Indian children from their homes, ... the most tragic aspect of Indian life today." *Indian Child Welfare Program, Hearings before the Subcommittee on Indian Affairs of the Senate Committee on Interior and Insular Affairs*, 93d Cong., 2d Sess., 3 (hereinafter *1974 Hearings*) (statement of William Byler). Studies undertaken by the Association on American Indian Affairs in 1969 and 1974, and presented in the Senate hearings, showed that 25 to 35 percent of all Indian children had been separated from their families and placed in adoptive families, foster care, or institutions. *Id.*, at 15. Adoptive placements counted significantly in this total: in the State of Minnesota, for example, one in eight Indian children under the age of 18 was in an adoptive home, and during the year 1971–1972 nearly one in every four infants under one year of age was placed for adoption. The adoption rate of Indian children was eight times that of non-Indian children. Approximately 90% of the Indian placements were in non-Indian homes. *1974 Hearings*, at 75–83. A number of witnesses also testified to the serious adjustment problems encountered by such children during adolescence, as well as the impact of the adoptions on Indian parents and the tribes themselves.

Further hearings, covering much the same ground, were held during 1977 and 1978 on the bill that became the ICWA. While much of the testimony again focused on the harm to Indian parents and their children who were involuntarily separated by decisions of local welfare authorities, there was also considerable emphasis on the impact on the tribes themselves of the massive removal of their children. For example, Mr. Calvin Isaac, Tribal Chief of the Mississippi Band of Choctaw Indians and representative of the National Tribal Chairmen's Association, testified as follows:

> Culturally, the chances of Indian survival are significantly reduced if our children, the only real means for the transmission of the tribal heritage, are to be raised in non-Indian homes and denied exposure to the ways of their People. Furthermore, these practices seriously undercut the tribes' ability to continue as self-governing communities. Probably in no area is it more important that tribal sovereignty be respected than in an area as socially and culturally determinative as family relationships. *1978 Hearings*, at 193.

See also *id.*, at 62. Chief Isaac also summarized succinctly what numerous witnesses saw as the principal reason for the high rates of removal of Indian children:

> One of the most serious failings of the present system is that Indian children are removed from the custody of their natural parents by nontribal govern-

ment authorities who have no basis for intelligently evaluating the cultural and social premises underlying Indian home life and childrearing. Many of the individuals who decide the fate of our children are at best ignorant of our cultural values, and at worst contemptful of the Indian way and convinced that removal, usually to a non-Indian household or institution, can only benefit an Indian child. *Id.*, at 191–92.[4]

The congressional findings that were incorporated into the ICWA reflect these sentiments. The Congress found:

(3) that there is no resource that is more vital to the continued existence and integrity of Indian tribes than their children . . .;
(4) that an alarmingly high percentage of Indian families are broken up by the

removal, often unwarranted, of their children from them by nontribal public and private agencies and that an alarmingly high percentage of such children are placed in non-Indian foster and adoptive homes and institutions; and
(5) that the States, exercising their recognized jurisdiction over Indian child custody proceedings through administrative and judicial bodies, have often failed to recognize the essential tribal relations of Indian people and the cultural and social standards prevailing in Indian communities and families. 25 U.S.C. § 1901.

At the heart of the ICWA are its provisions concerning jurisdiction over Indian child custody proceedings. Section 1911 lays out a dual jurisdictional scheme. Section 1911(a) establishes exclusive jurisdiction in the tribal courts for proceedings concerning an Indian child "who resides or is domiciled within the reservation of such tribe," as well as for wards of tribal courts regardless of domicile. Section 1911(b), on the other hand, creates concurrent but presumptively tribal jurisdiction in the case of children not domiciled on the reservation: on petition of either parent or the tribe, state-court proceedings for foster care placement or termination of parental rights are to be transferred to the tribal court, except in cases of "good cause," objection by either parent, or declination of jurisdiction by the tribal court.

. . . The most important substantive requirement imposed on state courts is that of § 1915(a), which, absent "good cause" to the contrary, mandates that adoptive placements be made preferentially with (1) members of the child's extended family, (2) other members of the same tribe, or (3) other Indian families.

---

4. One of the particular points of concern was the failure of non-Indian child welfare workers to understand the role of the extended family in Indian society. The House Report on the ICWA noted: "An Indian child may have scores of, perhaps more than a hundred, relatives who are counted as close, responsible members of the family. Many social workers, untutored in the ways of Indian family life or assuming them to be socially irresponsible, consider leaving the child with persons outside the nuclear family as neglect and thus as grounds for terminating parental rights." *House Report*, at 10, U.S. Code Cong. & Admin. News 1978, at 7532. At the conclusion of the 1974 Senate hearings, Senator Abourezk noted the role that such extended families played in the care of children: "We've had testimony here that in Indian communities throughout the Nation there is no such thing as an abandoned child because when a child does have a need for parents for one reason or another, a relative or a friend will take that child in. It's the extended family concept." *1974 Hearings* 473.

The ICWA thus, in the words of the House Report accompanying it, "seeks to protect the rights of the Indian child as an Indian and the rights of the Indian community and tribe in retaining its children in its society." *House Report*, at 23, U.S. Code Cong. & Admin. News 1978, at 7546. It does so by establishing "a Federal policy that, where possible, an Indian child should remain in the Indian community," *ibid.*, and by making sure that Indian child welfare determinations are not based on "a white, middle-class standard which, in many cases, forecloses placement with [an] Indian family." *Id.*, at 24, U.S. Code Cong. & Admin. News 1978, at 7546.

. . .

II

. . . In enacting the ICWA Congress confirmed that, in child custody proceedings involving Indian children domiciled on the reservation, tribal jurisdiction was exclusive as to the States . . . The sole issue in this case is, as the Supreme Court of Mississippi recognized, whether the twins were "domiciled" on the reservation.

A

[1] The meaning of "domicile" in the ICWA is, of course, a matter of Congress' intent. The ICWA itself does not define it. The initial question we must confront is whether there is any reason to believe that Congress intended the ICWA definition of "domicile" to be a matter of state law. . . . We . . . think it beyond dispute that Congress intended a uniform federal law of domicile for the ICWA.

B

It remains to give content to the term "domicile" in the circumstances of the present case. The holding of the Supreme Court of Mississippi that the twin babies were not domiciled on the Choctaw Reservation appears to have rested on two findings of fact by the trial court: (1) that they had never been physically present there, and (2) that they were "voluntarily surrendered" by their parents. 511 So.2d, at 921. . . .

"Domicile" is, of course, a concept widely used in both federal and state courts for jurisdiction and conflict-of-laws purposes, and its meaning is generally uncontroverted. . . . "Domicile" is not necessarily synonymous with "residence." For adults, domicile is established by physical presence in a place in connection with a certain state of mind concerning one's intent to remain there. . . . Since most minors are legally incapable of forming the requisite intent to establish a domicile, their domicile is determined by that of their parents. *Yarborough v. Yarborough*, 290 U.S. 202, 211 (1933). . . . Under these principles, it is entirely logical that "[o]n occasion, a child's domicile of origin will be in a place where the child has never been." *Restatement (Second) of Conflict of Laws* § 14, Comment *b* (1971) (hereinafter *Restatement*).

It is undisputed in this case that the domicile of the mother (as well as the father) has been, at all relevant times, on the Choctaw Reservation. Thus, it is clear that at their birth the twin babies were also domiciled on the reservation, even though they themselves had never been there. The statement of the Supreme Court of Mississippi that "[a]t no point in time can it be said the twins . . . were domiciled within the territory set aside for the reservation," 511 So. 2d, at 921, may be a correct statement of that State's law of domicile, but it is inconsistent with generally accepted doctrine in this country and cannot be what Congress had in mind when it used the term in the ICWA.

Nor can the result be any different simply because the twins were "voluntarily surrendered" by their mother. Tribal jurisdiction under § 1911(a) was not meant to be defeated by the actions of individual members of the tribe, for Congress was concerned not solely about the interests of Indian children and families, but also about the impact on the tribes themselves of the large numbers of Indian children adopted by non-Indians. See 25 U.S.C. §§ 1901(3) ("there is no resource that is more vital to the continued existence and integrity of Indian tribes than their children"), 1902 ("promote the stability and security of Indian tribes"). The numerous prerogatives accorded the tribes through the ICWA's substantive provisions ... must, accordingly, be seen as a means of protecting not only the interests of individual Indian children and families, but also of the tribes themselves.

In addition, it is clear that Congress' concern over the placement of Indian children in non-Indian homes was based in part on evidence of the detrimental impact on the children themselves of such placements outside their culture. Congress determined to subject such placements to the ICWA's jurisdictional and other provisions, even in cases where the parents consented to an adoption, because of concerns going beyond the wishes of individual parents....

These congressional objectives make clear that a rule of domicile that would permit individual Indian parents to defeat the ICWA's jurisdictional scheme is inconsistent with what Congress intended. The appellees in this case argue strenuously that the twins' mother went to great lengths to give birth off the reservation so that her children could be adopted by the Holyfields. But that was precisely part of Congress' concern. Permitting individual members of the tribe to avoid tribal exclusive jurisdiction by the simple expedient of giving birth off the reservation would, to a large extent, nullify the purpose the ICWA

was intended to accomplish. The Supreme Court of Utah expressed this well in its scholarly and sensitive opinion in what has become a leading case on the ICWA:

> To the extent that [state] abandonment law operates to permit [the child's] mother to change [the child's] domicile as part of a scheme to facilitate his adoption by non-Indians while she remains a domiciliary of the reservation, it conflicts with and undermines the operative scheme established by subsections [1911(a)] and [1913(a)] to deal with children of domiciliaries of the reservation and weakens considerably the tribe's ability to assert its interest in its children. The protection of this tribal interest is at the core of the ICWA, which recognizes that the tribe has an interest in the child which is distinct from but on a parity with the interest of the parents. This relationship between Indian tribes and Indian children domiciled on the reservation finds no parallel in other ethnic cultures found in the United States. It is a relationship that many non-Indians find difficult to understand and that non-Indian courts are slow to recognize. It is precisely in recognition of this relationship, however, that the ICWA designates the tribal court as the exclusive forum for the determination of custody and adoption matters for reservation-domiciled Indian children, and the preferred forum for nondomiciliary Indian children. [State] abandonment law cannot be used to frustrate the federal legislative judgment expressed in the ICWA that the interests of the tribe in custodial decisions made with respect to Indian children are as entitled to respect as the interests of the parents. *In re Adoption of Halloway,* 732 P.2d 962, 969–70 (1986).

We agree with the Supreme Court of Utah that the law of domicile Congress used in the ICWA cannot be one that permits individual reservation-domiciled tribal members to defeat the tribe's exclusive jurisdiction by the simple expedient of giving birth and placing the child for adoption off the reservation. Since, for purposes of the ICWA, the twin babies in this case were domiciled on the reservation when adoption proceedings were begun, the Choctaw tribal court possessed exclusive jurisdiction pursuant to 25 U.S.C. § 1911(a). The Chancery Court of Harrison County was, accordingly, without jurisdiction to enter a decree of adoption; under ICWA § 1914 its decree of January 28, 1986, must be vacated.

III

We are not unaware that over three years have passed since the twin babies were born and placed in the Holyfield home, and that a court deciding their fate today is not writing on a blank slate in the same way it would have in January 1986. Three years' development of family ties cannot be undone, and a separation at this point would doubtless cause considerable pain.

Whatever feelings we might have as to where the twins should live, however, it is not for us to decide that question. We have been asked to decide the legal question of *who* should make the custody determination concerning these children—not what the outcome of that determination should be. The law places that decision in the hands of the Choctaw tribal court. Had the mandate of the ICWA been followed in 1986, of course, much potential anguish might have been avoided, and in any case the law cannot be applied so as automatically to "reward those who obtain custody, whether lawfully or otherwise, and maintain it during any ensuing (and protracted)

litigation." *Halloway, supra,* at 972. It is not ours to say whether the trauma that might result from removing these children from their adoptive family should outweigh the interest of the Tribe—and perhaps the children themselves—in having them raised as part of the Choctaw community. Rather, "we must defer to the experience, wisdom, and compassion of the [Choctaw] tribal courts to fashion an appropriate remedy." *Ibid.*

The judgment of the Supreme Court of Mississippi is reversed. . . .

JUSTICE STEVENS, with whom THE CHIEF JUSTICE and JUSTICE KENNEDY join, dissenting.

The parents of these twin babies unquestionably expressed their intention to have the state court exercise jurisdiction over them. J.B. gave birth to the twins at a hospital 200 miles from the Reservation, even though a closer hospital was available. Both parents gave their written advance consent to the adoption and, when the adoption was later challenged by the Tribe, they reaffirmed their desire that the Holyfields adopt the two children. . . . Indeed, both parents appear before us today, urging that Vivian Holyfield be allowed to retain custody of B.B. and G.B.

Because J.B.'s domicile is on the reservation and the children are eligible for membership in the Tribe, the Court today closes the state courthouse door to her. I agree with the Court that Congress intended a uniform federal law of domicile for the Indian Child Welfare Act of 1978 (ICWA), 92 Stat. 3069, 25 U.S.C. §§ 1901–1963, and that domicile should be defined with reference to the objectives of the congressional scheme. . . . I cannot agree, however, with the cramped definition the Court gives that term. To preclude parents domiciled on a reservation from deliberately invoking the adoption procedures of state court, the Court gives "domicile" a meaning that Congress could not have intended and distorts the delicate balance between individual rights and group rights recognized by the ICWA.

The ICWA was passed in 1978 in response to congressional findings that "an alarmingly high percentage of Indian families are broken up by the *removal*, often unwarranted, of their children from them by nontribal public and private agencies" and that "the States, exercising their recognized jurisdiction over Indian child custody proceedings through administrative and judicial bodies, have often failed to recognize the essential tribal relations of Indian people and the cultural and social standards prevailing in Indian communities and families." 25 U.S.C. § 1901(4), (5). (Emphasis added.) The Act is thus primarily addressed to the unjustified removal of Indian children from their families through the application of standards that inadequately recognized the distinct Indian culture.[1]

The most important provisions of the ICWA are those setting forth minimum standards for the placement of Indian children by state courts and providing procedural safeguards to insure that parental rights are protected.[2] The Act provides that

1. The House Report found that "Indian families face vastly greater risks of involuntary separation than are typical of our society as a whole." H.R.Rep. No. 95–1386, p. 9 (1978) (hereinafter *House Report*).

2. "The purpose of the bill (H.R. 12533), introduced by Mr. Udall et al., is to protect the best interests of Indian children and to promote the stability and security of Indian tribes and families. . ." *House Report*, at 8. See also 124 Cong. Rec. 38102 (1978) (remarks of Rep. Udall) ("[The Act] clarifies the allocation of jurisdiction over Indian child custody proceedings between Indian tribes and the States. More importantly, it establishes minimum Federal standards and procedural safeguards to protect Indian families

any party seeking to effect a foster care placement of, or involuntary termination of parental rights to, an Indian child must establish by stringent standards of proof that efforts have been made to prevent the breakup of the Indian family and that the continued custody of the child by the parent is likely to result in serious emotional or physical damage to the child. §§ 1912(d), (e), (f) . . . In the case of a voluntary termination, the ICWA provides that consent is valid only if given after the terms and consequences of the consent have been fully explained, may be withdrawn at any time up to the final entry of a decree of termination or adoption, and even then may be collaterally attacked on the grounds that it was obtained through fraud or duress. § 1913. Finally, because the Act protects not only the rights of the parents, but also the interests of the tribe and the Indian children, the Act sets forth criteria for adoptive, foster care, and preadoptive placements that favor the Indian child's extended family or tribe, and that can be altered by resolution of the tribe. § 1915.

The Act gives Indian tribes certain rights, not to restrict the rights of parents of Indian children, but to complement and help effect them. The Indian tribe may petition to transfer an action in state court to the tribal court, but the Indian parent may veto the transfer. § 1911(b). The Act provides for a tribal right of notice and intervention in involuntary proceedings but not in voluntary ones. §§ 1911(c), 1912(a). Finally, the tribe may petition the court to set aside a parental termination action upon a showing that the provisions of the ICWA that are designed to protect parents and Indian children have been violated. § 1914.[5]

___

when faced with child custody proceedings against them in State agencies or courts").

5. Significantly, the tribe can not set aside a termination of parental rights on the grounds that the adoptive placement provisions of § 1915,

While the Act's substantive and procedural provisions effect a major change in state child custody proceedings, its jurisdictional provision is designed primarily to preserve tribal sovereignty over the domestic relations of tribe members and to confirm a developing line of cases which held that the tribe's exclusive jurisdiction could not be defeated by the temporary presence of an Indian child off the reservation. . . . The apparent intent of Congress was to overrule such decisions as that in *In re Cantrell*, 159 Mont. 66, 495 P.2d 179 (1972), in which the State placed an Indian child, who had lived on a Reservation with his mother, in a foster home only three days after he left the Reservation to accompany his father on a trip. Jones, *Indian Child Welfare: A Jurisdictional Approach*, 21 Ariz. L. Rev. 1123, 1129 (1979). Congress specifically approved a series of cases in which the state courts declined jurisdiction over Indian children who were wards of the tribal court, *In re Adoption of Buehl*, 87 Wash.2d 649, 555 P.2d 1334 (1976); *Wakefield v. Little Light*, 276 Md. 333, 347 A.2d 228 (1975), or whose parents were temporarily residing off the reservation, *Wisconsin Potowatomies of Hannahville Indian Community v. Houston*, 393 F. Supp. 719 (W.D. Mich. 1973), but exercised jurisdiction over Indian children who had never lived on a reservation and whose Indian parents were not then residing on a reservation. *In re Greybull*, 23 Or. App. 674, 543 P.2d 1079 (1975); see *House Report*, at 21, U.S. Code Cong. & Admin. News 1978, at 7543.[6] It did not express any disapproval of decisions such

as that of the United States Court of Appeals for the Ninth Circuit in *United States ex rel. Cobell v. Cobell*, 503 F.2d 790 (9th Cir. 1974), *cert. denied*, 421 U.S. 999 (1975), which indicated that a Montana state court could exercise jurisdiction over an Indian child custody dispute because the parents "by voluntarily invoking the state court's jurisdiction for divorce purposes, . . . clearly submitted the question of their children's custody to the judgment of the Montana state courts." 503 F.2d, at 795. . . .

Although parents of Indian children are shielded from the exercise of state jurisdiction when they are temporarily off the reservation, the Act also reflects a recognition that allowing the tribe to defeat the parents' deliberate choice of jurisdiction would be conducive neither to the best interests of the child nor to the stability and security of Indian tribes and families. Section 1911(b), providing for the exercise of concurrent jurisdiction by state and tribal courts when the Indian child is not domiciled on the reservation, gives the Indian parents a veto to prevent the transfer of a state court action to tribal court. "By allowing the Indian parents to 'choose' the forum that will decide whether to sever the parent-child relationship, Congress promotes the security of Indian families by allowing the Indian parents to defend in the court system that most reflects the parents' familial standards." Jones, 21 Ariz. L. Rev., at 1141. As Mr. Calvin Isaac, Tribal Chief of the Mississippi Band of Choctaw Indians stated in testimony to the House Subcommittee on Indian Affairs and Public Lands with respect to a different provision:

> The ultimate responsibility for child welfare rests with the parents and we would not support legislation which

---

favoring placement with the tribe, have not been followed.

6. None of the cases cited approvingly by Congress involved a deliberate abandonment. . . .

interfered with that basic relationship. Hearings on S. 1214 before the Subcommittee on Indian Affairs and Public Lands of the House Committee on Interior and Insular Affairs, 95th Cong., 2d Sess., 62 (1978).

If J.B. and W.J. had established a domicile off the Reservation, the state courts would have been required to give effect to their choice of jurisdiction; there should not be a different result when the parents have not changed their own domicile, but have expressed an unequivocal intent to establish a domicile for their children off the Reservation. The law of abandonment, as enunciated by the Mississippi Supreme Court in this case, does not defeat, but serves the purposes of the Act. An abandonment occurs when a parent deserts a child and places the child with another with an intent to relinquish all parental rights and obligations. *Restatement* § 22, Comment *e* . . . If a child is abandoned by his mother, he takes on the domicile of his father; if the child is abandoned by his father, he takes on the domicile of his mother. *Restatement* § 22, Comment *e* . . .

. . . The ICWA expresses the intent that exclusive tribal jurisdiction is not so frail that it should be defeated as soon as the Indian child steps off the reservation. Similarly, when the child is abandoned by one parent to a person off the reservation, the tribe and the other parent domiciled on the reservation may still have an interest in the exercise of exclusive jurisdiction. That interest is protected by the rule that a child abandoned by one parent takes on the domicile of the other. But when an Indian child is deliberately abandoned by both parents to a person off the reservation, no purpose of the ICWA is served by closing the state courthouse door to them. . . .

The interpretation of domicile adopted by the Court requires the custodian of an Indian child who is off the reservation to haul the child to a potentially distant tribal court unfamiliar with the child's present living conditions and best interests. Moreover, it renders any custody decision made by a state court forever suspect, susceptible to challenge at any time as void for having been entered in the absence of jurisdiction.[12] Finally, it forces parents of Indian children who desire to invoke state court jurisdiction to establish a domicile off the reservation. Only if the custodial parent has the wealth and ability to establish a domicile off the reservation will the parent be able use the processes of state court. I fail to see how such a requirement serves the paramount congressional purpose of "promot[ing] the stability and security of Indian tribes and families." 25 U.S.C. § 1902.

The Court concludes its opinion with the observation that whatever anguish is suffered by the Indian children, their natural parents, and their adoptive parents because of its decision today is a result of their failure to initially follow the provisions of the ICWA. By holding that parents who are domiciled on the reservation cannot voluntarily avail themselves of the adoption procedures of state court and that all such proceedings will be void for lack of jurisdiction, however, the Court establishes a rule of law that is virtually certain to ensure that similar anguish will be suffered by other families in the future. . . . I respectfully dissent.

12. . . . As the Tribe acknowledged at oral argument, any adoption of an Indian child effected through a state court will be susceptible of challenge by the Indian tribe no matter how old the child and how long it has lived with its adoptive parents.

CASE QUESTIONS

1. The Utah Supreme Court, whose reasoning Justice Brennan follows, argues that this statute put Indian tribal rights in children "on a parity" with the interests of the parents in their children. Since the parents' wishes are being overridden by the tribe here, does "parity" seem like an accurate description?

2. Even fundamental constitutional rights can be restricted to the degree that the restriction is necessitated by a "compelling governmental interest." Is this decision best understood as suggesting that tribal preservation and avoiding adjustment difficulties for the adopted Indian child amount to compelling interests? Ought the biological parents be allowed to choose for their child between these potential adjustment difficulties in non-Indian families and the difficulties of life on the reservation? Could a state government, citing similar adjustment difficulties, pass a law forbidding all interracial adoption of Americans? (The same "compelling interest" test must be met for any law that discriminates on the basis of race.)

3. Does the fact that Native Americans who wish to avoid tribal courts can simply establish domicile off the reservation before giving birth mean that the restrictions of the ICWA as now interpreted are only minor obstacles? Consider Justice Stevens's dissent on this point.

CHAPTER 4   **Sex Discrimination**

The framework of national law, both constitutional and statutory, that governs sex discrimination cases in the nineties is radically different from what it was only three decades ago. In order to provide historical perspective on the current situation and current trends, a brief review of American law on this subject follows.

Historical Background

Sex discrimination was deeply embedded in Anglo-American law as recently as the middle of the twentieth century.[1] The U.S. Supreme Court was no exception.

The Court ruled in 1873 that neither the privileges or immunities clause nor the equal protection clause nor due process clause of the recently adopted Fourteenth Amendment[2] presented any constitutional obstacle to the state of Illinois's practice of forbidding women to practice law (even after they had passed the bar exam). One justice explained the rationale as follows:

> The . . . family organization, which is founded in the divine ordinance, as well as in the nature of things, indicates the domestic sphere as that which properly belongs to the domain and functions of womanhood. The harmony, not to say identity, of interests and views which belong or should belong to the family institution, is repugnant to the idea of a woman adopting a distinct and independent career from that of her husband. . . .
> . . . The paramount destiny and mission of woman are to fulfill the noble and benign offices of wife and mother. This is the law of the Creator. And the rules of civil society must be adapted to the general constitution of things, and cannot be based upon exceptional cases.[3]

Even as recently as 1961 the Court was voicing somewhat similar sentiments when it upheld the conviction by an all-male jury of a woman who killed her husband in a state where the jury selection system virtually always produced all-male juries. The Court explained,

> Despite the enlightened emancipation of women from the restrictions and protections of bygone years, and their entry into many parts of community life

205

formerly considered to be reserved to men, woman is still regarded as the center of home and family life. We cannot say that it is constitutionally impermissible for a State, acting in pursuit of the general welfare, to conclude that a woman should be relieved from the civic duty of jury service. . . .[4]

This decision was not overturned until 1975,[5] and then as part of a series of decisions in the 1970s that amounted to a judicial revolution in the constitutional law of women's rights. While the details of those decisions can be found elsewhere,[6] the principles of law that they produced are important for understanding the legal parameters of contemporary cases in women's rights. One of those principles of the seventies has already been elaborated at length in chapters 1, 2, and 3, namely, the rule that women have a right to procreative privacy which includes, among other things, the right to seek an abortion "free from unwarranted governmental intrusion."[7]

A second innovation of constitutional principle of the 1970s, and the one that set the framework for the concerns of this chapter, was the rule that gender discrimination in the law is frowned upon, by virtue of the equal protection clause of the Fourteenth Amendment. It is, precisely, "frowned upon," but not absolutely forbidden. The more technical terminology that the Court uses to express this principle and the historical background to the Court's adoption of it can be best understood in the context of the Court's interpretations of other (more explicit or more obvious) constitutional prohibitions.

In fact, virtually nothing under the Constitution is absolutely forbidden. Despite the sweeping phrases of the First Amendment, for instance, certain speech may be restricted if the government can show that the restriction is necessary for the attainment of a compelling governmental interest. Similarly, despite the unanimous understanding that forbidding racial discrimination in laws was the core purpose of the equal protection clause, laws that draw distinctions on racial lines are permitted when the government can prove that they are necessitated by a compelling governmental interest. Racially drawn lines are permitted, for example, for the compelling purpose of rectifying the segregation of public schools by race where it was originally mandated by law.[8]

Many statutes place people into categories; for instance, the purchase of alcoholic beverages is typically restricted to persons in the age category over twenty-one. Such categories in general are permitted despite the sweeping language of the equal protection clause ("nor [shall any state] deny to any person the equal protection of the laws"). The clause is understood ordinarily to permit the creation of legal categories as long as there is some valid reason for the categorization (i.e., some grounds for a rational person to believe sincerely that the law in some way promotes some aspect of public welfare). This standard is called "ordinary scrutiny," or the "rational basis" test.

Because of the historic purpose of the equal protection clause, race-based categories are treated differently; they are treated as "suspect classifications" and are subjected not to ordinary scrutiny but to "strict scrutiny." Thus, they must meet the very stringent, compelling-interest test described above if they are to be permitted. In the history of American legislation, nationality lines in law were often linked to race—as in the example of laws discriminating against the Chinese. The Supreme Court took account of this connection as early as 1886 when it added nationality-based categories to race-based ones as meriting the condemnation that is now called "suspect classification" status.[9] Legal lines drawn on the basis of gender or "sex,"[10] however, were not treated to this same early condemnation; indeed, leading forces of the nineteenth century women's movement successfully lobbied for such laws in the form of protective labor legislation for women.[11]

In 1964 Congress adopted a civil rights act of historic proportions. It prohibited racial discrimination in hiring, firing, compensation, and other "terms of employment." It also opened up public accommodations to members of all races and mandated that federal funds would be cut off from any *de jure* (by law) segregated school. In the process of Congressional debate on the bill, the employment sections were amended to include a prohibition on sex-based discrimination.[12] So amended, the 1964 Civil Rights Act in a stroke rendered a dead letter all existing protective labor legislation for women.

Thus, when the second women's movement in America became activated in the late 1960s, no protective labor laws were in force. Moreover, the leading voices of the movement, in contrast to those of the first women's movement, by this time opposed such laws on the grounds that they purported to place women on a pedestal but in fact functioned more as a cage, cutting women off from lucrative job opportunities. For the decade of the seventies these voices worked along two fronts to revolutionize the constitutional law of women's rights in the United States: (1) they brought a series of cases to the U.S. Supreme Court in an effort to persuade the justices to declare any gender-based category in law a "suspect classification";[13] (2) they attempted to have an Equal Rights Amendment (ERA) added to the U.S. Constitution. It read (in part): "Equality of rights under the law shall not be denied or abridged by the United States or by any State on account of sex." (Its other clauses gave Congress enforcement power and stated when it would take effect.) The amendment was generally understood to have the import of rendering gender a "suspect classification," just as the equal protection clause so rendered race.

The egalitarian women's movement of the seventies garnered enormous success in terms of legal change. While the ERA was not formally ratified, it was proposed by votes of more than 90 percent in favor in each house of Congress and it achieved ratification in 70 percent of the states, with public opinion polls showing majorities in favor in the other states as well.[14] In this atmosphere, it would have been difficult for the Supreme Court to continue to insist that sex discrimination in laws was basically acceptable, deserving only minimal, "ordinary scrutiny." For the period 1971–1975, while the ERA was actively pending, the Supreme Court spoke as though nothing had changed, as though all that was needed to justify sex discrimination in laws was any "rational" basis. Unlike its words, however, the Court's actions showed that much had changed, for the Court was striking down sex discriminations in laws that easily would have passed muster a decade earlier.[15] The Court appeared to be awaiting formal passage of the ERA so that it could change its tune, to make that tune match its steps.

By December of 1976, however, it was clear to observers that the ERA had ceased to progress toward ratification. At this point the Supreme Court admitted that a new rule was in play, and *had been* in play since 1971, namely, that to satisfy the equal protection clause, any law that discriminated on the basis of sex had to be *"substantially related* to an *important* government interest."[16] Called the *Craig* rule, after the case that gave rise to it, in effect (and in conscious purpose) this new mandate rendered sex a "semi-suspect" classification, because this test fell between ordinary scrutiny (*rationally related* to any *legitimate* government interest) and strict scrutiny (*necessary for* a *compelling* government interest). As worded, the *Craig* rule permitted judges to strike down the vast majority of sex-based classifications but to uphold those for which there appeared to be strong reasons. It also enabled the Court to maintain the appearance (if not, perhaps, the reality) of not entirely pre-empting the ERA.

The five most recent applications of this test were the following: The Court struck down as unconstitutional a state law that gave husbands unilateral control over marital property[17] and a state law excluding males from a state-run nursing college.[18] The Court upheld as not unconstitutional a state law defining as criminal the behavior of the male, but not the female, in a couple aged 14–17 who engage in sexual intercourse;[19] the federal government policy requiring males but not females to register for the draft;[20] and a five-year timing delay enacted by Congress for the implementation of a Supreme Court decision[21] that had struck down as sex discrimination, in 1977, a Social Security provision that gave certain benefits to widows but not to widowers.[22]

The Supreme Court has not taken up a Constitution-based sex discrimination case since 1984. Instead, for the past decade it has limited its dealings with sex discrimination to challenges brought under federal statutes, such as the 1964 Civil Rights Act. The reasons for this shift are not obvious. It may reflect a preference on the part of the justices for a less obviously activist role—when they interpret a federal statute, they are applying the expressed will of a recently elected majority, not just their own reading of an arguably malleable hundred-year-old clause. If Congress disagrees with the Court's reading of a statute, it can override that interpretation with relative ease, by amending the statute with a simple majority vote (assuming the absence of a presidential veto). Congress has done this three times in recent years, amending the 1964 Civil Rights Act with the Pregnancy Discrimination Act of 1978,[23] amending Title IX of the Education Amendments with the Civil Rights Restoration Act of 1987,[24] and overturning a series of 1989 interpretations of the 1964 Civil Rights Act and of an 1866 Civil Rights Act by the Civil Rights Act of 1991.[25] (The last was legislation that took a compromise form because a presidential veto was threatened. This compromise is explained later in this chapter.)

The Court's recent inclination to stay on the more democratically constrained terrain of statutory interpretation and off the shakier ground of constitutional interpretation may, alternatively, reflect the decline of a unified legal impetus within the feminist movement. The eighties and nineties brought a notable increase in the number of feminist legal scholars but a precipitous decline in unity within their ranks. Many feminists now frankly argue for what used to be called "protective" legislation for women, on the grounds that without such legislation women are unfairly disadvantaged by making them play by rules that were designed with men in mind, and that are ill-adapted to women's biology and life patterns.[26] In this climate, where the national consensus on what would be fair under the equal protection clause is not so clear as it appeared in the seventies, the Court restricts its policy declarations to issues where any public dissatisfaction that might be incurred is readily rectified by Congressional action.

Yet another possible explanation for this avoidance of constitution-based gender equity decisions is a more banal one: It is possible that in the years since 1976, the states have responded to the Supreme Court's clear signal by cleaning up their act and removing so much of the sex-based discrimination from their statute books that not many cases are left to be appealed to the Court.[27]

In any event, the recent gender discrimination cases all involve legislative interpretation. Consequently, the cases included in this chapter present contested interpretations of statutes adopted by Congress that affect women's legal right to freedom from gender discrimination. Lurking in the background of all these cases, however, are constitutional rights, because when Congress legislates it acts pursuant to its powers listed in the Constitution. One of those is the power allocated to it by section 5 of the Fourteenth Amendment, namely, the "power to enforce, by appropriate legislation, the provisions of [the Fourteenth Amendment, which include the equal protection clause]." Thus, when Congress legislates, for instance, a prohibition on sex discrimination in educational programs that receive federal funds, it is in part expressing its own interpretation of the meaning of the equal protection clause. And the Supreme Court is always supposed to be guided, when interpreting federal statutes, by the rule that if two readings of a statute are plausible, one constitutional and one not, the constitutional reading is the one to be followed.

Employment Opportunity

The equal employment opportunity cases of the late eighties and early nineties that have come to the Supreme Court have been considerably more subtle than the no-women-need-apply situations of an earlier era. Cases of recent years have involved discrimination based not on sex as such but on particular traits of selected women. One case involved an alleged deficiency in appropriately feminine behavior; another involved unwanted romantic overtures from a co-worker that left the female employee feeling uncomfortable in the workplace; a third involved workplace restrictions that kept potentially fertile women (but not women who were sterile) away from sections of the workplace where high concentrations of lead would endanger the well-being of a fetus with long-term exposure to the area. It is unlikely that any of these specific situations was in the mind of a Congressperson voting for the Civil Rights Act of 1964. But applying refinements to laws as new and unforeseen situations arise is precisely what judges are obliged to do with statutes that endure over time. These cases illustrate the most recent refinements to the gender equity aspect of Title VII.

Gender Stereotyping and the Workplace: *Price Waterhouse v. Hopkins* (1988)

One of the clauses of Title VII of the 1964 Civil Rights Act forbids discrimination "with respect to . . . compensation, terms, conditions, or privileges of employment, because of [an] individual's race, color, religion, sex, or national origin," and another makes it unlawful to "classify . . . employees . . . in any way which would deprive or tend to deprive any individual of equal employment opportunities because of such individual's race . . . sex [etc.]."[28] In a 1984 case, *Hishon v. Spaulding*,[29] the Supreme Court ruled that eligibility to be promoted to partnership in a law firm was properly viewed as a "term, condition, or privilege of employment," and First Amendment rights of association of the partners in the firm did not override this statutory right of employees of the firm. The decision was widely understood as applying to analogous sorts of professional partnerships, such as those of large accounting firms.

A case involving such a firm, the Price Waterhouse company, came before the Supreme Court in 1988, but with a new twist. The discrimination alleged was discrimination not against women as such but against a particular woman for behaving in an insufficiently feminine manner. The facts of this case highlight a problem with the Supreme Court's (and Congress's) practice of using the terms *sex discrimination* and *gender discrimination* interchangeably. Sociologists, by contrast, distinguish *sex* from *gender* by using *sex* to describe biological category and *gender* to describe societal expectations that are attached to one or another biological sex group. The Price Waterhouse case, in sociological terms, involved a corporate decision against promoting a female employee on the grounds of her gender nonconformity. The Supreme Court glided right past this innovative aspect of the case (discussing it as just another example of sex discrimination), but the dissenter in the federal circuit court of appeals did raise the issue.

The facts of the case contained numerous examples of what the Supreme Court called "sex stereotyping" in remarks made by supervisory personnel at Price Waterhouse who were examining the candidacy of Ann B. Hopkins for promotion to partnership. Both supporters and critics painted a mixed picture of her. She combined a stellar record of acquiring lucrative contracts for the firm as well as an outstanding number of billable hours, excellent integrity, communication skills, and intelligence, with some problems in the area of interpersonal skills. Those problems include being sometimes "overly aggressive, unduly harsh, impatient with staff, and very demanding." These personality flaws proved the fertile ground for the sex-stereotyped remarks. A man who opposed her promotion (in his written evaluation) suggested that she needed a "course at charm school." A member of the admissions committee (which plays a pivotal role in the promotion process) specifically investigated a complaint in Hopkins's personnel file that she used profane language and testified that her use of profanity had been regarded by "several . . . partners" as "one of the negatives." One of her supporters for promotion specifically responded to this issue by noting (in a written evaluation), "Many male partners are worse than Ann (language and tough personality)," and added that others were concerned about her profanity only "because she is a lady using foul language." Another of her supporters tried to head off this line of criticism by saying that she "had matured from a tough-talking, somewhat masculine, hard-nosed mgr. to an authoritative, formidable, but much more appealing lady partner candidate."

After the firm voted to postpone Ms. Hopkins's promotion decision for a year, she met with the head partner of her own division, Thomas Beyer, a firm supporter of her candidacy. He advised her (in sincerity) that the best avenue for improving her chances of promotion would be "to walk more femininely, dress more femininely, wear make-up, have her hair styled, and wear jewelry." Once her case was in court, Hopkins also presented some evidence of sex stereotyping in evaluations of candidates from previous years, including a comment from one partner the year prior to her own candidacy that he could never seriously consider a woman candidate for partner and believed women were not even capable of functioning as senior managers (the job Ann Hopkins already had). His evaluation and vote in that year had been counted in the process just like that of the other partners, even though his practice was clearly against the law. (There was no evidence that he personally had participated in Ann Hopkins's evaluation; his comments were introduced to show the general atmosphere at the company.)

Ann Hopkins was denied promotion at Price Waterhouse the second year as well as the first. She then resigned and sued the company for violating her rights under Title VII. At the district court level, the judge ruled that she had persuasively demonstrated that the presence of "stereotyped assumptions about women" in the selection process at Price Waterhouse meant that its evaluation system was "subject to sex bias" in the "double standard" being applied to partner candidates; this stereotyping violated Title VII. Because there were, however, legitimate nonsexist concerns about Ann Hopkins's lack of interpersonal skills, the company had to be given a chance to show "by clear and convincing evidence" that the decision would be the same absent the discrimination. Since the company failed to succeed in this demonstration, the court awarded to Hopkins appropriate economic relief.[30] Both sides appealed (Hopkins, because she wanted a more substantial award of damages).

At the federal circuit court of appeals, the three-judge panel upheld all of the district court rulings by a 2–1 vote. The majority commented that Hopkins had "made a substantial showing of the role . . . sexual stereotyping played in the selection system" and that such stereotyping had "played a significant role in blocking plaintiff's admission to partnership."[31] Once a plaintiff has demonstrated that "discriminatory animus played a significant or substantial role in the contested employment decision," the circuit court acknowledged, courts are divided over what is the next appropriate step. Some let the employer prove simply by the preponderance of evidence that the decision would have been the same even without any discrimination, but others agree with the district court below that the appropriate level of proof to be required is "clear and convincing evidence."[32] This circuit court (the D.C. Circuit) agreed with the district court that the appropriate standard was "clear and convincing evidence," and it is this aspect of the decision to which the U.S. Supreme Court directed its attention.

The U.S. Supreme Court totally neglected the host of questions that might be raised about the basic assumption that requiring gender conformity itself amounts to sex discrimination. Circuit Court Judge Stephen Williams, in dissent, had suggested this line of questions, but even the dissenters on the Supreme Court ignored his suggestion. He had complained: "Dismissal of a male employee because he routinely appeared for work in skirts and dresses would surely reflect a form of sexual stereotyping, but it would not, merely on that account, support Title VII liability. . . . The court makes no effort to delineate the theory, to draw a line between permissible and impermissible."[33] What the Supreme Court did say is excerpted below.

Price Waterhouse v. Hopkins, 490 U.S. 228 (1989)

Justice Brennan announced the judgment of the Court and delivered an opinion, in which Justice Marshall, Justice Blackmun, and Justice Stevens join.

. . .

II

The specification of the standard of causation under Title VII is a decision about the kind of conduct that violates that statute. According to Price Waterhouse, an employer violates Title VII only if it gives decisive consideration to an employee's gender, race, national origin, or religion in making a decision that affects that employee. On Price Waterhouse's theory, even if a plaintiff shows that her gender played a part in an employment decision, it is still her burden to show that the decision would have been different if the employer had not discriminated. In Hopkins' view, on the other hand, an employer violates the statute whenever it allows one of these attributes to play any part in an employment decision. Once a plaintiff shows that this occurred, according to Hopkins, the employer's proof that it would have made the same decision in the absence of discrimination can serve to limit equitable relief but not to avoid a finding of liability. We conclude that, as often happens, the truth lies somewhere in-between.

A

In passing Title VII, Congress made the simple but momentous announcement that sex, race, religion, and national origin are not relevant to the selection, evaluation, or compensation of employees.[3] . . .

. . . In now-familiar language, the statute forbids an employer to "fail or refuse to hire or to discharge any individual, or otherwise to discriminate with respect to his compensation, terms, conditions, or privileges of employment," or to "limit, segregate, or classify his employees or applicants for employment in any way which would deprive or tend to deprive any individual of employment opportunities or otherwise adversely affect his status as an employee, *because of* such individual's . . . sex." 42 U.S.C. §§ 2000e–2(a)(1), (2) (emphasis added). We take these words to mean that gender must be irrelevant to

3. We disregard, for purposes of this discussion, the special context of affirmative action.

employment decisions. To construe the words "because of" as colloquial shorthand for "but-for causation," as does Price Waterhouse, is to misunderstand them.

But-for causation is a hypothetical construct. In determining whether a particular factor was a but-for cause of a given event, we begin by assuming that that factor was present at the time of the event, and then ask whether, even if that factor had been absent, the event nevertheless would have transpired in the same way. The present, active tense of the operative verbs of § 703(a)(1) ("to fail or refuse"), in contrast, turns our attention to the actual moment of the event in question, the adverse employment decision. The critical inquiry, the one commanded by the words of § 703(a)(1), is whether gender was a factor in the employment decision *at the moment it was made.* Moreover, since we know that the words "because of" do not mean "*solely* because of," we also know that Title VII meant to condemn even those decisions based on a mixture of legitimate and illegitimate considerations. When, therefore, an employer considers both gender and legitimate factors at the time of making a decision, that decision was "because of" sex and the other, legitimate considerations—even if we may say later, in the context of litigation, that the decision would have been the same if gender had not been taken into account.

To attribute this meaning to the words "because of" does not, as the dissent asserts, divest them of causal significance. A simple example illustrates the point. Suppose two physical forces act upon and move an object, and suppose that either force acting alone would have moved the object. As the dissent would have it, *neither* physical force was a "cause" of the motion unless we can show that but for one or both of them, the object would not have moved; to use the dissent's terminology, both forces were simply "in the air" unless we can identify at least one of them as a but-for cause of the object's movement. Events that are causally overdetermined, in other words, may not have any "cause" at all. This cannot be so.

We need not leave our common sense at the doorstep when we interpret a statute. It is difficult for us to imagine that, in the simple words "because of," Congress meant to obligate a plaintiff to identify the precise causal role played by legitimate and illegitimate motivations in the employment decision she challenges. We conclude, instead, that Congress meant to obligate her to prove that the employer relied upon sex-based considerations in coming to its decision.

. . . To say that an employer may not take gender into account is not, however, the end of the matter, for that describes only one aspect of Title VII. The other important aspect of the statute is its preservation of an employer's remaining freedom of choice. We conclude that the preservation of this freedom means that an employer shall not be liable if it can prove that, even if it had not taken gender into account, it would have come to the same decision regarding a particular person. The statute's maintenance of employer prerogatives is evident from the statute itself and from its history, both in Congress and in this Court. . . .

. . . And our emphasis . . . on "legitimate, nondiscriminatory reason[s]" in disparate-treatment cases, see *McDonnell Douglas Corp. v. Green*, 411 U.S. 792, 802, (1973); *Texas Dept. of Community Affairs v. Burdine*, 450 U.S. 248 (1981), results from our awareness of Title VII's balance between employee rights and employer prerogatives . . .

When an employer ignored the attributes enumerated in the statute, Congress hoped, it naturally would focus on the qualifications of the applicant or em-

ployee. The intent to drive employers to focus on qualifications rather than on race, religion, sex, or national origin is the theme of a good deal of the statute's legislative history. An interpretive memorandum entered into the Congressional Record by Senators Case and Clark, comanagers of the bill in the Senate, is representative of this general theme. According to their memorandum, Title VII "expressly protects the employer's right to insist that any prospective applicant, Negro or white, must meet the applicable job qualifications. Indeed, the very purpose of Title VII is to promote hiring on the basis of job qualifications, rather than on the basis of race or color."[9] 110 Cong. Rec. 7247 (1964) . . .

Our holding casts no shadow on *Burdine*, in which we decided that, even after a plaintiff has made out a prima facie case of discrimination under Title VII, the burden of persuasion does not shift to the em-

---

9. Many of the legislators' statements, such as the memorandum quoted in text, focused specifically on race rather than on gender or religion or national origin. We do not, however, limit their statements to the context of race, but instead we take them as general statements on the meaning of Title VII. The somewhat bizarre path by which "sex" came to be included as a forbidden criterion for employment—it was included in an attempt to *defeat* the bill, see C. & B. Whalen, *The Longest Debate: A Legislative History of the 1964 Civil Rights Act* 115–117 (1985)—does not persuade us that the legislators' statements pertaining to race are irrelevant to cases alleging gender discrimination. The amendment that added "sex" as one of the forbidden criteria for employment was passed, of course, and the statute on its face treats each of the enumerated categories exactly the same.

By the same token, our specific references to gender throughout this opinion, and the principles we announce, apply with equal force to discrimination based on race, religion, or national origin.

ployer to show that its stated legitimate reason for the employment decision was the true reason. 450 U.S., at 256–58. We stress, first, that neither court below shifted the burden of persuasion to Price Waterhouse on this question, and in fact, the District Court found that Hopkins had not shown that the firm's stated reason for its decision was pretextual. 618 F. Supp., at 1114–15. Moreover, since we hold that the plaintiff retains the burden of persuasion on the issue whether gender played a part in the employment decision, the situation before us is not the one of "shifting burdens" that we addressed in *Burdine.* Instead, the employer's burden is most appropriately deemed an affirmative defense: the plaintiff must persuade the factfinder on one point, and then the employer, if it wishes to prevail, must persuade it on another. See *NLRB v. Transportation Management Corp.,* 462 U.S. 393, 400 (1983)[11]

---

11. Given that both the plaintiff and defendant bear a burden of proof in cases such as this one, it is surprising that the dissent insists that our approach requires the employer to bear "the ultimate burden of proof." It is, moreover, perfectly consistent to say *both* that gender was a factor in a particular decision when it was made *and* that, when the situation is viewed hypothetically and after the fact, the same decision would have been made even in the absence of discrimination. Thus, we do not see the "internal inconsistency" in our opinion that the dissent perceives. Finally, where liability is imposed because an employer is unable to prove that it would have made the same decision even if it had not discriminated, this is not an imposition of liability "where sex made no difference to the outcome." In our adversary system, where a party has the burden of proving a particular assertion and where that party is unable to meet its burden, we assume that that assertion is inaccurate. Thus, where an employer is unable to prove its claim that it would have made the same decision in the absence of discrimination,

Price Waterhouse's claim that the employer does not bear any burden of proof (if it bears one at all) until the plaintiff has shown "substantial evidence that Price Waterhouse's explanation for failing to promote Hopkins was not the 'true reason' for its action" merely restates its argument that the plaintiff in a mixed-motives case must squeeze her proof into *Burdine's* framework. Where a decision was the product of a mixture of legitimate and illegitimate motives, however, it simply makes no sense to ask whether the legitimate reason was "*the* 'true reason'" for the decision—which is the question asked by *Burdine.* See *Transportation Management, supra,* at 400, n. 5. Oblivious to this last point, the dissent would insist that *Burdine's* framework perform work that it was never intended to perform. It would require a plaintiff who challenges an adverse employment decision in which both legitimate and illegitimate considerations played a part to pretend that the decision, in fact, stemmed from a single source—for the premise of *Burdine* is that *either* a legitimate *or* an illegitimate set of considerations led to the challenged decision. To say that *Burdine's* evidentiary scheme will not help us decide a case admittedly involving *both* kinds of considerations is not to cast aspersions on the utility of that scheme in the circumstances for which it was designed.

B

In deciding as we do today, we do not traverse new ground. We have in the past confronted Title VII cases in which an employer has used an illegitimate criterion to distinguish among employees, and have held that it is the employer's burden to justify decisions resulting from that

---

we are entitled to conclude that gender *did* make a difference to the outcome.

practice. When an employer has asserted that gender is a bona fide occupational qualification within the meaning of § 703(e), for example, we have assumed that it is the employer who must show why it must use gender as a criterion in employment. See *Dothard v. Rawlinson*, 433 U.S. 321, 332–37 (1977). In a related context, although the Equal Pay Act expressly permits employers to pay different wages to women where disparate pay is the result of a "factor other than sex," see 29 U.S.C. § 206(d)(1), we have decided that it is the employer, not the employee, who must prove that the actual disparity is not sex-linked. See *Corning Glass Works v. Brennan*, 417 U.S. 188, 196 (1974). . . . As these examples demonstrate, our assumption always has been that if an employer allows gender to affect its decisionmaking process, then it must carry the burden of justifying its ultimate decision. We have not in the past required women whose gender has proved relevant to an employment decision to establish the negative proposition that they would not have been subject to that decision had they been men, and we do not do so today.

We have reached a similar conclusion in other contexts where the law announces that a certain characteristic is irrelevant to the allocation of burdens and benefits. In *Mt. Healthy City School Dist. Board of Education v. Doyle*, 429 U.S. 274 (1977), the plaintiff claimed that he had been discharged as a public school teacher for exercising his free-speech rights under the First Amendment. Because we did not wish to "place an employee in a better position as a result of the exercise of constitutionally protected conduct than he would have occupied had he done nothing," *id.*, at 285, we concluded that such an employee "ought not to be able, by engaging in such conduct, to prevent his employer from assessing his performance record and reaching a decision not to rehire on the basis of that record."

Id., at 286. We therefore held that once the plaintiff had shown that his constitutionally protected speech was a "substantial" or "motivating factor" in the adverse treatment of him by his employer, the employer was obligated to prove "by a preponderance of the evidence that it would have reached the same decision as to [the plaintiff] even in the absence of the protected conduct." *Id.*, at 287. A court that finds for a plaintiff under this standard has effectively concluded that an illegitimate motive was a "but-for" cause of the employment decision. See *Givhan v. Western Line Consolidated School District*, 439 U.S. 410, 417 (1979). . . .

In *Transportation Management*, we upheld the NLRB's interpretation of § 10(c) of the National Labor Relations Act, which forbids a court to order affirmative relief for discriminatory conduct against a union member "if such individual was suspended or discharged for cause." 29 U.S.C. § 160(c). The Board had decided that this provision meant that once an employee had shown that his suspension or discharge was based in part on hostility to unions, it was up to the employer to prove by a preponderance of the evidence that it would have made the same decision in the absence of this impermissible motive. In such a situation, we emphasized, "[t]he employer is a wrongdoer; he has acted out of a motive that is declared illegitimate by the statute. It is fair that he bear the risk that the influence of legal and illegal motives cannot be separated, because he knowingly created the risk and because the risk was created not by innocent activity but by his own wrongdoing." 462 U.S., at 403.

We have, in short, been here before. Each time, we have concluded that the plaintiff who shows that an impermissible motive played a motivating part in an adverse employment decision has thereby placed upon the defendant the burden to show that it would have made the same decision in the absence of the unlawful motive. Our decision today treads this well-worn path.

C

In saying that gender played a motivating part in an employment decision, we mean that, if we asked the employer at the moment of the decision what its reasons were and if we received a truthful response, one of those reasons would be that the applicant or employee was a woman.[13] In the specific context of sex stereotyping, an employer who acts on the basis of a belief that a woman cannot be aggressive, or that she must not be, has acted on the basis of gender.

Although the parties do not overtly dispute this last proposition, the placement by Price Waterhouse of "sex stereotyping" in quotation marks throughout its brief seems to us an insinuation either that such stereotyping was not present in this case or that it lacks legal relevance. We reject both possibilities. As to the existence of sex stereotyping in this case, we are not inclined to quarrel with the District Court's conclusion that a number of the partners' comments showed sex stereotyping at work. As for the legal relevance of sex stereotyping, we are beyond the day when an employer could evaluate employees by assuming or insisting that they matched the stereotype associated with their group, for " '[i]n forbidding employers to discriminate against individuals because of their sex, Congress intended to strike at the entire spectrum of disparate treatment of men and women resulting from sex stereotypes.' " *Los Angeles Dept. of Water & Power v. Manhart*, 435

13. After comparing this description of the plaintiff's proof to that offered by the concurring opinion, we do not understand why the concurrence suggests that they are meaningfully different from each other. . . .

U.S. 702, 707, n.13 (1978). An employer who objects to aggressiveness in women but whose positions require this trait places women in an intolerable and impermissible Catch-22: out of a job if they behave aggressively and out of a job if they don't. Title VII lifts women out of this bind.

Remarks at work that are based on sex stereotypes do not inevitably prove that gender played a part in a particular employment decision. The plaintiff must show that the employer actually relied on her gender in making its decision. In making this showing, stereotyped remarks can certainly be *evidence* that gender played a part. . . .

As to the employer's proof, in most cases, the employer should be able to present some objective evidence as to its probable decision in the absence of an impermissible motive. Moreover, proving "that the same decision would have been justified . . . is not the same as proving that the same decision would have been made." *Givhan*, 439 U.S., at 416. An employer may not, in other words, prevail in a mixed-motives case by offering a legitimate and sufficient reason for its decision if that reason did not motivate it at the time of the decision. Finally, an employer may not meet its burden in such a case by merely showing that at the time of the decision it was motivated only in part by a legitimate reason. The very premise of a mixed-motives case is that a legitimate reason was present, and indeed, in this case, Price Waterhouse already has made this showing by convincing Judge Gesell that Hopkins' interpersonal problems were a legitimate concern. The employer instead must show that its legitimate reason, standing alone, would have induced it to make the same decision.

III

The courts below held that an employer who has allowed a discriminatory impulse to play a motivating part in an employment decision must prove by clear and convincing evidence that it would have made the same decision in the absence of discrimination. We are persuaded that the better rule is that the employer must make this showing by a preponderance of the evidence.

Conventional rules of civil litigation generally apply in Title VII cases. . . .

Significantly, the cases from this Court that most resemble this one, *Mt. Healthy* and *Transportation Management*, did not require clear and convincing proof. *Mt. Healthy*, 429 U.S., at 287; *Transportation Management*, 462 U.S., at 400, 403. We are not inclined to say that the public policy against firing employees because they spoke out on issues of public concern or because they affiliated with a union is less important than the policy against discharging employees on the basis of their gender. Each of these policies is vitally important, and each is adequately served by requiring proof by a preponderance of the evidence.

Although Price Waterhouse does not concretely tell us how its proof was preponderant even if it was not clear and convincing, this general claim is implicit in its request for the less stringent standard. Since the lower courts required Price Waterhouse to make its proof by clear and convincing evidence, they did not determine whether Price Waterhouse had proved by a *preponderance of the evidence* that it would have placed Hopkins' candidacy on hold even if it had not permitted sex-linked evaluations to play a part in the decision-making process. Thus, we shall remand this case so that that determination can be made.

IV

. . . Price Waterhouse disputes both that stereotyping occurred and that it played any part in the decision to place Hopkins' candidacy on hold. In the firm's view, in other words, the District Court's factual conclusions are clearly erroneous. We do not agree. . . .

. . . It takes no special training to discern sex stereotyping in a description of an aggressive female employee as requiring "a course at charm school." Nor, turning to Thomas Beyer's memorable advice to Hopkins, does it require expertise in psychology to know that, if an employee's flawed "interpersonal skills" can be corrected by a soft-hued suit or a new shade of lipstick, perhaps it is the employee's sex and not her interpersonal skills that has drawn the criticism. . . .

Price Waterhouse appears to think that we cannot affirm the factual findings of the trial court without deciding that, instead of being overbearing and aggressive and curt, Hopkins is in fact kind and considerate and patient. If this is indeed its impression, petitioner misunderstands the theory on which Hopkins prevailed. The District Judge acknowledged that Hopkins' conduct justified complaints about her behavior as a senior manager. But he also concluded that the reactions of at least some of the partners were reactions to her as a *woman* manager. . . . Thus, even if we knew that Hopkins had "personality problems," this would not tell us that the partners who cast their evaluations of Hopkins in sex-based terms would have criticized her as sharply (or criticized her at all) if she had been a man. It is not our job to review the evidence and decide that the negative reactions to Hopkins were based on reality; our perception of Hopkins' character is irrelevant. We sit not to determine whether Ms. Hopkins is nice, but to decide whether the partners reacted negatively to her personality because she is a woman.

V

We hold that when a plaintiff in a Title VII case proves that her gender played a motivating part in an employment decision, the defendant may avoid a finding of liability only by proving by a preponderance of the evidence that it would have made the same decision even if it had not taken the plaintiff's gender into account. Because the courts below erred by deciding that the defendant must make this proof by clear and convincing evidence, we reverse the Court of Appeals' judgment against Price Waterhouse on liability and remand the case to that court for further proceedings.

JUSTICE WHITE, concurring in the judgment.

In my view, to determine the proper approach to causation in this case, we need look only to the Court's opinion in *Mt. Healthy City School District Bd. of Ed. v. Doyle*. . . . The Court rejected a rule of causation that focused "solely on whether protected conduct played a part, 'substantial' or otherwise, in a decision not to rehire," on the grounds that such a rule could make the employee better off by exercising his constitutional rights than by doing nothing at all. *Id.*, at 285. Instead, the Court outlined the following approach:

> Initially, in this case, the burden was properly placed upon respondent to show that his conduct was constitutionally protected, and that his conduct was a "substantial factor"—or, to put it in other words, that it was a "motivating factor" in the Board's decision not to rehire him. Respondent having carried that burden, however, the District Court should have gone on to determine whether the Board had shown by a preponderance of the evidence that it would have reached the same decision as to respondent's reemployment even in the absence of the protected conduct. *Id.*, at 287.

It is not necessary to get into semantic discussions on whether the *Mt. Healthy* approach is "but for" causation in another guise or creates an affirmative defense on the part of the employer to see its clear application to the issues before us in this case. As in *Mt. Healthy*, the District Court found that the employer was motivated by both legitimate and illegitimate factors. And here, as in *Mt. Healthy*, and as the Court now holds, Hopkins was not required to prove that the illegitimate factor was the only, principal, or true reason for the petitioner's action. Rather, as JUSTICE O'CONNOR states, her burden was to show that the unlawful motive was a *substantial* factor in the adverse employment action. The District Court, as its opinion was construed by the Court of Appeals, so found. 825 F.2d 458, 470, 471 (1987), and I agree that the finding was supported by the record. The burden of persuasion then should have shifted to Price Waterhouse to prove "by a preponderance of the evidence that it would have reached the same decision . . . in the absence of" the unlawful motive. *Mt. Healthy, supra*, 429 U.S., at 287. . . .

Because the Court of Appeals required Price Waterhouse to prove by clear and convincing evidence that it would have reached the same employment decision in the absence of the improper motive, rather than merely requiring proof by a preponderance of the evidence as in *Mt. Healthy*, I concur in the judgment reversing this case in part and remanding. With respect to the employer's burden, however, the plurality seems to require, at least in most cases, that the employer submit objective evidence that the same result would have occurred absent the unlawful motivation. In my view, however, there is no special requirement that the employer carry its burden by objective evidence. In a mixed motive case, where the legitimate motive found would have been ample grounds for the action taken, and the employer credibly testifies that the action would have been taken for the legitimate reasons alone, this should be ample proof.

JUSTICE O'CONNOR, concurring in the judgment.

I agree with the plurality that on the facts presented in this case, the burden of persuasion should shift to the employer to demonstrate by a preponderance of the evidence that it would have reached the same decision concerning Ann Hopkins' candidacy absent consideration of her gender. I further agree that this burden shift is properly part of the liability phase of the litigation. I thus concur in the judgment of the Court. My disagreement stems from the plurality's conclusions concerning the substantive requirement of causation under the statute and its broad statements regarding the applicability of the allocation of the burden of proof applied in this case. The evidentiary rule the Court adopts today should be viewed as a supplement to the careful framework established by our unanimous decisions in *McDonnell Douglas Corp. v. Green* and *Texas Dept. of Community Affairs v. Burdine* for use in cases such as this one where the employer has created uncertainty as to causation by knowingly giving substantial weight to an impermissible criterion. I write separately to explain why I believe such a departure from the *McDonnell Douglas* standard is justified in the circumstances presented by this and like cases, and to express my views as to when and how the strong medicine of requiring the employer to bear the burden of persuasion on the issue of causation should be administered.

I

... I disagree with the plurality's dictum that the words "because of" do not mean "but-for" causation; manifestly they do. See *Sheet Metal Workers v. EEOC*, 478 U.S. 421, 499 (1986) (WHITE, J., dissenting) ("[T]he general policy under Title VII is to limit relief for racial discrimination in employment practices to actual victims of the discrimination"). We should not, and need not, deviate from that policy today. The question for decision in this case is what allocation of the burden of persuasion on the issue of causation best conforms with the intent of Congress and the purposes behind Title VII.

... [As to who bears the burden of proof,] in the area of tort liability, from whence the dissent's "but-for" standard of causation is derived, the law has long recognized that in certain "civil cases" leaving the burden of persuasion on the plaintiff to prove "but-for" causation would be both unfair and destructive of the deterrent purposes embodied in the concept of duty of care. Thus, in multiple causation cases, where a breach of duty has been established, the common law of torts has long shifted the burden of proof to multiple defendants to prove that their negligent actions were not the "but-for" cause of the plaintiffs injury. See *e.g., Summers v. Tice*, 33 Cal. 2d 80, 84–87, 199 P.2d 1, 3–4 (1948). The same rule has been applied where the effect of a defendant's tortious conduct combines with a force of unknown or innocent origin to produce the harm to the plaintiff. See *Kingston v. Chicago & N.W.R. Co.*, 191 Wis. 610, 616, 211 N.W. 913, 915 (1927). ...

While requiring that the plaintiff in a tort suit or a Title VII action prove that the defendant's "breach of duty" was the "but-for" cause of an injury does not generally hamper effective enforcement of the policies behind those causes of action,

at other times the [but-for] test demands the impossible. It challenges the imagination of the trier to probe into a purely fanciful and unknowable state of affairs. He is invited to make an estimate concerning facts that concededly never existed. The very uncertainty as to what *might* have happened opens the door wide for conjecture. But when conjecture is demanded it can be given a direction that is consistent with the policy considerations that underlie the controversy. Malone, *Ruminations on Cause-In-Fact,* 9 Stan. L. Rev. 60, 67 (1956).

Like the common law of torts, the statutory employment "tort" created by Title VII has two basic purposes. The first is to deter conduct which has been identified as contrary to public policy and harmful to society as a whole.... The second goal of Title VII is "to make persons whole for injuries suffered on account of unlawful employment discrimination." *Albemarle Paper Co. v. Moody,* 422 U.S. 405, at 418 (1975)....

Where an individual disparate treatment plaintiff has shown by a preponderance of the evidence that an illegitimate criterion was a *substantial* factor in an adverse employment decision, the deterrent purpose of the statute has clearly been triggered. More importantly, as an evidentiary matter, a reasonable factfinder could conclude that absent further explanation, the employer's discriminatory motivation "caused" the employment decision. The employer has not yet been shown to be a violator, but neither is it entitled to the same presumption of good faith concerning its employment decisions which is accorded employers facing only circumstantial evidence of discrimination. Both the policies behind the statute, and the evidentiary principles developed in the analogous area of causation in the law of torts, suggest that at this point the employer may be

required to convince the factfinder that, despite the smoke, there is no fire.

... There has been a strong showing that the employer has done exactly what Title VII forbids, but the connection between the employer's illegitimate motivation and any injury to the individual plaintiff is unclear. At this point calling upon the employer to show that despite consideration of illegitimate factors the individual plaintiff would not have been hired or promoted in any event hardly seems "unfair" or contrary to the substantive command of the statute....

... In my view, nothing in the language, history, or purpose of Title VII prohibits adoption of an evidentiary rule which places the burden of persuasion on the defendant to demonstrate that legitimate concerns would have justified an adverse employment action where the plaintiff has convinced the factfinder that a forbidden factor played a substantial role in the employment decision....

II

The dissent's summary of our individual disparate treatment cases to date is fair and accurate, and amply demonstrates that the rule we adopt today is at least a change in direction from some of our prior precedents. We have indeed emphasized in the past that in an individual disparate treatment action the plaintiff bears the burden of persuasion throughout the litigation.... *McDonnell Douglas* and *Burdine* assumed that the plaintiff would bear the burden of persuasion, ... and we clearly depart from that framework today. Such a departure requires justification, and its outlines should be carefully drawn.

First, *McDonnell Douglas* itself dealt with a situation where the plaintiff presented no direct evidence that the employer had relied on a forbidden factor under Title VII in making an employment decision. . . . I do not think that the employer is entitled to the same presumption of good faith where there is direct evidence that it has placed substantial reliance on factors whose consideration is forbidden by Title VII. . . .

Second, the facts of this case, and a growing number like it decided by the Courts of Appeals, convince me that the evidentiary standard I propose is necessary to make real the promise of *McDonnell Douglas* that "[i]n the implementation of [employment] decisions, it is abundantly clear that Title VII tolerates no . . . discrimination, subtle or otherwise." 411 U.S., at 801. In this case, the District Court found that a number of the evaluations of Ann Hopkins submitted by partners in the firm overtly referred to her failure to conform to certain gender stereotypes as a factor militating against her election to the partnership. 618 F. Supp. 1109, 1116–17 (1985). The District Court further found that these evaluations were given "great weight" by the decisionmakers at Price Waterhouse. *Id.*, at 1118. In addition, the District Court found that the partner responsible for informing Hopkins of the factors which caused her candidacy to be placed on hold, indicated that her "professional" problems would be solved if she would "walk more femininely, talk more femininely, wear make-up, have her hair styled, and wear jewelry." *Id.*, at 1117 (footnote omitted). As the Court of Appeals characterized it, Ann Hopkins proved that Price Waterhouse "permitt[ed] stereotypical attitudes towards women to play a significant, though unquantifiable, role in its decision not to invite her to become a partner." 825 F.2d, at 461.

At this point Ann Hopkins had taken her proof as far as it could go. She had proved discriminatory input into the decisional process, and had proved that participants in the process considered her failure to conform to the stereotypes credited by a number of the decisionmakers had been a substantial factor in the decision. . . . [O]ne would be hard pressed to think of a situation where it would be more appropriate to require the defendant to show that its decision would have been justified by wholly legitimate concerns.

Moreover, there is mounting evidence in the decisions of the lower courts that respondent here is not alone in her inability to pinpoint discrimination as the precise cause of her injury, despite having shown that it played a significant role in the decisional process. Many of these courts, which deal with the evidentiary issues in Title VII cases on a regular basis, have concluded that placing the risk of nonpersuasion on the defendant in a situation where uncertainty as to causation has been created by its consideration of an illegitimate criterion makes sense as a rule of evidence and furthers the substantive command of Title VII. . . . Particularly in the context of the professional world, where decisions are often made by collegial bodies on the basis of largely subjective criteria, requiring the plaintiff to prove that *any* one factor was the definitive cause of the decisionmakers' action may be tantamount to declaring Title VII inapplicable to such decisions. . . .

Finally, I am convinced that a rule shifting the burden to the defendant where the plaintiff has shown that an illegitimate criterion was a "substantial factor" in the employment decision will not conflict with other congressional policies embodied in Title VII. . . .

I believe there are significant differences between shifting the burden of persuasion to the employer in a case resting purely on statistical proof as in the disparate impact setting and shifting the burden of persuasion in a case like this one, where an employee has demonstrated by direct evidence that an illegitimate factor played a substantial role in a particular employment decision. First, the explicit consideration of race, color, religion, sex, or national origin in making employment decisions "was the most obvious evil Congress had in mind when it enacted Title VII." *Teamsters v. United States*, 431 U.S. 324, at 335, n. 15 (1977).... Second, shifting the burden of persuasion to the employer in a situation like this one creates no incentive to preferential treatment in violation of § 2000e–2(j). To avoid bearing the burden of justifying its decision, the employer need not seek racial or sexual balance in its work force; rather, all it need do is avoid substantial reliance on forbidden criteria in making its employment decisions....

In my view, in order to justify shifting the burden on the issue of causation to the defendant, a disparate treatment plaintiff must show by direct evidence that an illegitimate criterion was a substantial factor in the decision.... Requiring that the plaintiff demonstrate that an illegitimate factor played a substantial role in the employment decision identifies those employment situations where the deterrent purpose of Title VII is most clearly implicated. As an evidentiary matter, where a plaintiff has made this type of strong showing of illicit motivation, the factfinder is entitled to presume that the employer's discriminatory animus made a difference to the outcome, absent proof to the contrary from the employer. Where a disparate treatment plaintiff has made such a showing, the burden then rests with the employer to convince the trier of fact that it is more likely than not that the decision would have been the same absent consideration of the illegitimate factor. The employer need not isolate the sole cause for the decision, rather it must demonstrate that with the illegitimate factor removed from the calculus, sufficient business reasons would have induced it to take the same employment action. This evidentiary scheme essentially

requires the employer to place the employee in the same position he or she would have occupied absent discrimination. Cf. *Mt. Healthy Board of Education v. Doyle*, 429 U.S. 274, 286 (1977). If the employer fails to carry this burden, the factfinder is justified in concluding that the decision was made "because of" consideration of the illegitimate factor and the substantive standard for liability under the statute is satisfied....

It should be obvious that the threshold standard I would adopt for shifting the burden of persuasion to the defendant differs substantially from that proposed by the plurality, the plurality's suggestion to the contrary notwithstanding. See *ante*, at n. 13. The plurality proceeds from the premise that the words "because of" in the statute do not embody any causal requirement at all. Under my approach, the plaintiff must produce evidence sufficient to show that an illegitimate criterion was a substantial factor in the particular employment decision such that a reasonable factfinder could draw an inference that the decision was made "because of" the plaintiff's protected status. Only then would the burden of proof shift to the defendant to prove that the decision would have been justified by other, wholly legitimate considerations....

In this case, I agree with the plurality that petitioner should be called upon to show that the outcome would have been the same if respondent's professional merit had been its only concern. On remand, the District Court should determine whether Price Waterhouse has shown by a preponderance of the evidence that if gender had not been part of the process, its employment decision concerning Ann Hopkins would nonetheless have been the same.

JUSTICE KENNEDY, with whom the CHIEF JUSTICE and JUSTICE SCALIA join, dissenting.

Today the Court manipulates existing and complex rules for employment discrimination cases in a way certain to result in confusion. Continued adherence to the evidentiary scheme established in *McDonnell Douglas* and *Burdine* is a wiser course than creation of more disarray in an area of the law already difficult for the bench and bar, and so I must dissent.

Before turning to my reasons for disagreement with the Court's disposition of the case, it is important to review the actual holding of today's decision. I read the opinions as establishing that in a limited number of cases Title VII plaintiffs, by presenting direct and substantial evidence of discriminatory animus, may shift the burden of persuasion to the defendant to show that an adverse employment decision would have been supported by legitimate reasons. The shift in the burden of persuasion occurs only where a plaintiff proves by direct evidence that an unlawful motive was a substantial factor actually relied upon in making the decision.

Where the plaintiff makes the requisite showing, the burden that shifts to the employer is to show that legitimate employment considerations would have justified the decision without reference to any impermissible motive. ([see] opinion of WHITE, J. [and] . . . opinion of O'CONNOR, J.). The employer's proof on the point is to be presented and reviewed just as with any other evidentiary question: the Court does not accept the plurality's suggestion that an employer's evidence need be "objective" or otherwise out of the ordinary. ([see] opinion of WHITE, J.).

In sum, the Court alters the evidentiary framework of *McDonnell Douglas* and *Burdine* for a closely defined set of cases. Although JUSTICE O'CONNOR advances some thoughtful arguments for this change, I remain convinced that it is unnecessary and unwise. . . .

I

The plurality describes this as a case about the standard of *causation* under Title VII, but I respectfully suggest that the description is misleading. Much of the plurality's rhetoric is spent denouncing a "but-for" standard of causation. The theory of Title VII liability the plurality adopts, however, essentially incorporates the but-for standard. The importance of today's decision is not the standard of causation it employs, but its shift to the defendant of the burden of proof. The plurality's causation analysis is misdirected, for it is clear that, whoever bears the burden of proof on the issue, Title VII liability requires a finding of but-for causation. . . .

The words of Title VII are not obscure. . . .

By any normal understanding, the phrase "because of" conveys the idea that the motive in question made a difference to the outcome. We use the words this way in everyday speech. . . .

Our decisions confirm that Title VII is not concerned with the mere presence of impermissible motives; it is directed to employment decisions that result from those motives. The verbal formulae we have used in our precedents are synonymous with but-for causation. Thus we have said that providing different insurance coverage to male and female employees violates the statute by treating the employee " 'in a manner which but-for that person's sex would be different.' " *Newport News Shipbuilding & Dry Dock Co. v. EEOC*, 462 U.S. 669, 683 (1983). . . .

. . . If a motive is not a but-for cause of an event, then by definition it did not make a difference to the outcome. The event would have occurred just the same without it. . . .

One of the principal reasons the plurality decision may sow confusion is that it claims Title VII liability is unrelated to but-for causation, yet it adopts a but-for standard once it has placed the burden of proof as to causation upon the employer. . . .

. . . The plurality seems to say that since we know the words "because of" do not mean "solely because of," they must not mean "because of" at all. This does not follow. . . .

. . . Labels aside, the import of today's decision is not that Title VII liability can arise without but-for causation, but that in certain cases it is not the plaintiff who must prove the presence of causation, but the defendant who must prove its absence.

II

We established the order of proof for individual Title VII disparate treatment cases in *McDonnell Douglas Corp. v. Green*, and reaffirmed this allocation in *Texas Dept. of Community Affairs v. Burdine*. Under *Burdine*, once the plaintiff presents a prima facie case, an inference of discrimination arises. The employer must rebut the inference by articulating a legitimate nondiscriminatory reason for its action. The final burden of persuasion, however, belongs to the plaintiff. *Burdine* makes clear that the "ultimate burden of persuading the trier of fact that the defendant intentionally discriminated against the plaintiff remains at all times with the plaintiff." *Id.*, at 253. . . . I would adhere to this established evidentiary framework, which provides the appropriate standard for this and other individual disparate treatment cases. Today's creation of a new set of rules for "mixed-motive" cases is not mandated by the statute itself. The Court's attempt at refinement provides limited practical benefits at the cost of confusion and complexity. . . .

Downplaying the novelty of its opinion, the plurality claims to have followed a "well-worn path" from our prior cases. The

path may be well-worn, but it is in the wrong forest. . . .

. . . [A]nalogies to the plurality's new approach are found in *Mt. Healthy Board of Education v. Doyle* and *NRLB v. Transportation Management Corp.*, but these cases were decided in different contexts. *Mt. Healthy* was a First Amendment case involving the firing of a teacher, and *Transportation Management* involved review of the NLRB's interpretation of the National Labor Relations Act. The *Transportation Management* decision was based on the deference that the Court traditionally accords NLRB interpretations of the statutes it administers. See 462 U.S., at 402–03. Neither case therefore tells us why the established *Burdine* framework should not continue to govern the order of proof under Title VII.

. . . These analogies demonstrate that shifts in the burden of proof are not unprecedented in the law of torts or employment discrimination. Nonetheless, I believe continued adherence to the *Burdine* framework is more consistent with the statutory mandate. Congress' manifest concern with preventing imposition of liability in cases where discriminatory animus did not actually cause an adverse action suggests to me that an affirmative showing of causation should be required.

III

. . . Some of the plurality's comments with respect to the District Court's findings in this case . . . are potentially misleading. . . .

. . . I think it important to stress that Title VII creates no independent cause of action for sex stereotyping. Evidence of use by decisionmakers of sex stereotypes is, of course, quite relevant to the question of discriminatory intent. The ultimate question, however, is whether discrimination caused the plaintiff's harm.

. . . In this case, Hopkins plainly presented a strong case both of her own professional qualifications and of the presence of discrimination in Price Waterhouse's partnership process. Had the District Court found on this record that sex discrimination caused the adverse decision, I doubt it would have been reversible error. That decision was for the finder of fact, however, and the District Court made plain that sex discrimination was not a but-for cause of the decision to place Hopkin's partnership candidacy on hold. . . .

IV

. . . Here the District Court found that . . . "[b]ecause plaintiff has considerable problems dealing with staff and peers, the Court cannot say that she would have been elected to partnership if the Policy Board's decision had not been tainted by sexually based evaluations," 618 F. Supp., at 1120. Hopkins thus failed to meet the requisite standard of proof after a full trial. I would remand the case for entry of judgment in favor of Price Waterhouse.

CASE QUESTIONS

1. If firing a woman for failing to wear make-up or feminine jewelry or certain colors of clothing is illegal sex discrimination, would it be similarly illegal to fire a man for wearing obvious make-up—say, heavy lipstick and eye shadow; wearing skirts to work; wearing men's suits but in the color of red or pink (say, to a law office); wearing long, dangling earrings and prominent necklaces?

   Would it be illegal for a company to fire a lesbian who appeared at a company picnic holding hands with her female sweetheart? A gay male who did the same with a male companion? (Discrimination on the basis of sexual orientation is not forbidden under federal law, but could the plaintiff not argue that only "sex stereotypes" are offended when men hold hands with men?) Could a company fire a woman for failure to remove or cover up a large and prominently dark mustache?

   In Ann Hopkins's case, testimony was unanimous that she excelled at garnering business for the firm. Would the situation be different if some of the hypothetical

practices suggested here could be shown to have cost a company clients? (Note that under Title VII such an argument would not be treated as valid justification for a blanket refusal to hire women or blacks.[34] Are these hypotheticals different because they involve behavior that is alterable, rather than an immutable characteristic such as race or sex?)

2. Is the requirement that the employer prove that it would have had (and acted upon) sufficient legitimate motives for firing someone in Ann Hopkins's position akin to treating the employer as guilty until proven innocent? Would requiring Ann Hopkins to prove that she would not have been fired if the employers did not harbor views that certain behavior was especially inappropriate for women impose on her an impossible burden of proof?

3. The four-justice plurality proposes a rule that shifts the burden of proof of innocent motive to the employer once the employee shows that a forbidden

motive, such as racial or gender bias, "played a motivating part in an employment decision." Justices White and O'Connor, either of whose vote is needed to make a majority, argue that the language from precedents such as *Mt. Healthy* establish that the phrase "motivating factor" should be interpreted to mean "substantial factor," and thus they stress that courts should require evidence that the forbidden motive played a "substantial" role in the employment decision before requiring that the employer prove a legitimate, alternative motive. In the Civil Rights Act of 1991, which is further discussed below, Congress adopted into law this explicit rule: "[A]n unlawful employment practice is established when the complaining party demonstrates that race, color, religion, sex, or national origin was a motivating factor for any employment practice, even though other factors also motivated the practice."[35] What is the significance of Congress's choice of language?

4. The four-justice plurality argues that the employer ought to be required to prove

that he *would* have made the same employment decision on legitimate grounds, even if the illegitimate one had not been present. Justices White and O'Connor seem to argue that the employer should only have to prove that its decision "would have been justified" on wholly legitimate grounds—in other words, that it *could* have made the same employment decision legitimately. Such evidence, White argues, plus "credibl[e] testi[mony]" that the employer would have so acted even without the influence of bias should satisfy the law. Does the distinction between the two positions have much practical significance?

In the Civil Rights Act of 1991 Congress legislated that an employer shown to have been influenced by an "impermissible motivating factor" could avoid liability for any employment decision for which the employer can "demonstrate" that it "would have taken the same action in the absence of the impermissible motivating factor."[36] Does this language seem to side with the plurality against Justice White?

The Civil Rights Act of 1991

Dissenting Justice Kennedy's frequent reference to the absence of a statutory mandate for the standards of proof that the Court was establishing in *Price Waterhouse* was met head on by a Congressional response; the Civil Rights Act of 1991 codified the language from the plurality's opinion into explicit statutory mandate (as noted in questions 3 and 4 above). In addition to a direct congressional response to divisions within the *Price Waterhouse* Court, the act contained corrective Congressional reactions to three 1989 Supreme Court decisions on equal employment opportunity.

This congressional reply to these Court decisions took as long as it did because President Bush vetoed Congress's initial response, the Civil Rights Act of 1990, on the ostensible grounds that the legislation would, despite Congress's expressed intention to the contrary, pressure employers into hiring on the basis of affirmative "quotas." Congress then repassed quite similar legislation as the Civil Rights Act of 1991. This time, facing an election only one year away and aware that many women voters were angered by the Anita Hill/Clarence Thomas hearings, President Bush agreed to sign the act and did so on November 21, 1991.[37]

The first of the three 1989 decisions altered by this law, *Wards Cove Packing v. Atonio*,[38] concerned the clause in the 1964 Civil Rights Act that made it unlawful to "classify . . . applicants for employment in any way which would deprive *or tend to deprive* any individual of employment opportunities . . . because of such individual's race . . . or sex" (emphasis added).[39] In a number of cases involving employment practices that operated with a disproportionately negative impact on women or on racial minorities, the Supreme Court by 1989 had evolved certain procedural rules for applying this clause.[40]

If a plaintiff wants to claim that a particular job requirement, which looks neutral (nondiscriminatory) on the surface, in fact has a *tendency* to discriminate against one sex (or one race), the plaintiff can present general statistical evidence on the disproportionate impact that the particular requirement has on one sex (or one race). In other words, if something like 98 percent of males meet a particular job requirement but only 2 percent of females meet the requirement, clear evidence of a sex-linked disproportionate impact of the requirement would be present.

Once such evidence has been presented, however, the Court's work has only begun. This evidence creates what is called a *prima facie* case of sex discrimination; consequently, the job requirement in question is presumed to be discriminatory until proven otherwise. The burden of proof then shifts from the plaintiff to the defendant-employer. If the employer can prove that the requirement reflects "business necessity" and bears "a manifest relation to the employment in question,"[41] or that the requirement is "essential to effective job performance,"[42] the employer can succeed in shifting the burden of proof back to the plaintiff. At this point the plaintiff must show that other, nondiscriminatory (or less discriminatory) selection devices are available that would achieve the same goal as the discriminatory one. If the plaintiff can do this, the Court is supposed to strike down the discriminatory requirement.

In the *Wards Cove* case the 5–4 majority opinion by Justice White appeared to water down some of the language from these rules in a way that made it more difficult for plaintiff-employees to prevail against defendant-employers. Instead of requiring from the employer "proof" of "business necessity," the Court said that the employer had only to "produce evidence" that the "challenged practice serves, in a significant way, the legitimate employment goals of the employer."[43] The corrective to this judicial decision that was mandated into law by Congress in 1991 was the rule that the respondent must "demonstrate that the challenged practice is job related for the position in question and consistent with business necessity."[44] (If the employer succeeds in this, the employee can still prevail if he or she can prove that an alternative with a less discriminatory impact is available that still achieves the same business purpose.)

The second 1989 judicial decision that prompted Congressional reversal was handed down, again 5-4, in *Martin v. Wilks*.[45] There the majority had permitted some white firefighters to bring a lawsuit challenging a "consent decree" to which two groups of black plaintiff employees, the federal government, and the employer had all consented as a way of settling a job discrimination lawsuit. Consent decrees have long been an important weapon in the arsenal of women fighting employment discrimination. For instance, in January 1973 the American Telephone and Telegraph Company (AT&T) consented to pay $15 million in back pay to thousands of discriminated-against female employees.[46]

The lawsuit that led to the decree challenged in *Martin v. Wilks* had been initiated by the federal government in combination with the two groups of black employees in 1974 and 1975. After the employer had been found guilty of discrimination in hiring and promotions, the various parties to the case and the federal district court approved the negotiated "consent decree," which specified an affirmative hiring plan for minorities. After granting provisional approval for the plan, the district court ordered that "all interested parties" be notified of it and of their right to file objections to it. Two months later, the district court held a fairness hearing, at which both white and black employees presented objections (from different directions) to the plan. The district court overruled the objections and put the plan into effect in 1981. Various groups of white firefighters, believing that less meritorious blacks were starting to receive promotions ahead of the whites, began bringing a series of legal actions against the consent decree within several months. These various legal actions were consolidated in the district court, which in 1985 rejected the various challenges to the consent decree. This decision was appealed, and by the time it reached the U.S. Supreme Court the issue had narrowed down to the question of which parties are free to challenge a remedial Title VII consent decree after it has gone into effect. Five justices answered that question in a way that the four dissenters found much too expansive of the previous rules limiting such challenges.

In 1991 Congress turned around and legislated explicitly what the dissenters had claimed were the pre-existing rules on the subject: Persons are forbidden to challenge a remedial consent decree "that resolves a claim of employment discrimination under the Constitution or Federal civil rights laws" if such persons prior to the effective date of the decree have already had available to them "actual notice of the proposed . . . order sufficient to apprise such person[s] that such . . . order might adversely affect the interests and legal rights of such person[s] and that an opportunity was available to present objections to such . . . order by a future date certain," and "a reasonable opportunity to present objections to [the] . . . order."[47] In other words, Congress stepped in to eliminate the specter, provoked by the majority decision in *Martin v. Wilks*, of a "never-ending stream of litigation" against remedial consent decrees.[48]

At first glance, the third Supreme Court decision overturned in the 1991 Civil Rights Act, *Patterson v. McLean Credit Union*,[49] appeared to have everything to do with race and nothing to do with gender, although it did involve discrimination against a black woman, Brenda Patterson. In a much older law, the Civil Rights Act of 1866 ("Section 1981"),[50] Congress had prohibited specifically discrimination against nonwhites, with its mandate, "All persons . . . shall have the same right . . . to make and enforce contracts . . . as is enjoyed by white citizens." While the Supreme Court was unanimous in *Patterson* in its willingness to apply this command to an initial hiring contract or to an employment contract signed pursuant to a promotion, a majority of five[51] refused to extend this language to cover racial disparities in the "terms or conditions" of employment—which disparities would be forbidden, as to either race or gender, under Title VII of the 1964 Civil Rights Act. Brenda Patterson had several reasons for preferring a Section 1981 lawsuit to a Title VII one. Title VII limited back-pay awards to two years and did not allow extra, compensatory and punitive damages; Section 1981 does not impose these limits. (Also, Section 1981 covers all employers, including those who have fewer than fifteen employees, whereas Title VII exempts this 15 percent of the workforce from its coverage.)

Brenda Patterson alleged a ten-year pattern of on-the-job harassment; she was subjected to racial slurs, given more work than white fellow employees and assigned the most demeaning tasks, and singled out for scrutiny and criticism. The Supreme Court had ruled in 1986 that race-based or sex-based harassment that is sufficiently severe or pervasive to "create an abusive working environment" must be viewed as affecting a "condition of employment" under Title VII.[52] But in *Patterson v. McLean* the Court majority refused to read the Section 1981 phrase "the same right to make contracts" as covering conditions of employment; the majority opinion by Justice Kennedy restricted the reach of that phrase to the explicit terms of an initial hiring or separate promotion contract.

When civil rights lobbyists went to work in Congress against this decision, they did not keep their attack within the narrow confines of the terms of Section 1981. Instead, they urged that all the sorts of discrimination condemned by current mores be rendered just as punishable (through civil suits) as was race discrimination in hiring and promotions. They succeeded up to a point. The Civil Rights Act of 1991 did amend Section 1981 so that it covers "the enjoyment of all benefits, privileges, terms, and conditions of the contractual relationship."[53] In other words, on-the-job *racial* harassment is now actionable even for employers of fewer than fifteen and without the limits on damages awards contained in Title VII. Section 1981 was also amended to allow compensatory and punitive damages for victims of the other kinds of intentional discrimination forbidden by Title VII; this change allows victims of sex-based (or religion-based) job discrimination (including harassment) to sue for punitive and compensatory damages.[54] These damages are limited, however, by the rule that firms of fewer than fifteen employees are still exempted from coverage; firms of 15–100 employees have a damage ceiling of $50,000; firms of 101–200 employees, a ceiling of $100,000; firms of 201–500 employees, a ceiling of $200,000; and firms of more than 500 employees, a ceiling of $300,000.[55] In short, as a matter of explicit federal law, employers who engage in sex-based discrimination are at less financial risk than employers who engage in race-based discrimination.

This difference between the penalties for racist discrimination and for sexist discrimination was opposed by Congressional Democrats and added to the bill in order to overcome (Republican) President Bush's determination to veto the bill if some limits were not imposed. The resulting limits were the most significant sense in which the bill was a compromise, since President Bush had argued for a $150,000 limit and the Democrats had opposed all limits (on the grounds that the two kinds of discrimination should be equally punishable).[56]

Overall, one can conclude from the pattern exhibited in the judicial-legislative dialogue of 1988–1991, especially in light of the precedent for that pattern that took place between the judicial *Grove City* decision of 1984[57] and the congressional Civil Rights Restoration Act of 1987,[58] that the 1980s and early 1990s showed Congress to be more staunchly dedicated to protecting the rights of racial minorities and of women than was the U.S. Supreme Court. This pattern runs contrary to the prediction by Alexander Hamilton in *The Federalist* No. 78 that the Supreme Court, because it could not be voted out of office, would prove to be the special protector of rights of "the minor party" and of individuals against "the oppressions" that a majority might otherwise impose. The pattern of the 1980s obviously has something to do with the judicial appointing power of Republican presidents Reagan and Bush and with the evidently effective position of racial minorities and women (or of their supporters) in the electoral coalition that backs congressional Democrats. (The effective role that minorities can play in national majority coalitions was itself predicted by James Madison in *The Federalist* No. 10.)

This pattern of the 1980s is not necessarily a pattern for all times; the Supreme Court that produced the school desegregation decisions of the 1950s was certainly more protective of racial minorities than were the political branches (i.e., Congress and the President) of that era. Still, one can infer from the experience of the 1980s that the institutional pattern predicted by Alexander Hamilton (with its special role for the Supreme Court) for protecting individual and minority rights in the United States is not always the one that prevails.

Protection of the Fetus vs. Opportunity for Women: *UAW v. Johnson Controls* (1991)

In March of 1991, the Supreme Court handed down a decision that interpreted yet another section of Title VII of the 1964 Civil Rights Act.[59] The challenged employment practice in question, unlike that in the *Wards Cove* case, was not a hiring practice that looked neutral on its face but struck with a group-disproportionate impact. Nor was it a practice like the one dealt with in *Price Waterhouse* that combined a mixture of nondiscriminatory motives with forbidden, discriminatory ones. It was straightforward sex discrimination that took the United Autoworkers Union (UAW) into court against the Johnson Controls company, a manufacturer of lead batteries. Although the challenged policy did not discriminate against all women workers, it did discriminate against all women workers who could not provide medical documentation certifying that they were sterile. Such women were barred from working in any "jobs involving lead exposure or which could expose them to lead through ... transfer or promotion." This description covered all industrial jobs at the company. While Title VII does forbid job discrimination "because of ... race, color, religion, sex, or national origin," it also builds in some employer leeway on the topics of "religion, sex, [and] national origin." Title VII states that an employer *may* discriminate on the basis of "religion, sex, or national origin in those certain instances where religion, sex, or national origin is a bona fide occupational qualification reasonably necessary to the normal operation of that particular business or enterprise."[60] (For instance, religious affiliation for certain teachers might count as "reasonably necessary to the normal operation" of a seminary.) Essentially *Johnson Controls* turned on the Court's understanding of the meaning of the "bona fide occupational qualification"—or BFOQ in Court parlance—rule. For this particular case, an additional clause of Title VII also bore some relevance: in 1978 in the Pregnancy Discrimination Act, Congress had amended Title VII to say that the phrases "because of sex" and "on the basis of sex," which referred to forbidden job discrimination, "include, but are not limited to, because of or on the basis of pregnancy, childbirth, or related medical conditions; and women affected by pregnancy, childbirth, or related medical conditions shall be treated the same for all employment-related purposes ... as other persons not so affected but similar in their ability or inability to work."[61]

Johnson Controls had a history of clear-cut sex discrimination. Before the 1964 Civil Rights Act the company employed no women in any battery-manufacturing job. Finally, in June of 1977, Johnson Controls changed its approach.[62] The company announced, with regard to the employment of women in jobs where they would be exposed to the lead used in making batteries,

> [P]rotection of the health of the unborn child is the immediate and direct responsibility of the prospective parents. While the medical profession and the company can support them in the exercise of this responsibility, it cannot assume it for them without simultaneously infringing their rights as persons. ...
>
> ... Since not all women who can become mothers wish to become mothers (or will become mothers), it would appear to be illegal discrimination to treat all who are capable of pregnancy as though they will become pregnant.

Johnson supplemented this announcement with a written warning to its women employees stating that there was evidence "that women exposed to lead have a higher rate of abortion" but that this evidence was "not as clear . . . as the relationship between cigarette smoking and cancer," and that, still, it was "medically speaking, just good sense not to run that risk if you want children and do not want to expose the unborn child to risk, however small. . . ." Any woman who wished to be considered for employment at Johnson Products thereafter had to sign a statement indicating that she had read this warning.

Five years later the company changed from a policy of warning to one of prohibition. The federal Occupational Safety and Health Administration (OSHA) indicates that blood lead levels in excess of thirty micrograms per deciliter are dangerous for women who are pregnant (but also that such levels endanger the reproductive capacity of men).[63] Johnson Controls adopted this standard and said that any work station where over the past year an employee had registered a blood lead level in this range would henceforth be off-limits to any woman capable of pregnancy.[64] (In general, only one third of the workers at these stations registered at this level; careful washing after work could minimize lead risk, and some workers protected themselves better than others. In the years from 1979 to 1983, eight employees became pregnant with blood lead levels in this range. Only one of the babies born to this group later was shown to have this elevated blood lead level.)

In response to the 1982 prohibition, in 1984 a group of employees and their union initiated a lawsuit against Johnson Controls. Two of the employees were female; one had become sterilized in order to keep her job, and the other had suffered a paycut as a result of a transfer pursuant to the new policy. A third was a male who had been refused a leave of absence from a high lead-exposure job because he wanted to lower his blood lead level in preparation for conceiving a child.

The federal district court issued a summary judgment for the employer, citing ample expert opinion that exposure to lead is much more dangerous to a fetus than to an adult, and concluding that concern for protecting the safety of the fetus is a legitimate business consideration of the company. This court treated the company policy as one of disparate impact and ruled that Johnson Controls had satisfactorily demonstrated a "business necessity" for it. The circuit court of appeals affirmed in a 7–4 vote, ruling that whether the test was business necessity or BFOQ, either way the company had an adequate basis for its policy of excluding fertile women from these jobs. Both courts reasoned essentially that lead exposure presents a substantial health risk to the fetus, and no "less discriminatory alternative" exists to protect the fetus from this hazard. They both found avoidance of this health risk to be a legitimate business concern, and one essential enough to count as either "business necessity" or "bona fide occupational qualification." The circuit court dissenters presented a number of arguments that the U.S. Supreme Court reiterated (see below). One that was not mentioned by the Supreme Court, however, was Judge Easterbrook's description of the drastic impact that fetal protection policies of a blanket exclusionary nature (like this one) would have on women's job opportunities if universally adopted in the United States: More than twenty million jobs would be closed to (most) women workers.

On appeal, the U.S. Supreme Court reversed unanimously but with three different factions utilizing three different lines of reasoning. The various opinions appear below.

UAW v. Johnson Controls, 111 S. Ct. 1196 (1991)

JUSTICE BLACKMUN delivered the opinion of the Court.

. . .

III

The bias in Johnson Controls' policy is obvious. Fertile men, but not fertile women, are given a choice as to whether they wish to risk their reproductive health for a particular job. Section 703(a) of the Civil Rights Act of 1964 prohibits sex-based classifications in terms and conditions of employment, in hiring and discharging decisions, and in other employment decisions that adversely affect an employee's status. . . . Respondent does not seek to protect the unconceived children of all its employees. Despite evidence in the record about the debilitating effect of lead exposure on the male reproductive system, Johnson Controls is concerned only with the harms that may befall the unborn offspring of its female employees. . . . Johnson Controls' policy is facially discriminatory because it requires only a female employee to produce proof that she is not capable of reproducing.

Our conclusion is bolstered by the Pregnancy Discrimination Act of 1978

(PDA). . . . "The Pregnancy Discrimination Act has now made clear that, for all Title VII purposes, discrimination based on a woman's pregnancy is, on its face, discrimination because of her sex." *Newport News Shipbuilding & Dry Dock Co. v. EEOC*, 462 U.S. 669, 684 (1983). In its use of the words "capable of bearing children" in the 1982 policy statement as the criterion for exclusion, Johnson Controls explicitly classifies on the basis of potential for pregnancy. Under the PDA, such a classification must be regarded, for Title VII purposes, in the same light as explicit sex discrimination. . . .

We concluded above that Johnson Controls' policy is not neutral because it does not apply to the reproductive capacity of the company's male employees in the same way as it applies to that of the females. . . .

In sum, Johnson Controls' policy "does not pass the simple test of whether the evidence shows 'treatment of a person in a manner which but for that person's sex would be different.'" *Los Angeles Dept. of Water & Power v. Manhart*, 435 U.S. 702, 711 (1978). . . . We hold that Johnson Controls' fetal-protection policy is sex discrimination forbidden under Title VII unless respondent can establish that sex is a "bona fide occupational qualification."

IV

Under § 703(e)(1) of Title VII, an employer may discriminate on the basis of "religion, sex, or national origin in those certain instances where religion, sex, or national origin is a bona fide occupational qualification reasonably necessary to the normal operation of that particular business or enterprise." 42 U.S.C. § 2000e–2(e)(1). . . .

The BFOQ defense is written narrowly, and this Court has read it narrowly. See, e.g., *Dothard v. Rawlinson*, 433 U.S. 321, 332–37 (1977); *Trans World Airlines, Inc. v. Thurston*, 469 U.S. 111, 122–25 (1985). We have read the BFOQ language of § 4(f) of the Age Discrimination in Employment Act of 1967 (ADEA), which tracks the BFOQ provision in Title VII, just as narrowly. See *Western Air Lines, Inc. v. Criswell*, 472 U.S. 400 (1985). Our emphasis on the restrictive scope of the BFOQ defense is grounded on both the language and the legislative history of § 703.

The wording of the BFOQ defense contains several terms of restriction that indicate that the exception reaches only special situations. The statute thus limits the situations in which discrimination is permissible to "certain instances" where sex discrimination is "reasonably necessary" to the "normal operation" of the "particular" business. Each one of these terms—certain, normal, particular—prevents the use of general subjective standards and favors an objective, verifiable requirement. But the most telling term is "occupational"; this indicates that these objective, verifiable requirements must concern job-related skills and aptitudes.

The concurrence defines "occupational" as meaning related to a job. *Post*, at n. 1. According to the concurrence, any discriminatory requirement imposed by an employer is "job-related" simply because the employer has chosen to make the requirement a condition of employment. In effect, the concurrence argues that sterility may be an occupational qualification for women because Johnson Controls has chosen to require it. This reading of "occupational" renders the word mere surplusage. . . . By modifying "qualification" with "occupational," Congress narrowed the term to qualifications that affect an employee's ability to do the job.

Johnson Controls argues that its fetal-protection policy falls within the so-called safety exception to the BFOQ. Our cases have stressed that discrimination on the basis of sex because of safety concerns is allowed only in narrow circumstances. In *Dothard v. Rawlinson*, this Court indicated that danger to a woman herself does not justify discrimination. 433 U.S., at 335.´ . . . We there allowed the employer to hire only male guards in contact areas of maximum-security male penitentiaries only because more was at stake than the "individual woman's decision to weigh and accept the risks of employment." *Ibid.* We found sex to be a BFOQ inasmuch as the employment of a female guard would create real risks of safety to others if violence broke out because the guard was a woman. Sex discrimination was tolerated because sex was related to the guard's ability to do the job—maintaining prison security. . . .

Similarly, some courts have approved airlines' layoffs of pregnant flight attendants at different points during the first five months of pregnancy on the ground that the employer's policy was necessary to ensure the safety of passengers. . . .

We considered safety to third parties in *Western Airlines, Inc. v. Criswell, supra,* in the context of the ADEA. We focused upon "the nature of the flight engineer's tasks," and the "actual capabilities of persons over age 60" in relation to those tasks. 472 U.S., at 406. Our safety concerns were not independent of the individual's ability to perform the assigned tasks, but rather involved the possibility that, because of age-connected debility, a flight engineer might not properly assist the pilot, and might thereby cause a safety emergency. Furthermore, although we considered the safety of third parties in *Dothard* and *Criswell*, those third parties were indispensable to the particular business at issue. In *Dothard*, the third parties were the inmates; in *Criswell*, the third parties were the passengers on the plane. We stressed that in order to qualify as a BFOQ, a job qualification must relate to the "essence," *Dothard*, 433 U.S., at 333, or to the "central mission of the employer's business," *Criswell*, 472 U.S., at 413.

The concurrence ignores the "essence of the business" test and so concludes that "the safety to fetuses in carrying out the duties of battery manufacturing is as much a legitimate concern as is safety to third parties in guarding prisons (*Dothard*) or flying airplanes (*Criswell*)." By limiting its discussion to cost and safety concerns and rejecting the "essence of the business" test that our case law has established, the concurrence seeks to expand what is now the narrow BFOQ defense. Third-party safety considerations properly entered into the BFOQ analysis in *Dothard* and *Criswell* because they went to the core of the employee's job performance. Moreover, that performance involved the central purpose of the enterprise. *Dothard*, 433 U.S., at 335 ("The essence of a correctional counselor's job is to maintain prison security"); *Criswell*, 472 U.S., at 413 (the central mission of the airline's business was the safe transportation of its passengers). The concurrence attempts to transform this case into one of customer safety. The unconceived fetuses of Johnson Controls' female employees, however, are neither customers nor third parties whose safety is essential to the business of battery manufacturing.

No one can disregard the possibility of injury to future children; the BFOQ, however, is not so broad that it transforms this deep social concern into an essential aspect of batterymaking.

Our case law, therefore, makes clear that the safety exception is limited to instances in which sex or pregnancy actually interferes with the employee's ability to perform the job. This approach is consistent with the language of the BFOQ provision itself, for it suggests that permissible distinctions based on sex must relate to ability to perform the duties of the job. Johnson Controls suggests, however, that we expand the exception to allow fetal-protection policies that mandate particular standards for pregnant or fertile women. We decline to do so. Such an expansion contradicts not only the language of the BFOQ and the narrowness of its exception but the plain language and history of the Pregnancy Discrimination Act.

The PDA's amendment to Title VII contains a BFOQ standard of its own: unless pregnant employees differ from others "in their ability or inability to work," they must be "treated the same" as other employees "for all employment-related purposes." ... In other words, women as capable of doing their jobs as their male counterparts may not be forced to choose between having a child and having a job.

... The concurrence ... [ignores] the second clause of the Act which states that "women affected by pregnancy, childbirth, or related medical conditions shall be treated the same for all employment-related purposes ... as other persons not so affected but similar in their ability or inability to work." ... The concurrence now seeks to read the second clause out of the Act.

The legislative history confirms what the language of the Pregnancy Discrimination Act compels. ... The Senate Report [on the PDA] states that employers may not require a pregnant woman to stop working at any time during her pregnancy unless she is unable to do her work. Employment late in pregnancy often imposes risks on the unborn child, *see* Chavkin, "Walking a Tightrope: Pregnancy, Parenting, and Work," in *Double Exposure* 196, 196–202 (W. Chavkin ed. 1984), but Congress indicated that the employer may take into account only the woman's ability to get her job done. *See* Becker, *From* Muller v. Oregon *to Fetal Vulnerability Policies*, 53 U. Chi. L. Rev. 1219, 1255–56 (1986). With the PDA, Congress made clear that the decision to become pregnant or to work while being either pregnant or capable of becoming pregnant was reserved for each individual woman to make for herself. . . .[4]

V

We have no difficulty concluding that Johnson Controls cannot establish a BFOQ. Fertile women, as far as appears in the record, participate in the manufacture of batteries as efficiently as anyone else. Johnson Controls' professed moral and ethical concerns about the welfare of the next generation do not suffice to establish a BFOQ of female sterility. Decisions about the welfare of future children must be left to the parents who conceive, bear, support, and raise them rather than to the employers who hire those parents. Congress has

4. The concurrence predicts that our reaffirmation of the narrowness of the BFOQ defense will preclude considerations of privacy as a basis for sex-based discrimination. *Post*, at n.6. Nothing in our discussion of the "essence of the business test," however, suggests that sex could not constitute a BFOQ when privacy interests are implicated. See, *e.g.*, *Backus v. Baptist Medical Center*, 510 F. Supp. 1191 (E.D. Ark. 1981), *vacated as moot*, 671 F.2d 1100 (8th Cir. 1982) (essence of obstetrics nurse's business is to provide sensitive care for patient's intimate and private concerns).

mandated this choice through Title VII, as amended by the Pregnancy Discrimination Act. Johnson Controls has attempted to exclude women because of their reproductive capacity. Title VII and the PDA simply do not allow a woman's dismissal because of her failure to submit to sterilization.

Nor can concerns about the welfare of the next generation be considered a part of the "essence" of Johnson Controls' business. Judge Easterbrook in this case pertinently observed: "It is word play to say that 'the job' at Johnson [Controls] is to make batteries without risk to fetuses in the same way 'the job' at Western Air Lines is to fly planes without crashing." 886 F.2d, at 913.

. . . [I]t perhaps is worth noting . . . that Johnson Controls has shown no "factual basis for believing that all or substantially all women would be unable to perform safely and efficiently the duties of the job involved." *Dothard*, 433 U.S., at 333. . . . Of the eight pregnancies reported among the female employees, it has not been shown that any of the babies have birth defects or other abnormalities. The record does not reveal the birth rate for Johnson Controls' female workers but national statistics show that approximately nine percent of all fertile women become pregnant each year. The birthrate drops to two percent for blue collar workers over age 30. See Becker, 53 U. Chi. L. Rev., at 1233. Johnson Controls' fear of prenatal injury, no matter how sincere, does not begin to show that substantially all of its fertile women employees are incapable of doing their jobs.

VI

A word about tort liability and the increased cost of fertile women in the workplace is perhaps necessary. One of the dissenting judges in this case expressed concern about an employer's tort liability and concluded that liability for a potential injury to a fetus is a social cost that Title VII does not require a company to ignore. 886 F.2d, at 904–05. It is correct to say that Title VII does not prevent the employer from having a conscience. The statute, however, does prevent sex-specific fetal-protection policies. These two aspects of Title VII do not conflict.

More than 40 States currently recognize a right to recover for a prenatal injury based either on negligence or on wrongful death. . . . According to Johnson Controls, however, the company complies with the lead standard developed by OSHA and warns its female employees about the damaging effects of lead. It is worth noting that OSHA gave the problem of lead lengthy consideration and concluded that "there is no basis whatsoever for the claim that women of childbearing age should be excluded from the workplace in order to protect the fetus or the course of pregnancy." 43 Fed. Reg. 52952, 52966 (1978). See also *id.*, at 54354, 54398. Instead, OSHA established a series of mandatory protections which, taken together, "should effectively minimize any risk to the fetus and newborn child." *Id.*, at 52966. See 29 CFR § 1910.125(k)(ii) (1989). Without negligence, it would be difficult for a court to find liability on the part of the employer. If, under general tort principles, Title VII bans sex-specific fetal-protection policies, the employer fully informs the woman of the risk, and the employer has not acted negligently, the basis for holding an employer liable seems remote at best.

Although the issue is not before us, the concurrence observes that "it is far from clear that compliance with Title VII will preempt state tort liability." The cases relied upon by the concurrence to support its prediction, however, are inapposite. . . . When it is impossible for an employer to comply with both state and federal requirements, this Court has ruled that federal law

pre-empts that of the States. See, *e.g.*, *Florida Lime & Avocado Growers, Inc. v. Paul*, 373 U.S. 132, 142–43 (1963).

This Court faced a similar situation in *Farmers Union v. WDAY, Inc.*, 360 U.S. 525 (1959). In *WDAY*, it held that § 315(a) of the Federal Communications Act of 1934 barred a broadcasting station from removing defamatory statements contained in speeches broadcast by candidates for public office. It then considered a libel action which arose as a result of a speech made over the radio and television facilities of WDAY by a candidate for the 1956 senatorial race in North Dakota. It held that the statutory prohibition of censorship carried with it an immunity from liability for defamatory statements made by the speaker. To allow libel actions "would sanction the unconscionable result of permitting civil and perhaps criminal liability to be imposed for the very conduct the statute demands of the licensee." *Id.*, at 531. . . .

If state tort law furthers discrimination in the workplace and prevents employers from hiring women who are capable of manufacturing the product as efficiently as men, then it will impede the accomplishment of Congress' goals in enacting Title VII. Because Johnson Controls has not argued that it faces any costs from tort liability, not to mention crippling ones, the preemption question is not before us. We therefore say no more than that the concurrence's speculation appears unfounded as well as premature.

. . . Title VII plainly forbids illegal sex discrimination as a method of diverting attention from an employer's obligation to police the workplace. Second, the spectre of an award of damages reflects a fear that hiring fertile women will cost more. The extra cost of employing members of one sex, however, does not provide an affirmative Title VII defense for a discriminatory refusal to hire members of that gender. See

Manhart, 435 U.S., at 716–18, and n. 32. Indeed, in passing the PDA, Congress considered at length the considerable cost of providing equal treatment of pregnancy and related conditions, but made the "decision to forbid special treatment of pregnancy despite the social costs associated therewith." *Arizona Governing Committee v. Norris,* 463 U.S. 1073, 1084, n.14 (1983) (opinion of MARSHALL, J.).

We, of course, are not presented with, nor do we decide, a case in which costs would be so prohibitive as to threaten the survival of the employer's business. We merely reiterate our prior holdings that the incremental cost of hiring women cannot justify discriminating against them.

VII

It is no more appropriate for the courts than it is for individual employers to decide whether a woman's reproductive role is more important to herself and her family than her economic role. Congress has left this choice to the woman as hers to make.

The judgment of the Court of Appeals is reversed and the case is remanded for further proceedings consistent with this opinion.

JUSTICE WHITE, with whom THE CHIEF JUSTICE and JUSTICE KENNEDY join, concurring in part and concurring in the judgment.

The Court properly holds that Johnson Controls' fetal protection policy overtly discriminates against women, and thus is prohibited by Title VII unless it falls within the bona fide occupational qualification (BFOQ) exception, set forth at 42 U.S.C. § 2000e–2(e). The Court erroneously holds, however, that the BFOQ defense is so narrow that it could never justify a sex-specific fetal protection policy. I nevertheless concur in the judgment of reversal because on the record before us summary judgment in favor of Johnson Controls was improperly

entered by the District Court and affirmed by the Court of Appeals.

I

In evaluating the scope of the BFOQ defense, the proper starting point is the language of the statute. . . . [T]herefore, the policy must be "reasonably necessary" to the "normal operation" of making batteries, which is Johnson Controls' "particular business."

. . . [A] fetal protection policy would be justified under the terms of the statute if, for example, an employer could show that exclusion of women from certain jobs was reasonably necessary to avoid substantial tort liability. Common sense tells us that it is part of the normal operation of business concerns to avoid causing injury to third parties, as well as to employees, if for no other reason than to avoid tort liability and its substantial costs. This possibility of tort liability is not hypothetical; every State currently allows children born alive to recover in tort for prenatal injuries caused by third parties, *see* W. Keeton, D. Dobbs, R. Keeton, & D. Owen, *Prosser and Keeton on Law of Torts* § 55 p. 368 (5th ed. 1984), and an increasing number of courts have recognized a right to recover even for prenatal injuries caused by torts committed prior to conception.

The Court dismisses the possibility of tort liability by no more than speculating. . . . Such speculation will be small comfort to employers. First, it is far from clear that compliance with Title VII will pre-empt state tort liability, and the Court offers no support for that proposition.[2]

2. Cf. *English v. General Electric Co.,* 496 U.S. 72. (1990) (state law action for intentional infliction of emotional distress not preempted by Energy Reorganization Act of 1974); *California Federal Savings and Loan Assn. v. Guerra,* 479 U.S. 272, 290–92 (1987) (state statute requiring the provision of leave and pregnancy to employees disabled by pregnancy not preempted by the PDA);

Second, although warnings may preclude claims by injured *employees*, they will not preclude claims by injured children because the general rule is that parents cannot waive causes of action on behalf of their children, and the parents' negligence will not be imputed to the children. Finally, although state tort liability for prenatal injuries generally requires negligence, it will be difficult for employers to determine in advance what will constitute negligence. Compliance with OSHA standards, for example, has been held not to be a defense to state tort or criminal liability. . . . Moreover, it is possible that employers will be held strictly liable, if, for example, their manufacturing process is considered "abnormally dangerous." See *Restatement (Second) of Torts* § 869, comment *b* (1979).

Relying on *Los Angeles Dept. of Water and Power v. Manhart*, 435 U.S. 702 (1978), the Court contends that tort liability cannot justify a fetal protection policy because the extra costs of hiring women is not a defense under Title VII. This contention misrepresents our decision in *Manhart*. There, we held that a requirement that female employees contribute more than male employees to a pension fund, in order to reflect the greater longevity of women, constituted discrimination against women under Title VII because it treated them as a class rather than as individuals. 435 U.S., at 708, 716–17. We did not in that case address in any detail the nature of the BFOQ defense, and we certainly did not hold that cost was irrelevant to the BFOQ analysis. Rather, we

Silkwood v. Kerr-McGee Corp., 464 U.S. 238, 256 (1984) (state punitive damage claim not preempted by federal laws regulating nuclear power plants); *Bernstein v. Aetna Life & Cas.*, 843 F.2d 359, 364–65 (9th Cir. 1988) ("It is well-established that Title VII does not preempt state common law remedies"); see also 42 U.S.C. § 2000e-7.

merely stated in a footnote that "there has been no showing that sex distinctions are reasonably necessary to the normal operation of the Department's retirement plan." *Id.*, at 716, n.30. We further noted that although Title VII does not contain a "cost-justification defense comparable to the affirmative defense available in a price discrimination suit," "no defense based on the *total* cost of employing men and women was attempted in this case." *Id.*, at 716–17, and n.32.

Prior decisions construing the BFOQ defense confirm that the defense is broad enough to include considerations of cost and safety of the sort that could form the basis for an employer's adoption of a fetal protection policy. In *Dothard v. Rawlinson*, 433 U.S. 321 (1977), the Court held that being male was a BFOQ for "contact" guard positions in Alabama's maximum-security male penitentiaries. The Court first took note of the actual conditions of the prison environment: "In a prison system where violence is the order of the day, where inmate access to guards is facilitated by dormitory living arrangements, where every institution is understaffed, and where a substantial portion of the inmate population is composed of sex offenders mixed at random with other prisoners, there are few visible deterrents to inmate assaults on women custodians." *Id.*, at 335–36. The Court also stressed that "[m]ore [was] at stake" than a risk to individual female employees: "The likelihood that inmates would assault a woman because she was a woman would pose a real threat not only to the victim of the assault but also to the basic control of the penitentiary and protection of its inmates and the other security personnel." *Ibid.* Under those circumstances, the Court observed that "it would be an oversimplification to characterize [the exclusion of women] as an exercise in 'romantic paternalism.'" *Id.*, 433 U.S., at 335.

We revisited the BFOQ defense in *Western Air Lines, Inc. v. Criswell*, 472 U.S. 400 (1985), this time in the context of the Age Discrimination in Employment Act of 1967 (ADEA). There, we endorsed the two-part inquiry for evaluating a BFOQ defense. . . . First, the job qualification must not be "so peripheral to the central mission of the employer's business" that no discrimination could be " 'reasonably *necessary* to the normal operation of the particular business.' " 472 U.S., at 413. Although safety is *not* such a peripheral concern, *id.*, at 413, 419, the inquiry " 'adjusts to the safety factor' "— " '[t]he greater the safety factor, measured by the likelihood of harm and the probable severity of that harm in case of an accident, the more stringent may be the job qualifications,' " *id.*, at 413. Second, the employer must show either that all or substantially all persons excluded "would be unable to perform safely and efficiently the duties of the job involved," or that it is "impossible or highly impractical" to deal with them on an individual basis. 472 U.S., at 414. We further observed that this inquiry properly takes into account an employer's interest in safety—"[w]hen an employer establishes that a job qualification has been carefully formulated to respond to documented concerns for public safety, it will not be overly burdensome to persuade a trier of fact that the qualification is 'reasonably necessary' to safe operation of the business." 472 U.S., at 419.

Dothard and *Criswell* make clear that avoidance of substantial safety risks to third parties is *inherently* part of both an employee's ability to perform a job and an employer's "normal operation" of its business. Indeed, in both cases, the Court approved the statement in *Weeks v. Southern Bell Telephone & Telegraph Co.*, 408 F.2d 228 (5th Cir. 1969), that an employer could establish a BFOQ defense by showing that "all or substantially all women would be unable to perform *safely and efficiently* the duties of the job involved." *Id.*, at 235 (emphasis added). See *Criswell*, 472 U.S., at 414; *Dothard*, 433 U.S., at 333. The Court's statement in this case that "the safety exception is limited to instances in which sex or pregnancy actually interferes with the employee's ability to perform the job," therefore adds no support to its conclusion that a fetal protection policy could never be justified as a BFOQ. On the facts of this case, for example, protecting fetal safety while carrying out the duties of battery manufacturing is as much a legitimate concern as is safety to third parties in guarding prisons (*Dothard*) or flying airplanes (*Criswell*).[5]

Dothard and *Criswell* also confirm that costs are relevant in determining whether a discriminatory policy is reasonably necessary for the normal operation of a business. In *Dothard*, the safety problem that justified exclusion of women from the prison guard positions was largely a result of inadequate staff and facilities. See 433 U.S., at 335. If the cost of employing women could not be considered, the employer there should have been required to hire more staff and restructure the prison environment rather than exclude women. Similarly, in *Criswell* the airline could have been required to hire more pilots and install expensive monitoring devices rather than discriminate

5. I do not, as the Court asserts, reject the "essence of the business" test. Rather, I merely reaffirm the obvious—that safety to third parties is part of the "essence" of most if not all businesses. Of course, the BFOQ inquiry " 'adjusts to the safety factor.' " *Criswell*, 472 U.S., at 413. As a result, more stringent occupational qualifications may be justified for jobs involving higher safety risks, such as flying airplanes. But a recognition that the importance of safety varies among businesses does not mean that safety is completely irrelevant to the essence of a job such as battery manufacturing.

against older employees. The BFOQ statute, however, reflects "Congress' unwillingness to require employers to change the
very nature of their operations." *Price Waterhouse v. Hopkins*, 490 U.S. 228, 242, (1989)
(plurality opinion).

The Pregnancy Discrimination Act
(PDA), 42 U.S.C. § 2000e(k), contrary to the
Court's assertion, did not restrict the scope
of the BFOQ defense. The PDA was only an
amendment to the "Definitions" section of
Title VII, 42 U.S.C. § 2000e, and did not
purport to eliminate or alter the BFOQ
defense. Rather, it merely clarified Title VII
to make it clear that pregnancy and related
conditions are included within Title VII's
antidiscrimination provisions. As we have
already recognized, "the purpose of the
PDA was simply to make the treatment of
pregnancy consistent with general Title VII
principles." *Arizona Governing Committee for
Tax Deferred Annuity and Deferred Compensation Plans v. Norris*, 463 U.S. 1073, 1085, n.14.
. . . The Court's narrow interpretation
of the BFOQ defense in this case, however,
means that an employer cannot exclude
even *pregnant* women from an environment
highly toxic to their fetuses. It is foolish to
think that Congress intended such a result,
and neither the language of the BFOQ
exception nor our cases require it.[8]

II

Despite my disagreement with the
Court concerning the scope of the BFOQ
defense, I concur in reversing the Court of
Appeals. First, the Court of Appeals erred
in failing to consider the level of risk-
avoidance that was part of Johnson Controls' "normal operation." Although the
court did conclude that there was a "substantial risk" to fetuses from lead exposure
in fertile women, 886 F.2d 871, 879–83, 898
(7th Cir. 1989), it merely meant that there
was a high risk that *some* fetal injury would
occur absent a fetal protection policy. That
analysis, of course, fails to address the
extent of fetal injury that is likely to occur. If
the fetal protection policy insists on a risk-
avoidance level substantially higher than
other risk levels tolerated by Johnson Controls such as risks to employees and consumers, the policy should not constitute a
BFOQ.[10]

Second, even without more information about the normal level of risk at
Johnson Controls, the fetal protection policy at issue here reaches too far. This is
evident both in its presumption that, absent medical documentation to the contrary, all women are fertile regardless of

---

8. The Court's cramped reading of the BFOQ
defense is also belied by the legislative history of
Title VII, in which three examples of permissible
sex discrimination were mentioned—a female
nurse hired to care for an elderly woman, an
all-male professional baseball team, and a mas-
seur. See 110 Cong. Rec. 2718 (1964) (Rep. Good-
ell); *id.*, at 7212–13 (interpretive memorandum
introduced by Sens. Clark and Case); *id.*, at 2720
(Rep. Multer). In none of those situations would
gender "actually interfer[e] with the employee's
ability to perform the job," as required today by
the Court.

The Court's interpretation of the BFOQ standard also would seem to preclude considerations
of privacy as a basis for sex-based discrimination, since those considerations do not relate
directly to an employee's physical ability to
perform the duties of the job. The lower federal
courts, however, have consistently recognized
that privacy interests may justify sex-based requirements for certain jobs.

10. It is possible, for example, that alternatives
to exclusion of women, such as warnings combined with frequent bloodtestings, would sufficiently minimize the risk such that it would be
comparable to other risks tolerated by Johnson
Controls.

their age, see *id.*, at 876, n.8, and in its exclusion of presumptively fertile women from positions that might result in a promotion to a position involving high lead exposure, *id.*, at 877. There has been no showing that either of those aspects of the policy is reasonably necessary to ensure safe and efficient operation of Johnson Controls' battery-manufacturing business. Of course, these infirmities in the company's policy do not warrant invalidating the entire fetal protection program.

Third, it should be recalled that until 1982 Johnson Controls operated without an exclusionary policy, and it has not identified any grounds for believing that its current policy is reasonably necessary to its normal operations. Although it is now more aware of some of the dangers of lead exposure, *id.*, at 899, it has not shown that the risks of fetal harm or the costs associated with it have substantially increased. Cf. *Manhart*, 435 U.S., at 716, n.30, in which we rejected a BFOQ defense because the employer had operated prior to the discrimination with no significant adverse effects.

Finally, the Court of Appeals failed to consider properly petitioners' evidence of harm to offspring caused by lead exposure in males. The court considered that evidence only in its discussion of the business necessity standard, in which it focused on whether *petitioners* had met their burden of proof. 886 F.2d, at 889–90. The burden of proving that a discriminatory qualification is a BFOQ, however, rests with the employer. Thus, the court should have analyzed whether the evidence was sufficient for petitioners to survive summary judgment in light of *respondent's* burden of proof to establish a BFOQ. Moreover, the court should not have discounted the evidence as "speculative," 886 F.2d, at 889, merely because it was based on animal studies. We have approved the use of animal studies to assess risks, see *Industrial*

Union Dept. v. American Petroleum Institute, 448 U.S. 607, 657, n.64 (1980), and OSHA uses animal studies in establishing its lead control regulations, see *United Steelworkers of America, AFL-CIO-CLC v. Marshall*, 647 F.2d 1189, 1257, n.97 (1980), *cert. denied*, 453 U.S. 913 (1981).

JUSTICE SCALIA, concurring in the judgment.

I generally agree with the Court's analysis, but have some reservations, several of which bear mention.

First, I think it irrelevant that there was "evidence in the record about the debilitating effect of lead exposure on the male reproductive system." Even without such evidence, treating women differently "on the basis of pregnancy" constitutes discrimination "on the basis of sex," because Congress has unequivocally said so. Pregnancy Discrimination Act of 1978.

Second, the Court points out that "Johnson Controls has shown no factual basis for believing that all or substantially all women would be unable to perform safely . . . the duties of the job involved." In my view, this is . . . entirely irrelevant. By reason of the Pregnancy Discrimination Act, it would not matter if all pregnant women placed their children at risk in taking these jobs, just as it does not matter if no men do so. As Judge Easterbrook put it in his dissent below, "Title VII gives parents the power to make occupational decisions affecting their families. A legislative forum is available to those who believe that such decisions should be made elsewhere." 886 F.2d 871, 915 (7th Cir. 1989) (Easterbrook, J., dissenting).

Third, I am willing to assume, as the Court intimates, that any action required by Title VII cannot give rise to liability under state tort law. That assumption, however, does not answer the question whether an action *is* required by Title VII (including the BFOQ provision) even if it is subject to liability under state tort law. It is perfectly reasonable to believe that Title VII has *accommodated* state tort law through the BFOQ exception. However, all that need be said in the present case is that Johnson has not demonstrated a substantial risk of tort liability—which is alone enough to defeat a tort-based assertion of the BFOQ exception.

Last, the Court goes far afield, it seems to me, in suggesting that increased cost alone—short of "costs . . . so prohibitive as to threaten survival of the employer's business,"—cannot support a BFOQ defense. I agree with Justice White's concurrence, that nothing in our prior cases suggests this, and in my view it is wrong. I think, for example, that a shipping company may refuse to hire pregnant women as crew members on long voyages because the on-board facilities for foreseeable emergencies, though quite feasible, would be inordinately expensive. In the present case, however, Johnson has not asserted a cost-based BFOQ.

I concur in the judgment of the Court.

CASE QUESTIONS

1. Compare the majority's description of the *Dothard v. Rawlinson* decision with Justice White's description of the same case. Who seems to be persuasive about whether cost considerations were or were not implicit in the resolution of that case?

2. Four justices grant that genuine necessity for avoiding substantial tort liability should count in determining what is a BFOQ. The other five justices reject that assertion but admit that the analysis might be different if "cost would be so prohibitive as to threaten the survival of the employer's business." Does this acknowledgment undermine the rest of their logic on tort liability?

3. The majority and Justice Scalia reject the argument that employer concerns about the safety of to-be-born babies is a legitimate consideration in deciding what is a BFOQ, although they do grant that financial threat to the employer (see question 2) is a legitimate consideration. Is there anything troubling about a statutory scheme that honors an employer's pocketbook but not his/her conscience?

4. Are the six justices who do not concur with Justice White correct in their belief that he is ignoring the basic thrust of the Pregnancy Discrimination Act?

5. If a woman could document that her lung cancer stemmed from the passive smoke she inhaled from her chain-smoking parents, should she be permitted to sue them for damages? Sue the cigarette manufacturer? (Even if for most of the years her parents smoked the packages contained warnings about the dangers of passive smoke?) Is her situation analogous to that of a child born deformed as a result of its mother's exposure to toxic chemicals in the workplace? Should it be an adequate corporate defense in such cases that the parents could have taken care to smoke outdoors, and

the mother could have taken a leave from work until her blood lead levels subsided to a safe point for pregnancy?

6. Why do you suppose this conscience-stricken company ignored the OSHA safety levels for the reproductive systems of male employees?

7. Suppose a toxic industrial chemical were discovered that could be shown to be not harmful to adults or to their reproductive systems but highly toxic to fetuses, causing, say, cancer in two thirds of the children born to women who had been exposed to the chemical at close range for more than twenty hours per week during pregnancy. Should this degree of harm be viewed as a BFOQ eliminating pregnant workers from those close-range jobs?

Sexual Harassment as Sex Discrimination

Supreme Court Guidelines: *Meritor Savings Bank v. Vinson* (1986)

As early as 1971 federal courts were reading the 1964 Civil Rights Act's prohibition on race discrimination in the "terms, conditions, or privileges of employment" to contain an implied prohibition on racial harassment in the workplace.[65] In a series of decisions in the seventies, federal courts made clear that the act forbade such employee behavior as placing drawings of caricatured blacks being lynched by Klansmen on the desk or locker door of black employees and that employers who did not take steps to halt such behavior would be actionable under the law, just as though they had openly discriminated against the black.[66] Placing severe psychological pressure on an employee, on racial grounds, to quit his or her job was close enough to firing the employee on racial grounds that the law would treat them as similar. This principle treating discriminatory harassment as discrimination under the law was also applied in those years to harassment based on religion[67] and on national origin.[68]

While employee harassment of women on the job sometimes took a form that was directly analogous to that to which racial or ethnic minorities were exposed—as when, for instance, firemen angry at including women in their ranks tried to pressure them into quitting—sexual harassment of women often took a different form. This other form, *unwelcome sexual advances*, from the perpetrator's point of view was frequently (perhaps even usually) the opposite of hostile; it was, in fact, affectionate. But from the recipient's point of view, it was an additional source of psychic discomfort in the workplace, one to which other employees were not subjected, and for that reason, arguably discriminatory. Both the Equal Opportunity Employment Commission (EEOC) and several (but not all) federal courts[69] agreed that it was, and in 1986 the U.S. Supreme Court added its voice to this chorus of disapproval.

In the case that went to the Supreme Court, a woman named Mechelle Vinson complained that for four years her supervisor at the bank where she worked subjected her to sexual harassment.[70] Shortly after her probationary period as a teller-trainee had ended, he had started dating her. Her description of the situation, as paraphrased in Justice Rehnquist's opinion for the Supreme Court, went as follows:

> [H]e invited her out to dinner and, during the course of the meal, suggested that they go to a motel and have sexual relations. At first she refused, but out of what she described as fear of losing her job she eventually agreed. According to respondent, Taylor [the supervisor] thereafter made repeated demands upon her for sexual favors, usually at the branch, both during and after business hours; she estimated that over the next several years she had intercourse with him some 40 or 50 times. In addition, respondent testified that Taylor fondled her in front of other employees, followed her into the women's restroom when she went there alone, exposed himself to her, and even forcibly raped her on several occasions. These activities ceased after 1977 ... when she started going with a steady boyfriend. [Taylor denied that there had ever been a sexual relationship between them or that he had ever asked her for sexual favors.][71]

The federal district court that had heard Mechelle Vinson's complaint had rejected it on the grounds that the relationship she described struck that court as "voluntary" and that sexual compliance had never been made an explicit condition for her to keep her job or get a promotion. Both the circuit court of appeals and the U.S. Supreme Court rejected this narrow view of the kind of sexual harassment that was prohibited.

Instead, the Supreme Court reasoned that, in addition to *quid pro quo* harassment, also forbidden was " '[s]exual harassment which creates a hostile or offensive environment for members of one sex.' "[72] Such harassment would be actionable whenever it was "sufficiently severe or pervasive 'to alter the conditions of [the victim's] employment and create an abusive working environment.' "[73] The Court endorsed the EEOC rule that "employees have a right to work in an environment free from discriminatory intimidation, ridicule, and insult."[74] It also specifically disapproved of the district court's basing its decision on Vinson's technical consent to the sexual relationship; Justice Rehnquist reasoned that the central issue was not whether she was forced into sex against her will but rather whether the on-the-job advances were "unwelcome." Finally, the U.S. Supreme Court agreed with the circuit court that company management is liable for sexual harassment among its employees and is responsible for adopting policies aimed at checking such harassment. The high Court declined to issue "definitive" guidelines concerning employer liability, however, because the record in *Meritor Savings* was scanty in that regard.

Once the Supreme Court issues a ruling like this, it then must be applied by private employers, federal executive branch officials, and lower federal courts. In any application of a set of rules, there is some discretionary leeway. The following circuit court of appeals decision from 1991 is presented to illustrate the kind of innovation that can take place at the hands of a court that is ostensibly "implementing" rules from a higher court; it is presented also to encourage the reader to consider the substantive issue that separates the dissenter from the majority.

Lower Court Innovation: *Ellison v. Brady* (1991)[75]

This recent decision from the Ninth Circuit Court of Appeals is much discussed by legal scholars because it endorses a "reasonable woman" test for deciding whether sexual harassment has occurred. Indeed, that endorsement is precisely what provoked discussion from the dissenting judge in the same case. Because the outcome of the case is so fact-dependent, the excerpt presented below reprints the facts, virtually verbatim, as the circuit court majority described them.

Kerry Ellison v. Nicholas F. Brady,* Secretary of the Treasury, 924 F.2d 872 (9th Cir. 1991)

ROBERT R. BEEZER, Circuit Judge:

. . .

I

Kerry Ellison worked as a revenue agent for the Internal Revenue Service in San Mateo, California. During her initial training in 1984 she met Sterling Gray, another trainee, who was also assigned to the San Mateo office. The two co-workers never became friends, and they did not work closely together.

Gray's desk was twenty feet from Ellison's desk, two rows behind and one row over. Revenue agents in the San Mateo office often went to lunch in groups. In June of 1986 when no one else was in the office, Gray asked Ellison to lunch. She

*Nicholas F. Brady is substituted for James A. Baker III as Secretary of the Treasury. . . .

accepted. Gray had to pick up his son's forgotten lunch, so they stopped by Gray's house. He gave Ellison a tour of his house.

Ellison alleges that after the June lunch Gray started to pester her with unnecessary questions and hang around her desk. On October 9, 1986, Gray asked Ellison out for a drink after work. She declined, but she suggested that they have lunch the following week. She did not want to have lunch alone with him, and she tried to stay away from the office during lunch time. One day during the following week, Gray uncharacteristically dressed in a three-piece suit and asked Ellison out for lunch. Again, she did not accept.

On October 22, 1986, Gray handed Ellison a note he wrote on a telephone message slip which read:

I cried over you last night and I'm totally drained today. I have never been in such constant term oil (sic).

Thank you for talking with me. I could not stand to feel your hatred for another day.

When Ellison realized that Gray wrote the note, she became shocked and frightened and left the room. Gray followed her into the hallway and demanded that she talk to him, but she left the building.

Ellison later showed the note to Bonnie Miller, who supervised both Ellison and Gray. Miller said "this is sexual harassment." Ellison asked Miller not to do anything about it. She wanted to try to handle it herself. Ellison asked a male co-worker to talk to Gray, to tell him that she was not interested in him and to leave her alone. The next day, Thursday, Gray called in sick.

Ellison did not work on Friday, and on the following Monday, she started four weeks of training in St. Louis, Missouri. Gray mailed her a card and a typed, single-spaced, three-page letter. She describes this letter as "twenty times, a hundred times weirder" than the prior note. Gray wrote, in part:

I know that you are worth knowing with or without sex. . . . Leaving aside the hassles and disasters of recent weeks. I have enjoyed you so much over these past few months. Watching you. Experiencing you from O so far away. Admiring your style and elan. . . . Don't you think it odd that two people who have never even talked together, alone, are striking off such intense sparks . . . I will [write] another letter in the near future.[1]

Explaining her reaction, Ellison stated: "I just thought he was crazy. I thought he

was nuts. I didn't know what he would do next. I was frightened."

She immediately telephoned Miller. Ellison told her supervisor that she was frightened and really upset. She requested that Miller transfer either her or Gray because she would not be comfortable working in the same office with him. Miller asked Ellison to send a copy of the card and letter to San Mateo.

Miller then telephoned her supervisor, Joe Benton, and discussed the problem. That same day she had a counseling session with Gray. She informed him that he was entitled to union representation. During this meeting, she told Gray to leave Ellison alone.

At Benton's request, Miller apprised the labor relations department of the situation. She also reminded Gray many times over the next few weeks that he must not contact Ellison in any way. Gray subsequently transferred to the San Francisco office on November 24, 1986. Ellison returned from St. Louis in late November and did not discuss the matter further with Miller.

After three weeks in San Francisco, Gray filed union grievances requesting a return to the San Mateo office. The IRS and the union settled the grievances in Gray's favor, agreeing to allow him to transfer back to the San Mateo office provided that he spend four more months in San Francisco and promise not to bother Ellison. On January 28, 1987, Ellison first learned of Gray's request in a letter from Miller explaining that Gray would return to the San Mateo office. The letter indicated that management decided to resolve Ellison's problem with a six-month separation, and that it would take additional action if the problem recurred.

---

1. In the middle of the long letter Gray did say "I am obligated to you so much that if you want me to leave you alone I will. . . . If you want me to forget you entirely, I can not do that."

After receiving the letter, Ellison was "frantic." She filed a formal complaint alleging sexual harassment on January 30, 1987 with the IRS. She also obtained permission to transfer to San Francisco temporarily when Gray returned.

Gray sought joint counseling. He wrote Ellison another letter which still sought to maintain the idea that he and Ellison had some type of relationship.

The IRS employee investigating the allegation agreed with Ellison's supervisor that Gray's conduct constituted sexual harassment. In its final decision, however, the Treasury Department rejected Ellison's complaint because it believed that the complaint did not describe a pattern or practice of sexual harassment covered by the EEOC regulations. After an appeal, the EEOC affirmed the Treasury Department's decision on a different ground. It concluded that the agency took adequate action to prevent the repetition of Gray's conduct.

Ellison filed a complaint in September of 1987 in federal district court. The court granted the government's motion for summary judgment on the ground that Ellison had failed to state a prima facie case of sexual harassment due to a hostile working environment. Ellison appeals.

. . .

III

The parties ask us to determine if Gray's conduct, as alleged by Ellison, was sufficiently severe or pervasive to alter the conditions of Ellison's employment and create an abusive working environment. The district court, with little Ninth Circuit case law to look to for guidance, held that Ellison did not state a prima facie case of sexual harassment due to a hostile working environment. It believed that Gray's con-duct was "isolated and genuinely trivial." We disagree.

. . . The Supreme Court in *Meritor* explained that courts may properly look to guidelines issued by the Equal Employment Opportunity Commission (EEOC) for guidance when examining hostile environment claims of sexual harassment. 477 U.S. at 65. The EEOC guidelines describe hostile environment harassment as "conduct [which] has the purpose or effect of unreasonably interfering with an individual's work performance or creating an intimidating, hostile, or offensive working environment." 29 C.F.R. § 1604.11(a)(3). The EEOC, in accord with a substantial body of judicial decisions, has concluded that "Title VII affords employees the right to work in an environment free from discriminatory intimidation, ridicule, and insult." 477 U.S. at 65.

The Supreme Court cautioned, however, that not all harassment affects a "term, condition, or privilege" of employment within the meaning of Title VII. For example, the "mere utterance of an ethnic or racial epithet which engenders offensive feelings in an employee" is not, by itself, actionable under Title VII. *Id.* at 67. To state a claim under Title VII, sexual harassment "must be sufficiently severe or pervasive to alter the conditions of the victim's employment and create an abusive working environment." *Id.*

. . .

Although *Meritor* and our previous cases establish the framework for the resolution of hostile environment cases, they do not dictate the outcome of this case. Gray's conduct falls somewhere between forcible rape and the mere utterance of an epithet. 477 U.S. at 60, 67

The government asks us to apply the reasoning of other courts which have declined to find Title VII violations on more egregious facts. In *Scott v. Sears, Roebuck & Co.*, 798 F.2d 210, 212 (7th Cir. 1986), the Seventh Circuit analyzed a female employee's working conditions for sexual harassment. It noted that she was repeatedly propositioned and winked at by her supervisor. When she asked for assistance, he asked "what will I get for it?" Co-workers slapped her buttocks and commented that she must moan and groan during sex. The court examined the evidence to see if "the demeaning conduct and sexual stereotyping cause[d] such anxiety and debilitation to the plaintiff that working conditions were 'poisoned' within the meaning of Title VII." *Id.* at 213. The court did not consider the environment sufficiently hostile. *Id.* at 214.

Similarly, in *Rabidue v. Osceola Refining Co.*, 805 F.2d 611 (6th Cir. 1986), *cert. denied*, 481 U.S. 1041 (1987), the Sixth Circuit refused to find a hostile environment where the workplace contained posters of naked and partially dressed women, and where a male employee customarily called women "whores," "cunt," "pussy," and "tits," referred to plaintiff as "fat ass," and specifically stated, "All that bitch needs is a good lay." Over a strong dissent, the majority held that the sexist remarks and the pin-up posters had only a de minimis effect and did not seriously affect the plaintiff's psychological well-being.

We do not agree with the standards set forth in *Scott* and *Rabidue*,[6] and we choose not to follow those decisions. Neither *Scott's* search for "anxiety and debilitation" sufficient to "poison" a working environment nor *Rabidue's* requirement that a plaintiff's psychological well-being be "seriously affected" follows directly from language in *Meritor*. It is the harasser's conduct which must be pervasive or severe, not the alteration in the conditions of employment. Surely, employees need not endure sexual harassment until their psychological well-being is seriously affected to the extent that they suffer anxiety and debilitation. . . . Title VII's protection of employees from sex discrimination comes into play long before the point where victims of sexual harassment require psychiatric assistance.

We have closely examined *Meritor* and our previous cases, and we believe that Gray's conduct was sufficiently severe and pervasive to alter the conditions of Ellison's employment and create an abusive working environment. We first note that the required showing of severity or seriousness of the harassing conduct varies inversely with the pervasiveness or frequency of the conduct. . . .

Next, we believe that in evaluating the severity and pervasiveness of sexual harassment, we should focus on the perspective of the victim. . . . If we only examined whether a reasonable person would engage in allegedly harassing conduct, we would run the risk of reinforcing the prevailing level of discrimination. Harassers could continue to harass merely because a partic-

---

6. We note that the Sixth Circuit has called *Rabidue* into question in at least two subsequent opinions. In *Yates v. Avco Corp.*, 819 F.2d 630, 637 (6th Cir. 1987), a panel of the Sixth Circuit expressly adopted one of the main arguments in the *Rabidue* dissent, that sexual harassment actions should be viewed from the victim's perspective. In *Davis v. Monsanto Chemical Co.*, 858 F.2d 345, 350 (6th Cir. 1988), *cert. denied*, 490 U.S. 1110 (1989), the Sixth Circuit once again criticized *Rabidue's* limited reading of Title VII. *See also Andrews v. City of Philadelphia*, 895 F.2d 1469, 1485 (3d Cir. 1990) (explicitly rejecting *Rabidue* and holding that derogatory language directed at women and pornographic pictures of women serve as evidence of a hostile working environment).

ular discriminatory practice was common, and victims of harassment would have no remedy.

We therefore prefer to analyze harassment from the victim's perspective. A complete understanding of the victim's view requires, among other things, an analysis of the different perspectives of men and women. Conduct that many men consider unobjectionable may offend many women. *See, e.g., Lipsett v. University of Puerto Rico,* 864 F.2d 881, 898 (1st Cir. 1988)....

We realize that there is a broad range of viewpoints among women as a group, but we believe that many women share common concerns which men do not necessarily share. For example, because women are disproportionately victims of rape and sexual assault, women have a stronger incentive to be concerned with sexual behavior. Women who are victims of mild forms of sexual harassment may understandably worry whether a harasser's conduct is merely a prelude to violent sexual assault. Men, who are rarely victims of sexual assault, may view sexual conduct in a vacuum without a full appreciation of the social setting or the underlying threat of violence that a woman may perceive.

In order to shield employers from having to accommodate the idiosyncratic concerns of the rare hyper-sensitive employee, we hold that a female plaintiff states a prima facie case of hostile environment sexual harassment when she alleges conduct which a reasonable woman would consider sufficiently severe or pervasive to alter the conditions of employment and create an abusive working environment....

We adopt the perspective of a reasonable woman primarily because we believe that a sex-blind reasonable person standard tends to be male-biased and tends to systematically ignore the experiences of women. The reasonable woman standard does not establish a higher level of protection for women than men.... Instead, a gender-conscious examination of sexual harassment enables women to participate in the workplace on an equal footing with men. By acknowledging and not trivializing the effects of sexual harassment on reasonable women, courts can work towards ensuring that neither men nor women will have to "run a gauntlet of sexual abuse in return for the privilege of being allowed to work and make a living." *Henson v. Dundee,* 682 F.2d 897, 902 (11th Cir. 1982).

We note that the reasonable victim standard we adopt today classifies conduct as unlawful sexual harassment even when harassers do not realize that their conduct creates a hostile working environment. Well-intentioned compliments by co-workers or supervisors can form the basis of a sexual harassment cause of action if a reasonable victim of the same sex as the plaintiff would consider the comments sufficiently severe or pervasive to alter a condition of employment and create an abusive working environment. That is because Title VII is not a fault-based tort scheme. "Title VII is aimed at the consequences or effects of an employment practice and not at the ... motivation" of co-workers or employers. *Rogers,* 454 F.2d at 239; *see also Griggs v. Duke Power Co.,* 401 U.S. 424, 432 (1971) (the absence of discriminatory intent does not redeem an otherwise unlawful employment practice). To avoid liability under Title VII, employers may have to educate and sensitize their workforce to eliminate conduct which a reasonable victim would consider unlawful sexual harassment....

The facts of this case illustrate the importance of considering the victim's perspective. Analyzing the facts from the alleged harasser's viewpoint, Gray could be portrayed as a modern-day Cyrano de

Bergerac wishing no more than to woo Ellison with his words. There is no evidence that Gray harbored ill will toward Ellison. He even offered in his "love letter" to leave her alone if she wished. Examined in this light, it is not difficult to see why the district court characterized Gray's conduct as isolated and trivial.

Ellison, however, did not consider the acts to be trivial. Gray's first note shocked and frightened her. After receiving the three-page letter, she became really upset and frightened again. She immediately requested that she or Gray be transferred. Her supervisor's prompt response suggests that she too did not consider the conduct trivial. When Ellison learned that Gray arranged to return to San Mateo, she immediately asked to transfer, and she immediately filed an official complaint.

We cannot say as a matter of law that Ellison's reaction was idiosyncratic or hyper-sensitive. We believe that a reasonable woman could have had a similar reaction. After receiving the first bizarre note from Gray, a person she barely knew, Ellison asked a co-worker to tell Gray to leave her alone. Despite her request, Gray sent her a long, passionate, disturbing letter. He told her he had been "watching" and "experiencing" her; he made repeated references to sex; he said he would write again. Ellison had no way of knowing what Gray would do next. A reasonable woman could consider Gray's conduct, as alleged by Ellison, sufficiently severe and pervasive to alter a condition of employment and create an abusive working environment.

Sexual harassment is a major problem in the workplace.[15] Adopting the victim's perspective ensures that courts will not

"sustain ingrained notions of reasonable behavior fashioned by the offenders." *Lipsett,* 864 F.2d at 898. . . . We hope that over time both men and women will learn what conduct offends reasonable members of the other sex. When employers and employees internalize the standard of workplace conduct we establish today, the current gap in perception between the sexes will be bridged.

IV

We next must determine what remedial actions by employers shield them from liability under Title VII for sexual harassment by co-workers. . . .

We . . . believe that remedies should be reasonably calculated to end the harassment. . . . In essence, . . . we think that the reasonableness of an employer's remedy will depend on its ability to stop harassment by the person who engaged in harassment. In evaluating the adequacy of the remedy, the court may also take into account the remedy's ability to persuade potential harassers to refrain from unlawful conduct. Indeed, meting out punishments that do not take into account the need to maintain a harassment-free working environment may subject the employer to suit by the EEOC. . . .

We decline to accept the government's argument that its decision to return Gray to San Mateo did not create a hostile environment for Ellison because the government

---

15. Over 40 percent of female federal employees reported incidents of sexual harassment in 1987, roughly the same number as in 1980. United States Merit Systems Protection Board, *Sexual*

Harassment in the Federal Government: An Update 11 (1988). Victims of sexual harassment "pay all the intangible emotional costs inflicted by anger, humiliation, frustration, withdrawal, dysfunction in family life," as well as medical expenses, litigation expenses, job search expenses, and the loss of valuable sick leave and annual leave. *Id.* at 42. Sexual harassment cost the federal government $267 million from May 1985 to May 1987 for losses in productivity, sick leave costs, and employee replacement costs. *Id.* at 39.

granted Ellison's request for a temporary transfer to San Francisco. Ellison preferred to work in San Mateo over San Francisco. We strongly believe that the victim of sexual harassment should not be punished for the conduct of the harasser. We wholeheartedly agree with the EEOC that a victim of sexual harassment should not have to work in a less desirable location as a result of an employer's remedy for sexual harassment.

Ellison maintains that the government's remedy was insufficient because it did not discipline Gray and because it allowed Gray to return to San Mateo after only a six-month separation. Even though the hostile environment had been eliminated when Gray began working in San Francisco, we cannot say that the government's response was reasonable under Title VII. The record on appeal suggests that Ellison's employer did not express strong disapproval of Gray's conduct, did not reprimand Gray, did not put him on probation, and did not inform him that repeated harassment would result in suspension or termination. Apparently, Gray's employer only told him to stop harassing Ellison. Title VII requires more than a mere request to refrain from discriminatory conduct. Employers send the wrong message to potential harassers when they do not discipline employees for sexual harassment. If Ellison can prove on remand that Gray knew or should have known that his conduct was unlawful and that the government failed to take even the mildest form of disciplinary action, the district court should hold that the government's initial remedy was insufficient under Title VII. At this point, genuine issues of material fact remain concerning whether the government properly disciplined Gray.

Ellison further maintains that her employer's decision to allow Gray to transfer back to the San Mateo office after a six-month cooling-off period rendered the gov-

ernment's remedy insufficient. She argues that Gray's *mere presence* would create a hostile working environment.

... To avoid liability under Title VII for failing to remedy a hostile environment, employers may even have to remove employees from the workplace if their mere presence would render the working environment hostile. Once again, we examine whether the mere presence of a harasser would create a hostile environment from the perspective of a reasonable woman.

The district court did not reach the issue of the reasonableness of the government's remedy. Given the scant record on appeal, we cannot determine whether a reasonable woman could conclude that Gray's mere presence at San Mateo six months after the alleged harassment would create an abusive environment.... [W]e do not know how often Ellison and Gray would have to interact at San Mateo.

Moreover, it is not clear to us that the six-month cooling-off period was reasonably calculated to end the harassment or assessed proportionately to the seriousness of Gray's conduct. There is evidence in the record which suggests that the government intended to transfer Gray to San Francisco permanently and only allowed Gray to return to San Mateo because he promised to drop some union grievances. We do know that the IRS did not request Ellison's input or even inform her of the proceedings before agreeing to let Gray return to San Mateo. This failure to even attempt to determine what impact Gray's return would have on Ellison shows an insufficient regard for the victim's interest in avoiding a hostile working environment. On remand, the district court should fully explore the facts concerning the government's decision to return Gray to San Mateo.

V

We reverse the district court's decision that Ellison did not allege a prima facie case of sexual harassment due to a hostile working environment, and we remand for further proceedings consistent with this opinion. . . .

ALBERT LEE STEPHENS JR., District Judge, dissenting:

This case comes to us on appeal in the wake of the granting of a summary judgment motion. There was no trial, therefore no opportunities for cross examination of the witnesses. In addition, there are factual gaps in the record that can only lead by speculation. Consequently, I believe that it is an inappropriate case with which to establish a new legal precedent which will be binding in all subsequent cases of like nature in the Ninth Circuit. I refer to the majority's use of the term "reasonable woman," a term I find ambiguous and therefore inadequate.

Nowhere in section 2000e of Title VII, the section under which the plaintiff in this case brought suit, is there any indication that Congress intended to provide for any other than equal treatment in the area of civil rights. The legislation is designed to achieve a balanced and generally gender neutral and harmonious workplace which would improve production and the quality of the employees' lives. In fact, the Supreme Court has shown a preference against systems that are not gender or race neutral, such as hiring quotas. *See City of Richmond v. J. A. Croson Co.,* 488 U.S. 469 (1989). While women may be the most frequent targets of this type of conduct that is at issue in this case, they are not the only targets. I believe that it is incumbent upon the court in this case to use terminology that will meet the needs of all who seek recourse under this section of Title VII. Possible alternatives that are more in line with a gender neutral approach include "victim," "target," or "person."

The term "reasonable man" as it is used in the law of torts, traditionally refers to the average adult person, regardless of gender, and the conduct that can reasonably be expected of him or her. For the purposes of the legal issues that are being addressed, such a term assumes that it is applicable to all persons. Section 2000e of Title VII presupposes the use of a legal term that can apply to all persons and the impossibility of a more individually tailored standard. It is clear that the authors of the majority opinion intend a difference between the "reasonable woman" and the "reasonable man" in Title VII cases on the assumption that men do not have the same sensibilities as women. This is not necessarily true. . . . [C]ircumstances faced by women and their effect upon women can be and in given circumstances may be expected to be understood by men.

. . . Application of the "new standard" presents a puzzlement which is born of the assumption that men's eyes do not see what a woman sees through her eyes. I find it surprising that the majority finds no need for evidence on any of these subjects. I am not sure whether the majority also concludes that the woman and the man in question are also reasonable without evidence on this subject. . . . [T]he workplace itself should be examined as affected, among other things, by the conduct of the people working there as to whether the workplace as existing is conducive to fulfilling the goals of Title VII. In any event, these are unresolved factual issues which preclude summary judgment. . . .

It is my opinion that the case should be reversed with instructions to proceed to trial. This would certainly lead to filling in the factual gaps left by the scanty record, such as what happened at the time of or after the visit of Ellison to Gray's house to cause her to be subsequently fearful of his presence. The circumstances existing in the work place where only men are employed are different than they are where there are both male and female employees. The existence of the differences is readily recognizable and the conduct of employees can be changed appropriately. This is what Title VII requires. Whether a man or a woman has sensibilities peculiar to the person and what they are is not necessarily known. Until they become known by manifesting themselves in an obvious way, they do not become part of the circumstances of the work place. Consequently, the governing element in the equation is the workplace itself, not concepts or viewpoints of individual employees. This does not conflict with existing legal concepts.

The creation of the proposed "new standard" which applies only to women will not necessarily come to the aid of all potential victims of the type of misconduct that is at issue in this case. I believe that a gender neutral standard would greatly contribute to the clarity of this and future cases in the same area. . . .

CASE QUESTIONS

1. In the *Rabidue* case, which the majority cites with disapproval (and which had since been disavowed even in its own circuit, as explained in footnote 6), extremely vulgar language (as quoted by the *Ellison* majority) had been judged not a violation of Title VII on the grounds that such language had been a part of "the lexicon of obscenity that pervaded the environment of the workplace both before and after the [female] plaintiff" went to work there, and that Title VII was not "designed to bring about a magical transformation in the social mores of American workers."[75] Is that a wrong-headed view of Title VII? Is it plausible, as the dissenter in *Ellison* argues, that any reasonable *person* (male or female) can figure out that certain terms are offensive to women and should not be addressed to them in a work setting? Should a woman who knowingly enters a work environment where "sexual jokes, sexual conversations and girlie magazines . . . abound"[76] be prepared to tolerate such things, as long as they are not addressed to her in a harassing way (e.g., by placing *Playboy* centerfolds on *her* locker door, etc.)?

2. Does the "reasonable woman" standard espoused here mean that conduct which *some* reasonable women *might* find intimidating is now forbidden in the workplace, or only that conduct which *every* reasonable woman *would* so find is now forbidden? Even from a woman's point of view, does being pestered with questions, asked out for a drink (once), asked out for lunch (once), and being sent a card, two love notes (one long and one short, and one of which agrees to stop writing if so requested), and then another letter after the sender has promised "not to bother" the recipient again, add up to "a gauntlet of sexual abuse"? An "intimidating" environment? Suppose that in response to this decision, the employer put Gray on probation with the warning that any further communication addressed to Ellison would get him suspended or fired, but still let

him work two rows behind her where he could stare at her all day. If Ellison insisted that this response was inadequate because she still felt great discomfort in his presence, would her demand that he be transferred out of her office be something the employer had to honor under a "reasonable woman standard"? Under a reasonable person standard?

3. Do men and women in fact have different sensibilities? Even if they do, does that make what is "reasonable" for one differ from what is "reasonable" for the other? Is a unisex standard, as advocated by the dissent, impossible? Undesirable? The majority granted (in a footnote omitted from this excerpt) that if a man were claiming harassment of himself, then a

"reasonable man" standard would apply. Is there really a difference between what a male victim would find harassing and what a female victim would find harassing? If your imagination fails you in conceiving of a man truly not wanting someone's sexual attention, try imagining that he is being harassed by a gay supervisor. Would a man who received these love notes from such a supervisor have good cause for complaint? Does a judge really need the "reasonable woman" standard to decide these cases fairly?

4. Do the judges in this case seem insufficiently attentive to First Amendment freedom of speech concerns (which may conflict with the prohibition on sexual harassment, as the judges interpret it)?

Educational Opportunity: Franklin v. Gwinnett County Schools (1992)

Congress's rebuff of the Supreme Court in the Civil Rights Act of November 1991 was expressed in no uncertain terms. The Supreme Court evidently got the message. In a case argued only one month later, the Court faced a choice between a broad and a narrow reading of plaintiff's rights under Title IX of the Education Amendments of 1972, which forbids sex discrimination in educational programs that receive federal funds.[77] Apparently the Court knew which choice would avoid congressional ire, for when it handed down its decision on February 26, 1992, it made that choice (despite the Bush Administration's sending its solicitor general to Court to argue for the contrary outcome). Not only did the Court make the choice that was the more hostile to sex discrimination; it made the choice unanimously.

The specific issue posed in the case, *Christine Franklin v. Gwinnett County Schools,* was whether money damages were permitted in a suit by a victim of sex discrimination under Title IX.[78] Whether a plaintiff in such a lawsuit could ask just for injunctive relief—i.e., a court order to cease the discrimination—or whether monetary damages would also be allowed was not just a narrow, technical question for Christine Franklin. The Court's answer would make a sizable difference in her life.

Franklin claimed that she had been the victim of sexual harassment by a high school teacher (and sports coach), Andrew Hill, and that despite her complaints, the school administration had done nothing to stop his behavior. She stated that beginning in tenth grade he engaged her frequently in unwelcome conversation about her sexual tastes and behavior, that he forcibly kissed her on the mouth in the school parking lot, and that three times during her junior year he took her to his private office and subjected her to "coercive intercourse."[79] Despite her complaints, she claimed, the school did nothing to stop Hill's behavior and discouraged her from pressing criminal charges against him. The school did investigate up to the point that Hill agreed to resign if all matters pending against him be dropped. He did resign and the investigation then ceased. By August of 1989, Christine Franklin had graduated from high school, so a corrective injunction would have been useless to her. Thus, she wanted the chance to sue for monetary damages.

Like Title VI of the 1964 Civil Rights Act, which forbids race discrimination in programs that receive federal funds, Title IX is silent on the question of whether individual victims (of sex discrimination in educational programs that receive federal funds) may sue schools that discriminate against them. But the U.S. Supreme Court had ruled in a number of precedents that individual victims do have a cause of action for such discrimination. In 1979 the Supreme Court first ruled that individual victims may take schools to court for sex discrimination under Title IX[80] (at that point it was not clear whether the suit could ask just for injunctive relief or for damages as well). Then two cases in 1983[81] and 1984,[82] respectively, established that victims of race discrimination under Title VI could take perpetrators to court, and that monetary damages could be sought under Title VI.

Congress itself followed up by enacting the Civil Rights Remedies Equalization Amendment of 1986,[83] which essentially took away the states' Eleventh Amendment immunity against lawsuits from private citizens when such lawsuits were brought under either Title VI or Title IX (or also the 1973 prohibition on discrimination against the disabled or the 1975 prohibition on age discrimination). (Normally Congress cannot legislate away parts of the Constitution; Congress evidently believes that the Fourteenth Amendment, adopted later than the Eleventh, and which Congress is charged with enforcing, limits the reach of the Eleventh Amendment.) This 1986 act states that under the aforementioned laws "remedies . . . are available for such a violation to the same extent as such remedies are available for such a violation in the suit against any public or private entity other than a State."

All the members of the Supreme Court in *Franklin v. Gwinnett County* treated this 1986 act of Congress as implicit endorsement of the judicial precedents described above and as itself implying a right of action for damages under Titles VI and IX,[84] and they unanimously overruled the district and circuit court decisions to the contrary. When Congress expresses itself with clarity on the matter of discrimination, the Supreme Court of the 1990s appears quite willing to apply the legislative mandate.

CHAPTER 5

Sexual Violence
and Pornography

After feminist legal activists achieved relatively quick success in the 1970s in establishing the anti-discrimination principle for gender equity, as explained in the discussion of the *Craig* rule in the first section of the last chapter, their attention turned increasingly to more intractable issues related to sexuality. In a sense, sexual harassment is one of those issues. The law, however, has dealt with sexual harassment as an example of discrimination against one gender group rather than as a legal harm involving the expression of sexuality (akin to, say, the offense committed by a "Peeping Tom"). Indeed, even though the harassment case that went to the U.S. Supreme Court, *Meritor Savings Bank v. Vinson*, contained allegations of rape (a harsh example of sexual violence), its presentation was framed not in terms of sexual violence but in terms of gender equity, i.e., the prohibition on sex discrimination.

A number of other legal issues involving sexuality in the form of sexual violence against women have aroused the concern of feminists and produced some important judicial developments. Three that are dealt with in this chapter are rape, wife-battering, and pornography.

Rape

Rape law has been a section of the criminal code to receive considerable attention from feminists. For these statutes the bulk of feminists' efforts, in contrast to other areas of the law, has not been toward making these laws gender-neutral, but rather toward reforming testimonial aspects of rape law that have rendered rape prosecutions both difficult to win and taxing on the victims. Anglo-American common law long proceeded on the assumption that women might lightly and falsely charge rape. Consequently, in many state jurisdictions, even into the 1970s, the victim's word alone, unlike the situation with such crimes as robbery or assault, was not adequate to bring rape charges. Instead, the fact of the crime needed independent corroboration, before prosecution could proceed, of three elements of the crime: (1) force, (2) sexual penetration, and (3) the

identity of the rapist. Since eyewitnesses were rarely available, these requirements drastically reduced the number of prosecutable rapes. The feminist
movement successfully reformed most such statutes. Moreover, almost all the
states have adopted statutes that in most circumstances forbid testimony about
the sexual history of the rape victim.[1]

In addition, feminists also achieved some success in sensitizing police and
prosecutors' offices to the needs of rape victims. Beyond these, other legal
reforms have included (1) a decision by the U.S. Supreme Court that the death
sentence is unconstitutionally harsh in rape cases (favored by reformers as
making conviction more readily obtainable)[2] and (2) laws in a number of states
making rape by a husband a punishable offense.

Before this latter reform—and presently in a majority of the states, as long as
the couple are not in divorce proceedings or separated—forcible sexual intercourse between a husband and his wife was not punishable. Traditionally, the
legal core of marriage in Anglo-American law has been that the wife has conjugal
duties of sexual and social companionship and of domestic (i.e., household)
service. The husband has the duty of financial support. These duties were
reciprocal rather than equal. For instance, even if a wife came from wealthy
parents and the husband did not, it was his duty to support her, and not the
reverse. In consenting to marriage, people were legally presumed to be consenting to this system, and since rape was sex without the woman's consent, there
could therefore be no rape in marriage.

In 1979, the U.S. Supreme Court, applying the *Craig* rule described in
chapter 4, declared unconstitutional this husband-only support obligation in the
context of alimony laws. States, however, were still free to impose alimony if
they did so in a gender-neutral way, i.e., by requiring the more financially able
spouse to support the other. It was not clear, therefore, that this decision
undermined the notion of conjugal duties; it may have simply made the concept
of conjugal duties applicable to both spouses. In that sense it had no obvious
import concerning the constitutionality of exempting husbands from rape
liability. The reforms that came on this subject, therefore, had to come
state-by-state and by statutory reform. Stories of extraordinary brutality in
husbands' rapes of their wives, such as by the use of painful implements, were
used to persuade legislatures that the presumption of consent sometimes made
no sense.

Statutory Rape and Sexual Violence: *Michael M. v. Sonoma County* (1981)

Some feminists wanted to go beyond these changes and render all rape laws
gender-neutral, and they succeeded in doing so in a number of states. In other
states, where the political climate was not ripe for total gender neutrality, a
particularly likely target of such reformers was "statutory rape" legislation. Most

states had laws punishing males for sex with females deemed too young to give informed consent to sexual intercourse.

The age of such consent was 18 in California, where *Michael M. v. Sonoma County* began.[3] A 17-1/2-year-old male, Michael M., was prosecuted in Sonoma County for sex with a 16-1/2-year-old-female, Sharon, in June 1978. He challenged the proceedings on the grounds that California's statutory rape law denied him equal protection, in violation of the Fourteenth Amendment. The California Supreme Court, using a strict-scrutiny-compelling-interest test, as required by their own reading of their state constitution, nonetheless upheld the law (as had two lower courts). Using the *Craig* test (demanding of gender discrimination a substantial relation to an important governmental interest), the U.S. Supreme Court also upheld the law.

Although this case was prosecuted as consensual intercourse, facts revealed in the lengthy footnote to Justice Blackmun's opinion indicated that it was arguably a forcible rape (although he seems to think otherwise). Statutory rape laws function not infrequently as a practical, back-up alternative for prosecutors for these cases where forcible rape convictions appear to have uncertain chances of success, and this need comprised one of California's arguments on behalf of the statute. Indeed, the argument was persuasive to all of the justices in the majority.

As is perhaps evident from this introduction, the Supreme Court treated the case as one presenting a gender equity/sex discrimination issue. Yet the Court ended up not requiring strict equality of treatment, in part because women face problems of sexual violence to a degree not encountered by men. This case is being included in this chapter on sexual violence (rather than in the previous chapter on sex discrimination) in order to highlight the problem faced in prosecuting cases like this one, cases of what Justice Stevens terms "nonforcible, but nonetheless coerced, sexual intercourse."

Michael M. v. Sonoma County, 450 U.S. 464 (1981)

JUSTICE REHNQUIST announced the judgment of the Court and delivered an opinion, in which THE CHIEF JUSTICE, JUSTICE STEWART, and JUSTICE POWELL joined.

The question presented in this case is whether California's "statutory rape" law, §261.5 of the California Penal Code, violates the Equal Protection Clause of the Fourteenth Amendment. Section 261.5 defines unlawful sexual intercourse as "an act of sexual intercourse accomplished with a female not the wife of the perpetrator, where the female is under the age of 18 years." The statute thus makes men alone criminally liable for the act of sexual intercourse.

. . .

. . . Unlike the California Supreme Court, we have not held that gender-based classifications are "inherently suspect" and thus we do not apply so-called "strict scrutiny" to those classifications. *See Stanton v. Stanton*, 421 U.S. 7 (1975). Our cases have held, however, that the traditional minimum rationality test takes on a somewhat "sharper focus" when gender-based classifications are challenged. *See Craig v. Boren*, 429 U.S. 190, 210 n.* (1976) (POWELL, J., concurring). . . . [I]n *Craig v. Boren*, at 197, the Court [stated] the test to require the classification to bear a "substantial relationship" to "important governmental objectives."

Underlying these decisions is the principle that a legislature not "make overbroad generalizations based on sex which are entirely unrelated to any differences between men and women or which demean the ability or social status of the affected class." *Parham v. Hughes*, 441 U.S. 347, 354 (1979) (STEWART, J., plurality). But because the Equal Protection Clause does not "demand that a statute necessarily apply equally to all persons" or require "things which are different in fact . . . to be treated in law as though they were the same," *Rinaldi v. Yeager*, 384 U.S. 305, 309 (1966), *quoting Tigner v. Texas*, 310 U.S. 141, 147 (1940), this Court has consistently upheld statutes where the gender classification is not invidious, but rather realistically reflects the fact that the sexes are not similarly situated in certain circumstances. *Parham v. Hughes, supra; Califano v. Webster*, 430 U.S. 313 (1977); *Schlesinger v. Ballard*, 419 U.S. 498 (1975); *Kahn v. Shevin*, 416 U.S. 351 (1974). As the Court has stated, a legislature may "provide for the special problems of women." *Weinberger v. Wiesenfeld*, 420 U.S. 636, 653 (1975).

Applying those principles to this case, the fact that the California Legislature criminalized the act of illicit sexual intercourse with a minor female is a sure indication of its intent or purpose to discourage that conduct. Precisely why the legislature desired that result is of course somewhat less clear. . . . Here, for example, the individual legislators may have voted for the statute for a variety of reasons. Some legislators may have been concerned about preventing teenage pregnancies, others about protecting young females from physical injury or from the loss of "chastity," and still others about promoting various religious and moral attitudes towards premarital sex.

The justification for the statute offered by the State, and accepted by the Supreme Court of California, is that the legislature sought to prevent illegitimate teenage pregnancies. That finding, of course, is entitled to great deference. *Reitman v. Mulkey*, 387 U.S. 369, 373-74 (1967). And although our cases establish that the State's asserted reason for the enactment of a statute may be rejected, "if it could not have been a goal of the legislation," *Weinberger v. Wiesenfeld, supra*, at 648, n.16, this is not such a case.

We are satisfied not only that the prevention of illegitimate pregnancy is at least one of the "purposes" of the statute, but that the State has a strong interest in preventing such pregnancy. At the risk of stating the obvious, teenage pregnancies, which have increased dramatically over the last two decades, have significant social, medical and economic consequences for both the mother and her child, and the State. Of particular concern to the State is that approximately half of all teenage pregnancies end in abortion. And of those children who are born, their illegitimacy makes them likely candidates to become wards of the State.

We need not be medical doctors to discern that young men and young women are not similarly situated with respect to the problems and the risks of sexual intercourse. Only women may become pregnant and they suffer disproportionately the profound physical, emotional, and psychological consequences of sexual activity. The statute at issue here protects women from sexual intercourse at an age when those consequences are particularly severe.

The question thus boils down to whether a State may attack the problem of sexual intercourse and teenage pregnancy directly by prohibiting a male from having sexual intercourse with a minor female. We hold that such a statute is sufficiently related to the State's objectives to pass constitutional muster.

Because virtually all of the significant harmful and inescapably identifiable consequences of teenage pregnancy fall on the young female, a legislature acts well within its authority when it elects to punish only the participant who, by nature, suffers few of the consequences of his conduct. It is hardly unreasonable for a legislature acting to protect minor females to exclude them from punishment. Moreover, the risk of pregnancy itself constitutes a substantial deterrence to young females. No similar natural sanctions deter males. A criminal sanction imposed solely on males thus serves to roughly "equalize" the deterrents on the sexes.

We are unable to accept petitioner's contention that the statute is impermissibly underinclusive and must, in order to pass judicial scrutiny, be *broadened* so as to hold the female as criminally liable as the male. It is argued that this statute is not *necessary* to deter teenage pregnancy because a gender-neutral statute, where both male and female would be subject to prosecution, would serve that goal equally well. . . .

. . . [W]e cannot say that a gender-neutral statute would be as effective as the statute California has chosen to enact. The State persuasively contends that a gender-neutral statute would frustrate its interest in effective enforcement. Its view is that a female is surely less likely to report violations of the statute if she herself would be subject to criminal prosecution.[9] In an area already fraught with prosecutorial difficulties, we decline to hold that the Equal Protection Clause requires a legislature to enact a statute so broad that it may well be incapable of enforcement.[10]

. . . Petitioner argues that the statute is flawed because it presumes that as between two persons under eighteen, the male is the culpable aggressor. We find petitioner's con-

9. Petitioner contends that a gender-neutral statute would not hinder prosecutions because the prosecutor could take into account the relative burdens on females and males and generally only prosecute males. But to concede this is to concede all. If the prosecutor, in exercising discretion, will virtually always prosecute just the man and not the woman, we do not see why it is impermissible for the legislature to enact a statute to the same effect.

10. The question whether a statute is *substantially* related to its asserted goals is at best an opaque one. It can be plausibly argued that a gender-neutral statute would produce fewer prosecutions than the statute at issue here. *See* Stewart, J., concurring. The dissent argues, on the other hand, that "even assuming that a gender neutral statute would be more difficult to enforce. . . . Common sense . . . suggests that a gender-neutral statutory rape law is potentially a greater deterrent of sexual activity than a gender-based law, for the simple reason that a gender-neutral law subjects both men and women to criminal sanctions and thus arguably has a deterrent effect on twice as many potential violators." *Post.* Where such differing speculations as to the effect of a statute are plausible, we think it appropriate to defer to the decision of the California

tentions unpersuasive. Contrary to his assertions, the statute does not rest on the assumption that males are generally the aggressors. It is instead an attempt by a legislature to prevent illegitimate teenage pregnancy by providing an additional deterrent for men. The age of the man is irrelevant since young men are as capable as older men of inflicting the harm sought to be prevented.

... As we have held, the statute ... reasonably reflects the fact that the consequences of sexual intercourse and pregnancy fall more heavily on the female than on the male.

Accordingly, the judgment of the California Supreme Court is affirmed.

Affirmed.

JUSTICE STEWART, concurring.

. . .

A

At the outset, it should be noted that the statutory discrimination, when viewed as part of the wider scheme of California law, is not as clearcut as might at first appear. Females are not freed from criminal liability in California for engaging in sexual activity that may be harmful. It is unlawful, for example, for any person, of either sex, to molest, annoy, or contribute to the delinquency of anyone under eighteen years of age. All persons are prohibited from committing "any lewd or lascivious act," including consensual intercourse, with a child under fourteen. And members of both sexes may be convicted for engaging in

Supreme Court, "armed as it was with the knowledge of the facts and the circumstances concerning the passage and potential impact of [the statute], and familiar with the milieu in which that provision would operate." *Reitman v. Mulkey*, 387 U.S. 369, 378-79 (1967). . . .

deviant sexual acts with anyone under eighteen. Finally, females may be brought within the proscription of § 261.5 itself, since a female may be charged with aiding and abetting its violation.

Section 261.5 is thus but one part of a broad statutory scheme that protects all minors from the problems and risks attendant upon adolescent sexual activity. To be sure, § 261.5 creates an additional measure of punishment for males who engage in sexual intercourse with females between the ages of fourteen and seventeen. The question then is whether the Constitution prohibits a state legislature from imposing this *additional* sanction on a gender-specific basis.

. . .

C

As the California Supreme Court's catalogue shows, the pregnant unmarried female confronts problems more numerous and more severe than any faced by her male partner. She alone endures the medical risks of pregnancy or abortion. She suffers disproportionately the social, educational, and emotional consequences of pregnancy. Recognizing this disproportion, California has attempted to protect teenage females by prohibiting males from participating in the act necessary for conception.

... Experienced observation confirms the common-sense notion that adolescent males disregard the possibility of pregnancy far more than do adolescent females. And to the extent that § 261.5 may punish males for intercourse with prepubescent females, that punishment is justifiable because of the substantial physical risks for prepubescent females that are not shared by their male counterparts.

. . .

E

In short, the Equal Protection Clause does not mean that the physiological differences between men and women must be disregarded. While those differences must never be permitted to become a pretext for invidious discrimination, no such discrimination is presented by this case. The Constitution surely does not require a State to pretend that demonstrable differences between men and women do not really exist.

JUSTICE BLACKMUN, concurring in the judgment.

. . .

I . . . cannot vote to strike down the California statutory rape law, for I think it is a sufficiently reasoned and constitutional effort to control the problem at its inception. . . .

I think, too, that it is only fair, with respect to this particular petitioner, to point out that his partner, Sharon, appears not to have been an unwilling participant in at least the initial stages of the intimacies that took place the night of June 3, 1978.*

*Sharon at the preliminary hearing testified as follows:

"Q [by the Deputy District Attorney]. On June the 4th, at approximately midnight—midnight of June the 3rd, were you in Rohnert Park?

"A [by Sharon]. Yes.

. . .

"Q. Now, after you met the defendant, what happened?

"A. We walked down to the railroad tracks.

"Q. What happened at the railroad tracks?

"A. We were drinking at the railroad tracks and we walked over to this bush and he started kissing me and stuff, and I was kissing him back, too, at first. Then, I was telling him to stop—

"Q. Yes.

Petitioner's and Sharon's nonacquaintance with each other before the incident; their drinking; their withdrawal from the others of the group; their foreplay, in which she

———

"A.—and I was telling him to slow down and stop. He said, 'Okay, okay.' But then he just kept doing it. He just kept doing it and then my sister and two other guys came over to where we were and my sister said—told me to get up and come home. And then I didn't—

"Q. Yes.

"A.—and then my sister and—

. . .

"The Witness: Yeah. We was laying there and we were kissing each other, and then he asked me if I wanted to walk him over to the park; so we walked over to the park and we sat down on a bench and then he started kissing me again and we were laying on the bench. And he told me to take my pants off.

"I said, 'No,' and I was trying to get up and he hit me back down on the bench and then I just said to myself, 'Forget it,' and I let him do what he wanted to do and he took my pants off and he was telling me to put my legs around him and stuff—

. . .

"Q. Did you have sexual intercourse with the defendant?

"A. Yeah.

"Q. He did put his penis into your vagina?

"A. Yes.

"Q. You said that he hit you?

"A. Yeah. He slugged me in the face.

"Q. With what did he slug you?

"A. His fist.

"Q. Where abouts in the face?

"A. On my chin.

"Q. As a result of that, did you have any bruises or any kind of an injury?

"A. Yeah.

"Q. What happened?

"A. I had bruises.

"The Court: Did he hit you one time or did he hit you more than once?

willingly participated and seems to have encouraged; and the closeness of their ages (a difference of only one year and 18 days) are factors that should make this case an unattractive one to prosecute at all, and especially to prosecute as a felony, rather than as a misdemeanor chargeable under § 261.5. But the State has chosen to prosecute in that manner, and the facts, I reluctantly conclude, may fit the crime.

"The Witness: He hit me about two or three times.

. . .

"Q. Now, during the course of that evening, did the defendant ask you your age?
"A. Yeah.
"Q. And what did you tell him?
"A. Sixteen.
"Q. Did you tell him you were sixteen?
"A. Yes.
"Q. Now, you said you had been drinking, is that correct?
"A. Yes.
"Q. Would you describe your condition as a result of the drinking?
"A. I was a little drunk." App. 20-23.
CROSS-EXAMINATION
"Q. Did you go off with Mr. M. away from the others?
"A. Yeah.
"Q. Why did you do that?
"A. I don't know. I guess I wanted to.
"Q. Did you have any need to go to the bathroom when you were there.
"A. Yes.
"Q. And what did you do?
"A. Me and my sister walked down the railroad tracks to some bushes and went to the bathroom.
"Q. Now, you and Mr. M., as I understand it, went off into the bushes, is that correct?
"A. Yes.
"Q. Okay. And what did you do when you and Mr. M. were there in the bushes?
"A. We were kissing and hugging.
"Q. Were you sitting up?
"A. We were laying down.
"Q. You were lying down. This was in the bushes?
"A. Yes.

"Q. How far away from the rest of them were you ?
"A. They were just bushes right next the railroad tracks. We just walked off into the bushes; not very far.
"Q. So your sister and the other two boys came over to where you were, you and Michael were, is that right?
"A. Yeah.
"Q. What did they say to you, if you remember?
"A. My sister didn't say anything. She said, 'Come on, Sharon, let's go home.'
"Q. She asked you to go home with her?
"A. (Affirmative nod.)
"Q. Did you go home with her?
"A. No.
"Q. You wanted to stay with Mr. M.?
"A. I don't know.
"Q. Was this before or after he hit you?
"A. Before.

. . .

Q. What happened in the five minutes that Bruce stayed there with you and Michael?
"A. I don't remember.
"Q. You don't remember at all?
"A. (Negative head shake.)
"Q. Did you have occasion at that time to kiss Bruce?
"A. Yeah.
"Q. You did? You were kissing Bruce at that time?
"A. (Affirmative nod.)
"Q. Was Bruce kissing you?
"A. Yes.

Justice Brennan, with whom Justices White and Marshall join, dissenting.

I

It is disturbing to find the Court so splintered on a case that presents such a straightforward issue: whether the admittedly gender-based classification in Cal. Pe-

---

"Q. And were you standing up at this time?
"A. No, we were sitting down.
                . . .
"Q. Okay. So at this point in time you had left Mr. M. and you were hugging and kissing with Bruce, is that right?
"A. Yeah.
"Q. And you were sitting up.
"A. Yes.
"Q. Was your sister still there then?
"A. No. Yeah, she was at first.
"Q. What was she doing?
"A. She was standing up with Michael and David.
"Q. Yes. Was she doing anything with Michael and David?
"A. No. I don't think so.
"Q. Whose idea was it for you and Bruce to kiss? Did you initiate that?
"A. Yes.
"Q. What happened after Bruce left?
"A. Michael asked me if I wanted to go walk to the park.
"Q. And what did you say?
"A. I said, "Yes."
"Q. And then what happened?
"A. We walked to the park.
                . . .
"Q. How long did it take you to get to the park?
"A. About ten or fifteen minutes.
"Q. And did you walk there?
"A. Yes.

---

nal Code § 261.5 bears a sufficient relationship to the State's asserted goal of preventing teenage pregnancies to survive the "mid-level" constitutional scrutiny mandated by *Craig v. Boren,* 429 U.S. 190 (1976). Applying the analytical framework provided by our precedents, I am convinced that there is only one proper resolution of this issue: the classification must be declared unconstitutional. I fear that the plurality and Justices Stewart and Blackmun reach the opposite result by placing too much emphasis on the desirability of achieving the State's asserted statutory goal—prevention of teenage pregnancy— and not enough emphasis on the fundamental question of whether the sex-based discrimination in the California statute is *substantially* related to the achievement of that goal.

                . . .

The State of California vigorously asserts that the "important governmental objective" to be served by § 261.5 is the prevention of teenage pregnancy. It claims that its statute furthers this goal by deterring sexual activity by males—the class of persons it considers more responsible for causing those pregnancies. But even assuming that prevention of teenage pregnancy is an important governmental objective and that it is in fact an objective of § 261.5, California still has the burden of proving that there are fewer teenage pregnancies under its gender-based statutory rape law than there would be if the law were gender-neutral. To meet this burden, the State must show that because its statutory rape law punishes only males, and not females, it more effectively deters minor females from having sexual intercourse.

The plurality assumes that a gender-neutral statute would be less effective than § 261.5 in deterring sexual activity because a gender-neutral statute would create significant enforcement problems. The plurality thus accepts the State's assertion that. . .

> a female is surely less likely to report violations of the statute if she herself would be subject to criminal prosecution. In an area already fraught with prosecutorial difficulties, we decline to hold that the Equal Protection Clause requires a legislature to enact a statute so broad that it may well be incapable of enforcement. (*Ante.*)

. . . [T]here are a least two serious flaws in the State's assertion. . . .

First, the experience of other jurisdictions, and California itself, belies the plurality's conclusion that a gender-neutral statutory rape law "may well be incapable of enforcement." There are now at least 37 States that have enacted gender-neutral statutory rape laws. Although most of these laws protect young persons (of either sex) from the sexual exploitation of older individuals, the laws of Arizona, Florida, and Illinois permit prosecution of both minor females and minor males for engaging in mutual sexual conduct. California has introduced no evidence that those states have been handicapped by the enforcement problems the plurality finds so persuasive. Surely, if those States could provide such evidence, we might expect that California would have introduced it.

. . .

The second flaw in the State's assertion is that even assuming that a gender-neutral statute would be more difficult to enforce, the State has still not shown that those enforcement problems would make such a statute less effective than a gender-based statute in deterring minor females from engaging in sexual intercourse. Common sense, however, suggests that a gender-neutral statutory rape law is potentially a greater deterrent of sexual activity than a gender-based law, for the simple reason that a gender-neutral law subjects both men and women to criminal sanctions and thus arguably has a deterrent effect on twice as many potential violators. . . .

JUSTICE STEVENS, dissenting.

Local custom and belief—rather than statutory laws of venerable but doubtful ancestry—will determine the volume of sexual activity among unmarried teenagers. The empirical evidence cited by the plurality demonstrates the futility of the notion that a statutory prohibition will significantly affect the volume of that activity or provide a meaningful solution to the problems created by it. Nevertheless, as a matter of constitutional power, unlike my Brother BRENNAN at n.5, I would have no doubt about the validity of a state law prohibiting all unmarried teenagers from engaging in sexual intercourse. The societal interests in reducing the incidence of venereal disease and teenage pregnancy are sufficient, in my judgment, to justify a prohibition of conduct that increases the risk of those harms.

My conclusion that a nondiscriminatory prohibition would be constitutional does not help me answer the question whether a prohibition applicable to only half of the joint participants in the risk-creating conduct is also valid. It cannot be true that the validity of a total ban is an adequate justification for a selective prohibition; otherwise, the constitutional objection to discriminatory rules would be meaningless. The question in this case is whether the difference between males and females justifies this statutory discrimination based entirely on sex. . . .

In my judgment, the fact that a class of persons is especially vulnerable to a risk that a statute is designed to avoid is a reason for making the statute applicable to that class. The argument that a special need for protection provides a rational explanation for an exemption is one I simply do not comprehend.

In this case, the fact that a female confronts a greater risk of harm than a male is a reason for applying the prohibition to her—not a reason for granting her a license to use her own judgment on whether or not to assume the risk. Surely, if we examine the problem from the point of view of society's interest in preventing the risk-creating conduct from occurring at all, it is irrational to exempt 50 percent of the potential violators. *See* Dissent of JUSTICE BRENNAN. And, if we view the government's interest as that of a *parens patriae* seeking to protect its subjects from harming themselves, the discrimination is actually perverse. Would a rational parent making rules for the conduct of twin children of opposite sex simultaneously forbid the son and authorize the daughter to engage in conduct that is especially harmful to the daughter? That is the effect of this statutory classification. . . .

I cannot accept the State's argument that the constitutionality of the discriminatory rule can be saved by an assumption that prosecutors will commonly invoke this statute only in cases that actually involve a forcible rape, but one that cannot be established by proof beyond a reasonable doubt.[8] That assumption implies that a State has a legitimate interest in convicting a defendant on evidence that is constitutionally insufficient. . . .

Nor do I find at all persuasive the suggestion that this discrimination is adequately justified by the desire to encourage females to inform against their male partners. Even if the concept of a wholesale informant's exemption were an acceptable enforcement device, what is the justification for defining the exempt class entirely by reference to sex rather than by reference to a more neutral criterion such as relative innocence? Indeed, if the exempt class is to be composed entirely of members of one sex, what is there to support the view that the statutory purpose will be better served by granting the informing license to females rather than to males? If a discarded male partner informs on a promiscuous female, a timely threat of prosecution might well prevent the precise harm the statute is intended to minimize.

Finally, even if my logic is faulty and there actually is some speculative basis for treating equally guilty males and females differently, I still believe that any such speculative justification would be outweighed by the paramount interest in even-handed enforcement of the law. A rule that authorizes punishment of only one of two equally guilty wrongdoers violates the essence of the constitutional requirement that the sovereign must govern impartially.

I respectfully dissent.

---

8. According to the State of California: "The statute is commonly employed in situations involving force, prostitution, pornography or coercion due to status relationships, and the state's

interest in these situations is apparent." Brief for the Respondent . . . . The State's interest in these situations is indeed apparent and certainly sufficient to justify statutory prohibition of forcible rape, prostitution, pornography and nonforcible, but nonetheless coerced, sexual intercourse. However, it is not at all apparent to me how this state interest can justify a statute not specifically directed to any of these offenses.

CASE QUESTIONS

1. Would the sorts of rules suggested by Justice Stevens, making guilty the party more "responsible" for the intercourse, or the person initiating the intercourse, be readily applicable? How would one prove who the initiator was?

2. Do laws like this one harm women more than they help them?

Nonviolent, Coerced Intercourse: *State v. Rusk* (1981)

In footnote 8 of his dissenting opinion in *Michael M.,* Justice Stevens refers to the problem of "nonforcible, but nonetheless coerced, sexual intercourse," and suggests that states might wish to directly target a statutory prohibition against such conduct, rather than using the roundabout and partial solution of the kind of law applied to *Michael M.* Indeed, even persons sympathetic to California's approach would have to acknowledge that it would not have been effective if precisely the same incident had taken place when both parties were one and a half years older. Under those hypothetical circumstances, despite the coercive (as well as violent) behavior of punching his victim in the face twice, Michael apparently stood a good chance of being found innocent of rape charges.

These conviction difficulties, typified by Michael M.'s situation, that continue to face prosecutors of rape have produced a variety of suggestions for reform. In her book *Real Rape,* Susan Estrich has argued that rape statutes should be changed such that " '[c]onsent' should be defined so that no means no. . . . [T]he threshold of liability—whether phrased in terms of 'consent,' 'force,' and 'coercion' or some combination of the three—should be understood to include at least those nontraditional rapes where the woman *says* no or submits only in response to lies or threats which would be prohibited were money sought instead."[4] Other reformers have endorsed the "reasonable woman" standard, as advocated by the judge in the *Ellison* case from the last chapter, as a guide to deciding whether consent was denied and whether "force" was either used or threatened.

A much-debated case that illustrates the issues addressed by these reformers is *State v. Rusk.*[5] The rapist, Edward Rusk, was first convicted by a Baltimore jury. On appeal, the court of special appeals in an 8–5 vote reversed his conviction on the grounds that the original trial judge should have ruled that the evidence was insufficient under Maryland law for the charge of rape to go to a jury. Then

Maryland's highest court, the court of appeals, voted 4–3 to reinstate the conviction. One of those four votes was a woman judge, the only woman out of twenty-one judges who dealt with the case.[6] (Of the twenty-one, a total of eleven favored releasing the defendant, and only ten favored conviction. By the luck of the draw, in a sense, Rusk stayed convicted.)

Rusk had been convicted of raping a woman referred to by the judges as "Pat." Pat's story was that she met Rusk in a bar where he appeared to be acquainted with a friend of hers. He asked her for a ride home, and she agreed, although she warned him not to think of it as anything more than a ride. When they reached his house, around 1 A.M., he invited her up. She refused. He persisted. She repeatedly refused. He then reached over, grabbed her car keys, pocketed them, got out, and said, "Now will you come up?" Fearing to walk alone in the middle of the night in an unfamiliar urban neighborhood, and already fearing that he might rape her because of a look on his face, Pat followed him up to his one-room apartment. She waited a few minutes while he went into the bathroom, and when he returned asked if she could now leave. She reminded him that she had not wanted to come up. He told her to stay and pulled her onto the bed where he then took off her blouse and bra and unzipped her slacks. He asked her to remove her slacks and his pants, and she did so. He then started kissing her as she lay on the bed. Meanwhile she was begging him to let her leave, to return her keys. She was "really scared," she reported, because of the "look in his eyes," and said to him, "If I do what you want, will you let me go without killing me?" because she had no idea what he might do. She then started to cry. At this point he placed his hands on her throat and started (in her description) "lightly to choke" her. She repeated her question (omitting the "without killing me" phrase) and he said yes, after which she submitted to fellatio and vaginal sex. Immediately after that she again asked if she could leave. He said yes and gave back her car keys. He also answered her request for directions how to drive home. She went home, thought a bit about the incident, and about an hour later reported it to the police. They picked her up, she led them to his apartment, and he was arrested for rape.

Rusk's story was that she was lying from beginning to end. In his version, she had cuddled with him en route to her car, eagerly petted with him on the way to his home, eagerly followed him in, eagerly had sex with him, and only became distraught after the fact. And he had never taken her car keys.

The judges who argued against convicting Rusk *assumed* Pat's story was true and still argued that this was not a rape situation. Maryland law (Article 27, section 463 [a] [1]) defined rape as "vaginal intercourse with another person by force or threat of force against the will and without the consent of the other person." The court of special appeals majority reasoned that this law required either evidence of nonconsent in the form of "resistance" or evidence that the victim "was prevented from resisting by threats to her safety."[7] As debated on the (higher) court of appeals, then, the central question turned out to be whether there had been force or a threat of force against Pat, and if she believed there had, did her belief itself have to be reasonable. Whether the standard of reasonable fear varied as between women and men was not a question articulated by the judges. The court of appeals debate is excerpted below.

State v. Rusk, 424 A.2d 720 (1981)

[ROBERT C.] MURPHY, Chief Judge.

. . .

On appeal, the Court of Special Appeals, sitting en banc, reversed the conviction; it concluded by an 8–5 majority that in view of the prevailing law as set forth in *Hazel v. State*, 221 Md. 464, 157 A.2d 922 (1960), insufficient evidence of Rusk's guilt had been adduced at the trial to permit the case to go to the jury. *Rusk v. State*, 43 Md. App. 476, 406 A.2d 624 (1979).

. . .

In reversing Rusk's second degree rape conviction, . . . Judge Thompson said:

In all of the victim's testimony we have been unable to see any resistance on her part to the sex acts and certainly can we see no fear as would overcome her attempt to resist or escape as required by *Hazel*. Possession of the keys by the accused may have deterred her vehicular escape but hardly a departure seeking help in the rooming house or in the street. We must say that "the way he looked" fails utterly to support the fear required by *Hazel*. 43 Md. App. at 480.

The Court of Special Appeals interpreted *Hazel* as requiring a showing of a reasonable apprehension of fear in instances where the prosecutrix did not resist. It concluded:

. . . We do not believe that "lightly choking" along with all the facts and circumstances in the case, were sufficient to cause a reasonable fear which overcame her ability to resist. In the absence of any other evidence showing force used by appellant, we find that the evidence was insufficient to convict appellant of rape. *Id.* at 484.

In argument before us on the merits of the case, the parties agreed that the issue was whether, in light of the principles of *Hazel*, there was evidence before the jury legally sufficient to prove beyond a reasonable doubt that the intercourse was "[b]y force or threat of force against the will and without the consent" of the victim in violation of Art. 27, § 463(a)(1). . . .
[*Hazel* established:]

Force is an essential element of the crime and to justify a conviction, the evidence must warrant a conclusion either that the victim resisted and her resistance was overcome by force or that she was prevented from resisting by threats to her safety. But no particular amount of force, either actual or constructive, is required to constitute rape. Necessarily, that fact must

depend upon the prevailing circumstances. As in this case force may exist
without violence. If the acts and
threats of the defendant were reasonably calculated to create in the mind of
the victim—having regard to the circumstances in which she was placed—a
real apprehension, due to fear, of imminent bodily harm, serious enough to
impair or overcome her will to resist,
then such acts and threats are the
equivalent of force. *Id.* at 469.

As to the element of lack of consent,
the Court said in *Hazel*:

[I]t is true, of course, that however
reluctantly given, consent to the act at
any time prior to penetration deprives
the subsequent intercourse of its criminal character. There is, however, a
wide difference between consent and a
submission to the act. Consent may
involve submission, but submission
does not necessarily imply consent.
Furthermore, submission to a compelling force, or as a result of being put in
fear, is not consent. *Id.*

. . . The degree of fear necessary to
obviate the need to prove resistance, and
thereby establish lack of consent, was defined in the following manner:

The kind of fear which would render
resistance by a woman unnecessary to
support a conviction of rape includes,
but is not necessarily limited to, a fear of
death or serious bodily harm, or a fear
so extreme as to preclude resistance, or a
fear which would well nigh render her
mind incapable of continuing to resist,
or a fear that so overpowers her that she
does not dare resist. *Id.* at 470.

. . .

Hazel did not expressly determine
whether the victim's fear must be "reasonable." . . . While *Hazel* made it clear that the
victim's fear had to be genuine, it did not
pass upon whether a real but unreasonable
fear of imminent death or serious bodily
harm would suffice. The vast majority of
jurisdictions have required that the victim's fear be reasonably grounded in order
to obviate the need for either proof of
actual force on the part of the assailant or
physical resistance on the part of the victim. We think that, generally, this is the
correct standard.

As earlier indicated, the Court of Special Appeals held that a showing of a reasonable apprehension of fear was essential
under *Hazel* to establish the elements of the
offense where the victim did not resist. The
Court did not believe, however, that the evidence was legally sufficient to demonstrate
the existence of "a reasonable fear" which
overcame Pat's ability to resist. . . .

We think the reversal of Rusk's conviction by the Court of Special Appeals was in
error for the fundamental reason so well
expressed in the dissenting opinion by
Judge Wilner when he observed that the
majority had "trampled upon the first principle of appellate restraint . . . [because it
had] substituted [its] own view of the evidence (and the inferences that may fairly
be drawn from it) for that of the judge and
jury . . . [and had thereby] improperly invaded the province allotted to those tribunals." 43 Md. App. at 484–85. In view of
the evidence adduced at the trial, the reasonableness of Pat's apprehension of fear
was plainly a question of fact for the jury to
determine. . . . Applying the constitutional
standard of review articulated in *Jackson v.
Virginia*, 443 U.S. 307, 319 (1979), i.e.—
whether after considering the evidence in
the light most favorable to the prosecution,
any rational trier of fact could have found
the essential elements of the crime beyond

a reasonable doubt—it is readily apparent to us that the trier of fact could rationally find that the elements of force and non-consent had been established and that Rusk was guilty of the offense beyond a reasonable doubt. Of course, it was for the jury to observe the witnesses and their demeanor, and to judge their credibility and weigh their testimony. Quite obviously, the jury disbelieved Rusk and believed Pat's testimony. From her testimony, the jury could have reasonably concluded that the taking of her car keys was intended by Rusk to immobilize her alone, late at night, in a neighborhood with which she was not familiar; that after Pat had repeatedly refused to enter his apartment, Rusk commanded in firm tones that she do so; that Pat was badly frightened and feared that Rusk intended to rape her; that unable to think clearly and believing that she had no other choice in the circumstances, Pat entered Rusk's apartment; that once inside Pat asked permission to leave but Rusk told her to stay; that he then pulled Pat by the arms to the bed and undressed her; that Pat was afraid that Rusk would kill her unless she submitted; that she began to cry and Rusk then put his hands on her throat and began " 'lightly to choke' " her; that Pat asked him if he would let her go without killing her if she complied with his demands; that Rusk gave an affirmative response, after which she finally submitted.

Just where persuasion ends and force begins in cases like the present is essentially a factual issue, to be resolved in light of the controlling legal precepts. That threats of force need not be made in any particular manner in order to put a person in fear of bodily harm is well established. Indeed, conduct, rather than words, may convey the threat. That a victim did not scream out for help or attempt to escape, while bearing on the question of consent, is

unnecessary where she is restrained by fear of violence.

Considering all of the evidence in the case, with particular focus upon the actual force applied by Rusk to Pat's neck, we conclude that the jury could rationally find that the essential elements of second degree rape had been established and that Rusk was guilty of that offense beyond a reasonable doubt.

Judgment of the Court of Special Appeals reversed; case remanded to that court with directions that it affirm the Judgment of the Criminal Court of Baltimore; costs to be paid by the appellee.

[Marvin H.] Smith, [J. Dudley] Digges and [Harry A.] Cole, JJ., dissent.

Cole, Judge, dissenting.

I agree with the Court of Special Appeals that the evidence adduced at the trial of Edward Salvatore Rusk was insufficient to convict him of rape. I, therefore, respectfully dissent.

The standard of appellate review in deciding a question of sufficiency, as the majority correctly notes, is "whether, after viewing the evidence in the light most favorable to the prosecution, *any* rational trier of fact could have found the essential elements of the crime beyond a reasonable doubt." *Jackson v. Virginia* (emphasis in original). However, it is equally well settled that when one of the essential elements of a crime is not sustained by the evidence, the conviction of the defendant cannot stand as a matter of law.

The majority, in applying this standard, concludes that "[i]n view of the evidence adduced at the trial, the reasonableness of Pat's apprehension of fear was plainly a question of fact for the jury to determine." In so concluding, the majority has skipped over the crucial issue. It seems to me that whether the prosecutrix's fear is reasonable becomes a question only after the court determines that the defendant's conduct under the circumstances was reasonably calculated to give rise to a fear on her part to the extent that she was unable to resist. In other words, the fear must stem from his articulable conduct, and equally, if not more importantly, cannot be inconsistent with her own contemporaneous reaction to that conduct. The conduct of the defendant, in and of itself, must clearly indicate force or the threat of force such as to overpower the prosecutrix's ability to resist or will to resist. In my view, there is no evidence to support the majority's conclusion that the prosecutrix was forced to submit to sexual intercourse, certainly not fellatio. . . .

[Fifty years of precedents from rape cases around the country] make plain that *Hazel* intended to require clear and cognizable evidence of force or the threat of force sufficient to overcome or prevent resistance by the female before there would arise a jury question of whether the prosecutrix had a reasonable apprehension of harm. The majority today departs from this requirement and places its imprimatur on the female's conclusory statements that she was in fear, as sufficient to support a conviction of rape.

. . .

While courts no longer require a female to resist to the utmost or to resist where resistance would be foolhardy, they do require her acquiescence in the act of intercourse to stem from fear generated by something of substance. She may not simply say, "I was really scared," and thereby transform consent *or mere unwillingness* into submission by force. These words do not transform a seducer into a rapist. She must follow the natural instinct of every proud female *to resist, by more than mere words*, the violation

of her person by a stranger or an unwelcomed friend. She must make it plain that she regards such sexual acts as abhorrent and repugnant to her natural sense of pride. She must resist unless the defendant has objectively manifested his intent to use physical force to accomplish his purpose. The law regards rape as a crime of violence. The majority today attenuates this proposition. It declares the innocence of an at best distraught young woman. It does not demonstrate the defendant's guilt of the crime of rape. [Emphasis added.—Au.]

My examination of the evidence in a light most favorable to the State reveals no conduct by the defendant reasonably calculated to cause the prosecutrix to be so fearful that she should fail to resist and thus, the element of force is lacking in the State's proof.

Here we have a full grown married woman who meets the defendant in a bar under friendly circumstances. They drink and talk together. She agrees to give him a ride home in her car. When they arrive at his house, located in an area with which she was unfamiliar but which was certainly not isolated, he invites her to come up to his apartment and she refuses. According to her testimony he takes her keys, walks around to her side of the car, and says "Now will you come up?" She answers, "yes." The majority suggests that "from her testimony the jury could have reasonably concluded that the taking of her keys was intended by Rusk to immobilize her alone, late at night, in a neighborhood with which she was unfamiliar. . . ." But on what facts does the majority so conclude? There is no evidence descriptive of the tone of his voice; her testimony indicates only the bare statement quoted above. How can the majority extract from this conduct a threat reasonably calculated to create a fear of imminent bodily harm? There was no weapon, no threat to inflict physical injury.

She also testified that she was afraid of "the way he looked," and afraid of his statement, "come on up, come on up." But what can the majority conclude from this statement coupled with a "look" that remained undescribed? There is no evidence whatsoever to suggest that this was anything other than a pattern of conduct consistent with the *ordinary seduction* of a female acquaintance who at first suggests her disinclination. . . .[Emphasis added.—Au.]

She then testified that she started to cry and he "started lightly to choke" her, whatever that means. Obviously, the choking was not of any persuasive significance. During this "choking" she was able to talk. She said "If I do what you want will you let me go?" It was at this point that the defendant said yes.

I find it incredible for the majority to conclude that on these facts, without more, a woman was *forced* to commit oral sex upon the defendant and then to engage in vaginal intercourse. In the absence of any verbal threat to do her grievous bodily harm or the display of any weapon and threat to use it, I find it difficult to understand how a victim could participate in these sexual activities and not be willing.

What was the nature and extent of her fear anyhow? . . . She was afraid because she didn't know him and she was afraid he was going to "rape" her. But there are no acts or conduct on the part of the defendant to suggest that these fears were created by

the defendant or that he made any objective, identifiable threats to her which would give rise to this woman's failure to flee, summon help, scream, or make physical resistance.

As the defendant well knew, this was not a child. This was a married woman with children, a woman familiar with the social setting in which these two actors met. It was an ordinary city street, not an isolated spot. He had not forced his way into her car; he had not taken advantage of a difference in years or any state of intoxication or mental or physical incapacity on her part. He did not grapple with her. She got out of the car, *walked with him* across the street and *followed* him up the stairs to his room. She certainly had to realize that they were not going upstairs to play *Scrabble.* . . .

The record does not disclose the basis for this young woman's misgivings about her experience with the defendant. The only substantive fear she had was that she would be late arriving home. The objective facts make it inherently improbable that the defendant's conduct generated any fear for her physical well-being.

In my judgment the State failed to prove the essential element of force beyond a reasonable doubt and, therefore, the judgment of conviction should be reversed.

Judges Smith and Digges have authorized me to state that they concur in the views expressed herein.

CASE QUESTIONS

1. If Rusk's actions were not calculated to instill enough fear in Pat that she comply with his demands, why did he lie about what happened? If it is Pat who is lying, why wouldn't she just claim that he threatened to kill her?

2. Pat said no several times to Rusk's invitations and even begged for her keys and cried, but she complied with his commands to undress, etc. The dissent concedes that this behavior might be accurately characterized as "unwilling" submission (see phrases I have italicized—Au.) but says this does not amount to rape. If sex against a person's will is not rape, then what is? Should a reasonable man in Rusk's situation believe that Pat had become willing to have sex? The dissent says that for a rape to be proven, there must be evidence of "resistance beyond mere words." (See italics.) Do you agree? Should weeping count as "beyond mere words"? Does Rusk's behavior strike you as "ordinary seduction"? (See italics.)

3. Does the scenario between Pat and Rusk strike you as materially different from the following hypothetical, and if so, in what respects?

A carjacker opens a woman's car door at a red light, grabs her keys, and demands that she get out. (No weapon is displayed.) She tells him she is terrified of being on foot in this neighborhood late at night and she will do anything he asks if he just gives her back her car keys. He says, "Okay, come with me." He drives her to his nearby apartment where they go in and have sex, then he gives back her car keys, and she leaves. She reports him to the police, who arrest him.

Wife Abuse and Husband Homicide: State v. Stewart (1988)

In October of 1990, shortly before he left office, Governor Richard Celeste of Ohio issued a mass clemency of twenty-five battered women who had been convicted of killing or assaulting the man in their lives.[8] This set off what has since been dubbed the "clemency movement." Governor William Schaefer of Maryland granted clemency for eight similar inmates in 1991.[9] The women who were freed had been convicted following trials in which the judge had not permitted testimony presenting the fact that they had been battered.[10] By the end of 1992, governors in seven states had granted clemency to thirty-eight women convicted of assaulting or killing their partners after having been battered by them.[11]

Resorting to homicide even to alleviate a desperate situation is generally frowned upon in the law. Still, battered women may be validly perceiving an imminent danger to their lives, and homicide in self-defense is permitted throughout the United States. Between 1985 and 1991, according to FBI figures, 28 percent of all women killed were the victims of present or former husbands or boyfriends.[12]

Publicity about a particularly egregious example of such a murder by a husband in Massachusetts prompted Governor William Weld of that state to recommend parole one month later for another battered woman who had resorted to killing her former boyfriend, who had stalked and battered her for months. In the publicized case that seems to have motivated Governor Weld, a woman had followed every prescribed procedure for protecting herself from her husband: she had obtained a permanent court restraining order against his contacting her, she had filed for divorce (despite his threat to kill her if she did), she had hired a private detective to follow her husband, she had joined a women's support group and taken self-defense lessons, and she even kept her whereabouts secret. When she went to pick up her mail, her husband shot first her and then himself.[13]

American judges are divided on how to treat self-defense claims by women who kill their batterers. Here, too, the question has been raised of whether there should be a "reasonable woman" standard for judging the options available to a woman who is often outweighed by a hundred pounds and outsized by several inches by her husband. The traditional legal notion of fending off a man's attack with "equal force" may simply not be available to such a woman facing her husband's fists. The question might best be posed as, "What should be done by a reasonable person *who finds herself in the same situation as the battered wife?*" (with "same situation" including such particular factors as size and strength differences compared to the husband).

Some battered women have a particularly difficult time invoking a self-defense claim because they kill their husband when he is not in the midst of a battering episode, say, while he sleeps. In these situations, the traditional legal duty to flee, many people would suggest, would seem more appropriate than homicide. A case illustrating the perplexities of these situations is *State v. Stewart*, below. The grisly details of Mike Stewart's long history of battering and otherwise abusing his wife Peggy and his stepdaughters are presented in full in the majority's opinion. This case was decided by a 5–2 majority in the Supreme Court of Kansas, and the majority was reversing the trial court's verdict of not guilty by reason of self-defense.

State v. Stewart, 763 P.2d 572 (Kan. 1988)

TYLER C. LOCKETT, Justice.

A direct appeal by the prosecution upon a question reserved asks whether the statutory justification for the use of deadly force in self-defense provided by K.S.A. 21-3211 excuses a homicide committed by a battered wife where there is no evidence of a deadly threat or imminent danger contemporaneous with the killing. . . .

Peggy Stewart fatally shot her husband, Mike Stewart, while he was sleeping. She was charged with murder in the first degree, K.S.A. 21-3401. Defendant pled not guilty, contending that she shot her husband in self-defense. Expert evidence showed that Peggy Stewart suffered from the battered woman syndrome. Based upon the battered woman syndrome, the trial judge instructed the jury on self-defense. The jury found Peggy Stewart not guilty.

The State stipulates that Stewart "suffered considerable abuse at the hands of her husband," but contends that the trial court erred in giving a self-defense instruction since Peggy Stewart was in no imminent danger when she shot her sleeping husband. We agree that under the facts of this case the giving of the self-defense instruction was erroneous. We further hold that the trial judge's self-defense instruction improperly allowed the jury to determine the reasonableness of defendant's belief that she was in imminent danger from her individual subjective viewpoint rather than the viewpoint of a reasonable person in her circumstances.

Following an annulment from her first husband and two subsequent divorces in which she was the petitioner, Peggy Stewart married Mike Stewart in 1974. Evidence at trial disclosed a long history of abuse by Mike against Peggy and her two daughters from one of her prior marriages. Laura, one of Peggy's daughters, testified that early in the marriage Mike hit and kicked Peggy, and that after the first year of the marriage Peggy exhibited signs of severe psychological problems. Subsequently, Peggy was hospitalized and diagnosed as having symptoms of paranoid schizophrenia; she responded to treatment and was soon released. It appeared to Laura, however, that Mike was encouraging Peggy to take more than her prescribed dosage of medication.

In 1977, two social workers informed Peggy that they had received reports that Mike was taking indecent liberties with her daughters. Because the social workers did not want Mike to be left alone with the girls, Peggy quit her job. In 1978, Mike began to taunt Peggy by stating that Carla, her 12-year-old daughter, was "more of a wife" to him than Peggy.

Later, Carla was placed in a detention center, and Mike forbade Peggy and Laura to visit her. When Mike finally allowed Carla to return home in the middle of summer, he forced her to sleep in an un-air conditioned room with the windows nailed shut, to wear a heavy flannel nightgown, and to cover herself with heavy blankets. Mike would then wake Carla at 5:30 A.M. and force her to do all the housework. Peggy and Laura were not allowed to help Carla or speak to her.

When Peggy confronted Mike and demanded that the situation cease, Mike responded by holding a shotgun to Peggy's head and threatening to kill her. Mike once kicked Peggy so violently in the chest and ribs that she required hospitalization. Finally, when Mike ordered Peggy to kill and bury Carla, she filed for divorce. Peggy's attorney in the divorce action testified in the murder trial that Peggy was afraid for both her and her children's lives.

One night, in a fit of anger, Mike threw Carla out of the house. Carla, who was not yet in her teens, was forced out of the home with no money, no coat, and no place to go. When the family heard that Carla was in Colorado, Mike refused to allow Peggy to contact or even talk about Carla.

Mike's intimidation of Peggy continued to escalate. One morning, Laura found her mother hiding on the school bus, terrified and begging the driver to take her to a neighbor's home. That Christmas, Mike threw the turkey dinner to the floor, chased Peggy outside, grabbed her by the hair, rubbed her face in the dirt, and then kicked and beat her.

After Laura moved away, Peggy's life became even more isolated. Once, when Peggy was working at a cafe, Mike came in and ran all the customers off with a gun because he wanted Peggy to go home and have sex with him right that minute. He abused both drugs and alcohol, and amused himself by terrifying Peggy, once waking her from a sound sleep by beating her with a baseball bat. He shot one of Peggy's pet cats, and then held the gun against her head and threatened to pull the trigger. Peggy told friends that Mike would hold a shotgun to her head and threaten to blow it off, and indicated that one day he would probably do it.

In May 1986, Peggy left Mike and ran away to Laura's home in Oklahoma. It was the first time Peggy had left Mike without telling him. Because Peggy was suicidal, Laura had her admitted to a hospital. There, she was diagnosed as having toxic psychosis as a result of an overdose of her medication. On May 30, 1986, Mike called to say he was coming to get her. Peggy agreed to return to Kansas. Peggy told a nurse she felt like she wanted to shoot her husband. At trial, she testified that she decided to return with Mike because she was not able to get the medical help she needed in Oklahoma.

When Mike arrived at the hospital, he told the staff that he "needed his housekeeper." The hospital released Peggy to Mike's care, and he immediately drove her back to Kansas. Mike told Peggy that all her problems were in her head and he would be the one to tell her what was good for her, not the doctors. Peggy testified that Mike threatened to kill her if she ever ran away again. As soon as they arrived at the house, Mike forced Peggy into the house and forced her to have oral sex several times.

The next morning, Peggy discovered a loaded .357 magnum. She testified she was afraid of the gun. She hid the gun under the mattress of the bed in a spare room. Later that morning, as she cleaned house, Mike kept making remarks that she should not bother because she would not be there long, or that she should not bother with her things because she could not take them

with her. She testified she was afraid Mike was going to kill her.

Mike's parents visited Mike and Peggy that afternoon. Mike's father testified that Peggy and Mike were affectionate with each other during the visit. Later, after Mike's parents had left, Mike forced Peggy to perform oral sex. After watching television, Mike and Peggy went to bed at 8:00 P.M. As Mike slept, Peggy thought about suicide and heard voices in her head repeating over and over, "kill or be killed." At this time, there were two vehicles in the driveway and Peggy had access to the car keys. About 10:00 P.M., Peggy went to the spare bedroom and removed the gun from under the mattress, walked back to the bedroom, and killed her husband while he slept. She then ran to the home of a neighbor, who called the police.

When the police questioned Peggy regarding the events leading up to the shooting, Peggy stated that things had not gone quite right that day, and that when she got the chance she hid the gun under the mattress. She stated that she shot Mike to "get this over with, this misery and this torment." When asked why she got the gun out, Peggy stated to the police:

> I'm not sure exactly what . . . led up to it . . . and my head started playing games with me and I got to thinking about things and I said I didn't want to be by myself again. . . . I got the gun out because there had been remarks made about me being out there alone. It was as if Mike was going to do something again like had been done before. He had gotten me down here from McPherson one time and he went and told them that I had done something and he had me put out of the house and was taking everything I had. And it was like he was going to pull the same thing over again.

Two expert witnesses testified during the trial. The expert for the defense, psychologist Marilyn Hutchinson, diagnosed Peggy as suffering from "battered woman syndrome," or post-traumatic stress syndrome. Dr. Hutchinson testified that Mike was preparing to escalate the violence in retaliation for Peggy's running away. She testified that loaded guns, veiled threats, and increased sexual demands are indicators of the escalation of the cycle. Dr. Hutchinson believed Peggy had a repressed knowledge that she was in a "really grave lethal situation."

The State's expert, psychiatrist Herbert Modlin, neither subscribed to a belief in the battered woman syndrome nor to a theory of learned helplessness as an explanation for why women do not leave an abusive relationship. Dr. Modlin testified that abuse such as repeated forced oral sex would not be trauma sufficient to trigger a post-traumatic stress disorder. He also believed Peggy was erroneously diagnosed as suffering from toxic psychosis. He stated that Peggy was unable to escape the abuse because she suffered from schizophrenia, rather than the battered woman syndrome.

At defense counsel's request, the trial judge gave an instruction on self-defense to the jury. The jury found Peggy not guilty.

. . .

The State claims that under the facts the instruction should not have been given because there was no lethal threat to defendant contemporaneous with the killing. The State points out that Peggy's annulment and divorces from former husbands, and her filing for divorce after leaving Mike, proved that Peggy knew there were non-lethal methods by which she could extricate herself from the abusive relationship.

Under the common law, the excuse for killing in self-defense is founded upon ne-

cessity, be it real or apparent. 40 Am. Jur.2d, Homicide § 151, p. 439. Early Kansas cases held that killing in self-defense was justifiable when the defendant had reasonable grounds to believe that an aggressor (1) had a design to take the defendant's life, (2) attempted to execute the design or was in an apparent situation to do so, and (3) induced in the defendant a reasonable belief that he intended to do so immediately. *State v. Horne*, 9 Kan. * 119, * 129 (1872). . . .

These common-law principles were codified in K.S.A. 21-3211, which provides:

A person is justified in the use of force against an aggressor when and to the extent it appears to him and he reasonably believes that such conduct is necessary to defend himself or another against such aggressor's imminent use of unlawful force.

The traditional concept of self-defense has posited one-time conflicts between persons of somewhat equal size and strength. When the defendant claiming self-defense is a victim of long-term domestic violence, such as a battered spouse, such traditional concepts may not apply. Because of the prior history of abuse, and the difference in strength and size between the abused and the abuser, the accused in such cases may choose to defend during a momentary lull in the abuse, rather than during a conflict. However, in order to warrant the giving of a self-defense instruction, the facts of the case must still show that the spouse was in imminent danger close to the time of the killing.

A person is justified in using force against an aggressor when it appears to that person and he or she reasonably believes such force to be necessary. A reasonable belief implies both an honest belief and the existence of facts which would persuade a reasonable person to that belief. K.S.A. 21-3211; *State v. Childers*, 222 Kan. 32, 48, 563 P.2d 999 (1977). A self-defense instruction must be given if there is any evidence to support a claim of self-defense, even if that evidence consists solely of the defendant's testimony. *State v. Hill*, 242 Kan. 68, 78, 744 P.2d 1228 (1987).

Where self-defense is asserted, evidence of the deceased's long-term cruelty and violence towards the defendant is admissible. *State v. Hundley*, 236 Kan. 461, 464, 693 P.2d 475 (1985); *State v. Gray*, 179 Kan. 133, 292 P.2d 698 (1956). In cases involving battered spouses, expert evidence of the battered woman syndrome is relevant to a determination of the reasonableness of the defendant's perception of danger. *State v. Hodges*, 239 Kan. 63, 716 P.2d 563 (1986). Other courts which have allowed such evidence to be introduced include those in Florida, Georgia, Illinois, Maine, New Jersey, New York, Pennsylvania, Washington, and Wisconsin. *See* Johann & Osanka, *I Didn't Mean to Kill Him!*, 14 Barrister 19, 20 (Fall 1987). However, no jurisdictions have held that the existence of the battered woman syndrome in and of itself operates as a defense to murder.

In order to instruct a jury on self-defense, there must be some showing of an imminent threat or a confrontational circumstance involving an overt act by an aggressor. There is no exception to this requirement where the defendant has suffered long-term domestic abuse and the victim is the abuser. In such cases, the issue is not whether the defendant believes homicide is the solution to past or future problems with the batterer, but rather whether circumstances surrounding the killing were sufficient to create a reasonable belief in the defendant that the use of deadly force was necessary.

. . . Here there is an absence of imminent danger to defendant: Peggy told a nurse at the Oklahoma hospital of her desire to kill Mike. She later voluntarily agreed to return home with Mike when he telephoned her. She stated that after leaving the hospital Mike threatened to kill her if she left him again. Peggy showed no inclination to leave. In fact, immediately after the shooting, Peggy told the police that she was upset because she thought Mike would leave her. Prior to the shooting, Peggy hid the loaded gun. The cars were in the driveway and Peggy had access to the car keys. After being abused, Peggy went to bed with Mike at 8 P.M. Peggy lay there for two hours, then retrieved the gun from where she had hidden it and shot Mike while he slept.

Under these facts, the giving of the self-defense instruction was erroneous. Under such circumstances, a battered woman cannot reasonably fear imminent life-threatening danger from her sleeping spouse. We note that other courts have held that the sole fact that the victim was asleep does not preclude a self-defense instruction. In *State v. Norman*, 89 N.C. App. 384, 366 S.E.2d 586 (1988), cited by defendant, the defendant's evidence disclosed a long history of abuse. Each time defendant attempted to escape, her husband found and beat her. On the day of the shooting, the husband beat defendant continually throughout the day, and threatened either to cut her throat, kill her, or cut off her breast. In the afternoon, defendant shot her husband while he napped. The North Carolina Court of Appeals held it was reversible error to fail to instruct on self-defense. The court found that, although decedent was napping at the time defendant shot him, defendant's unlawful act was closely related in time to an assault and threat of death by decedent against defendant and that the decedent's nap was "but a momentary hiatus in a continuous reign of terror." 89 N.C. App. at 394, 366 S.E.2d 586.

. . .[Still,] as one court has stated: "To permit capital punishment to be imposed upon the subjective conclusion of the [abused] individual that prior acts and conduct of the deceased justified the killing would amount to a leap into the abyss of anarchy." *Jahnke v. State*, 682 P.2d 991, 997 (Wyo. 1984). Finally, our legislature has not provided for capital punishment for even the most heinous crimes. We must, therefore, hold that when a battered woman kills her sleeping spouse when there is no imminent danger, the killing is not reasonably necessary and a self-defense instruction may not be given. To hold otherwise in this case would in effect allow the execution of the abuser for past or future acts and conduct.

One additional issue must be addressed. . . . We . . . believe it is necessary to clarify certain portions of our opinion in *State v. Hodges*.

Here, the trial judge gave the instruction approved in *State v. Simon*, 231 Kan. 572, 575, 646 P.2d 1119 (1982), stating:

The defendant has claimed her conduct was justified as self-defense. A person is justified in the use of force against an aggressor when and to the extent it appears to him and he reasonably believes that such conduct is necessary to defend himself or another against such aggressor's imminent use of unlawful force. Such justification requires both a belief on the part of the defendant and the existence of facts that would persuade a reasonable person to that belief.

The trial judge then added the following:

You must determine, from the viewpoint of the defendant's mental state, whether the defendant's belief in the need to defend herself was reasonable in light of her subjective impressions and the facts and circumstances known to her.

This addition was apparently encouraged by the following language in *State v. Hodges:*

Where the battered woman syndrome is an issue in the case, the standard for reasonableness concerning an accused's belief in asserting self-defense is not an objective, but a subjective standard. The jury must determine, from the viewpoint of defendant's mental state, whether defendant's belief in the need to defend herself was reasonable.

The statement that the reasonableness of defendant's belief in asserting self-defense should be measured from the defendant's own individual subjective viewpoint conflicts with prior law. Our test for self-defense is a two-pronged one. We first use a subjective standard to determine whether the defendant sincerely and honestly believed it necessary to kill in order to defend. We then use an objective standard to determine whether defendant's belief was reasonable—specifically, whether a reasonable person in defendant's circumstances would have perceived self-defense as necessary. In *State v. Hundley*, 236 Kan. at 467, we stated that, in cases involving battered spouses, "[t]he objective test is how a reasonably prudent battered wife would perceive [the aggressor's] demeanor."

Hundley makes clear that it was error for the trial court to instruct the jury to employ solely a subjective test in determining the reasonableness of defendant's actions. Insofar as the above-quoted language in *State v. Hodges* can be read to sanction a subjective test, this language is disapproved.

The appeal is sustained.

PRAGER, C.J., dissents.

HERD, Justice, dissenting:

The sole issue before us on the question reserved is whether the trial court erred in giving a jury instruction on self-defense. We have a well-established rule that a defendant is entitled to a self-defense instruction if there is any evidence to support it, even though the evidence consists solely of the defendant's testimony. It is for the jury to determine the sincerity of the defendant's belief she needed to act in self-defense, and the reasonableness of that belief in light of all the circumstances.

It is not within the scope of appellate review to weigh the evidence. An appellate court's function is to merely examine the record and determine if there is *any* evidence to support the theory of self-defense. If the record discloses any competent evidence upon which self-defense could be based, then the instruction must be given. In judging the evidence for this purpose, all inferences should be resolved in favor of the defendant. *State v. Hill*, 242 Kan. at 79, 744 P.2d 1228.

It is evident from prior case law appellee met her burden of showing some competent evidence that she acted in self-defense, thus making her defense a jury question. She testified she acted in fear for her life, and Dr. Hutchinson corroborated this testimony. The evidence of Mike's past abuse, the escalation of violence, his threat of killing her should she attempt to leave him, and Dr. Hutchinson's testimony that appellee was indeed in a "lethal situation" more than met the minimal standard of "any evidence" to allow an instruction to be given to the jury. See *State v. Hill*, 242 Kan. at 78.

Appellee introduced much uncontroverted evidence of the violent nature of the deceased and how he had brutalized her throughout their married life. It is well settled in Kansas that when self-defense is asserted, evidence of the cruel and violent nature of the deceased toward the defendant is admissible. The evidence showed Mike had a "Dr. Jekyll and Mr. Hyde" personality. He was usually very friendly and ingratiating when non-family persons were around, but was belligerent and domineering to family members. He had a violent temper and would blow up without reason. Mike was cruel to his two stepdaughters, Carla and Laura, as well as to the appellee. He took pride in hurting them or anything they held dear, such as their pets. Mike's violence toward appellee and her daughters caused appellee to have emotional problems with symptoms of paranoid schizophrenia. He would overdose appellee on her medication and then cut her off it altogether. Mike's cruelty would culminate in an outburst of violence, and then he would suddenly become very loving and considerate. This was very confusing to appellee. She lived in constant dread of the next outburst.

Appellee became progressively more passive and helpless during the marriage but finally became desperate enough to confront Mike and tell him the cruelty to her daughters had to stop. Mike responded by holding a shotgun to her head and threatening to kill her in front of the girls. The violence escalated. At one point, Mike kicked appellee so violently in the chest and ribs that she required hospitalization.

. . . Mike would not let appellee see her daughters and ran Laura off with a shotgun when she tried to visit. Appellee's life became even more isolated. Towards the end, both the phone and utilities were disconnected from the house.

Appellee finally took the car and ran away to Laura's home in Oklahoma. It was the first time she had ever left Mike without telling him. She was suicidal and again hearing voices, and Laura had her admitted to a hospital. She was diagnosed as having toxic psychosis from a bad reaction to her medication. She soon felt better, but was not fully recovered, when Mike found out where she was and called her to say he was coming to get her. She told a nurse she felt like she wanted to shoot him, but the nurse noted her major emotion was one of hopelessness.

The hospital nevertheless released appellee to Mike's care, and he immediately drove her back to Kansas, telling her on the way she was going to have to "settle down now" and listen to him because he was the boss. *He said if she ever ran away again, he would kill her.*

When they reached the house, Mike would not let appellee bring in her suitcases and forced her to have oral sex four or five times in the next 36 hours, with such violence that the inside of her mouth was bruised. The next morning, appellee found a box of bullets in the car that had not been there before. She then discovered a loaded .357 magnum. This frightened her, because Mike had promised to keep his guns unloaded. She did not know how to unload the gun, so she hid it under the mattress of the bed in a spare room. As she cleaned house, Mike remarked she should not bother, because she would not be there long. He told her she should not bother with her things, because she could not take them with her. She took these statements to mean she would soon be dead and she grew progressively more terrified. Throughout the day Mike continued to force her to have oral sex, while telling her how he preferred sex with other women.

The sexual abuse stopped when Mike's parents came to visit. Mike's father testified everything seemed normal during their stay. After the visit, Mike again forced appellee to perform oral sex and then demanded at 8:00 P.M. she come to bed with him. The cumulative effect of Mike's past history, coupled with his current abusive conduct, justified appellee's belief that a violent explosion was imminent. As he slept, appellee was terrified and thought about suicide and heard voices in her head repeating over and over, "kill or be killed." The voices warned her there was going to be killing and to get away.

She went to the spare bedroom and removed the gun from under the mattress, walked back to the bedroom, and fatally shot Mike. After the first shot, she thought he was coming after her so she shot again and fled wildly outside, barefoot, wearing only her underwear. Ignoring the truck and car outside, although she had the keys in her purse inside, she ran over a mile to the neighbors' house and pled with them to keep Mike from killing her. She thought she had heard him chasing her. The neighbor woman took the gun from appellee's hand and gave her a robe while her husband called the sheriff. The neighbor testified appellee appeared frightened for her life and was certain Mike was alive and looking for her.

. . .

The majority implies its decision is necessary to keep the battered woman syndrome from operating as a defense in and of itself. It has always been clear the syndrome is not a defense itself. Evidence of the syndrome is admissible only because of its relevance to the issue of self-defense. The majority of jurisdictions have held it beyond the ordinary jury's understanding why a battered woman may feel she cannot escape, and have held evidence of the battered woman syndrome proper to explain it. The expert testimony ... assists the jury in evaluating the sincerity of the defendant's belief she was in imminent danger requiring self-defense and whether she was in fact in imminent danger.

Dr. Hutchinson explained to the jury at appellee's trial the "cycle of violence" which induces a state of "learned helplessness" and keeps a battered woman in the relationship.... The woman becomes conditioned to trying to make it through one more violent explosion with its battering in order to be rewarded by the "honeymoon phase," with its expressions of remorse and eternal love and the standard promise of "never again." After all promises are broken time after time and she is beaten again and again, the battered woman falls into a state of learned helplessness where she gives up trying to extract herself from the cycle of violence. She learns fighting back only delays the honeymoon and escalates the violence. If she tries to leave the relationship, she is located and returned and the violence increases. She is a captive. She begins to believe her husband is omnipotent, and resistance will be futile at best.

It is a jury question to determine if the battered woman who kills her husband as he sleeps fears he will find and kill her if she leaves, as is usually claimed. Under such circumstances the battered woman is not under actual physical attack when she kills but such attack is imminent, and as a result she believes her life is in imminent danger. She may kill during the tension-building stage when the abuse is apparently not as severe as it sometimes has been, but nevertheless has escalated so that she is afraid the acute stage to come will be fatal to her. She only acts on such fear if she has some survival instinct remaining after the husband-induced "learned helplessness."...

It was Dr. Hutchinson's opinion Mike was planning to escalate his violence in retaliation against appellee for running away. She testified that Mike's threats against appellee's life, his brutal sexual acts, and appellee's discovery of the loaded gun were all indicators to appellee the violence had escalated and she was in danger. Dr. Hutchinson believed appellee had a repressed knowledge she was in what was really a gravely lethal situation. She testified appellee was convinced she must "kill or be killed."...

The majority claims permitting a jury to consider self-defense under these facts would permit anarchy. This underestimates the jury's ability to recognize an invalid claim of self-defense. Although this is a case of first impression where an appeal by the State has been allowed, there have been several similar cases in which the defendant appealed on other grounds. In each of these cases where a battered woman killed the sleeping batterer, a self-defense instruction has been given when requested by the defendant....

The majority bases its opinion on its conclusion appellee was not in imminent danger, usurping the right of the jury to make that determination of fact. The majority believes a person could not be in imminent danger from an aggressor merely because the aggressor dropped off to sleep. This is a fallacious conclusion. For instance, picture a hostage situation where the armed guard inadvertently drops off to sleep and the hostage grabs his gun and shoots him. The majority opinion would preclude the use of self-defense in such a case.

The majority attempts to buttress its conclusion appellee was not in imminent danger by citing 19th Century law. The old requirement of "immediate" danger is not in accord with our statute on self-defense, K.S.A. 21-3211, and has been emphatically overruled by case law. Yet this standard permeates the majority's reasoning. A review of the law in this state on the requirement of imminent rather than immediate danger to justify self-defense is therefore required. I will limit my discussion to those cases involving battered wives.

The first case, *State v. Hundley*, 236 Kan. 461, 693 P.2d 475 (1985), involved a battered wife who shot her husband when he threatened her and reached for a beer bottle. Hundley pled self-defense. We held it was error for the trial court to instruct that self-defense was justified if a defendant reasonably believed his conduct was necessary to defend himself against an aggressor's *immediate* use of force. We held this instruction improperly excluded from the jury's consideration the effect that Hundley's many years as a battered wife had upon her perception of the dangerousness of her husband's actions. We held the statutory word "imminent" should be used, rather than "immediate."

The next case in which a battered wife claimed self-defense was *State v. Osbey*, 238 Kan. 280, 710 P.2d 676 (1985). The husband had a gun and had threatened to kill Osbey. After an argument while the husband was moving out, Osbey threw a chair towards his van. She shot him when he walked towards her and reached behind some record albums he was carrying. We again held the trial court erred in using the word "immediate" rather than "imminent" in the self-defense instruction to the jury.

In the most recent case, *State v. Hodges*, 239 Kan. 63, 716 P.2d 563 (1986), the battered wife was kicked and beaten before making her way into another room. When her husband ordered her to return to him, she shot him. When her first trial resulted in a hung jury, she was retried and convicted of voluntary manslaughter.

On appeal, we again held the trial court's use of "immediate" in instructing the jury on self-defense was reversible er-

ror. Such usage "places undue emphasis on the decedent's immediate conduct and obliterates the build-up of terror and fear the decedent systematically injected into the relationship over a long period of time." 239 Kan. at 74. We also held the trial court erred in not permitting expert testimony on the battered woman syndrome. We found it appropriate that the testimony be offered to prove the reasonableness of the defendant's belief she was in imminent danger. . . .

The majority disapproves *State v. Hodges*, where we adopted the subjective test for self-defense in battered wife cases. We adopted the subjective test because there is a contradiction in the terms "reasonably prudent battered wife." One battered into "learned helplessness" cannot be characterized as reasonably prudent. Hence, the *Hodges* modification of *State v. Hundley* was necessary and properly states the law.

In *State v. Hundley*, we joined other enlightened jurisdictions in recognizing that the jury in homicide cases where a battered woman ultimately kills her batterer is entitled to all the facts about the battering relationship in rendering its verdict. The jury also needs to know about the nature of the cumulative terror under which a battered woman exists and that a batterer's threats and brutality can make life-threatening danger imminent to the victim of that brutality even though, at the moment, the batterer is passive. Where a person believes she must kill or be killed, and there is the slightest basis in fact for this belief, it is a question for the jury as to whether the danger was imminent. I confess I am an advocate for the constitutional principle that in a criminal prosecution determination of the facts is a function of the jury, not the appellate court.

I would deny this appeal.

CASE QUESTIONS

1. Was it objectively reasonable for Peggy Stewart to fear that her life was in imminent danger when her husband had just recaptured her after she had run away, had threatened to kill her if she ever ran away again, had a loaded gun in the car, had repeatedly implied that she would soon be dead (e.g., by saying that she would not be around for long), and had previously subjected her to numerous brutal injuries? The majority stresses that she could have taken the car and driven away. Was it reasonable for her to expect that a second escape would be more successful? Might she have simply driven to the police and told them of the threats? In light of her history of mental illness and Mike's success at being "friendly and ingratiating to nonfamily persons," might she reasonably expect failure at having the police restrain Mike?

2. Why did the majority not view Dr. Hutchinson's assessment that Peggy was in a "really grave lethal situation" as indicating "evidence sufficient to create a reasonable belief.... [that Peggy faced] imminent life-threatening danger"? Why didn't such statements as "You won't be here for long, anyway" count as an "imminent threat"?

3. Is the phrase "reasonably prudent battered wife" in fact a contradiction in terms? What is the meaning of "reasonable in light of [a given person's] subjective impressions"?

4. The majority warns against "self-defense" rules that would free every battered wife to kill her husband. Why should that be a concern in a case where shortly before the killing, the battering husband had threatened both explicitly and implicitly to kill his wife?

Pornography, Obscenity, and Hate Speech

Since the Supreme Court's earliest exposition of First Amendment law, the Court has consistently held that not all uses of words are covered by the phrase "freedom of speech or of the press." If a particular use of words has "the effect of force"—as in, for instance, inciting a murder-prone person to murder—those words in those circumstances are not considered protected by the Constitution.[14] About fifty years ago, the Supreme Court added to this rule, the additional rule that certain categories of speech and press are not protected by the First Amendment. The Court explained:

> There are certain well-defined and narrowly limited classes of speech, the prevention and punishment of which have never been thought to raise any

Constitutional problem. These include the lewd and obscene, the profane, the libelous, and the insulting or "fighting" words—those which by their very utterance inflict injury or tend to incite an immediate breach of the peace. It has been well observed that such utterances are no essential part of any exposition of ideas, and are of such slight social value as a step to truth that any benefit that may be derived from them is clearly outweighed by the social interest in order and morality. [They] . . . are not in any proper sense communication of information or opinion . . ."[15]

As of 1993, the Court continues to rule (and has never ruled otherwise) that the libelous, the obscene, and "fighting" words remain unprotected categories of speech or press. However, the justices have varied the definitions of these terms over the years and in that way have expanded or contracted the freedom to say things that are arguably "fighting" words or to print the arguably libelous or obscene.

Obscenity Doctrine

While feminists were by no means unanimous on the subject, numerous feminists in the 1970s and 1980s engaged in a variety of campaigns against the multibillion dollar pornography industry on the grounds that pornography, in depicting women as mere body parts meant for men's pleasure, debased women in the minds of the public and encouraged, both implicitly and explicitly, sexual violence against women. Since legally "obscene" books, pamphlets, and movies are *not* protected by the First Amendment, and are in fact outlawed in every state, one might wonder why there is a pornography problem in the first place.

The answer to this is twofold. Beginning in 1966, part of the problem could be blamed on a Supreme Court opinion that defined "obscenity" so narrowly that virtually nothing could be squeezed into the definition.[16] In that case obscenity was said to be, among other things, material that was "*utterly* without redeeming social importance." Since even the most hard-core pornography has entertainment value for someone, this standard ended up opening the commercial floodgates for pornography.

Reacting to the situation, the Supreme Court in 1973 widened the definition somewhat.[17] The Court replaced the rule "utterly without importance" with a rule that said that to be judged obscene a work would have to, "taken as a whole, lack[] serious literary, artistic, political, or scientific value."[18] In addition, two other tests have to be applied to determine obscenity. First, the judge must determine "whether the average [adult] person applying contemporary community standards would find that the work, taken as a whole, appeals to the prurient interest [in sex]."[19] In an earlier case, the Court had referred readers to a dictionary definition of *prurient*; in part it read: "Itching; longing; uneasy with desire or longing . . . ."[20] Second, the judge must decide "whether the work depicts or describes, in a patently offensive way, sexual conduct specifically defined by applicable state law."²¹ (One of several examples of "sexual conduct" that the Court listed as possibilities for inclusion in state statutes that itemize what may not be offensively depicted was "lewd exhibition of the genitals.")²² If a work fails both these tests and also lacks "serious importance," then it is legally obscene and may be banned.

In addition to altering the legal definition of the obscene, so as to make more works proscribable, the Court in 1973 also reiterated why obscenity was punishable under the First Amendment. It was not, Chief Justice Burger explained, in any meaningful sense "communication of ideas"; rather, it was "crass commercial exploitation of sex." People who buy and sell obscenity are not engaged in the exchange of ideas (or money for the expression of ideas) but rather are simply trafficking in titillation.²³ Moreover, there is an identifiable harm or set of harms attributable to obscenity; it debases the public environment in our commercial centers; one can reasonably believe that it promotes antisocial behavior; and, because what people read and view affects their attitudes, "a sensitive key relationship of human existence [i.e., the intimate one between a man and a woman] . . . can be debased and distorted,"²⁴ through the prevalence of pornographic works in our society. Thus, it was punishable, despite the First Amendment.

Since it is obvious that much if not all of hard-core pornography can be easily judged obscene under the three-part test adopted in these 1973 cases, one may wonder why so much of it is still openly marketed. While judicial leniency is useful for explaining the 1966–1973 pornography boom, it really cannot carry the explanatory burden after this point. To do that, societal attitudes have to be brought into the picture. Most communities and most prosecutors in the 1970s and 1980s were not interested in spending scarce public funds to prosecute and imprison pornographers. And many juries were simply unwilling to convict, even for showing films of the standard porn genre, such as *Deep Throat.* ·

Anti-Pornography Ordinances: *American Booksellers Association v. Hudnut* (1985)

Two feminist authors and activists, Catharine MacKinnon and Andrea Dworkin, who are firmly convinced that the widespread availability and viewing of pornography really do hurt women, have developed an anti-pornography strategy aimed at coping with the apparent reluctance of the American public to apply the machinery of the criminal justice system to censor pornography. They define "pornography" somewhat differently from the Court's definition of obscenity, and they have argued for making such pornography actionable in civil suits brought by individual women who felt they were being harmed or had been harmed by pornography. The civil suits could pursue both "cease and desist" court orders and compensatory damages. Thus, MacKinnon argued, women, rather than government as such, would be empowered. And something that does harm to women could be checked.

Moreover, in the model ordinance that they proposed, MacKinnon and Dworkin described pornography as illegal on the grounds that it was *sex discrimination*. This legal strategy, taking a species of speech with some linkage to sexual violence and defining it in law as forbidden sex discrimination, had proved strikingly effective for MacKinnon with regard to sexual harassment. She had advocated precisely that approach in a 1979 book, *Sexual Harassment of Working Women: A Case of Sex Discrimination*,[25] and the U.S. Supreme Court embraced the idea as the law of the land by 1986 (as described in chapter 4 above). When applied to pornography, however, this strategy was not to prove so successful with the judiciary.

After extensive lobbying in conjunction with a variegated coalition of interest groups (some feminist, some church-related, some extremely traditional conservative), MacKinnon and Dworkin did succeed in persuading the city of Indianapolis to adopt an anti-pornography ordinance along the lines described above.

The phenomenon of *pornography* as defined in the Indianapolis ordinance differed from the judicial definition of *obscenity* in a number of respects. A comparison of the two terms follows the description of the Indianapolis statute, below.

The Indianapolis law defined *pornography* as the *graphic sexually explicit* subordination of women [emphasis added], whether in pictures or words, that also includes one or more of the following:

(1) Women are presented as sexual objects who enjoy pain or humiliation; or
(2) Women are presented as sexual objects who experience sexual pleasure in being raped; or
(3) Women are presented as sexual objects tied up or cut up or mutilated or bruised or physically hurt, or as dismembered or truncated or fragmented or severed into body parts; or
(4) Women are presented as being penetrated by objects or animals; or
(5) Women are presented in scenarios of degradation, injury, abasement, torture, shown as filthy or inferior, bleeding, bruised, or hurt in a context that makes these conditions sexual; or
(6) Women are presented as sexual objects for domination, conquest, violation, exploitation, possession, or use, or through postures or positions of servility or submission or display.[26]

The statute added that the "use of men, children, or transsexuals in the place of women" in these six paragraphs also would constitute pornography.

The ordinance then prohibited four acts with regard to pornography as so defined. The first was "trafficking," defined as "production, sale, exhibition [except in special displays in libraries], or distribution of pornography [of the types described in categories 1-5 above][27] The second was "coercion into pornographic performance," defined as "coercing, intimidating, or fraudulently inducing someone into performing for pornography."[28] Third was "forcing pornography on any woman, man, child, or transsexual in any place of employment, in education, in a home, or in any public place."[29] Finally, the production or sale of any piece of pornography that "directly causes" an "assault, physical attack, or injury" of anyone renders the producer or seller of that pornography liable to the injured person for damages.[30]

The concept of pornography that is employed in this statute differs from judicially defined obscenity in three ways. First, where obscenity speaks of the [mysterious and paradoxical] combination of *appeal* to prurient interest in sex, with patent *offensiveness* in degree of explicitness about sex, the pornography definition speaks simply of being "graphic [and] sexually explicit" (avoiding the seemingly contradictory rule that a thing be appealing and repellent at the same time). However, while the phraseology differs, up to this point there does not seem to be a difference of principle between the two terms. In other words, they describe essentially the same material.

The second difference is one of substance. The Supreme Court takes the general category of material that is offensively explicit about sex in a way that arouses a longing for sex—i.e., that is erotically explicit—and divides it into two parts: that which is obscene—the part that lacks serious artistic or other importance—and that which is not obscene—those works of serious literary, artistic, political, or scientific importance that happen to be erotically explicit. The Indianapolis ordinance did not make this division; *all* erotically explicit work was eligible for the pornography label if it had the additional trait of displaying the subordination of women through this graphic sexual portrayal.

This last trait made for the third difference between the two concepts. Some material that was legally obscene (because it was erotically explicit and lacked artistic or other serious value)—in other words, that was constitutionally punishable—would not be punished by the Indianapolis ordinance because it had an egalitarian message. Only if it somehow endorsed the subjugation of women through sex was it actionable as pornography. On the other hand some material that was not constitutionally punishable—that the First Amendment protected *because* it was the serious exchange of ideas, despite its sexually explicit medium—would be punishable under the Indianapolis ordinance (because it was sexually explicit and downgraded women). Because of this last fact, it was utterly predictable that federal courts would throw out the law. This prediction would not surprise the authors of the statute; their hope was to persuade the federal courts to alter existing First Amendment doctrine on the grounds that pornography causes great harm. While they did not succeed, the anti-pornography campaign is by no means over. The *American Booksellers* case is best thought of as only the first major battle in a long-term war on pornography that continues even as this book goes to press.

This battle had three phases. In phase one, Federal District Court Judge Sara Evans Hughes threw out the ordinance as unconstitutional in response to a suit by the American Booksellers Association, the Association for American publishers, and various other interested parties against the Mayor of Indianapolis, William Hudnut.[31] In phase two, a three judge panel of the federal circuit court of appeals unanimously affirmed Hughes's judgment that the statute was unconstitutional (this opinion is excerpted below). In phase three, without even bothering to hear oral argument or to write an explanatory opinion, the U.S. Supreme Court affirmed the circuit court judgement.[32]

American Booksellers Ass'n, Inc. v. Hudnut, 771 F.2d 323 (7th Cir. 1985)

FRANK H. EASTERBROOK, Circuit Judge:

. . .

III

"If there is any fixed star in our constitutional constellation, it is that no official, high or petty, can prescribe what shall be orthodox in politics, nationalism, religion, or other matters of opinion or force citizens to confess by word or act their faith therein." *West Virginia State Board of Education v. Barnette*, 319 U.S. 624, 642 (1943). Under the First Amendment the government must leave to the people the evaluation of ideas. Bald or subtle, an idea is as powerful as the audience allows it to be. A belief may be pernicious—the beliefs of Nazis led to the death of millions, those of the Klan to the repression of millions. A pernicious belief may prevail. Totalitarian governments today rule much of the planet, practicing suppression of billions and spreading dogma that may enslave others. One of the things that separates our society from theirs is our absolute right to propagate opinions that the government finds wrong or even hateful.

The ideas of the Klan may be propagated. *Brandenburg v. Ohio*, 395 U.S. 444 (1969). Communists may speak freely and run for office. *DeJonge v. Oregon*, 299 U.S. 353 (1937). The Nazi Party may march through a city with a large Jewish population. *Collin v. Smith*, 578 F.2d 1197 (7th Cir.), *cert. denied*, 439 U.S. 916 (1978). People may criticize the President by misrepresenting his positions, and they have a right to post their misrepresentations on public property. *Lebron v. Washington Metropolitan Area Transit Authority*, 749 F.2d 893 (D.C. Cir. 1984) (Bork, J.). People may teach religions that others despise. People may seek to repeal laws guaranteeing equal opportunity in employment or to revoke the constitutional amendments granting the vote to blacks and women. They may do this because "above all else, the First Amendment means that government has no power to restrict expression because of its message [or] its ideas. . . ." *Police Department v. Mosley*, 408 U.S. 92, 95 (1972). *See also* Geoffrey R. Stone, *Content Regulation and the First Amendment*, 25 William & Mary L. Rev. 189 (1983); Paul B. Stephan, *The First Amendment and Content Discrimination*, 68 Va. L. Rev. 203, 233–36 (1982).

Under the ordinance graphic sexually explicit speech is "pornography" or not depending on the perspective the author adopts. Speech that "subordinates" women and also, for example, presents women as enjoying pain, humiliation, or rape, or even simply presents women in "positions of servility or submission or display" is forbidden, no matter how great the literary or political value of the work taken as a whole. Speech that portrays women in positions of equality is lawful, no matter how graphic the sexual content. This is thought control. It establishes an "approved" view of women, of how they may react to sexual encounters, of how the sexes may relate to each other. Those who espouse the approved view may use sexual images; those who do not, may not.

Indianapolis justifies the ordinance on the ground that pornography affects thoughts. Men who see women depicted as subordinate are more likely to treat them so. Pornography is an aspect of dominance.[1] It does not persuade people so much as change them. It works by socializing, by establishing the expected and the permissible. In this view pornography is not an idea; pornography is the injury.

There is much to this perspective. Beliefs are also facts. People often act in accordance with the images and patterns they find around them. People raised in a religion tend to accept the tenets of that religion, often without independent examination. People taught from birth that black people are fit only for slavery rarely rebelled against that creed; beliefs coupled with the self-interest of the masters established a social structure that inflicted great harm while enduring for centuries. Words and images act at the level of the subconscious before they persuade at the level of the conscious. Even the truth has little chance unless a statement fits within the framework of beliefs that may never have been subjected to rational study.

Therefore we accept the premises of this legislation. Depictions of subordination tend to perpetuate subordination. The subordinate status of women in turn leads to affront and lower pay at work, insult and injury at home, battery and rape on the streets.[2] In the language of the legislature, "[p]ornography is central in creating and

---

1. "Pornography constructs what a woman is in terms of its view of what men want sexually.... Pornography's world of equality is a harmonious and balanced place. Men and women are perfectly complementary and perfectly bipolar.... All the ways men love to take and violate women, women love to be taken and violated.... What pornography *does* goes beyond its content: It eroticizes hierarchy, it sexualizes inequality. It makes dominance and submission sex. Inequality is its central dynamic; the illusion of freedom coming together with the reality of force is central to its working.... [P]ornography is neither harmless fantasy nor a corrupt and confused misrepresentation of an otherwise neutral and healthy sexual situation. It institutionalizes the sexuality of male supremacy, fusing the erotization of dominance and submission with the social construction of male and female.... Men treat women as who they see women as

being. Pornography constructs who that is. Men's power over women means that the way men see women defines who women can be. Pornography ... is a sexual reality." Catharine MacKinnon, *Pornography, Civil Rights, and Speech,* 20 Harv. Civ. Rts.–Civ. Lib. L. Rev. 1, 17–18 (1985).*See also* Andrea Dworkin, *Pornography: Men Possessing Women* (1981)....

2. MacKinnon's article collects empirical work that supports this proposition. The social science studies are very difficult to interpret, however, and they conflict. Because much of the effect of speech comes through a process of socialization, it is difficult to measure incremental benefits and injuries caused by particular speech. Several psychologists have found, for example, that those who see violent, sexually explicit films tend to

maintaining sex as a basis of discrimination. Pornography is a systematic practice of exploitation and subordination based on sex which differentially harms women. The bigotry and contempt it produces, with the acts of aggression it fosters, harm women's opportunities for equality and rights [of all kinds]." Indianapolis Code § 16-1(a)(2).

Yet this simply demonstrates the power of pornography as speech. All of these unhappy effects depend on mental intermediation. Pornography affects how people see the world, their fellows, and social relations. If pornography is what pornography does, so is other speech. Hitler's orations affected how some Germans saw Jews. Communism is a world view, not simply a *Manifesto* by Marx and Engels or a set of speeches. Efforts to suppress communist speech in the United States were based on the belief that the public acceptability of such ideas would increase the likelihood of totalitarian government. Religions affect socialization in the most pervasive way. The opinion in *Wisconsin v. Yoder*, 406 U.S. 205 (1972), shows how a religion can dominate an entire approach to life, governing much more than the relation between the sexes. Many people believe that the existence of television, apart from the content of specific programs, leads to intellectual lazi-

---

have more violent thoughts. But how often does this lead to actual violence? National commissions on obscenity here, in the United Kingdom, and in Canada have found that it is not possible to demonstrate a direct link between obscenity and rape or exhibitionism. The several opinions in *Miller v. California* discuss the U.S. commission.... In saying that we accept the finding that pornography as the ordinance defines it leads to unhappy consequences, we mean only that there is evidence to this effect, that this evidence is consistent with much human experience, and that as judges we must accept the legislative resolution of such disputed empirical questions....

ness, to a penchant for violence, to many other ills. The Alien and Sedition Acts passed during the administration of John Adams rested on a sincerely held belief that disrespect for the government leads to social collapse and revolution—a belief with support in the history of many nations. Most governments of the world act on this empirical regularity, suppressing critical speech. In the United States, however, the strength of the support for this belief is irrelevant. Seditious libel is protected speech unless the danger is not only grave but also imminent. See *New York Times Co. v. Sullivan*, 376 U.S. 254 (1964); cf. *Brandenburg v. Ohio, supra; New York Times Co. v. United States*, 403 U.S. 713 (1971).

Racial bigotry, anti-semitism, violence on television, reporters' biases—these and many more influence the culture and shape our socialization. None is directly answerable by more speech, unless that speech too finds its place in the popular culture. Yet all is protected as speech, however insidious. Any other answer leaves the government in control of all of the institutions of culture, the great censor and director of which thoughts are good for us.

Sexual responses often are unthinking responses, and the association of sexual arousal with the subordination of women therefore may have a substantial effect. But almost all cultural stimuli provoke unconscious responses. Religious ceremonies condition their participants. Teachers convey messages by selecting what not to cover; the implicit message about what is off limits or unthinkable may be more powerful than the messages for which they present rational argument. Television scripts contain unarticulated assumptions. People may be conditioned in subtle ways. If the fact that speech plays a role in a process of conditioning were enough to permit governmental regulation, that would be the end of freedom of speech.

It is possible to interpret the claim that the pornography is the harm in a different way. Indianapolis emphasizes the injury that models in pornographic films and pictures may suffer. The record contains materials depicting sexual torture, penetration of women by red-hot irons and the like. These concerns have nothing to do with written materials subject to the statute, and physical injury can occur with or without the "subordination" of women. As we discuss in Part IV, a state may make injury in the course of producing a film unlawful independent of the viewpoint expressed in the film.

The more immediate point, however, is that the image of pain is not necessarily pain. In *Body Double*, a suspense film directed by Brian DePalma, a woman who has disrobed and presented a sexually explicit display is murdered by an intruder with a drill. The drill runs through the woman's body. The film is sexually explicit and a murder occurs—yet no one believes that the actress suffered pain or died. . . . Depictions may affect slavery, war, or sexual roles, but a book about slavery is not itself slavery, or a book about death by poison a murder. . . .

A power to limit speech on the ground that truth has not yet prevailed and is not likely to prevail implies the power to declare truth. At some point the government must be able to say (as Indianapolis has said): "We know what the truth is, yet a free exchange of speech has not driven out falsity, so that we must now prohibit falsity." If the government may declare the truth, why wait for the failure of speech? Under the First Amendment, however, there is no such thing as a false idea, *Gertz v. Robert Welch, Inc.*, 418 U.S. 323, 339 (1974) . . . .

We come, finally, to the argument that pornography is "low value" speech, that it is enough like obscenity that Indianapolis may prohibit it. Some cases hold that speech far removed from politics and other

subjects at the core of the Framers' concerns may be subjected to special regulation. E.g., *FCC v. Pacifica Foundation*, 438 U.S. 726 (1978); *Young v. American Mini Theatres, Inc.*, 427 U.S. 50, 67–70 (1976) (plurality opinion); *Chaplinsky v. New Hampshire*, 315 U.S. 568, 571–72 (1942). These cases do not sustain statutes that select among viewpoints, however. In *Pacifica* the FCC sought to keep vile language off the air during certain times. The Court held that it may; but the Court would not have sustained a regulation prohibiting scatological descriptions of Republicans but not scatological descriptions of Democrats, or any other form of selection among viewpoints.

At all events, "pornography" is not low value speech within the meaning of these cases. Indianapolis seeks to prohibit certain speech because it believes this speech influences social relations and politics on a grand scale, that it controls attitudes at home and in the legislature. This precludes a characterization of the speech as low value. True, pornography and obscenity have sex in common. But Indianapolis left out of its definition any reference to literary, artistic, political, or scientific value. The ordinance applies to graphic sexually explicit subordination in works great and small.[3] The Court sometimes balances the

3. Indianapolis briefly argues that *Beauharnais v. Illinois*, 343 U.S. 250 (1952), which allowed a state to penalize "group libel," supports the ordinance. In *Collin v. Smith, supra*, 578 F.2d at 1205, we concluded that cases such as *New York Times v. Sullivan* had so washed away the foundations of *Beauharnais* that it could not be considered authoritative. If we are wrong in this, however, the case still does not support the ordinance. It is not clear that depicting women as subordinate in sexually explicit ways, even combined with a depiction of pleasure in rape, would fit within the definition of a group libel. The well received film *Swept Away* used explicit

value of speech against the costs of its restriction, but it does this by category of speech and not by the content of particular works.... Indianapolis has created an approved point of view and so loses the support of these cases.

Any rationale we could imagine in support of this ordinance could not be limited to sex discrimination. Free speech has been on balance an ally of those seeking change. Governments that want stasis start by restricting speech. Culture is a powerful force of continuity; Indianapolis paints pornography as part of the culture of power. Change in any complex system ultimately depends on the ability of outsiders to challenge accepted views and the reigning institutions. Without a strong guarantee of freedom of speech, there is no effective right to challenge what is.

IV

The definition of "pornography" is unconstitutional. No construction or excision of particular terms could save it. The offense of trafficking in pornography necessarily falls with the definition....

Section 8 of the ordinance is a strong severability clause, and Indianapolis asks that we parse the ordinance to save what we can. If a court could do this by surgical excision, this might be possible. But a federal court may not completely reconstruct a

---

sex, plus taking pleasure in rape, to make a political statement, not to defame....

local ordinance, and we conclude that nothing short of rewriting could save anything.

The offense of coercion to engage in a pornographic performance, for example, has elements that might be constitutional. Without question a state may prohibit fraud, trickery, or the use of force to induce people to perform—in pornographic films or in any other films. Such a statute may be written without regard to the viewpoint depicted in the work....

But the Indianapolis ordinance, unlike our hypothetical statute, is not neutral with respect to viewpoint. The ban on distribution of works containing coerced performances is limited to pornography; coercion is irrelevant if the work is not "pornography," and we have held the definition of "pornography" to be defective root and branch. A legislature might replace "pornography" in § 16-3(g)(4) with "any film containing explicit sex" or some similar expression, but even the broadest severability clause does not permit a federal court to rewrite as opposed to excise. Rewriting is work for the legislature of Indianapolis....

No amount of struggle with particular words and phrases in this ordinance can leave anything in effect. The district court came to the same conclusion. Its judgment is therefore

Affirmed.

LUTHER M. SWYGERT, Senior Circuit Judge, concurring. [Opinion omitted. Au.]

CASE QUESTIONS

1. Suppose Indianapolis were to repass this ordinance but substitute the Supreme Court's obscenity definition (offensively explicit depictions of sex, calculated to appeal to prurient interest, and lacking a serious degree of redeeming impor-

tance) for the phrase "graphic, sexually explicit," while keeping all the other qualifiers about being degrading to women in one or another way. Would the law then be constitutional? In other words, would it be constitutional to ban only some (rather than all) materials that are legally obscene—those that eroticize violence toward women or that eroticize subjugation of women? If it would, why does Judge Easterbrook pay so much attention to the rule that the First Amendment does not allow laws that restrict the expression of particular points of view? Is

it because this law included in its proscription material that was of "serious literary, artistic, political, or scientific value" along with obvious trash?

2. Consider footnote 3. Libel, in current American law, is material that damages someone's reputation by falsehood. Is it plausible to claim that the kind of pornography punished in this statute is libelous to women as a group? Would it be more plausible if the statute exempted serious works of art, science, and so forth?

Hate Speech and the Future of Pornography Laws: *R.A.V. v. St. Paul* (1992)

In June of 1992, a five-justice majority that included the vote of Clarence Thomas (the lone black justice on the Supreme Court), in the face of heated criticism in a concurrence from the other four justices, handed down an implicit answer to "Case Question #1" above. According to the four critics, this answer contained "serious departures from the teaching of prior cases" and "cast[] aside long-established First Amendment doctrine."[33]

The legal question directly posed in the *R.A.V.* case involved not pornography but expressive conduct conveying hatred for certain kinds of groups. "R.A.V." was a juvenile who had, along with some other teenagers, burned a cross in the yard of a black family in violation of St. Paul's law making it a misdemeanor to place on any property "a symbol, object, appellation, characterization or graffiti, including but not limited to, a burning cross or Nazi swastika, which one knows or has reasonable grounds to know arouses anger, alarm or resentment in others on the basis of race, color, creed, religion or gender."[34] In interpreting this law the Minnesota Supreme Court had ruled that it covered only "fighting words," which are not protected by the First Amendment. The U.S. Supreme Court had earlier defined "fighting words" as "words which by their very nature inflict injury or tend to incite an immediate breach of the peace."[35] In *R.A.V.*, the five-justice majority on the U.S. Supreme Court ruled that even if the statute banned only (unprotected) fighting words, it was unconstitutional for a government to pick and choose among different viewpoints within the unprotected speech category.[36]

According to the *R.A.V.* majority, despite the Court's *Chaplinsky* precedent, which had established that the categories of unprotected speech (obscenity, fighting words, libel) "are no essential part of any exposition of ideas,"[37] it is nonetheless unconstitutional to ban a part of an unprotected category on the grounds of disapproval of the idea expressed in it.[38] The majority argued that such a ban was an attempt at governmental thought control and therefore disapproved by the First Amendment.

This argument by the *R.A.V.* majority seems to indicate that a statute that banned only those obscene materials showing sexual violence against women or subjugation of women would be unconstitutional (for the sorts of reasons outlined by Judge Easterbrook). On the other hand, the *R.A.V.* majority left a few loopholes against this inference.

One loophole they described as follows:

> When the basis for the content discrimination consists entirely of the very reason the entire class of speech at issue is proscribable, no significant danger of idea or viewpoint discrimination exists. . . . To illustrate: a State might choose to prohibit only that obscenity which is the most patently offensive *in its prurience—i.e.*, that which involves the most lascivious displays of sexual activity. But it may not prohibit, for example, only that obscenity which includes offensive *political* messages.[39]

In order to fit into this loophole, an Indianapolis-type ordinance modified along the lines already suggested (making it a partial ban on constitutionally unprotected "obscenity") would have to be defended on the grounds that those types of obscenity (the ones eroticizing violence toward, and subjugation of, women) were the most disruptive of "the social interest in order and morality" (taking "morality" in its broad sense—decent treatment of other people).

A second possible loophole into which modified Indianapolis-type ordinances might be fit was outlined by the Court majority as follows:

> [A] particular content-based subcategory of a proscribable class of speech can be swept up incidentally within the reach of a statute directed at conduct rather than speech. . . . Thus, for example, sexually-derogatory "fighting words," among other words, may produce a violation of Title VII's general prohibition against sexual discrimination in employment practices. . . . Where the government does not target conduct on the basis of its expressive content, acts are not shielded from regulation merely because they express a discriminatory idea or philosophy.[40]

Proponents of a modified Indianapolis-type ordinance who wanted to utilize this loophole would need to be able to make a persuasive case that the prevalence of the kinds of obscenity they were banning contributed in a substantial way to employment and educational discrimination against women (both of which are forbidden in federal law).

Neither of the efforts described here is in principle impossible, but it does appear that the *R.A.V.* decision has thrown new obstacles into the path of proponents of Indianapolis-style anti-obscenity laws.

Conclusion

Rather than conclude this study, my preference is to invite the reader to continue to explore the subject through other works. I will, however, offer a few concluding reflections.

A pattern is discernible in the willingness of the U.S. Supreme Court to announce policy innovations that expand the rights of women. The decade of the 1970s showed that willingness at a peak; the Burger Court announced dramatic changes in the meaning of the Constitution, such that women's rights to gender equity and to reproductive freedom both came into being and had a substantial impact on public policy. The decade of the 1980s was essentially an era of consolidation; the Supreme Court stayed away from innovating in constitutional interpretation on this subject. The Supreme Court has decided no constitutional gender equity case since 1984. On reproductive freedom, the Court in the late 1980s appeared willing to abandon *Roe v. Wade*, but by 1992, in *Planned Parenthood v. Casey*, declared that it would maintain the essential holding of *Roe* (a woman's right to seek an abortion, free from undue governmental interference, up to the point of fetal viability). While the Court upholds the basic right, it does allow what it views as minor restrictions on the right, such as a twenty-four-hour waiting period prior to the abortion and state rules commanding that a woman be told the various risks of abortion, the facts of fetal development, and so on.

Where the Supreme Court has shown, on at least some occasions, a continuing willingness to innovate on behalf of women's rights has been in statutory interpretation. In 1986, the Supreme Court endorsed the idea that sexual harassment of working women did count as sex discrimination under the Civil Rights Act of 1964 (*Meritor Savings v. Vinson*). In 1987, the Supreme Court upheld an employer's affirmative action plan for hiring women, despite a claim of a male job-seeker that the plan was forbidden by the Civil Rights Act's prohibition on sex discrimination in employment (*Johnson v. Transportation Agency*, 480 U.S. 616). In 1988 the Supreme Court indicated that employers who require female employees to conform to certain norms of ladylike behavior just because they are female are violating the Civil Rights Act's prohibition on sex discrimination in the terms of employment (*Price Waterhouse v. Hopkins*). And in 1992, the Supreme Court reasoned that a student who felt she had been the victim of sex discrimination (specifically, sexual harassment) by her public school authorities could bring a lawsuit for monetary damages under Title IX of the Education Amendments of 1972, even though Title IX mentions neither lawsuits by victims of discrimination nor suits for money damages (*Franklin v. Gwinnett County*). While the Court's recent willingness to innovate on behalf of pro-woman's-rights readings of statutes has not been unwavering, it is safe to say that the contemporary Supreme Court generally arrives at these readings when it feels confident that Congress will go along with them (even if Congress may not have had the particular interpretation in mind when it first adopted the law in question—as with, for example, sexual harassment).

On the other hand, the arena where one witnesses more daring innovations expanding the legal rights of women in the 1980s and 1990s is at the level of state supreme courts, and even in lower level federal courts. There one sees courts proclaiming such things as a substitution of a "reasonable woman" test in place of the old "reasonable man" test in the context of rape or of husband-killing by battered women, a right of women to refuse compulsory caesarean operations even when they are needed to save the life of a near-term fetus, and a right of the natural mother to retain custody of her child even if she has signed a pre-birth contract abandoning such custody. The lower courts are not uniform in these proclamations, but this pattern does show that these courts are functioning as laboratories for experimentation and policy innovation.

The reader is invited to pursue these and other matters further. Good overviews are available on the general subject of women and American law, among them Deborah Rhode's *Justice and Gender: Sex Discrimination and the Law*, Judith Baer's *Women in American Law*, and Susan Gluck Mezey's *In Pursuit of Equality: Women, Public Policy, and the Federal Courts*. On particular topics, the reader may wish to explore subjects that did not fit into the contours of this book, such as women and the criminal law. (Good starting points are Nicole Hahn Rafter and Elizabeth Anne Stanko, eds., *Judge, Lawyer, Victim, Thief: Women, Gender Roles, and Criminal Justice*, and Susette Talarico's "Women as Offenders and Victims in Criminal Justice" in Beverly B. Cook et al., *Women in the Judicial Process*.) Another important topic is the set of inequities facing women in the law of divorce and child custody. (See, for example, Lenore Weitzman's *The Divorce Revolution* and Martha Fineman's *The Illusion of Equality: The Rhetoric and Reality of Divorce Reform*.) And a number of good collections are available on the more theoretical topic of feminist jurisprudence (Patricia Smith, ed., *Feminist Jurisprudence*; Katharine Bartlett and Roseanne Kennedy, eds., *Feminist Legal Theory*; Leslie F. Goldstein, ed., *Feminist Jurisprudence: The Difference Debate*; Linda Nicholson, ed. *Feminism/Post-Modernism*; and Catharine MacKinnon, *Toward a Feminist Theory of the State*).

The cases collected here reveal what is really only the tip of a sizable iceberg of the body of law on the subject of women's rights. The collection is offered in the hope that it has tempted the reader to delve more deeply into the subject.

Notes

Appendices

Case Index

Notes

Chapter 1. Historical Evolution of the Right of Privacy

1. 410 U.S. 113. *Roe* was decided as part of a pair of cases; the other was *Doe v. Bolton* 410 U.S. 179. Before these U.S. Supreme Court rulings, four states had legalized abortion by statute in 1970: Hawaii, Alaska, New York, and Washington. Also, federal or state courts had declared unconstitutional the criminal abortion laws of the District of Columbia and eight states in the period 1969-1972: California, Texas, Wisconsin, Georgia, Florida, New Jersey, Connecticut, and South Dakota. A number of those decisions were on appeal in January 1973, when the appeal of two of them produced *Roe v. Wade* (Texas) and *Doe v. Bolton* (Georgia).

2. 492 U.S. 490.

3. 111 S. Ct. 1759.

4. 112 S. Ct. 2791 (1992).

5. Insider rumors indicated that a number of justices had been especially mortified at the crassness of the televised hearings of the debate over the nomination of Clarence Thomas to the Supreme Court. Those hearings showed University of Oklahoma Law School Professor Anita Hill accusing Thomas, her former supervisor at the Equal Employment Opportunity Commission, of having verbally pressured her on a number of occasions to go with him on dates to see pornographic movies. Shortly thereafter Thomas, confirmed in the Senate by a narrow margin, gave a cover story interview to *People* magazine. According to the rumors, this cover story, too, was regarded as beneath the dignity of the U.S. Supreme Court. These rumors were reported by a panelist and a number of members of the audience at a panel on the Thomas nomination which was presented at the annual meeting of the American Political Science Asssociation (Chicago, 1992).

In addition, justices on all sides of the question are annoyed by the massive demonstrations that both pro-choicers and pro-lifers have been holding outside the Supreme Court building. They like to believe that they do their job of interpreting the law of the Constitution according to the highest professional standards, and not in response to political pressure of any kind. In their *Casey* opinions, both majority and dissenting justices openly expressed this annoyance.

6. While he does support the legality of abortion, Clinton as governor of Arkansas signed a bill that requires a minor who wants an abortion to obtain the prior consent of her parents (as long as they have both been in touch for the past year; otherwise one parent suffices) or of a judge. Also, Arkansas is one of the (majority of) states that do not provide public funding for abortions for poor people.

7. In the 1992 congressional races thirteen anti-abortion candidates employed

controversial, graphic television commercials depicting aborted fetuses. All thirteen lost their elections. Michael deCourcy Hinds, "Senator Who Wouldn't Run Has Victory," *New York Times*, Dec. 6, 1992, A26, col. 1.

8. The case in which this happened was *The Slaughter-House Cases*, 83 U.S. (16 Wall.) 36 (1872). For a more detailed explanation of this development, see Leslie F. Goldstein, *The Constitutional Rights of Women* 4–7 (Madison: University of Wisconsin Press, 1988).

9. *Slaughter-House Cases*.

10. 166 U.S. 226.

11. 198 U.S. 45.

12. *Muller v. Oregon*, 208 U.S. 412 (1908).

13. *Bunting v. Oregon*, 243 U.S. 426 (1917).

14. *Adkins v. Children's Hospital*, 261 U.S. 525.

15. *Morehead v. New York ex rel. Tipaldo*, 298 U.S. 587.

16. *West Coast Hotel v. Parrish*, 300 U.S. 379 (1937).

17. Major decisions upholding New Deal legislation were *N.L.R.B. v. Jones & Laughlin Steel*, 301 U.S. 1 (1937); *Steward Machine v. Davis*, 301 U.S. 548 (1937); *U.S. v. Darby*, 312 U.S. 100 (1941); and *Wickard v. Filburn*, 317 U.S. 111 (1942).

18. See *Gitlow v. New York*, 268 U.S. 652 (1925).

19. *Near v. Minnesota*, 283 U.S. 697 (1931).

20. 304 U.S. 144 (1938).

21. 262 U.S. 390, 399.

22. 268 U.S. 510, 534–35 (1925).

23. 316 U.S. 535.

24. This is the final clause in the indented excerpt from the Fourteenth Amendment, which is printed above at p. 4.

25. Skinner was a man. In 1927, when the Supreme Court had confronted a compulsory sterilization involving a woman, it had not occurred to the Court that procreation is "a basic liberty." The woman in the case, Carrie Buck, had just given birth out of wedlock and herself had been born out of wedlock (so this was not a case of marriage-and-procreation). The Supreme Court was told that Carrie Buck and her mother and child were "feeble-minded." No real evidence of this supposed feeblemindedness was presented in court (and researchers have since uncovered much evidence of their normalcy). But the Supreme Court accepted the word of the state of Virginia and upheld the law permitting sterilization of inmates of state institutions for the feeble-minded who were "afflicted with hereditary forms of insanity, imbecility, etc." Justice Holmes's opinion for eight of the nine justices upholding this sterilization included the remarkably callous remark: "Three generations of imbeciles are enough." The case was *Buck v. Bell*, 274 U.S. 200 (1927), and further details can be found in Goldstein, *Constitutional Rights of Women* 303–5. *Skinner v. Oklahoma* did not overrule *Buck v. Bell*. Justices in *Skinner* insisted that, in terms of constitutional significance, hereditary feeble-mindedness was different from criminal recidivism.

26. C. Thomas Dienes, *Law, Politics, and Birth Control* 139–40 (Urbana: University of Illinois Press, 1972). Tileston actually first filed suit in New Haven in 1941, the year before *Skinner*, but he must have been encouraged when, one month after his appeal lost at the Connecticut Supreme Court, the U.S. Supreme Court announced that procreation is a basic national liberty. He appealed his case to the U.S. Supreme Court with the help of the nationally prominent attorney and civil liberties advocate Morris Ernst.

27. *Tileston v. Ullman*, 318 U.S. 44 (1943).

28. 367 U.S. 497. Poe was the name used by an anonymous patient of Dr. C. Lee Buxton who joined Buxton's suit against the statute, claiming that her health would be seriously threatened by a pregnancy

(and therefore she had a personal and substantial stake in the liberty to use contraceptives).

29. 367 U.S. 497, 515–22.

30. 367 U.S. 497, 539–55.

31. In short, Justice Goldberg used the Ninth Amendment to justify construing the due process clause as protecting unwritten fundamental rights (381 U.S. 479, 486–99, concurring). Since Justice Douglas in *Poe v. Ullman* had construed this clause the same way, it is not clear why his *Griswold* opinion did not concur with Goldberg but instead emphasized "penumbras" of (written) clauses of the Bill of Rights. The answer may be that Douglas was responding to the dissents of Black and Stewart, which emphasized "written rights." In any case, Goldberg's group of three plus the concurrences of Harlan and White put a *Griswold* majority of five on record as favoring the use of the due process clause to protect unwritten rights fundamental to American traditions. Justice Douglas, a sixth, had gone on record the same way four years earlier in *Poe v. Ullman.*

32. This is a traditional premise of American constitutional law, and no Supreme Court justice has ever openly disputed it.

33. It is true that although Harlan does not discuss the marriage/family precedents in his brief *Griswold* concurrence, he had gone over them in his *Poe v. Ullman* dissent, to which he refers readers of *Griswold.*

34. 405 U.S. 438 (1972). He did not explain his *Eisenstadt* vote (one of four that made up the bare 4–3 majority) until his concurrence in *Roe v. Wade* a year later. 410 U.S. 113, 167–71.

35. 410 U.S. 113, 171–78, Justice Rehnquist dissenting.

36. He so indicated in a dissent in *Carey v. Population Services*, 431 U.S. 678, 718.

37. See his opinion for *Michael H. v. Gerald D.* (1989) in the Parenthood chapter below.

38. 405 U.S. 438 (1972).

39. The Court was not to decide those cases until January 22, 1973, more than a year later. *Roe v. Wade*, 410 U.S. 113; *Doe v. Bolton*, 410 U.S. 179.

40. For a review of the cases of this period, see Lee Epstein and Joseph Kobylka, *The Supreme Court and Legal Change* 160–86 (Chapel Hill: University of North Carolina Press, 1992).

41. *Ibid.*

42. For details, see Goldstein, *Constitutional Rights of Women* 334–36.

43. *U.S. v. Vuitch*, 402 U.S. 62.

44. *Roe v. Wade*, 314 F. Supp. 1217, and *Doe v. Bolton*, 319 F. Supp. 1048. The arguments and the strategies of the litigants in this round at the Supreme Court are described in Epstein and Kobylka, *Supreme Court and Legal Change* 167–82; the internal decisionmaking on the Supreme Court is described in *ibid.*, 182–86, and in Bernard Schwartz, *The Unpublished Opinions of the Burger Court* chapter 4 (New York: Oxford University Press, 1988).

45. *Eisenstadt*, 405 U.S. 438, 453.

46. *Moore v. East Cleveland*, 431 U.S. 494.

47. *Bowers v. Hardwick*, 478 U.S. 186.

48. For a detailed account of her story, see Marian Faux, *Roe v. Wade* (New York: Macmillan, 1988).

49. See explanation of standing at p. 8 above.

50. For the precise wording of the model, see Epstein and Kobylka, *Supreme Court and Legal Change* 142.

51. Justice Blackmun, who wrote for the Court, produced a separate opinion for each case. Rehnquist wrote a separate dissent for each case, and White wrote a combined dissent for the two. Burger and Douglas each authored a combined concurrence for the pair of cases. And Stewart wrote a separate concurrence for *Roe*. Since Burger, Stewart, and Douglas, however, all concurred with Blackmun's opinion also,

the vote in the cases was 7–2 on behalf of both the reasoning and the result.

52. The states were California, Wisconsin, Texas, Georgia, Illinois, Florida, New Jersey, Connecticut, and South Dakota. See details in Goldstein, Constitutional Rights of Women 334–35, and Epstein and Kobylka, *Supreme Court and Legal Change* 164–66. A number of those decisions were on appeal at the time of *Roe*.

53. The Supreme Court defined *viability* as "potentially able to live outside the mother's womb, albeit with artificial aid." Sec. IX.B of Blackmun's *Roe* opinion (410 U.S. at 160).

54. Blackmun opinion, Section VIII (410 U.S. at 153).

55. Section VII (410 U.S. at 149).

56. *Ibid.*

57. *Ibid.*

58. Section IX.B (410 U.S. at 159).

59. Section X (410 U.S. at 163–64).

60. Section X (410 U.S. at 163).

61. Section XI (410 U.S. at 165).

62. Section XI (410 U.S. at 164–65).

63. This clause states: "The citizens of each State shall be entitled to all privileges and immunities of citizens in the several States."

64. 428 U.S. 52 (1976).

65. Mo. H.B. 1211, § 2(2), enacted June 14, 1974.

66. § 6(1).

67. Section IV.B (428 U.S. at 67).

68. Section IV.F (428 U.S. at 81).

69. Section IV.C (428 U.S. at 71).

70. At this point the judicial line-up vis-à-vis abortion restrictions was the following: 3, Brennan, Marshall, and Blackmun opposed to all but the most incidental restrictions on pre-viability abortion; 3, Powell, Stewart, and Stevens generally opposed to restricting pre-viability abortion but willing to uphold parental consent for minors if a judicial bypass is allowed; 3, Burger, White, and Rehnquist generally in favor of abortion restrictions of all kinds, with Burger making an exception for outright prohibition (as a violation of the right to privacy).

71. See *Bellotti v. Baird I*, 428 U.S. 132 (1976), announcing the same rule requiring the option of a judicial bypass; *Bellotti v. Baird II*, 443 U.S. 622 (1979), applying the rule to strike down an overly restrictive parental consent requirement; *H.L. v. Matheson*, 450 U.S. 398 (1981), upholding a law requiring pre-abortion notification, "if possible," for an unmarried minor, at least as applied to an immature minor living with her parents (i.e., legally "unemancipated"); *Planned Parenthood v. Ashcroft*, 462 U.S. 476 (1983), upholding a parental consent provision that permitted a judicial bypass; *Ohio v. Akron Center for Reproductive Health (Akron II)*, 497 U.S. 502 (1990), upholding a requirement that either a parent be notified or "a court order of approval" be obtained prior to giving an abortion to an unmarried, unemancipated minor; and *Hodgson v. Minnesota*, 497 U.S. 417 (1990), declaring unconstitutional, on the grounds of patent unreasonableness, a law requiring that unemancipated, unmarried minors before getting an abortion notify both parents, irrespective of whether both of them have participated in any way in rearing the minor in question, but upholding a companion, substitute provision that required the same two-parent notification but allowed for the standard judicial bypass.

72. See note 71.

73. *Colautti v. Franklin*, 439 U.S. 379, 388 (1979).

74. 462 U.S. 416 (1983).

75. O'Connor dissent, Section II (462 U.S. at 461).

76. Abortions needed to save a mother's life further the compelling interest in preserving *actual* lives; O'Connor, Rehnquist, and White would presumably acknowledge this to be even more compelling than preserving "potential" life.

77. O'Connor dissent, Section III (462 U.S. at 461), quoting *Maher v. Roe*, 432 U.S. 464, 473–74 (1977). Emphasis added.

78. O'Connor dissent, Section III (462 U.S. at 466).

79. Section III of Powell opinion.

80. Justice O'Connor dissented on this point as on the others, but she added a footnote (number 16) indicating that physicians may present persuasive First Amendment objections to this part of the statute, but that none had done so in this case.

Her (and the other dissenters') views on the other regulations were that, except for parental consent, none imposed an undue burden on the abortion decision and thus, since there was some reason for them, they were constitutional. She argued that reviewing the constitutionality of the parental consent provision was premature because it had yet to be authoritatively construed by state judges.

81. 462 U.S. 506.

82. 462 U.S. 476.

83. 476 U.S. 747 (1986).

84. White dissent, Section I.A (476 U.S. at 791–92).

85. *Ibid.*

86. White dissent, Section I.B (476 U.S. at 795).

87. 476 U.S. at 776–79.

88. The Kennedy appointment was made on the heels of two failed nominations. The first was that of Robert Bork, a highly regarded, strongly conservative judge, who was rejected by the Senate on the grounds that his views were too extreme, or outside the American mainstream. The second was that of Douglas Ginsburg, a Harvard law professor (also very conservative in his politics) who withdrew his name from consideration after the press carried reports that he smoked marijuana with his students at Harvard (as well as some other rumors of impropriety in terms of judicial ethics).

89. 492 U.S. 490 (1989).

90. 432 U.S. 438 (1977).

91. This principle stems from the supremacy clause found in Article VI of the Constitution.

92. 52 U.S.C. § 1396(a)(17).

93. 42 U.S.C. § 1396.

94. 432 U.S. 464 (1977).

95. Of the phrase "medically necessary," the Connecticut statute said only that it included psychiatric necessity, as determined by the attending physician.

96. *Doe v. Rose*, 499 F.2d 1112 (10th Cir. 1974); *Wulff v. Singleton*, 508 F.2d 1211 (8th Cir. 1975); *Doe v. Westby*, 383 F. Supp. 1143 (1974) and 402 F. Supp. 140 (1975); *Doe v. Wohlgemuth*, 376 F. Supp. 173 (1974) (this case became *Beal v. Doe*); *Doe v. Rampton*, 366 F. Supp. 189 (1973); and *Klein v. Nassau County Medical Center*, 347 F. Supp. 496 (1972) and 409 F. Supp. 731 (1976).

97. *Edwards v. California*, 314 U.S. 160 (1941).

98. *Griffin v. Illinois*, 351 U.S. 12 (1956); *Burns v. Ohio*, 360 U.S. 252 (1959); *Smith v. Bennett*, 365 U.S. 708 (1961); *Long v. District Court*, 385 U.S. 192 (1966); *Roberts v. La-Vallee*, 389 U.S. 40 (1967); *Mayer v. Chicago*, 404 U.S. 189 (1971).

99. *Gideon v. Wainwright*, 372 U.S. 335 (1963); *Douglas v. California*, 372 U.S. 353 (1963); *Argersinger v. Hamlin*, 407 U.S. 25 (1972).

100. *Harper v. Board of Elections*, 383 U.S. 663 (1966).

101. *Turner v. Fouche*, 396 U.S. 346 (1970).

102. *Boddie v. Connecticut*, 401 U.S. 371 (1971).

103. *Harper v. Board of Elections*, 383 U.S. at 668.

104. *United States v. Kras*, 409 U.S. 434 (1973).

105. *Maher v. Roe*, 432 U.S. at 477.

106. 432 U.S. 519 (1977).

107. The Fourteenth Amendment restricts only the states, so parties wanting to

claim that a national law violates equal protection of the law typically argue that this idea is implied in the Fifth Amendment phrase "due process of law." This strategy was first endorsed by the Supreme Court in *Korematsu v. U.S.*, 323 U.S. 214 (1944).

108. 448 U.S. 297 (1980).

109. Nonetheless, fourteen states continued to finance Medicaid abortions with their own state funds.

110. *Harris v. McRae*, 448 U.S. at 351.

Chapter 2. Current Trends in Abortion

1. 492 U.S. 490.

2. 111 S. Ct. 1759.

3. Patrick Sheeran, *Women, Society, the State, and Abortion* 52–53 (New York: Praeger, 1987). Church doctrine did hold abortion a sin, and it was a more serious sin after ensoulment (thought to be forty days post-conception for a male fetus, and eighty days for a female); the church imposed penances, which varied in severity by locality.

4. 497 U.S. 417 (1990).

5. 497 U.S. 502 (1990).

6. *Hodgson*, note 5 of Stevens opinion.

7. Section V (497 U.S. at 519–20). Justices Rehnquist, White, and Scalia joined in this part of the opinion.

8. He appears to have come up with this logic about the right of privacy in the case of *Michael H. v. Gerald D.*, 491 U.S. 110 (1989), which is included in the Parenthood chapter below.

9. *Hodgson v. Minnesota*, 497 U.S. at 480 (Justice Scalia concurring in part and dissenting in part).

10. 111 S. Ct. 1759.

11. 42 U.S.C. § 300a-6.

12. 42 C.F.R. § 59.5(a)(9) (1972).

13. 42 C.F.R. § 59.8(a)(1) (1989).

14. 42 C.F.R. §§ 59.8(a)(2) and 59.8(a)(3).

15. 42 C.F.R. § 59.8(b)(5).

16. 42 C.F.R. § 59.10(a).

17. 42 C.F.R. § 59.9.

18. *Massachusetts v. Secretary of Health and Human Services*, 899 F.2d 53 (1st Cir. 1990);

Planned Parenthood Federation of America v. Sullivan, 913 F.2d 1492 (10th Cir. 1990).

19. *Rust v. Sullivan* and *New York v. Sullivan*, 889 F.2d 401 (2d Cir. 1989).

20. The question is not discussed by any of the justices, but the dissenting views of Justices Stevens, Blackmun, and Marshall implicitly assume the continuing validity of *Roe v. Wade*.

21. 59 U.S.L.W. 3338.

22. 112 S. Ct. 2791.

23. The only other jointly authored U.S. Supreme Court opinion of which I am aware is *Cooper v. Aaron*, 358 U.S. 1 (1958). All nine justices signed the opinion, which responded to a request for slowing school desegregation in Little Rock with the reply that widespread and intense community opposition can never be valid grounds for denying people their constitutional rights. The co-authoring of an opinion by all nine justices is unique in U.S. history.

24. The court reached that conclusion because in *Akron II* and *Hodgson* a majority supported the "undue burden" test, and in *Webster* support for the "undue burden" test was the tipping point that, added to either plurality, made a majority.

25. *Lee v. Weisman*, 112 S. Ct. 2649 (1992).

26. *Bray v. Alexandria Women's Health Clinic*. After argument in October 1991 and reargument in October 1992, the case was decided on January 13, 1993. 61 U.S.L.W. 4080. In a 5–4 vote, the Supreme Court ruled that abortion clinic blockades do not

violate any current federal statute, thus leaving their punishment to state and local authorities.

27. *Ada v. Guam*, 61 U.S.L.W. 3399 (1992) (No. 92-104).

28. *Edwards v. Sojourner T.*, 61 U.S.L.W. 3615 (1993) (No. 92-1066).

29. *Barnes v. Moore*, 61 U.S.L.W. 3418 (1992) (No. 92-588).

Chapter 3. Parenthood and Privacy: Contemporary Applications

1. 262 U.S. 390 (1923)

2. 268 U.S. 510 (1925).

3. *Pierce*, 268 U.S. at 534–35.

4. *Prince v. Massachusetts*, 321 U.S. 158 (1944).

5. *Jacobson v. Massachusetts*, 197 U.S. 11 (1905).

6. *Raleigh-Fitkin Paul Morgan Hospital v. Anderson*, 201 A.2d 537 (1964) (ordering a transfusion to a woman in her thirty-second week of pregnancy); *Crouse Irving Memorial Hospital v. Paddock*, 485 N.Y.S.2d 443 (ordering a transfusion for a fetus that was to be prematurely delivered), and *In re Jamaica Hospital*, 491 N.Y.S.2d 898 (1985) (ordering a transfusion to a woman eighteen weeks pregnant). In a somewhat different situation, *In re President and Directors of Georgetown College*, 331 F.2d 1000, 1008 (D.C.Cir. 1964), *cert. denied*, 377 U.S. 978 (1964), upheld the order of a transfusion to a woman on the grounds that she had a "responsibility to the community to care for her infant."

7. This is the group that brought the suit in *Thornburgh v. ACOG*, the 1986 Supreme Court abortion case.

8. 573 A.2d 1235 (1990).

9. Reprinted at 573 A.2d 1259. In that case, the woman had been already in labor and refused on religious grounds to allow a caesarean. A blockage made birth canal delivery dangerous to both mother and child; the child faced serious danger of death or brain damage, and the mother faced risk of serious infection. The moth-er's (and father's) religious claim was that Muslims believe that a mother may choose to avoid a risk to her own health even if it means a threat to her fetus. Doctors had placed the risk to the woman of undergoing a caesarean at 0.25 percent but the risk to the fetus from attempting vaginal delivery at 50–75 percent. Caesarean delivery took place, pursuant to court order, and a healthy child was born, without injury to the mother's health.

10. *Stanley v. Illinois*, 405 U.S. 645, 651 (1972) (Section II). The Court referred to the due process and equal protection clauses of the Fourteenth Amendment for this protection and also to the Ninth Amendment.

11. See *Fiallo v. Bell*, 430 U.S. 787 (1977) (upholding, on the grounds of Congress's special authority over international relations, preferred immigrant status for unwed mothers but not unwed fathers of American citizens, and for the illegitimate offspring of American mothers but not for such offspring of American fathers); *Quilloin v. Walcott*, 434 U.S. 246 (1978) (upholding state law that failed to allow unwed father to block adoption of his own child by the child's stepfather [although divorced fathers and unwed mothers were given such power in comparable situations], as applied to a situation where the father had never sought or held custody of the child, and according to a statutory "best interest of the child" standard); *Caban v. Mohammed*, 441 U.S. 380 (1979) (holding unconstitutional a state law requiring mother's but

not father's permission to release illegitimate child for adoption, at least in situation where father had shared in rearing the child); *Parham v. Hughes,* 441 U.S. 347 (1979) (upholding state law permitting mothers but not fathers to sue for wrongful death of illegitimate child, in a case involving a father who had acknowledged and regularly visited but had never legitimated his child); *Lehr v. Robertson,* 463 U.S. 248 (1983) (upholding state law that, as applied, denied to unmarried father opportunity for a legitimation hearing for purposes of blocking adoption of child by its stepfather, although mother had refused to allow father to develop a relationship with the child, on grounds that other procedures were open to the father [which he had failed to use] that would have enabled him to claim paternity at the adoption hearing). For cases dealing with required procedures for termination of parental rights but that do not pit mothers against fathers, see *Santosky v. Kramer,* 455 U.S. 745 (1982) (state must prove unfitness by "clear and convincing evidence," rather than a mere preponderance of evidence), and *Lassiter v. North Carolina,* 452 U.S. 18 (1981) (flexible, case-by-case standard of fundamental fairness is acceptable for procedures governing hearings for termination of parental rights).

12. *In the Matter of Baby Girl, L. J.,* 505 N.Y.S.2d 813 (1986).

13. *Surrogate Parenting v. Commonwealth ex rel. Armstrong,* 704 S.W.2d 209 (1986). The court in this case added that the mother's promise to give up her child was revocable up until five days after birth, just as in the case of adoption within that state.

14. *Doe v. Kelley,* 307 N.W.2d 438 (1981), *cert. denied,* 459 U.S. 1183 (1983).

15. U.S., Department of Commerce, Census Bureau, Current Population Reports, Consumer Income, Series P-60, no. 174, Table 24.

16. 491 U.S. 110 (1989).

17. The argument of "Victoria" was developed and presented by a court-appointed attorney.

18. The Supreme Court saw little merit in Victoria's equal protection argument (concerning the statute's granting to her lawful parents, but not to her, permission to challenge Gerald's paternity), and Scalia's brief discussion of it is omitted from the excerpt below.

19. See note 11 for case citations and *Michael H.* opinions for discussion of the cases involving these fathers.

20. 490 U.S. 30 (1989).

21. *Baby M* concerned interpretation of a state law, while *Mississippi Choctaw* dealt with federal law.

22. Pub. L. No. 90-284, 82 Stat. 73, Title II, Sec. 202 (1968).

23. Or more precisely, the statutory rights of Native Americans, which are constitutional rights of other Americans.

24. For brevity's sake the case is referred to herein as *Mississippi Choctaw v. Holyfield,* although the appellees in the case actually included both adoptive parents, Mr. and Mrs. Holyfield, and the birth parents, J. B. and W. J. Mr. Holyfield died during the litigation.

25. 511 So. 2d 918 (1987).

Chapter 4. Sex Discrimination

1. For an excellent survey *see,* Leo Kanowitz, *Women and the Law: The Unfinished Revolution* (Albuquerque: University of New Mexico Press, 1969).

2. "No State shall make or enforce any law which shall abridge the *privileges or immunities* of citizens of the United States; nor shall any State deprive any person of

life, liberty, or property, without *due process* of law; nor deny to any person within its jurisdiction the *equal protection* of the laws." (Emphasis added to indicate names of clauses.)

3. *Bradwell v. Illinois*, 83 U.S. 130, 141–42 (1873) (Justice Bradley concurring).

4. *Hoyt v. Florida*, 368 U.S. 57, 61–62 (1961).

5. *Taylor v. Louisiana*, 419 U.S. 522 (1975).

6. See, for instance, Leslie Friedman Goldstein, "Women as Litigants," in Beverly Blair Cook et al., *Women in the Judicial Process* 40–49 (Washington, D.C.: American Political Science Association, 1988).

7. *Eisenstadt v. Baird*, 405 U.S. 438, 453 (1972), a case that concerned unmarried persons' right to use birth control.

8. *Swann v. Charlotte-Mecklenburg*, 402 U.S. 1 (1971); *North Carolina v. Swann*, 402 U.S. 43 (1971).

9. *Yick Wo v. Hopkins*, 118 U.S. 356 (1886).

10. American courts use the terms *gender* and *sex* interchangeably. That usage can obscure certain problems, as will be illustrated in the discussion of the *Price Waterhouse* case below.

11. A detailed discussion of Supreme Court cases involving such laws appears in Leslie F. Goldstein, *The Constitutional Rights of Women*, 8–65 (Madison: University of Wisconsin Press, 1988).

12. This amendment was originally proposed by opponents of the bill, in hopes that it would make defeat more likely. Women members of Congress, however, liked the amendment, took up its active support, and persuaded their colleagues to keep it in the (successfully adopted) law.

13. For an examination of this litigation strategy, *see* Karen O'Connor, *Women's Organizations' Use of the Courts* (Lexington, Mass.: Lexington Books, 1980).

14. For details *see*, Leslie Goldstein, "Women as Litigants"; "Constitutional Inequality: The Political Fortunes of the Equal Rights Amendment" (book review), *Constitutional Commentary* 3 (1986):558–76; and

"The ERA and the U.S. Supreme Court," *Research in Law and Policy Studies* 1 (1987):145–61.

15. *Ibid.*

16. *Craig v. Boren*, 429 U.S. 190 (1976).

17. *Kirchberg v. Feenstra*, 450 U.S. 455 (1981).

18. *Mississippi University for Women v. Hogan*, 458 U.S. 718 (1982).

19. *Michael M. v. Sonoma County*, 450 U.S. 464 (1981). The female would be innocent of the crime of "unlawful sexual intercourse," but might be prosecuted for the lesser offense of contributing to the delinquency of a minor. The "important government interest" identified by the Court as substantially furthered by this law was the state interest in combatting teenage pregnancy. The Court reasoned that nature provides, in pregnancy itself, a stronger deterrent for females than males to the behavior that produces teen pregnancy (so it makes sense for the law to add a deterrent for males), and the Court accepted the state's argument that making both members of the couple guilty of the crime would make enforcement nearly impossible because the crime would never get reported. See next chapter for further discussion of this case.

20. *Rostker v. Goldberg*, 453 U.S. 57 (1981). The important government interest identified in this case in support of the law was the general need for extra leeway for the political branches (i.e., Congress and the President) in foreign, and especially defense, policymaking. The Court majority accepted the military's argument that the draft, if it were activated, would be for combat purposes only, and that, in light of the prohibition on sending women into combat, the military would have no need to draft women (and therefore registering them would be a sheer waste of money).

21. *Califano v. Goldfarb*, 430 U.S. 199 (1977).

22. *Heckler v. Mathews*, 465 U.S. 728 (1984). In this decision the Court unanimously accepted the Congressional rationale that the delay was carefully designed

to protect reasonable expectations of people who had been planning their retirement with pre-1977 assumptions.

23. § 701(k) of Title VII of the Civil Rights Act of 1964, 42 U.S.C. § 2000e *et seq.* This law overrode the ruling of *General Electric v. Gilbert,* 429 U.S. 125 (1976), that pregnancy discrimination was not sex discrimination.

24. Pub. L. No. 100-259, 102 Stat. 28 (1988). This law overrode the decision in *Grove City v. Bell,* 465 U.S. 555 (1984), which had given a narrow reading to the word *program* in Title IX's prohibition on sex discrimination in any educational program that receives federal funds.

25. The interpretive decisions overturned were *Patterson v. McLean Credit Union,* 491 U.S. 164 (1989); *Wards Cove Packing v. Atonio,* 490 U.S. 642 (1989); and *Martin v. Wilks,* 490 U.S. 755 (1989). The Civil Rights Act of 1991 is Pub. L. No. 102-166, 105 Stat. 1071 (1991). This statute is discussed in detail in the next subsection of this chapter.

26. For an exploration of this new trend and the opposition to it, *see* Leslie Goldstein, ed., *Feminist Jurisprudence: The Difference Debate* (Lanham, Md.: Rowman & Littlefield, 1992). A prominent case that pitted one group of feminists against the other on this issue was *California Federal Savings and Loan v. Guerra,* 479 U.S. 272 (1987).

27. A first step for verifying this particular explanation would be to compare the number of cases involving gender discrimination for which *certiorari* (agreement to review a case) by the Supreme Court was requested in the 1970s with the number requested in the 1980s. All the cases for which "cert" is requested are described in *United States Law Week.* So far as I know, no one has yet done this research.

28. 42 U.S.C. § 2000e-2(a)(1) and (2).

29. 467 U.S. 69.

30. *Ann B. Hopkins v. Price Waterhouse,* 618 F. Supp. 1109 (1985).

31. *Hopkins v. Price Waterhouse,* 825 F.2d 458, 468–69 (D.C.Cir. 1987).

32. See citations described in *Hopkins,* 825 F.2d 458, 471.

33. *Ibid.,* 474.

34. 42 U.S.C. § 2000e-2(k)(2). In § 105(a) of the Civil Rights Act of 1991, at 105 Stat. 1075.

35. Pub. L. No. 102-166, 105 Stat. 1071, § 107(a). This will become 42 U.S.C. 2000e-2(m), or § 703(m) of the 1964 Civil Rights Act.

36. *Ibid.,* § 107(b). This will become 42 U.S.C. § 2000e-5(g)(2)(B).

37. The president insisted that the 1991 law was a compromise product that took into account his most important concerns. News analysis generally viewed this claim as mostly a face-saving gesture. See, *e.g.,* "The Compromise on Civil Rights," *New York Times,* Oct. 26, 1991, A7, col. 3. But see also text for note 56.

38. 490 U.S. 642 (1989).

39. 42 U.S.C. § 2000e-2(a)(2).

40. *Griggs v. Duke Power,* 401 U.S. 424 (1971), and *Albemarle Paper v. Moody,* 422 U.S. 405 (1975), concerned disparate impact by race; *Dothard v. Rawlinson,* 433 U.S. 321 (1977), concerned disparate impact by gender.

41. *Griggs,* 401 U.S. 431, 432.

42. *Dothard,* 433 U.S. 321, 331.

43. 490 U.S. 642, 658–60.

44. 42 U.S.C. § 2000e-2(k)(1)(A)(i), § 105(a) of Civil Rights Act of 1991.

45. 490 U.S. 755 (1989). The dissenters in both this case and *Wards Cove* were Stevens, Blackmun, Brennan, and Marshall.

46. Lisa Cronin Wohl, "Liberating Ma Bell," *Ms.,* Nov. 1973, at 52.

47. 42 U.S.C. § 2000e-2(n)(1)(B)(i)(I)-(II), amended at § 108, Civil Rights Act of 1991, 105 Stat. 1076.

48. The quote is from Justice Steven's dissenting opinion, 490 U.S. at 791.

49. 491 U.S. 164 (1989).

50. Now 42 U.S.C. § 1981.

51. Again the dissenters were Stevens, Blackmun, Marshall, and Brennan.

52. *Meritor Savings v. Vinson,* 477 U.S. 57 (1986). See next chapter for further discussion of this topic.

53. 42 U.S.C. § 1981(b), amended at § 101, Civil Rights Act of 1991, 105 Stat. 1071-72.

54. Similar changes were adopted to allow damage awards for victims of discrimination against disabled persons, which discrimination is prohibited by the Americans with Disabilities Act of 1990 and by Section 501 of the Rehabilitation Act of 1973.

55. 42 U.S.C. § 1981a(a) and (b), amended at § 102 of Civil Rights Act of 1991, 105 Stat. 1072-73.

56. "The Compromise on Civil Rights."

57. 465 U.S. 555.

58. Additional support for this pattern can be seen in the Voting Rights Act of 1982, which concerns the rights of blacks, but not of women as such.

59. *International Union, United Automobile, Aerospace and Agricultural Implement Workers of America, U.A.W. et al. v. Johnson Controls*, 111 S. Ct. 1196 (1991).

60. 42 U.S.C. § 2000e-2(e)(1).

61. 42 U.S.C. § 2000e(k).

62. While sex discrimination in employment was officially prohibited in 1964, it was not until 1972 that a federal agency, the Equal Employment Opportunity Commission, was given power to take employers to court for violations. Coincidentally (perhaps), 1977 was also the year that the U.S. Senate voted 75-11 for the Pregnancy Discrimination Act. (The House of Representatives did not concur until 1978.)

63. Males at the higher levels risked lowered sperm count, decreased sperm motility, increased danger of malformed sperm, and impotence. *UAW v. Johnson Controls*, 886 F.2d 871, 918-19.

64. The company also declared off-limits to women work stations where the air level showed lead in excess of thirty micrograms per cubic meter.

65. *Rogers v. EEOC*, 454 F.2d 234 (5th Cir. 1971), *cert. denied*, 406 U.S. 957 (1972).

66. *Firefighters Institute for Racial Equality v. St. Louis*, 549 F.2d 506, 514–15 (8th Cir. 1977); *Gray v. Greyhound Lines, East*, 545 F.2d 169, 176 (D.C. Cir. 1976).

67. *Compston v. Borden*, 424 F. Supp. 157 (S.D. Ohio 1976).

68. *Cariddi v. Kansas City Chiefs Football Club*, 568 F.2d 87, 88 (8th Cir. 1977).

69. E.g., *Henson v. Dundee*, 682 F.2d 897, 902 (11th Cir. 1982).

70. *Meritor Savings Bank v. Vinson* 477 U.S. 57.

71. 477 U.S. at 60.

72. 477 U.S. at 67, quoting *Henson v. Dundee*, 682 F.2d 897, 902.

73. *Ibid.* (quoting *Henson*, 682 F.2d at 904).

74. 477 U.S. at 65.

75. *Rabidue v. Osceola Refining*, 805 F.2d 611, 620–21 (6th Cir. 1986).

76. *Ibid.*

77. 20 U.S.C. §§ 1681–88. The statute allows certain exceptions, including an exception for traditionally one-sex colleges that continue to admit only one sex.

78. 112 S. Ct. 1028 (1992).

79. The phrase is from the Supreme Court opinion, 112 S. Ct. 1028, 1031.

80. *Cannon v. University of Chicago*, 441 U.S. 677 (1979).

81. *Guardians Assn. v. Civil Service*, 463 U.S. 582 (1983).

82. *Consolidated Rail v. Darrone*, 465 U.S. 624, 630, n.9 (1984).

83. 42 U.S.C. § 2000d-7.

84. Certain other lines of reasoning divided the Court, but on this one they were all agreed.

Chapter 5. Sexual Violence and Pornography

1. According to the *New York Times*, Utah is the only state still lacking such a statute. Tamar Lewin, "Rape and the Accuser: A Debate Still Rages On Citing Sexual Past," *New York Times*, Feb. 12, 1993, B16, col. 1.

2. *Coker v. Georgia*, 433 U.S. 584 (1977).

3. 450 U.S. 464 (1981).

4. Susan Estrich, *Real Rape* 102–03 (Cambridge: Harvard University Press, 1987).

5. 424 A.2d 720 (1981).

6. *Real Rape* 130 n.23.

7. *Rusk v. State*, 43 Md. App. 476, 480, 406 A.2d 624 (1979).

8. Deborah Sontag, "Clemency Given Jean Harris Leaves Others Wondering," *New York Times*, Jan. 1, 1993, A1.

9. Ibid.

10. Dawn Browning, "The Paradoxical Battered Woman Syndrome," unpublished manuscript.

11. Fox Butterfield, "Parole Advised for Woman Who Killed Abusive Partner," *New York Times*, Jan. 21, 1993, A18, col. 1, citing the National Clearinghouse for the Defense of Battered Women, Philadelphia.

12. Ibid.

13. Ibid.

14. *Schenck v. U.S.*, 249 U.S. 47 (1919).

15. *Chaplinsky v. New Hampshire*, 315 U.S. 568, 571–72 (1942).

16. *Memoirs v. Massachusetts (The Fanny Hill Case)*, 383 U.S. 413.

17. *Miller v. California*, 413 U.S. 15 (1973), and *Paris Adult Theatre v. Slaton*, 413 U.S. 49 (1973).

18. *Miller*, 413 U.S. at 24–25.

19. Ibid.

20. *Roth v. U.S.*, 354 U.S. 476, 487 at n.20 (1957).

21. *Miller*, 413 U.S. at 24–25.

22. Ibid. at 25.

23. *Paris Adult Theatre*.

24. Ibid., 413 U.S. at 63.

25. New Haven, Ct: Yale University Press.

26. Indianapolis Code, § 16-3(q), cited in *American Booksellers Ass'n v. Hudnut*, 771 F.2d 323, 324 (7th Cir. 1985).

27. § 16-3(g)(4). For the trafficking provision a work had to be considered as a whole, not by isolated sections, so selling a magazine like *Playboy* would not be actionable. § 16-3(g)(4)(C). Also, for a plaintiff to recover damages, there had to be proof that the trafficker "knew or had reason to know" the material was pornographic.

28. § 16-3(g)(5).

29. § 16-3(g)(5).

30. § 16-3(g)(7). In an action for damages from the "seller, exhibitor, or distributor," in such a case, there must be proof that the respondent "knew or had reason to know" the material was pornographic.

31. 598 F. Supp. 1316.

32. *Hudnut v. American Booksellers Ass'n*, 475 U.S. 1001 (1986). Three justices dissented against the decision not to hear oral argument: Chief Justice Warren Burger, William Rehnquist, and Sandra Day O'Connor.

33. *R.A.V. v. St. Paul*, 112 S.Ct. 2538, 2551 (1992).

34. St. Paul, Minn. Legis. Code § 292.02 (1990).

35. *Chaplinsky*, 315 U.S. at 572.

36. The four concurring critics disagreed, insisting that if speech is unprotected a government, if it chose to, may ban whichever segment of it was most problematic. However, they also would strike down the St. Paul ordinance because they believed that a message could fall short of the true "fighting words" category and still "arouse anger or resentment."

37. 315 U.S. at 572.

38. The concurring justices noted the contradiction in assuming that ideas were being expressed in something defined as not part of the exchange of ideas. See 112 S. Ct. at 2553 (Justice White concurring.)

39. *R.A.V.*, 112 S. Ct. at 2545–46.

40. *R.A.V.*, 112 S. Ct. at 2546–47.

Appendix A

How the Supreme Court Operates

Jurisdiction

The Constitution mandates the establishment of a Supreme Court and grants that court jurisdiction over all "cases and controversies" involving diplomatic personnel, legal clashes on the seas, clashes between citizens or governments of two different states, legal disputes between Americans and foreigners, and all cases "arising under" any of the three forms of national law: federal statutes, treaties, or clauses of the Constitution. This grant of power in a variety of ways imposes limits on the Court's powers.

First, no legal dispute that is wholly an in-state matter may go to the federal courts. If the clash involves only the *state* law (and the bulk of laws affecting our daily lives *are* state laws), and the parties to the dispute all live within that state, no federal court may intervene. The federal courts may be brought in *only* if some element of federal law is at issue, such as, for example, the prohibition within the federal Constitution against unreasonable searches and seizures. (If a party in a local trial wishes to appeal the case later to a federal court, that party must raise the issue of federal law at the initial trial. People are not permitted to wait until they lose at the local level and then try to dream up new "federal" issues so that they can keep appealing to the federal courts.)

Second, the federal courts will hear only genuine, live "controversies"; that is, cases in which the court's ruling will settle someone's pending claim. The federal courts will not hand out "advisory opinions," that is, general opinions as to a law's merits or its constitutionality which do not settle actual live disputes between concrete individuals or groups. The Supreme Court, for this reason, avoids "moot" cases; these are cases in which the resolution of the initial legal claim has (usually by the passage of time) somehow been taken out of the power of the court. A mother who objects to prayers in public school but whose children have graduated from school by the time her case gets to the highest court would be one example of someone whose case had been "mooted" by the passage of time.

By inference from the "cases and controversies" phrase, the Supreme Court requires that the parties who present cases have an actual, tangible stake in the outcome. This requirement that the parties involved must somehow stand to gain or lose directly from the outcome of the case, is called the "standing" requirement. The federal courts apply it with a certain flexibility; it is one way for them to bow out tactfully from politically "hot" cases. For cases that the justices want to decide, they occasionally bend the rules of standing.

In all cases involving diplomatic personnel and in those where one state government is opposing another government or an out-of-state citizen, the Constitution gave the Supreme Court original jurisdiction. That means that the Supreme Court may hear the case on the initial round, before any other judicial body hears it. (Only about 150 cases in the entire history of the Supreme Court have been handled in this way.) All the rest of the Supreme Court's jurisdiction is appellate (cases come to it on appeal from the decision of lower courts, both state and federal). The Constitution gives Congress the power to make exceptions to these rules of jurisdiction and to create lower federal courts to supplement the work of the Supreme Court.

Congress also has the power to alter the number of justices on the Supreme Court, and it has done this on a number of occasions over the past 190 years. The official size of the Supreme Court has remained steadily at nine for more than a century.

The Supreme Court's appellate jurisdiction is now entirely discretionary. The Supreme Court exercises this discretion to select for decision only those cases of importance to the legal system of the country as a whole. In other words, the Supreme Court is more likely to accept a case for decision if that case presents a legal issue of national importance than if one of the parties in the case simply happened to receive unfair treatment.

Structure and Workload
of the Federal Courts

The vast majority of legal cases in the United States are handled in the state court system. (This system includes county and municipal courts.) In additon, about 150,000 cases each year are initiated in the federal court system at the level of the district courts.

The United States is divided into eighty-nine judicial districts, and the District of Columbia, Puerto Rico, Guam, Northern Mariana, and the Virgin Islands each constitute an additional district. Each of these has its own federal district court. There are 648 federal district judges. The district courts have original jurisdiction for cases arising under federal laws. They also have appellate jurisdiction to hear cases from the state courts in which a convicted criminal claims that his conviction process was in some way unconstitutional. Generally, district judges hear cases as individuals, but if a case presents a major constitutional issue, a panel of three district judges will hear it.

Anyone who loses at the district court level has a right to appeal to the one of the twelve U.S. circuit courts of appeals whose circuit includes the district of the original case. The courts of appeals must hear cases appealed to them. Roughly 10 percent of cases heard in district courts are taken to the circuit courts of appeals. There are 167 circuit court judges, plus a specialized federal circuit court (of 12) for customs and patent cases, and at the circuit level the use of three-judge panels to decide cases is much more typical than in the district courts. The number of court of appeals judges per circuit varies according to the size of the circuit. Whenever possible, the three-judge panels are designed so as to include at least two judges from states other than the one where the case arose. Very rarely (for the purpose of avoiding differing decisions by three-judge panels) all the judges of a circuit will hear a case together, or *en banc*.

Federal Court opinions are printed in the *Federal Supplement* (F. Supp.) or the *Fed-*

eral Reporter (F. 2d). State Supreme Court decisions are reprinted by region in collections such as *Northwest Reporter* (N.W.) or *Northeast Reporter Second Series* (N.E. 2d) or published in state collections such as *Idaho Reports* (Idaho).

Supreme Court Proceedings

About 5,000 cases each year are appealed to the Supreme Court. Some of these (about 30 percent) come from state supreme courts and a few directly from federal district courts, but most come from the circuit courts of appeals. Ninety percent of these appeals for Supreme Court review are rejected outright. A few hundred of them are disposed of in "summary" proceedings, in which no further argument is presented to the Supreme Court. Sometimes a summary disposition will have no explanatory opinion at all; the Supreme Court can just announce a summary affirmance or reversal. Often summary proceedings include very brief (three or four sentence) per curiam opinions authored anonymously for the Court as a group. Each year only about 150 cases are accepted for full argument at the United States Supreme Court.

To be accepted for review by the Supreme Court, a case must garner the votes of four of the nine justices in favor of its petition for review. About one hundred petitions arrive every week. These petitions are read by the justices (or their clerks), and any single justice can request that a particular petition be discussed at the next available conference. Seventy percent of the petitions never arouse such a request and are, therefore, rejected without any discussion.

The Supreme Court session begins on the first Monday in October and lasts until early July. The Court's sessions consists of alternating two-week periods in which the justices first hear oral arguments and then spend time drafting and re-drafting opinions to explain their decisions for the cases they have heard argued. Fridays are set aside for conferences.

These conferences begin at 9:30 A.M. with a series of handshakes between every justice and each of the other eight justices. The proceedings are kept completely secret. No one else is present. Only the chief justice takes notes (and these are not made public). If any books or papers are needed, the most "junior" justice (based on the date of appointment to the Court) goes to the door and hands a message to the bailiff, who is always waiting there.

The chief justice starts the discussion of each case, and the other justices then comment in order of descending seniority. When each justice speaks he or she indicates a tentative vote on the case, or on the petition for review. Once all nine have spoken, an official vote is taken, but this time in reverse order of seniority. In other words, the chief justice can see how everyone else has voted before he casts his vote. Any petition for review that obtains four votes in this process is then scheduled for full briefing and oral argument, usually several months hence.

The attorneys on both sides of cases accepted by the Court then submit written "briefs" (often hundreds of pages long), detailing their legal arguments. In addition, other parties (individuals, groups or government agencies) who feel they have a stake in the outcome of the case, often request the opportunity to submit *amicus curiae* ("friend of the court") briefs, supplementing the original brief with arguments presenting their own perspective on the case. These briefs may be submitted either by permission of both parties or by permission of the Supreme Court.

Once the Supreme Court justices have read the briefs and have had time, with the help of their (three or four per justice) law clerks (generally people who recently graduated at the top of their law school class) to research the cases further, they then hear oral argument. Oral argument is usually limited to thirty minutes for each side. The process of oral argument is a rather awesome spectacle. All nine justices sit in a row of high-backed chairs on an elevated platform behind a long table. They all wear black robes and the solicitor general, who argues cases for the federal government, dons a formal morning coat. The attorney stands facing the justices (with back to the small audience) and begins his or her argument. He or she generally manages no more than a few sentences before the justices begin to pepper him or her with questions. The rest of the "argument" then consists of a lively interchange between justices and attorney.

On the Friday following oral argument, the case is again discussed in conference. The justices follow the same procedures of speaking and voting, and, of course, a majority (rather than a vote of four) is now decisive. If the chief justice votes with the majority, he assigns the job of writing the "Court" opinion. If the chief justice is in the minority, the most senior of the associate justices assigns the Court opinion. Some effort is made to distribute the opinion-writing responsibility evenly around the Court; each justice authors about thirteen to eighteen majority opinions a year. Once the selected justice has drafted the intended majority opinion, he or she circulates this rough version to every other justice. At this point the other justices jot down various suggestions for changing the draft; a justice in the original minority, for example, may offer to change sides if a particular point is added or deleted, strengthened or weakened. Likewise, an original member of the majority may threaten to break ranks if the opinion is not

modified to his or her specifications. Meanwhile, if the vote on the case was non-unanimous (as 75 percent of them are), a dissenting opinion will also be circulating. Occasionally, a dissent is so persuasive, or a majority opinion so unpersuasive, that the initial dissent becomes a majority opinion before the consulting process has ended. These tk;2opinion drafts are frequently revised several times, and any justice is free to change sides until the official decision is announced in open court. Any justice who wants to may also write his or her own concurring or dissenting opinion.

Opinions are "read aloud" in Court, often on Mondays and Tuesdays. These days, justices generally summarize their main arguments and read only selected portions of the opinion. When the opinion is being announced, complete copies of it are distributed to journalists from the news media and are also mailed to the litigants and the lower courts involved, and are also available through electronic computer mail.

Supreme Court opinions are reprinted every week in a journal called *U.S. Law Week: Supreme Court Section* (abbreviated U.S.L.W. or L.W.), which is available in every law library. All law schools have law libraries, as do all county seats. Eventually the opinions are also reprinted in each of three ed-ited series: *United States Supreme Court Reports* (abbreviated U.S.), the official version of the Government Printing Office; *The Supreme Court Reporter* (abbreviated S. Ct.), and *United States Supreme Court, Lawyers' Edition* (abbreviated L. Ed.), both published by West Publishing, a private company. At least one of these editions is always available in law libraries.

Court cases use a legal notation form for citing cases. For example, in the citation 198 U.S. 45, 47, the letters U.S. are the abbreviation of the title of the collection in which the case can be found (in this instance, United States Supreme Court Reports); the first number, 198, refers to the volume number in that collection; the second number, 45, refers to the page on which the case begins; the third number, 47, refers to the page on which the particular quotation is found. For other forms of citation and further help, see a legal handbook or *A Uniform System of Citation* (currently in the fifteenth edition).

Appendix B

The Constitution of the United States

Preamble

We the People of the United States, in Order to form a more perfect Union, establish Justice, ensure domestic Tranquility, provide for the common defence, promote the general Welfare, and secure the Blessings of Liberty to ourselves and our Posterity, do ordain and establish this Constitution for the United States of America.

Article 1

Section 1. All legislative Powers herein granted shall be vested in a Congress of the United States, which shall consist of a Senate and House of Representatives.

Section 2. [1] The House of Representatives shall be composed of Members chosen every second Year by the People of the several States, and the Electors in each State shall have the Qualifications requisite for Electors of the most numerous Branch of the State Legislature.

[2] No Person shall be a Representative who shall not have attained to the Age of twenty five Years, and been seven Years a Citizen of the United States, and who shall not, when elected, be an Inhabitant of that State in which he shall be chosen.

[3] Representatives and direct Taxes shall be apportioned among the several States which may be included within this Union, according to their respective Numbers, which shall be determined by adding to the whole Number of free Persons, including those bound to Service for a Term of Years, and excluding Indians not taxed, three fifths of all other Persons. The actual Enumeration shall be made within three Years after the first Meeting of the Congress of the United States, and within every subsequent Term of ten Years, in such Manner as they shall by Law direct. The Number of Representatives shall not exceed one for every thirty Thousand, but each State shall have at Least one Representative; and until such enumeration shall be made, the State of New Hampshire shall be entitled to chuse three, Massachusetts eight. Rhode Island and Providence Plantations one, Connecticut five, New York six, New Jersey four, Pennsylvania eight, Delaware one, Maryland six, Virginia ten, North Carolina five, South Carolina five, and Georgia three.

[4] When vacancies happen in the Representation from any State, the Executive Authority thereof shall issue Writs of Election to fill such Vacancies.

[5] The House of Representatives shall chuse their Speaker and other Officers; and shall have the sole Power of Impeachment.

Section 3. [1] The Senate of the United States shall be composed of two Senators from each State, chosen by the Legislature thereof, for six Years; and each Senator shall have one Vote.

[2] Immediately after they shall be assembled in Consequence of the first Election, they shall be divided as equally as may be into three Classes. The Seats of the Senators of the first Class shall be vacated at the Expiration of the Second Year, of the second Class at the Expiration of the fourth Year, and of the third Class at the Expiration of the sixth Year, so that one third may be chosen every second Year; and if Vacancies happen by Resignation, or otherwise, during the Recess of the Legislature of any State, the Executive thereof may make temporary Appointments until the next Meeting of the Legislature, which shall then fill such Vacancies.

[3] No Person shall be a Senator who shall not have attained to the Age of thirty Years, and been nine Years a Citizen of the United States, and who shall not, when elected, be an Inhabitant of that State for which he shall be chosen.

[4] The Vice President of the United States shall be President of the Senate, but shall have no Vote, unless they be equally divided.

[5] The Senate shall chuse their other Officers, and also a President pro tempore, in the Absence of the Vice President, or when he shall exercise the Office of President of the United States.

[6] The Senate shall have the sole Power to try all Impeachments. When sitting for that Purpose, they shall be on Oath or Affirmation. When the President of the United States is tried, the Chief Justice shall preside: And no Person shall be convicted without the Concurrence of two thirds of the Members present.

[7] Judgment in Cases of Impeachment shall not extend further than to removal from Office, and disqualification to hold and employ any Office of honor, Trust, or Profit under the United States: but the Party convicted shall nevertheless be liable and subject to Indictment, Trial, Judgment, and Punishment, according to Law.

Section 4. [1] The Times, Places and Manner of holding Elections for Senators and Representatives, shall be prescribed in each State by the Legislature thereof; but the Congress may at any time by Law make or alter such Regulations, except as to the Places of chusing Senators.

[2] The Congress shall assemble at least once in every Year, and such Meeting shall be on the first Monday in December, unless they shall by Law appoint a different Day.

Section 5. [1] Each House shall be the Judge of the Elections, Returns, and Qualifications of its own Members, and a Majority of each shall constitute a Quorum to do Business; but a smaller Number may adjourn from day to day, and may be authorized to compel the Attendance of absent Members, in such Manner, and under such Penalties as each House may provide.

[2] Each House may determine the Rules of its Proceedings, punish its Members for disorderly Behavior, and, with the Concurrence of two thirds, expel a Member.

[3] Each House shall keep a Journal of its Proceedings, and from time to time publish the same, excepting such Parts as may in their Judgment require Secrecy; and the Yeas and Nays of the Members of either House on any question shall, at the Desire of one fifth of those Present, be entered on the Journal.

[4] Neither House, during the Session of Congress, shall, without the Consent of the other, adjourn for more than three days, nor to any other Place than that in which the two Houses shall be sitting.

Section 6. [1] The Senators and Representatives shall receive a Compensation for their Services, to be ascertained by Law, and paid out of the Treasury of the United

States. They shall in all Cases, except Treason, Felony and Breach of the Peace, be privileged from Arrest during their Attendance at the Session of their respective Houses, and in going to and returning from the same; and for any Speech and Debate in either House, they shall not be questioned in any other Place.

[2] No Senator or Representative shall, during the Time for which he was elected, be appointed to any civil Office under the Authority of the United States, which shall have been created, or the Emoluments whereof shall have been increased during such time; and no Person holding any Office under the United States, shall be a Member of either House during his Continuance in Office.

Section 7. [1] All Bills for raising Revenue shall originate in the House of Representatives; but the Senate may propose or concur with Amendments as on other Bills.

[2] Every Bill which shall have passed the House of Representatives and the Senate, shall, before it become a Law, be presented to the President of the United States; If he approve he shall sign it, but if not he shall return it, with his Objections to the House in which it shall have originated, who shall enter the Objections at large on their Journal, and proceed to reconsider it. If after such Reconsideration two thirds of that House shall agree to pass the Bill, it shall be sent together with the Objections, to the other House, by which it shall likewise be reconsidered, and if approved by two thirds of that House, it shall become a Law. But in all such Cases the Votes of both Houses shall be determined by Yeas and Nays, and the Names of the Persons voting for and against the Bill shall be entered on the Journal of each House respectively. If any Bill shall not be returned by the President within ten Days (Sundays excepted) after it shall have been presented to him, the Same shall be a Law, in like Manner as

if he had signed it, unless the Congress by their Adjournment prevent its Return in which Case it shall not be a Law.

[3] Every Order, Resolution, or Vote, to Which the Concurrence of the Senate and House of Representatives may be necessary (except on a question of Adjournment) shall be presented to the President of the United States; and before the Same shall take Effect, shall be approved by him, or being disapproved by him, shall be repassed by two thirds of the Senate and House of Representatives, according to the Rules and Limitations prescribed in the Case of a Bill.

Section 8. [1] The Congress shall have Power To lay and collect Taxes, Duties, Imposts and Excises, to pay the Debts and provide for the common Defence and general Welfare of the United States; but all Duties, Imposts and Excises shall be uniform throughout the United States;

[2] To borrow money on the credit of the United States;

[3] To regulate Commerce with foreign Nations, and among the several States, and with the Indian Tribes;

[4] To establish an uniform Rule of Naturalization, and uniform Laws on the subject of Bankruptcies throughout the United States;

[5] To coin Money, regulate the Value thereof, and of foreign Coin, and fix the Standard of Weights and Measures;

[6] To provide for the Punishment of counterfeiting the Securities and current Coin of the United States;

[7] To Establish Post Offices and Post Roads;

[8] To promote the Progress of Science and useful Arts, by securing for limited Times to Authors and Inventors the exclusive Right to their respective Writings and Discoveries;

[9] To constitute Tribunals inferior to the supreme Court;

[10] To define and punish Piracies and Felonies committed on the high Seas, and Offenses against the Law of Nations;

[11] To declare War, grant Letters of Marque and Reprisal, and make Rules concerning Captures on Land and Water;

[12] To raise and support Armies, but no Appropriation of Money to that Use shall be for a longer Term than two Years;

[13] To provide and maintain a Navy;

[14] To make Rules for the Government and Regulation of the land and naval Forces;

[15] To provide for calling forth the Militia to execute the Laws of the Union, suppress Insurrections and repel Invasions;

[16] To provide for organizing, arming, and disciplining, the Militia, and for governing such Part of them as may be employed in the Service of the United States, reserving to the States respectively, the Appointment of the Officers, and the Authority of training the Militia according to the discipline prescribed by Congress;

[17] To exercise exclusive Legislation in all Cases whatsoever, over such District (not exceeding ten Miles square) as may, by Cession of particular States, and the Acceptance of Congress, become the Seat of the Government of the United States, and to exercise like Authority over all Places purchased by the Consent of the Legislature of the State in which the Same shall be, for the Erection of Forts, Magazines, Arsenals, dock-Yards, and other needful Buildings;—And

[18] To make all Laws which shall be necessary and proper for carrying into Execution the foregoing Powers, and all other Powers vested by this Constitution in the Government of the United States, or in any Department or Officer thereof.

Section 9. [1] The Migration or Importation of Such Persons as any of the States now existing shall think proper to admit, shall not be prohibited by the Congress prior to the Year one thousand eight hundred and eight, but a Tax or duty may be imposed on such importation, not exceeding ten dollars for each Person.

[2] The privilege of the Writ of Habeas Corpus shall not be suspended, unless when in Cases of Rebellion or Invasion the public Safety may require it.

[3] No Bill of Attainder or ex post facto Law shall be passed.

[4] No Capitation, or other direct, Tax shall be laid, unless in Proportion to the Census or Enumeration herein before directed to be taken.

[5] No Tax or Duty shall be laid on Articles exported from any State.

[6] No Preference shall be given by any Regulation of Commerce or Revenue to the Ports of one State over those of another: nor shall Vessels bound to, or from, one State be obliged to enter, clear, or pay Duties in another.

[7] No money shall be drawn from the Treasury, but in Consequence of Appropriations made by Law; and a regular Statement and Account of the Receipts and Expenditures of all public Money shall be published from time to time.

[8] No Title of Nobility shall be granted by the United States; And no Person holding any Office of Profit or Trust under them, shall, without the Consent of the Congress, accept of any present, Emolument, Office, or Title, of any kind whatever, from any King, Prince, or foreign State.

Section 10. [1] No State shall enter into any Treaty, Alliance, or Confederation; grant Letters of Marque and Reprisal; coin Money; emit Bills of Credit; make any Things but gold and silver Coin a Tender in Payment of Debts; pass any Bill of Attainder, ex post facto Law, or Law impairing the Obligation of Contracts, or grant any Title of Nobility.

[2] No State shall, without the Consent of the Congress, lay any Imposts or Duties on Imports or Exports, except what may be

absolutely necessary for executing its inspection Laws: and the net Produce of all Duties and Imposts, laid by any State on Imports or Exports, shall be for the Use of the Treasury of the United States; and all such Laws shall be subject to the Revision and Controul of the Congress.

[3] No State shall, without the Consent of Congress, lay any Duty of Tonnage, keep Troops, or Ships of War in time of Peace, enter into any Agreement or Compact with another State or with a foreign Power, or engage in War, unless actually invaded, or in such imminent Danger as will not admit of delay.

Article 2

Section 1. [1] The executive Power shall be vested in a President of the United States of America. He shall hold his Office during the Term of four Years, and, together with the Vice President, chosen for the same Term, be elected, as follows:

[2] Each State shall appoint, in such Manner as the Legislature thereof may direct, a Number of Electors, equal to the whole Number of Senators and Representatives to which the State may be entitled in the Congress; but no Senator or Representative, or Person holding an Office of Trust or Profit under the United States, shall be appointed an Elector.

[3] The Electors shall meet in their respective States, and vote by Ballot for two Persons, of whom one at least shall not be an Inhabitant of the same State with themselves. And they shall make a List of all the Persons voted for, and of the number of Votes for each; which List they shall sign and certify, and transmit sealed to the Seat of the Government of the United States, directed to the President of the Senate. The President of the Senate shall, in the Presence of the Senate and House of Representatives, open all the Certificates, and the

Votes shall then be counted. The Person having the greatest Number of Votes shall be the President, if such Number be a Majority of the whole Number of Electors appointed; and if there be more than one who have such Majority, and have an equal Number of Votes, then the House of Representatives shall immediately chuse by Ballot one of them for President; and if no Person have a Majority, then from the five highest on the List the said House shall in like Manner chuse the President. But in chusing the President, the Votes shall be taken by States the Representation from each State having one Vote; A quorum for this Purpose shall consist of a Member or Members from two thirds of the States, and a Majority of all the States shall be necessary to a Choice. In every Case, after the Choice of the President, the Person having the greater Number of Votes of the Electors shall be the Vice President. But if there should remain two or more who have equal Votes, the Senate shall chuse from them by Ballot the Vice President.

[4] The Congress may determine the Time of chusing the Electors, and the Day on which they shall give their Votes; which Day shall be the same throughout the United States.

[5] No person except a natural born Citizen, or a Citizen of the United States, at the time of the Adoption of this Constitution, shall be eligible to the Office of President; neither shall any Person be eligible to that Office who shall not have attained to the Age of thirty five Years, and been fourteen Years a Resident within the United States.

[6] In case of the removal of the President from Office, or of his Death, Resignation or Inability to discharge the Powers and Duties of the said Office, the Same shall devolve on the Vice President, and the Congress may by Law provide for the Case of Removal, Death, Resignation

or Inability, both of the President and Vice President, declaring what Officer shall then act as President, and such Officer shall act accordingly, until the Disability be removed, or a President shall be elected.

[7] The President shall, at stated Times, receive for his Services, a Compensation, which shall neither be increased nor diminished during the Period for which he shall have been elected, and he shall not receive within that Period any other Emolument from the United States, or any of them.

[8] Before he enter on the Execution of his Office, he shall take the following Oath or Affirmation: "I do solemnly swear (or affirm) that I will faithfully execute the Office of President of the United States, and will to the best of my Ability, preserve, protect and defend the Constitution of the United States."

Section 2. [1] The President shall be Commander in Chief of the Army and Navy of the United States, and of the militia of the several States, when called into the actual Service of the United States; he may require the Opinion, in writing, of the principal Officer in each of the Executive Departments, upon any Subject relating to the Duties of their respective Offices, and he shall have Power to grant Reprieves and Pardons for Offenses against the United States, except in Cases of Impeachment.

[2] He shall have Power, by and with the Advice and Consent of the Senate to make Treaties, provided two thirds of the Senators present concur; and he shall nominate, and by and with the Advice and Consent of the Senate, shall appoint Ambassadors, other public Ministers and Consuls, Judges of the supreme Court, and all other Officers of the United States, whose Appointments are not herein otherwise provided for, and which shall be established by Law; but the Congress may by Law vest the Appointment of such inferior Officers, as they think proper, in the Presi-

dent alone, in the Courts of Law, or in the Heads of Departments.

[3] The President shall have Power to fill up all Vacancies that may happen during the Recess of the Senate, by granting Commissions which shall expire at the End of their next Session.

Section 3. He shall from time to time give to the Congress Information of the State of the Union, and recommend to their Consideration such Measures as he shall judge necessary and expedient; he may, on extraordinary Ocasions, convene both Houses, or either of them, and in Case of Disagreement between them, with Respect to the Time of Adjournment, he may, on extraordinary Occasions, convene both Houses, or either of them, and in and other public Ministers; he shall take Care that the Laws be faithfully executed, and shall Commission all the Officers of the United States.

Section 4. The President, Vice President and all civil Officers of the United States, shall be removed from Office on Impeachment for, and Conviction of, Treason, Bribery, or other high Crimes and Misdemeanors.

Article 3

Section 1. The judicial Power of the United States, shall be vested in one supreme Court, and in such inferior Courts as the Congress may from time to time ordain and establish. The Judges, both of the supreme and inferior Courts, shall hold their Offices during good Behaviour, and shall, at stated Times, receive for their Services a Compensation, which shall not be diminished during their Continuance in Office.

Section 2. [1] The judicial Power shall extend to all Cases, in Law and Equity, arising under this Constitution, the Laws of the United States, and Treaties made, or which shall be made, under their

Authority;—to all Cases affecting Ambassadors, other public Ministers and Consuls;—to all Cases of admiralty and maritime Jurisdiction;—to Controversies to which the United States shall be a Party;—to Controversies between two or more States;—between Citizens of the same State claiming Lands under the Grants of different States, and between a State, or the Citizens thereof, and foreign States, Citizens or Subjects.

[2] In all Cases affecting Ambassadors, other public Ministers and Consuls, and those in which a State shall be a Party, the Supreme Court shall have original Jurisdiction. In all the other Cases before mentioned, the supreme Court shall have appellate Jurisdiction, both as to Law and Fact, with such Exceptions, and under such Regulations as the Congress shall make.

[3] The trial of all Crime, except in Cases of Impeachment, shall be by Jury; and such Trial shall be held in the State where the said Crimes shall have been committed; but when not committed within any State, the Trial shall be at such Place or Places as the Congress may by Law have directed.

Section 3. [1] Treason against the United States, shall consist only in levying War against them, or, in adhering to their Enemies, giving them Aid and Comfort. No Person shall be convicted of Treason unless on the Testimony of two Witnesses to the same overt Act, or on Confession in open Court.

[2] The Congress shall have Power to declare the Punishment of Treason, but no Attainder of Treason shall work Corruption of Blood, or Forfeiture except during the Life of the Person attainted.

Article 4

*Section 1.*Full Faith and Credit shall be given in each State to the public Acts,

Records, and judicial Proceedings of every other State. And the Congress may be general Laws prescribe the Manner in which such Acts, Records and Proceedings shall be proved, and the Effect thereof.

Section 2. [1] The Citizens of each State shall be entitled to all Privileges and Immunities of Citizens in the several States.

[2] A Person charged in any State with Treason, Felony, or other Crime, who shall flee from Justice, and be found in another State, shall on demand of the executive Authority of the State from which he fled, be delivered up, to be removed to the State having Jurisdiction of the Crime.

[3] No Person held to Service or Labour in one State, under the Laws thereof, escaping into another, shall, in Consequence of any Law or Regulation therein, be discharged from such Service or Labour, but shall be delivered up on Claim of the Party to whom such Service or Labour may be due.

Section 3. [1] New States may be admitted by the Congress into this Union; but no new State shall be formed or erected within the Jurisdiction of any other State; nor any State be formed by the Junction of two or more States, or Parts of States, without the Consent of the Legislatures of the States concerned as well as of the Congress.

[2] The Congress shall have Power to dispose of and make all needful Rules and Regulations respecting the Territory or other Property belonging to the United States; and nothing in this Constitution shall be so construed as to Prejudice any Claims of the United States, or of any particular State.

Section 4. The United States shall guarantee to every State in this Union a Republican Form of Government, and shall protect each of them against Invasion; and on Application of the Legislature, or of the Executive (when the Legislature cannot be convened) against domestic Violence.

Article 5

The Congress, whenever two thirds of both Houses shall deem it necessary, shall propose Amendments to this Constitution, or, on the Application of the Legislatures of two thirds of the several States, shall call a Convention for proposing Amendments, which, in either Case, shall be valid to all Intents and Purposes, as part of this Constitution, when ratified by the Legislatures of three fourths of the several States, or by Conventions in three fourths thereof, as the one or the other Mode of Ratification may be proposed by the Congress; Provided that no Amendment which may be made prior to the Year One thousand eight hundred and eight shall in any Manner affect the first and fourth Clauses in the Ninth Section of the first Article; and that no State, without its Consent, shall be deprived of its equal Suffrage in the Senate.

Article 6

[1] All Debts contracted and Engagements entered into, before the Adoption of this Constitution shall be as valid against the United States under this Constitution, as under the Confederation.

[2] This Constitution, and the Laws of the United States which shall be made in Pursuance thereof; and all Treaties made, or which shall be made under the Authority of the United States, shall be the supreme Law of the Land; and the Judges in every State shall be bound thereby, any Things in the Constitution or Laws of any State to the Contrary notwithstanding.

[3] The Senators and Representatives before mentioned, and the Members of the several State Legislatures, and all executive and judicial Officers, both of the United States and of the several States, shall be bound by Oath or Affirmation, to support this Constitution; but no religious Test shall ever be required as a Qualification to any Office or public Trust under the United States.

Article 7

The Ratification of the Conventions of nine States shall be sufficient for the Establishment of this Constitution between the States so ratifying the Same.

ARTICLES IN ADDITION TO, AND AMENDMENT OF, THE CONSTITUTION OF THE UNITED STATES OF AMERICA, PROPOSED BY CONGRESS, AND RATIFIED BY THE LEGISLATURES OF THE SEVERAL STATES PURSUANT TO THE FIFTH ARTICLE OF THE ORIGINAL CONSTITUTION.

Amendment I [1791]

Congress shall make no law respecting an establishment of religion, or prohibiting the free exercise thereof; or abridging the freedom of speech, or of the press; or the right of the people peaceably to assemble, and to petition the Government for a redress of grievances.

Amendment II [1791]

A well regulated Militia, being necessary to the security of a free State, the right of the people to keep and bear Arms, shall not be infringed.

Amendment III [1791]

No Soldier shall, in time of peace be quartered in any house, without the consent of the Owner, nor in time of war, but in a manner to be prescribed by law.

Amendment IV [1791]

The right of the people to be secure in their persons, houses, papers, and effects, against unreasonable searches and sei-zures, shall not be violated, and no Warrants shall issue, but upon probable cause, supported by Oath or affirmation, and particularly describing the place to be searched, and the persons or things to be seized.

Amendment V [1791]

No person shall be held to answer for a capital, or otherwise infamous crime, unless on a presentment or indictment of a Grand Jury, except in cases arising in the land or naval forces, or in the Militia, when in actual service in time of War or public danger; nor shall any person be subject for the same offence to be twice put in jeopardy of life or limb; nor shall be compelled in any criminal case to be a witness against himself, nor be deprived of life, liberty, or property, without due process of law; nor shall private property be taken for public use, without just compensation.

Amendment VI [1791]

In all criminal prosecutions, the accused shall enjoy the right to a speedy and public trial, by an impartial jury of the State and district wherein the crime shall have been committed, which district shall have been previously ascertained by law, and to be informed of the nature and cause of the accusation; to be confronted with the wit-nesses against him; to have compulsory process for obtaining witnesses in his favor, and to have the Assistance of Counsel for his defence.

Amendment VII [1791]

In Suits at common law, where the value in controversy shall exceed twenty dollars, the right of trial by jury shall be preserved, and no fact tried by jury, shall be otherwise reexamined in any Court of the United States, than according to the rules of the common law.

Amendment VIII [1791]

Excessive bail shall not be required, nor excessive fines imposed, nor cruel and un-usual punishments inflicted.

Amendment IX [1791]

The enumeration in the Constitution, of certain rights, shall not be construed to deny or disparage others retained by the people.

Amendment X [1791]

The powers not delegated to the United States by the Constitution, nor prohibited by it to the States, are reserved to the States respectively, or to the people.

Amendment XI[1798]

The Judicial power of the United States shall not be construed to extend to any suit in law or equity, commenced or prosecuted against one of the United States by Citizens of another State, or by Citizens or Subjects of any Foreign State.

Amendment XII [1804]

The Electors shall meet in their respective states and vote by ballot for President and Vice-President, one of whom, at least, shall not be an inhabitant of the same state with themselves; they shall name in their ballots the person voted for as President, and in distinct ballots the person voted for as Vice-President, and they shall make distinct lists of all persons voted for as President, and of all persons voted for as Vice-President, and of the number of votes for each, which lists they shall sign and certify, and transmit sealed to the seat of the government of the United States, directed to the President of the Senate;—The President of the Senate shall, in the presence of the Senate and House of Representatives, open all the certificates and the votes shall then be counted;—The person having the greatest number of votes for President, shall be the President, if such number be a majority of the whole number of Electors appointed; and if no person have such majority, then from the persons having the highest numbers not exceeding three on the list of those voted for as President, the House of Representatives shall choose immediately, by ballot, the President. But in choosing the President, the votes shall be taken by states, the representation from each state having one vote; a quorum for this purpose shall consist of a member of members from two-thirds of the States, and a majority of all the states shall be necessary to a choice. And if the House of Representatives shall not choose a President whenever the right of choice shall devolve upon them before the fourth day of March next following, then the Vice-President shall act as President, as in the case of the death or other constitutional disability of the President.— The person having the greatest number of votes as Vice-President, shall be the Vice-President, if such number be a majority of the whole number of Electors appointed, and if no person have a majority, then from the two highest numbers on the list, the Senate shall choose the Vice-President; a quorum for the purpose shall consist of

two-thirds of the whole number of Senators, and a majority of the whole number shall be necessary to a choice. But no person constitutionally ineligible to the office of President shall be eligible to that of Vice-President of the United States.

Amendment XIII [1865]

Section 1. Neither slavery nor involuntary servitude, except as a punishment for crime whereof the party shall have been duly convicted, shall exist within the United States, or any place subject to their jurisdiction.

Section 2. Congress shall have power to enforce this article by appropriate legislation.

Amendment XIV [1868]

Section 1. All persons born or naturalized in the United States, and subject to the jurisdiction thereof, are citizens of the United States and of the State wherein they reside. No State shall make or enforce any law which shall abridge the privileges or immunities of citizens of the United States; nor shall any State deprive any person of life, liberty, or property, without due process of law; nor deny to any person within its jurisdiction the equal protection of the laws.

Section 2. Representatives shall be apportioned among the several States according to their respective numbers, counting the whole number of persons in each State, excluding Indians not taxed. But when the right to vote at any election for the choice of electors for President and Vice President of the United States, Representatives in Congress, the Executive and Judicial officers of a State, or the members of the Legislature thereof, is denied to any of the male inhabitants of such State, being twenty-one years of age, and citizens of the United

States, or in any way abridged, except for participation in rebellion, or other crime, the basis of representation therein shall be reduced in the proportion which the number of such male citizens shall bear to the whole number of male citizens twenty-one years of age in such State.

Section 3. No person shall be a Senator or Representative in Congress, or elector of President and Vice President, or hold any office, civil or military, under the United States, or under any State, who having previously taken an oath, as a member of Congress, or as an officer of the United States, or as a member of any State legislature, or as an executive or judicial officer of any State, to support the Constitution of the United States, shall have engaged in insurrection or rebellion against the same, or given aid or comfort to the enemies thereof. But Congress may by a vote of two-thirds of each House, remove such disability.

Section 4. The validity of the public debt of the United States, authorized by law, including debts incurred for payment of pensions and bounties for services in suppressing insurrection or rebellion, shall not be questioned. But neither the United States nor any State shall assume or pay any debt or obligation incurred in aid of insurrection or rebellion against the United States, or any claim for the loss or emancipation of any slave; but all such debts, obligations and claims shall be held illegal and void.

Section 5. The Congress shall have power to enforce, by appropriate legislation, the provisions of this article.

Amendment XV [1870]

Section 1. The right of citizens of the United States to vote shall not be denied or abridged by the United States or by any State on account of race, color, or previous condition of servitude.

Section 2. The Congress shall have power to enforce this article by appropriate legislation.

Amendment XVI [1913]

The Congress shall have power to lay and collect taxes on incomes, from whatever source derived, without apportionment among the several States, and without regard to any census or enumeration.

Amendment XVII [1914]

[1] The Senate of the United States shall be composed of two Senators from each State, elected by the people thereof, for six years; and each Senator shall have one vote. The electors in each State shall have the qualifications requisite for electors of the most numerous branch of the State legislatures.

[2] When vacancies happen in the representation of any State in the Senate, the executive authority of such State shall issue writs of election to fill such vacancies: *Provided,* That the legislature of any State may empower the executive thereof to make temporary appointments until the people fill the vacancies by election as the legislature may direct.

[3] This amendment shall not be so construed as to affect the election or term of any Senator chosen before it becomes valid as part of the Constitution.

Amendment XVIII [1919]

Section 1. After one year from the ratification of this article the manufacture, sale, or transportation of intoxicating liquors within, the importation thereof into, or the exportation thereof from the United States and all territory subject to the jurisdiction thereof for beverage purposes is hereby prohibited.

Section 2. The Congress and the several States shall have concurrent power to enforce this article by appropriate legislation.

Section 3. This article shall be inoperative unless it shall have been ratified as an amendment to the Constitution by the legislatures of the several States, as provided in the Constitution, within seven years from the date of the submission hereof to the States by the Congress.

Amendment XIX [1920]

[1] The right of citizens of the United States to vote shall not be denied or abridged by the United States or by any State on account of sex.

[2] Congress shall have power to enforce this article by appropriate legislation.

Amendment XX [1933]

Section 1. The terms of the President and Vice President shall end at noon on the 20th day of January, and the terms of Senators and Representatives at noon on the 3d day of January, of the years in which such terms would have ended if this article had not been ratified; and the terms of their successors shall then begin.

Section 2. The Congress shall assemble at least once in every year, and such meeting shall begin at noon on the 3d day of January, unless they shall by law appoint a different day.

Section 3. If, at the time fixed for the beginning of the term of the President, the President elect shall have died, the Vice President elect shall become President. If the President shall not have been chosen before the time fixed for the beginning of his term, or if the President elect shall have

failed to qualify, then the Vice President elect shall act as President until a President shall have qualified; and the Congress may by law provide for the case wherein neither a President elect nor a Vice President elect shall have qualified, declaring who shall then act as President, or the manner in which one who is to act shall be selected, and such person shall act accordingly until a President or Vice President shall have qualified.

Section 4. The Congress may by law provide for the case of the death of any of the persons from whom the House of Representatives may choose a President whenever the right of choice shall have devolved upon them, and for the case of the death of any of the persons from whom the Senate may choose a Vice President whenever the right of choice shall have devolved upon them.

Section 5. Sections 1 and 2 shall take effect on the 15th day of October following the ratification of this article.

Section 6. This article shall be inoperative unless it shall have been ratified as an amendment to the Constitution by the legislatures of three-fourths of the several States within seven years from the date of its submission.

Amendment XXI [1933]

Section 1. The eighteenth article of amendment to the Constitution of the United States is hereby repealed.

Section 2. The transportation or importation into any State, Territory, or possession of the United States for delivery or use therein of intoxicating liquors, in violation of the laws thereof, is hereby prohibited.

Section 3. This article shall be inoperative unless it shall have been ratified as an amendment to the Constitution by conventions in the several States, as provided in the Constitution, within seven years from the date of the submission hereof to the States by the Congress.

Amendment XXII [1951]

Section 1. No person shall be elected to the office of the President more than twice, and no person who has held the office of President, or acted as President, for more than two years of a term to which some other person was elected President shall be elected to the office of President more than once. But this Article shall not apply to any person holding the office of President when this Article was proposed by the Congress, and shall not prevent any person who may be holding the office of President, or acting as President, during the term within which this Article becomes operative from holding the office of President or acting as President during the remainder of such term.

Section 2. This article shall be inoperative unless it shall have been ratified as an amendment to the Constitution by the legislatures of three-fourths of the several States within seven years from the date of its submission to the States by the Congress.

Amendment XXIII [1961]

Section 1. The District constituting the seat of Government of the United States shall appoint in such manner as the Congress may direct:

A number of electors of President and Vice President equal to the whole number of Senators and Representatives in Congress to which the District would be entitled if it were a State, but in no event more than the least populous state; they shall be in addition to those appointed by the states, but they shall be considered, for the purposes of the election of President and Vice President, to be electors appointed by a state; and they shall meet in the District and perform such duties as provided by the twelfth article of amendment.

Section 2. The Congress shall have power to enforce this article by appropriate legislation.

Amendment XXIV [1964]

Section 1. The right of citizens of the United States to vote in any primary or other election for President or Vice President, for electors for President or Vice President, or for Senator or Representative in Congress, shall not be denied or abridged by the United States or any State by reason of failure to pay any poll tax or other tax.

Section 2. The Congress shall have power to enforce this article by appropriate legislation.

Amendment XXV [1967]

Section 1. In case of the removal of the President from office or of his death or resignation, the Vice President shall become President.

Section 2. Whenever there is a vacancy in the office of the Vice President, the President shall nominate a Vice President who shall take office upon confirmation by a majority vote of both Houses of Congress.

Section 3. Whenever the President transmits to the President pro tempore of the Senate and the Speaker of the House of Representatives his written declaration that he is unable to discharge the powers and duties of his office, and until he transmits to them a written declaration to the contrary, such powers and duties shall be discharged by the Vice President as Acting President.

Section 4. Whenever the Vice President and a majority of either the principal officers of the executive departments or of such other body as Congress may by law provide, transmit to the President pro tempore of the Senate and the Speaker of the House of Representatives their written declaration that the President is unable to discharge the powers and duties of his office, the Vice President shall immediately assume the powers and duties of the office as Acting President.

Thereafter, when the President transmits to the President pro tempore of the Senate and the Speaker of the House of Representatives his written declaration that no inability exists, he shall resume the powers and duties of his office unless the Vice President and a majority of either the principal officers of the executive department or of such other body as Congress may by law provide, transmit within four days to the President pro tempore of the Senate and the Speaker of the House of Representatives their written declaration that the President is unable to discharge the powers and duties of his office. Thereupon Congress shall decide the issue, assembling within forty-eight hours for that purpose if not in session. If the Congress, within twenty-one days after receipt of the latter written declaration, or, if Congress is not in session, within twenty-one days after Congress is required to assemble, determines by two-thirds vote of both Houses that the President is unable to discharge the powers and duties of his office, the Vice President shall continue to discharge the same as Acting President; otherwise, the President shall resume the powers and duties of his office.

Amendment XXVI [1971]

Section 1. The right of citizens of the United States, who are eighteen years of age or older, to vote shall not be denied or abridged by the United States or by any State on account of age.

Section 2. The Congress shall have power to enforce this article by appropriate legislation.

Amendment XXVII [1992]

No law varying the compensation for the services of the Senators and Representatives shall take effect, until an election of Representatives shall have intervened.

Equal Rights Amendment (ERA) [Proposed but not ratified]*

Section 1. Equality of rights under the law shall not be denied or abridged by the United States or by any State on account of sex.

Section 2. The Congress shall have the power to enforce, by appropriate legislation, the provisions of this article.

Section 3. This amendment shall take effect two years after the date of ratification.

---

*This amendment, proposed as the 27th, was submitted to the states on March 22, 1972. Although about half of the necessary number of states approved the Amendment in the first three months after submission, the drive for adoption of the Equal Rights Amendment slowed thereafter. By the ratification deadline, support for the Amendment still fell three short of the required 38 ratifying state legislatures. A three-year extension of the seven-year ratification period produced no additional state ratifications.

Case Index

Cases excerpted in this book are indicated by boldface type. The page numbers set in boldface type locate the excerpt.

DATE			